PUBLIC PROCUREMENT REGULATION IN AFRICA

Public procurement regulation in Africa is not widely researched. To address the shortage of scholarship in this area and to promote future research, this book analyses the law governing public procurement in a number of African systems and looks at key themes relevant to all African states. Part I discusses the regulatory regimes of nine African systems using a common framework, providing both a focused view of these African systems and an accessible comparative perspective. In Part II, key regulatory issues in public procurement that are particularly relevant in the African context are assessed through a comparative approach. The chapters consider the influence of international regulatory regimes (particularly the UNCITRAL Model Law on procurement) on African systems and provide insights into the way public procurement regulation is approached in Africa.

GEO QUINOT is Professor of Law in the Department of Public Law at Stellenbosch University, where he is also Director of the African Public Procurement Regulation Research Unit (APPRRU) and Co-Director of the Socio-Economic Rights and Administrative Justice Research Project (SERAJ).

SUE ARROWSMITH is Achilles Professor of Public Procurement Law and Policy at the University of Nottingham, where she is also Director of the Public Procurement Research Group and of the postgraduate Executive Programme in Public Procurement Law and Policy.

PUBLIC PROCUREMENT REGULATION IN AFRICA

Edited by

GEO QUINOT AND SUE ARROWSMITH

CAMBRIDGE
UNIVERSITY PRESS

CAMBRIDGE
UNIVERSITY PRESS

University Printing House, Cambridge CB2 8BS, United Kingdom

Cambridge University Press is part of the University of Cambridge.

It furthers the University's mission by disseminating knowledge in the pursuit of education, learning and research at the highest international levels of excellence.

www.cambridge.org
Information on this title: www.cambridge.org/9781107028326

First published 2013

A catalogue record for this publication is available from the British Library

Library of Congress Cataloguing in Publication data
Public procurement regulation in Africa / edited by Geo Quinot and Sue Arrowsmith.
p. cm.
Includes bibliographical references and index.
ISBN 978-1-107-02832-6 (hardback)
1. Government purchasing – Law and legislation – Africa, Sub-Saharan.
I. Quinot, Geo. II. Arrowsmith, Sue, 1962–
KQC234.3.P83 2013
352.5′30967 – dc23 2012027128

ISBN 978-1-107-02832-6 Hardback

CONTENTS

List of tables *page* vii
Notes on the contributors viii
Preface and acknowledgments xiii
List of abbreviations xvi

1 Introduction 1
GEO QUINOT AND SUE ARROWSMITH

PART I **Country studies** 23

2 The regulatory framework for public procurement in Botswana 25
REKHA A. KUMAR AND ELINOR CABORN

3 The regulatory framework for public procurement in Ethiopia 46
TECLE HAGOS BAHTA

4 The regulatory framework for public procurement in Ghana 77
DOMINIC N. DAGBANJA

5 The regulatory framework for public procurement in Kenya 100
KINGSLEY TOCHI UDEH

6 The regulatory framework for public procurement in Namibia 123
SAMUEL KWESI AMOO AND SCOTT DICKEN

7 The regulatory framework for public procurement in Nigeria 141
KINGSLEY TOCHI UDEH AND M. L. AHMADU

8 The regulatory framework for public procurement in Rwanda 162
IVAN RUGEMA

9 The regulatory framework for public procurement in South Africa 178
PHOEBE BOLTON

10 The regulatory framework for public procurement in Zimbabwe 200
JOEL ZOWA, NAISON MACHINGAUTA AND PHOEBE BOLTON

PART II Themes in public procurement regulation in Africa 217

11 Donors' influence on developing countries' procurement systems, rules and markets: a critical analysis 219
ANNAMARIA LA CHIMIA

12 Procurement methods in the public procurement systems of Africa 261
ELINOR CABORN AND SUE ARROWSMITH

13 A comparative perspective on supplier remedies in African public procurement systems 308
GEO QUINOT

14 A perspective on corruption and public procurement in Africa 336
SOPE WILLIAMS-ELEGBE

15 Promotion of social policy through public procurement in Africa 370
GEO QUINOT

Materials on public procurement regulation in Africa 404
Index 414

TABLES

5.1 Kenya, levels of usage of procurement methods *page* 116
11.1 Aid to Africa by DAC donors, 2002–2009 (US$ million) 227
11.2 Total ODA net disbursed to Africa, by DAC and non-DAC countries, multilateral donors and private donors, 2002–2009 229
11.3 Aid procurement granted for the government sector which has been spent using country systems, 2010 (US$ million) 256
15.1 Legal mechanisms aimed at implementing horizontal policies through procurement 375
15.2 Kenyan preferential procurement schemes 388
15.3 Preference points per B-BBEE status level 398

NOTES ON THE CONTRIBUTORS

Editors

PROFESSOR GEO QUINOT is Professor of Law in the Department of Public Law at Stellenbosch University, Director of the African Public Procurement Regulation Research Unit (APPRRU) and Co-Director of the Socio-Economic Rights and Administrative Justice Research Project (SERAJ). He mainly teaches administrative law and constitutional law. He also regularly instructs public administrators at Stellenbosch University's School of Public Leadership and in the University of Cape Town's Professional Development Project in both administrative law and public procurement regulation. His research focuses on general administrative law, including a particular focus on the regulation of state commercial activity. He is the author of various articles in academic journals and electronic publications such as *Juta's Quarterly Review of South African Law* to which he contributes quarterly updates on public procurement law, chapters in book publications such as the recent contribution 'Globalisation, State Commercial Activity and the Transformation of Administrative Law' in M. Faure and A. J. van der Walt (eds.), *Globalization and Private Law* (2010), two recent books, *Administrative Law Cases and Materials* (2008) and *State Commercial Activity: A Legal Framework* (2009), and an edited volume, *Law and Poverty: Perspectives from South Africa and Beyond* (2012), which he co-edited with Professor Sandra Liebenberg. He is currently the editor of the *Stellenbosch Law Review*.

PROFESSOR SUE ARROWSMITH is Achilles Professor of Public Procurement Law and Policy at the University of Nottingham, where she is also Director of the Public Procurement Research Group and of the postgraduate Executive Programme in Public Procurement Law and Policy (LLM/Diploma/Certificate). Her publications have been extensively cited by courts and legislators around the world. Authored books include *The Law of Public and Utilities Procurement* (2nd edn, 2005); (with J. Linarelli and D. Wallace Jr) *Regulating Public Procurement: National and International Perspectives* (2000); and *Government Procurement in the WTO* (2003). Recent collections of which she is editor include (with Peter Kunzlik) *Social and Environmental Policies in EC Procurement Law: New Directive and New Directions* (Cambridge University Press, 2009); (with R. D. Anderson), *The WTO Regime on Government Procurement: Challenge and Reform* (Cambridge University Press, 2011); and (with S.Treumer) *Competitive Dialogue in EU Procurement* (Cambridge University Press, 2012). In 1992, she launched the first international academic procurement journal, *Public Procurement Law Review*. In 2007, she was awarded the CIPS Swinbank Medal for thought innovation in purchasing and supply. She has taught university modules on procurement since 1995, and was Project Leader of the recent EU-funded project for developing a global academic network on procurement regulation (2008–11), which included setting up the global Procurement Law Academic Network (www.planpublicprocurement.org). She was principal investigator for the ongoing British Academy funded project on procurement in Africa in partnership with Stellenbosch University. She was a member for over twenty years of the European Commission's independent Advisory Committee on procurement; is a member of the UNCITRAL procurement Experts Group; and has been consultant on public procurement for, *inter alia*, the UK government, the UN, the WTO, the European Commission, the OECD, the EU, the European Central Bank and the ILO.

Other contributors

PROFESSOR MOHAMMED L. AHMADU is Dean of Law and the Coordinator, Arts and Humanities Complex, at Usmanu Dan Fodiyo University, Sokoto, Nigeria. He has worked in the Republic of Fiji Islands as a government lawyer, and has served as a lawyer in the Community Legal Centre in the Republic of Vanuatu. He has been called to the Nigerian Bar and also admitted as a barrister and solicitor in the Republic of the Fiji Islands and the Bar in the Republic of Vanuatu, and is an Associate of the Chartered Institute of Secretaries. He is author and editor of many law textbooks and articles and editor of the *Usmanu Dan Fodiyo Law Journal*.

MR S. K. AMOO is an advocate of the Supreme Court of Zambia and attorney of the High Court of Namibia, and is Senior Lecturer and acting director of the Justice Training Centre, Faculty of Law, University of

Namibia. He has written extensively on the Namibian legal system. He has served as a commissioner of the Namibia Law Reform and Development Commission, a member of the Board for Legal Education, on the National Council for Higher Education, on the Namibia Qualifications Authority Council and as a member of the Governing Board of and legal advisor to the Namibia Red Cross Society.

MR TECLE HAGOS BAHTA is Assistant Professor of Law at the University of Mekelle in Ethiopia. He has published articles in the areas of ADR and arbitration, construction and public procurement.

PROFESSOR PHOEBE BOLTON is Professor of Law at Stellenbosch University, South Africa. She is the author of a number of publications in the area of government contracts, supply chain management and government procurement, including *The Law of Government Procurement in South Africa* (2007).

MS ELINOR CABORN works for Crown Agents as a public procurement consultant and has spent the last ten years supporting national procurement reform programmes, predominantly in Africa. She has supported national governments in drafting procurement legislation, regulations, standard documents and guidance materials in Uganda, Zambia, Swaziland, Ethiopia and Malawi as well as Afghanistan, the Maldives and Barbados, and has done work on assessing and developing procurement capacity in Ghana, Botswana and Tanzania. She is a member of the Chartered Institute of Purchasing and Supply.

MR DOMINIC N. DAGBANJA is a lecturer in law at the Ghana Institute of Management and Public Administration in Accra, Ghana. He is the author of several articles and of the book, *The Law of Public Procurement in Ghana: Law, Policy and Practice* (2011). He has previously worked as, *inter alia*, Senior Legal Officer at the Public Procurement Authority of Ghana.

MR SCOTT DICKEN works for Crown Agents – USA as a Program and Procurement Manager and has over seven years of experience in private sector and international development and social programmes. He has provided procurement advisory and management support on large US government- and foundation-funded programmes and has worked on international donor-funded projects, including the Millennium Challenge Corporation, USAID, DfID, the Global Fund and JICA. His experience includes work on ODA-funded projects based in Tanzania, Namibia, Liberia, Colombia, Vietnam, Nigeria and the Gambia.

DR REKHA A. KUMAR teaches law in the Department of Law at the University of Botswana. Her research interests lie in the areas of public procurement and of health issues in Africa. She is a member of, among others, the Bagodi baRona Association, an NGO working for the elderly in Botswana, the Botswana Network on Ethics, Law and HIV/AIDS (BONELA) and the Botswana Network of AIDS Service Organizations (BONASO).

DR ANNAMARIA LA CHIMIA is a lecturer in law at the School of Law, University of Nottingham, and head of the Humanitarian and Development Procurement Unit of the Public Procurement Research Group (PPRG). She also teaches at the Universita' degli Studi di Roma Tre. She has previously worked as a lawyer in Italy and has acted as a consultant for the NGO ActionAid, the Commonwealth Secretariat and SIGMA. Her main research interests lie within the area of international development, international trade law and European law (especially external relations, public procurement, and internal market), and she is also interested in regional integration, developing countries' procurement policies, aid harmonisation, and the development of the European Partnership Agreements (EPAs).

MR NAISON MACHINGAUTA is a practising lawyer in Zimbabwe. He is currently working as a legal officer with the Constitution Select Committee (COPAC), a committee of parliament charged with the responsibility to produce a new Constitution for the Republic of Zimbabwe. He was co-editor of, and contributor to, the book, *Local Government Law Reform in Zimbabwe – A Policy Dialogue* (2010), and has a particular interest in public procurement law.

MR IVAN RUGEMA is a lecturer in the Department of Criminal Justice and Procedure at the Faculty of Law, University of the Western Cape, where he teaches advocacy and criminal law.

MR KINGSLEY TOCHI UDEH is a solicitor and advocate of the Supreme Court of Nigeria, and the Principal Partner of T. K. Udeh & Associates, a law and consultancy firm. Since 2008, he has worked as a consultant for the

Nigerian government on building capacity in public procurement, including coordinating public enlightenment programmes on the provisions of Nigeria's Public Procurement Act 2007 on behalf of the Bureau of Public Procurement, Nigeria. He has also coordinated a procurement capacity building programme for accounts and procurement officers of Nigeria's National Assembly in 2009, and is currently engaged as a consultant to conduct a procurement assessment under a UNICEF–EU partnership on Public Expenditure Management and Financial Accountability Review (PEMFAR) of the six EU states in Nigeria. He is a member of the Nigerian Bar Association and the Chartered Institute of Purchasing and Supply Management of Nigeria.

DR SOPE WILLIAMS-ELEGBE is a research fellow at the University of Stellenbosch, South Africa, a visiting scholar at the University of Lagos, Nigeria, and the Head of Research at the Nigerian Economic Summit Group in Lagos, Nigeria. She is a qualified barrister and solicitor. She is the author of *Fighting Corruption in Public Procurement: A Comparative Analysis of Disqualification or Disbarment Measures* (2012), and has advised international financial institutions and government bodies on public procurement and corruption issues. She is also an editor of the *Journal of African Law.*

MR JOEL ZOWA is a legal practitioner of the High Court of Zimbabwe and Deputy Chairman of the Law Development Commission of Zimbabwe. He also lectures in the Department of Procedural Law in the Faculty of Law at the University of Zimbabwe.

PREFACE AND ACKNOWLEDGMENTS

This book developed out of a three-year research partnership between the University of Nottingham and the University of Stellenbosch under the British Academy's UK–Africa Academic Partnerships scheme. The main aim of the project was to examine the current state of public procurement regulation in Africa, with an initial focus on Southern Africa, in key areas. The project was developed because of the extremely limited academic engagement to date with African public procurement systems. While public procurement regulation has recently developed as a distinct field of legal academic study in other continents and is increasingly playing a key role in international legal regimes, such as that of the WTO, the level of academic engagement with this area in Africa has been negligible. There have been only two comprehensive national studies published and a handful of academic articles, as indicated in the bibliography included in this book.

The goal of the project and hence of this book is to assist African domestic development and to inform legal research and policy-making, both through its short-term outputs, primarily in the form of this book, and long-term impact. In the latter respect, this project aims, *inter alia*: (i) to provide foundations for future research on African procurement regulation; (ii) to provide the foundation for specific research and teaching programmes to secure long-term academic capacity in Africa; and (iii) to provide a platform for African scholars to develop research partnerships and gain access to broader international scholarship. The project also seeks to provide interested parties outside Africa with access to materials on African procurement, so that they may incorporate African perspectives into academic work and policy-making activities.

From its inception, we realised that the project was an ambitious one and thus initially limited the focus to Southern Africa. In developing the book, however, we decided that a broader focus drawing on systems from across the continent would better serve the project's purposes. However, pragmatic problems such as access to materials, language barriers and finding research partners in different countries remained and played an important role in the final decision on which countries to include. Eventually, we included Botswana, Ethiopia, Ghana, Kenya, Namibia, Nigeria, Rwanda, South Africa and Zimbabwe, providing a good sample of sub-Saharan systems. Our aim is thus not to present either a full perspective – or even a representative view – of all African public procurement regulatory systems. In line with the objectives of the project, the book is only a starting point for further work to be done, and the systems included thus serve as examples of public procurement regulation in Africa.

The method used in the book is doctrinal legal analysis, covering both hard law (legislation and case law) and 'soft law' norms, since the latter play an important role in procurement in some countries. No new empirical work was done. As far as possible, the study of a particular system was done by local researchers working, in most cases, in collaboration with established researchers in the field of public procurement regulation.

Many persons contributed to the production of this book or otherwise provided necessary support. In the first place, we are grateful to the British Academy for the funding that made this project possible, as well as for the Academy's flexibility in allowing us to adapt the research programme as changing circumstances demanded. We are also grateful to the administrators at the University of Nottingham for providing excellent administrative support to the project and in particular to Anne Crump, Anne Snape, Jane Costa and Jill Gunn.

Early versions of some of the papers incorporated in the volume were presented at the Conference on 'Public Procurement – Global Revolution V' in Copenhagen in September 2010 and at the Conference on 'African Public Procurement Regulation' in Stellenbosch in October 2011. We are grateful to all those who made presentations at or assisted in the organisation of these events, or provided input on the material presented, and in particular to the sponsors of the latter event where the bulk of the research was presented: Achilles Information Ltd, the British Academy, Cambridge University Press, LexisNexis, the National Research Foundation (South Africa) and the Stellenbosch University Faculty of Law.

At the School of Law of the University of Nottingham and at the Stellenbosch Law Faculty thanks are due to all those who worked on technical aspects of the manuscript, in particular to Richard Craven, Megan Alberts, Gillian Armstrong, Michael Clark, Jan-Hugo Fyfer and Petrus Maree, for their very efficient contributions.

At Cambridge University Press we are grateful to Elizabeth Spicer and Kim Hughes, both for their enthusiasm for the project and patience in waiting for us to deliver on it, and to the many other staff at Cambridge for their able assistance in readying the manuscript for production.

We also record our very sincere thanks to the authors/co-authors of all the chapters of the book, who freely gave of their time and insights and whose contributions made the book possible, as well as to many administrators, practitioners and researchers in many African countries and beyond for providing us with relevant materials, answering questions and, where they could not help, putting us in contact with those who could.

Most of all, we express our appreciation to our spouses and children for their support and encouragement, without which this project could not have been completed. This book is for them.

Geo Quinot
and
Sue Arrowsmith

ABBREVIATIONS

AAA	Accra Agenda for Action
ACC	Anti-Corruption Commission (Namibia)
AfDB	African Development Bank
B-BBEE	Broad-Based Black Economic Empowerment (South Africa)
BEE	black economic empowerment (South Africa)
BPP	Bureau of Public Procurement (Nigeria)
COMESA	Common Market for Eastern and Southern Africa
CPAR	Country Procurement Assessment Report
CSO	civil society organisation
CUTS	Consumer Unity & Trust Society
DAC	Development Assistance Committee (OECD)
EAC	East African Community
ECOWAS	Economic Community of West African States
EFCC	Economic and Financial Crimes Commission (Nigeria)
FEC	Federal Executive Council (Nigeria)
FIDIC	Fédération Internationale des Ingénieurs-Conseils (International Federation of Consulting Engineers)
FPPA	Federal Public Procurement and Property Administration Agency (Ethiopia)
GDP	gross domestic product
GPA	Agreement on Government Procurement (WTO)
HDI	historically disadvantaged individual (South Africa)
HIPC	highly indebted poor country
IBRD	International Bank for Reconstruction and Development
ICRC	Independent Complaints Review Committee (Botswana)
IDA	International Development Association
IMF	International Monetary Fund
IRP	Independent Review Panels (Rwanda)
KENAO	Kenya National Audit Office
LDC	least developed country
MDA	ministries, departments and agencies
MSE	micro and small-scale enterprise

NGO	non-governmental organisation
NTB	National Tender Board (Rwanda)
ODA	official development assistance
OECD	Organization for Economic Co-operation and Development
PEC	Procurement Endorsing Committee (Ethiopia)
PPA	Public Procurement Act (Nigeria)
PPA	Public Procurement Agency (Ethiopia)
PPAD Act	Public Procurement and Asset Disposal Act (Botswana)
PPADB	Public Procurement and Asset Disposal Board (Botswana)
PPOA	Public Procurement Oversight Authority (Kenya)
PPP	public–private partnership
PPPFA	Preferential Procurement Policy Framework Act (South Africa)
RFP	request for proposal
RFQ	request for quotation
RPPA	Rwanda Public Procurement Agency
SACU	Southern African Customs Union
SADC	Southern African Development Community
SME	small and medium-sized enterprise / small, medium and micro enterprise
TIPEEG	Targeted Intervention Programme for Employment and Economic Growth (Namibia)
UNCITRAL	United Nations Commission on International Trade Law
UNCTAD	United Nations Conference on Trade and Development
UNICEF	United Nations Children's Fund
WAEMU	West African Economic and Monetary Union
WTO	World Trade Organization

1

Introduction

GEO QUINOT AND SUE ARROWSMITH

1. Background

'Public procurement' refers to the process through which the state acquires goods, works and services needed to fulfil its public functions. In its broadest definition, the function of procurement captures the entire process from the identification of the goods or services needed, through the course of identifying a supplier, to the maintenance (performance, administration, cancellation) of the contract concluded between the contracting authority and the supplier.[1] Unlike analogous commercial transacting in the private sector, public procurement is often governed and thus structured by specific detailed rules – the distinct field of law called public procurement law or public procurement regulation. Within this field of law, the focus of many regulatory instruments is on the rules governing the process leading up to the conclusion of the contract and in particular the process through which a supplier is identified and a contract awarded to that supplier.[2]

The development of this field of law and its academic study has gained significant momentum globally in the last two decades. Most recently, the two major international regulatory regimes on public procurement – the World Trade Organization's Agreement on Government Procurement and the UNCITRAL Model Law on the Procurement of Goods, Construction and Services – have both gone through comprehensive

1 See generally S. Arrowsmith, *The Law of Public and Utilities Procurement* (2nd edn, London: Sweet & Maxwell, 2005), p. 1; S. Arrowsmith, J. Linarelli and D. Wallace, *Regulating Public Procurement: National and International Perspectives* (The Hague; London: Kluwer Law International, 2000), pp. 1–2.

2 This is not to say that the focus in public procurement law is exclusively on this stage in the broader procurement process. Matters outside of this narrow focus have also been subjected to legal regulation, such as post-contractual variation of terms, particularly in countries of the civil law tradition.

revision.[3] Many African systems have also recently experienced major development in public procurement regulation.[4] As Stephen Karangizi notes, these developments have largely been in the form of 'the recognition of the need to enact specific legislation to provide for clear and unambiguous laws on procurement'.[5] While reforms in governance, including public procurement reforms, have been ongoing for some time on the African continent,[6] the current wave of reforms seems to have gathered momentum following the 1998 International Conference on Public Procurement Reform in Africa held in Abidjan[7] and continued to the most recent High Level Forum on Public Procurement Reform in Africa held in Tunis in November 2009,[8] both of which were sponsored by the African Development Bank Group (AfDB), the Common Market for Eastern and Southern Africa (COMESA), the West African Economic and Monetary Union (WAEMU), the African Capacity Building Foundation (ACBF), the Organization for Economic Co-operation and Development (OECD) and the World Bank.

The 1998 conference was attended by over thirty African governments and many more international development partners. At this conference, described as a 'watershed in bringing to the fore the importance of public

3 On the reform of the WTO's Agreement on Government Procurement, see S. Arrowsmith and R. D. Anderson (eds.), *The WTO Regime on Government Procurement: Challenge and Reform* (Cambridge University Press, 2011); and R. D. Anderson, 'The Conclusion of the Renegotiation of the WTO Agreement on Government Procurement in December 2011: What It Means for the Agreement and for the World Economy' (2012) 21 *Public Procurement Law Review* 83. On the UNCITRAL Model Law on Procurement, see J. Tillipman and S. Arrowsmith (eds.), *Reform of the UNCITRAL Model Law on Procurement: Procurement Regulation for the 21st Century* (Eagan, MN: West, 2010–11); C. Nicholas, 'The 2011 UNCITRAL Model Law on Public Procurement' (2012) 21 *Public Procurement Law Review* NA111.

4 S. Karangizi, 'Framework Arrangements in Public Procurement: A Perspective from Africa' in Tillipman and Arrowsmith (eds.), *Reform of the UNCITRAL Model Law on Procurement*, note 3 above.

5 *Ibid.*, p. 244.

6 See B. Basheka, 'Public Procurement Reforms in Africa: A Tool for Effective Governance and the Public Sector and Poverty Reduction' in K. V. Thai (ed.), *International Handbook of Public Procurement* (Boca Raton, FL: Taylor & Francis, 2009), p. 133.

7 See S. Karangizi, 'The COMESA Public Procurement Reform Initiative' (2005) 14 *Public Procurement Law Review* NA51, NA52; African Development Bank Group, *COMESA Public Procurement Reform and Capacity Building Projects, Project Performance Evaluation Report* (2012), pp. 2–3.

8 See the Tunis Declaration on Public Procurement Reforms in Africa, 17 November 2009, www.afdb.org/fileadmin/uploads/afdb/Documents/Generic-Documents/FINAL%20DECLARATION%20TRANSLATED%20ENGLISH_26-11-09.pdf (accessed 25 February 2012).

procurement, its linkages with governance and the far-reaching implications of its poor performance on African economies',[9] parties agreed to:

(a) the need for modernisation of public procurement in Africa to meet international standards and best practice;
(b) the need to forge a consensus among all stakeholders on the urgency of engaging in public procurement reforms; and
(c) the need to promote national reform programmes with a common strategic framework focusing on accountability, transparency and efficiency.[10]

The conference identified 'enabling legislation and regulations' as one of the four pillars of public procurement reform in Africa.[11] The scope of subsequent developments in public procurement regulation on the continent generally is staggering, with many African countries having adopted new regulatory regimes in the last ten years.[12] At the 2009 High Level Forum in Tunis, participants recognised the major developments in public procurement regulation since the 1998 Abidjan conference and renewed their commitment 'to consolidate the reforms and promote a multi-sector and participatory approach, mainstreaming public procurement into all State reforms in order to improve their economic impact, particularly in innovative sectors'.[13]

One of the most significant drivers of public procurement regulation reform has been the COMESA[14] Public Procurement Reform Project and its successor, the Enhancing Procurement Reforms and Capacity Project, both sponsored by the AfDB. Karangizi describes the 'twin objectives' of the reform initiative as follows:

9 S. R. Karangizi and I. Ndahiro, 'Public Procurement Reforms and Development in the Eastern and Southern Africa Region' in R. Hérnandez Garcia (ed.), *International Public Procurement: A Guide to Best Practice* (London: Globe Law and Business, 2009), p. 113.

10 African Development Bank Group, note 7 above, p. 3.

11 Karangizi, note 7 above, NA53.

12 See the chapters in Part I of this volume.

13 Tunis Declaration on Public Procurement Reform in Africa Sustaining Economic Development and Poverty Reduction (17 November 2009).

14 The member states of COMESA are Burundi, Comoros, Democratic Republic of the Congo, Djibouti, Egypt, Eritrea, Ethiopia, Kenya, Libya, Madagascar, Malawi, Mauritius, Rwanda, Seychelles, Sudan, Swaziland, Uganda, Zambia and Zimbabwe. This represents the largest economic zone in Africa, with an estimated annual public procurement market of US$50 billion: African Development Bank Group, note 7 above, pp. 1, 2.

> The first was to contribute to the liberalisation of trade in goods and services in the COMESA region. Secondly, the project had as its broad objective the contribution to enhancing good governance in the Member States. This involves laying the groundwork for ensuring accountability and transparency, combating corruption, and creating an enabling legal infrastructure in public procurement in the COMESA countries.[15]

These objectives include the need to 'modernise public procurement rules and practices throughout COMESA as well as to attain their uniformity and harmonisation'.[16] It is furthermore noteworthy that the project also aims to align such a uniform approach to 'practices that [are] of internationally accepted standards'.[17] This programme therefore not only exerts its own influence on local public procurement regimes, but also acts as a medium to transfer wider international influences on national systems in the region. Under this initiative, COMESA has developed a model strategy for public procurement reform in its member states, which includes a regulatory model.[18] Most recently, at its 26th meeting held in June 2009, the COMESA Council adopted a standard set of public procurement regulations that applies to all public procurement within set thresholds, which are conducted within the common market.[19] Member states are required to align their domestic procurement legislation to these regulations for procurement within the thresholds. The COMESA reform initiative has been particularly successful. By 2012, fourteen of the nineteen COMESA members states had aligned their procurement systems with the model developed under the initiative and the members had committed to implementing the regional procurement system under the 2009 COMESA Procurement Regulations by 2014.[20]

Another AfDB supported[21] regional public procurement reform project is that of WAEMU.[22] This initiative developed over two phases, with the first phase involving comprehensive reviews of member states' procurement regimes and resulting in the adoption of two regional public procurement directives in 2005 aimed at modernising and harmonising

15 Karangizi, note 7 above, NA52. 16 *Ibid.*, NA53. 17 *Ibid.* 18 *Ibid.*, NA56.

19 COMESA Legal Notice No. 3 of 2009, COMESA Official Gazette, vol. 15, No. 3, 9 June 2009.

20 African Development Bank Group, note 7 above, p. vi.

21 Other sponsors were the WAEMU Commission, ACBF and the International Organization of Francophone (OIF).

22 WAEMU, or UEMOA from its more commonly used French name, Union Economique et Monétaire Ouest-Africaine, consists of Benin, Burkina Faso, Côte d'Ivoire, Guinea-Bissau, Mali, Niger, Senegal and Togo.

national procurement systems of member states.[23] The second phase, starting in 2007, aims at implementing these directives in the national laws of member states.

While public procurement law reform in Africa has reflected international developments, the same cannot be said of the academic study of this area of law. Public procurement law is now an established field of study in the developed world. There are thriving research and teaching programmes in law schools in Europe and the United States of America in public procurement law and a substantial and ever expanding volume of literature on the topic.[24] In stark contrast, there are no comparable programmes on the African continent, and the literature dealing with public procurement law in Africa is almost negligible in comparison.[25] In many African states, there are no published studies of the local public procurement regulatory regime at all and neither has there been any major study of the topic on a cross-continental scale. The recent books by Phoebe Bolton[26] and Dominic Dagbanja,[27] setting out the public procurement regulatory regimes in South Africa and Ghana respectively, are rare exceptions. In addition, there have been a number of dedicated research studies[28] as well as chapters in books and articles published recently. However, these are still few and far between, with no published work on the topic in many African countries at all, as is indicated in

23 African Development Fund, *Appraisal Report Project in Support of Public Procurement Systems Reform in the WAEMU Zone (Phase II)* (2006), p. 1.

24 For institutions that focus on public procurement regulation in higher education, see the information on the Procurement Law Academic Network at www.planpublicprocurment.org, in the section on institutional membership. For literature, see the comprehensive global *Bibliography on Public Procurement Law and Regulation*, which aims to capture all major works on public procurement regulation published in English worldwide, developed by the EU Asia Inter-University Network for Teaching and Research in Public Procurement Regulation, www.nottingham.ac.uk/pprg/documentsarchive/bibliographies/co?mprehensivepublicprocurementbibliography.pdf (accessed 25 February 2012).

25 In the *Bibliography on Public Procurement Law and Regulation*, above, works dealing specifically with procurement in Africa comprise only nine pages of the 325-page document. In contrast, works dealing specifically with procurement in Europe cover ten times that amount of pages (totalling 91 pages).

26 P. Bolton, *The Law of Government Procurement in South Africa* (Durban: LexisNexis Butterworths, 2007).

27 D. N. Dagbanja, *The Law of Public Procurement in Ghana* (Saarbrücken: Lambert Academic Publishing, 2011).

28 See e.g. S. De la Harpe, 'Public Procurement Law: A Comparative Analysis' (unpublished doctoral thesis, University of South Africa, 2009); K. T. Udeh, 'A Critical Analysis of the Legal Framework for Supplier Remedies System of Kenya in the Light of International Standards' (unpublished LLM dissertation, University of Nottingham, 2008).

the 'Materials on public procurement regulation in Africa' section at the end of this volume. As a result, it is extremely difficult, if not impossible, at present to develop an understanding of the state of public procurement regulation on the continent. This state of affairs hampers effective legal development in Africa, and also limits the ability of those working in procurement outside Africa to incorporate African perspectives into their work, including in research and policy-making activities that have a potential impact on Africa (such as the World Trade Organization's Agreement on Government Procurement and the UNCITRAL Model Law on Public Procurement). In 2009, the Public Procurement Research Group at the University of Nottingham and the University of Stellenbosch Faculty of Law launched a three-year research partnership, funded by the British Academy, aimed at addressing this deficit in scholarly engagement with procurement regulation in Africa. This collection is the primary outcome of the partnership.

The aim of the book is to provide an analysis of the legal rules governing public procurement in a cross-section of African systems and to explore key issues emerging from such a comparative perspective. The objectives are to provide up-to-date information on the main legal rules governing public procurement in a number of African systems; to facilitate a comparative perspective on public procurement regulation on the African continent; to provide context-based analysis of the regulatory situation that is relevant for policy-making and academic debate in this field; to assist African domestic development and to inform legal research and policy-making; and to enable researchers outside Africa to incorporate African perspectives into their work.

2. Structure of the study

The book is divided into two parts. The first part comprises doctrinal analyses of the legal rules governing public procurement in nine African states. These states are Botswana (Chapter 2), Ethiopia (Chapter 3), Ghana (Chapter 4), Kenya (Chapter 5), Namibia (Chapter 6), Nigeria (Chapter 7), Rwanda (Chapter 8), South Africa (Chapter 9) and Zimbabwe (Chapter 10). While this collection of countries does not claim to be representative of the entire continent, it does contain examples from the major sub-Saharan geographical areas. The choice of systems to include has been guided by a desire to present a broad cross-section of African systems from across the continent, but has also been determined by the pragmatic factor of keeping the study to a manageable scope working within language and access constraints. These constraints have also meant that our focus has been primarily on English-speaking African countries and thus largely on common law systems. However, Ethiopia and Rwanda represent systems with a civil law tradition and a number of countries, including Namibia and South Africa, have mixed common law/civil law systems.

The analysis of each system considers both hard law (jurisprudence and legislation) and soft law in the form of guidance, which is important in some legal systems in this area. The analysis of the individual African country systems in Part I is organised in accordance with a detailed template that has been set up by the editors. This seeks to ensure that all chapters provide pertinent background information and use standard terminology to describe phenomena, and a standard approach to analysis, making the information clear to all readers; that all the chapters comment on all key issues; and, related to the above points, that the position of different African states can be compared and contrasted with ease.

In the second part of the book, the current state of procurement regulation in Africa is considered by reference to key themes in which regulation can play an important role using a comparative methodology based in part, but not exclusively, on the country-specific analyses in the first part. These are: the impact of development aid on procurement regulation and policy (Chapter 11); procurement methods (Chapter 12); supplier complaint (remedy) systems (Chapter 13); the use of regulatory techniques to address corruption (Chapter 14); and the use of procurement to promote social policy objectives (Chapter 15).

The remainder of this chapter sets out the basic principles of public procurement regulation to serve as a point of departure for the individual country studies in Part I and the thematic studies in Part II.

3. Principles and aims of public procurement regulation[29]

Public procurement regulation functions within the tension between the ostensibly private or commercial nature of the activity at hand, that is, the purchasing of goods, services and works in the market, and the public nature inherent in the contracting authority's existence and powers. A too narrow regulatory focus on the commercial nature of the activity

29 This section draws heavily from S. Arrowsmith (ed.), *Public Procurement Regulation: An Introduction* (2010), Chapter 1, which is freely available at www.nottingham.ac.uk/pprg/documentsarchive/asialinkmaterials/publicprocurementregulationintroduction.pdf (accessed 2 April 2012).

may lead one to lose sight of the public function necessarily underlying the procurement. Public procurement is thus never an end in itself, but always a means to a public end: for example, books are purchased from private publishers to provide public education or medicine from private pharmaceuticals to provide public health services. Public procurement regulation should thus effectively take account of these public functions. At the same time, it is obviously in the public interest for the contracting authority to obtain value for money in its procurement, that is, the best goods, services or works on the best terms. The latter perspective on public procurement focuses the attention more on the commercial nature of the conduct and emphasises the need to allow contracting authorities to benefit from the private market. The overarching objective of public procurement regulation is thus to obtain a balance between these competing aims.

Value for money has in many systems come to be considered the key objective of public procurement regulation.[30] This is also true of the African systems reviewed in this book as appears from the chapters in Part I.[31] While it is thus often argued that this is the primary objective of most public procurement systems, this is, however, by no means a universal view, nor perhaps true of every procurement system. Dekel, for example, considers that integrity rather than value for money is the overriding goal of competitive bidding in public procurement, and also that the principle of equal treatment as an independent objective of the procurement process should be equal in status to value for money.[32] Certainly, it is the case, however, that many of the regulatory rules that apply in public procurement – such as the basic requirements for transparency and competitive bidding – have the realisation of value for money as one of their aims. Such rules are designed, in particular, to ensure that value for money is not prejudiced by inefficient behaviour, and also that it is not prejudiced by certain deliberate conduct, notably corrupt behaviour and (in some systems) discrimination in favour of national firms.

For taxpayers, value for money is of obvious concern, not only to ensure that public funds achieve as much as possible, but also to ensure

30 See Arrowsmith, *The Law of Public and Utilities Procurement*, note 1 above, pp. 2–5; Arrowsmith, Linarelli and Wallace, *Regulating Public Procurement*, note 1 above, pp. 15, 28–31.

31 See section 2.1 of the respective chapters in Part I below, setting out the objectives of public procurement policy in each of the countries investigated.

32 O. Dekel, 'The Legal Theory of Competitive Bidding for Government Contracts' (2008) 37 *Public Contract Law Journal* 237.

general control over public spending. Value for money does not simply mean acquiring the goods at the lowest price. The quality of the goods and the terms upon which the goods are procured are also important considerations in achieving value for money.[33] The objective of value for money can thus be seen as consisting of three aspects:

(1) ensuring the goods, works or services acquired are suitable; this means both: (i) that they can meet the requirements for the task in question; and (ii) that they are not over-specified ('gold-plated');
(2) concluding an arrangement to secure what is needed on the best possible terms (which does not necessarily mean the lowest price); and
(3) ensuring the contracting partner is able to provide the goods, works or services on the agreed terms.

In order to achieve value for money, public procurement rules commonly require contracting authorities to purchase through some competitive method, allowing multiple suppliers to compete for the contract. Competition is thus a crucial means to achieve value for money (but not, however, an end in itself, as is discussed further below). From a legal perspective, the enforceability of clear rules requiring competition, which is often understood as part of the notion of transparency in procurement, is another key mechanism to ensure value for money.

However, efficiency in conducting the process of procurement is another important objective that also holds significant cost implications and that must be balanced against competition as a means to achieve value for money. From an efficiency perspective, it would not be sensible to approach hundreds of suppliers to buy an item of small value, since the better value for money that may be achieved through such a comprehensive procurement method will almost certainly be negated by the high cost of the procurement method.[34] An important objective of public procurement regulation is thus to define the trade-off between value for money and efficiency in procurement.

Value for money and procedural efficiency are not, of course, goals that are unique to public procurement, but are key considerations in private contracting as well. On their own, these two objectives would thus not justify the existence of distinct rules governing public procurement. The

33 See Arrowsmith, Linarelli and Wallace, *Regulating Public Procurement*, note 1 above, pp. 28–31.
34 *Ibid.*, pp. 31–2.

rationale for a distinct set of rules governing public contracting lies in the distinct nature of the procuring entities. Even in its commercial guise, that is, as a player in the private market, government has distinct characteristics setting it apart from other market participants.[35] Government is also, of course, subject to non-commercial requirements distinguishing it from other buyers. These public considerations play an important role in shaping public procurement regulation. In broad constitutional terms, government is accountable to the public for all its actions. It follows that the public has an interest in government conduct and that government is not simply free to pursue its own private interests in procurement as a private party would be.[36] From a regulatory perspective, this means that the public interest must be factored into the way that government procures, i.e. in the manner that procurement decisions are taken, as well as that there must be mechanisms for holding government accountable, including mechanisms to enforce public procurement rules.

Apart from the interest that the public has in state contracting, government is also often subject to higher standards of fairness and integrity as compared to private parties. A common view is that a higher standard of fair dealings should be expected of government, and even in commercial transactions government should remain the role model or 'moral exemplar' for society.[37] This perspective entails that procuring entities should treat bidders in a particular procurement fairly and equally. It also requires that government makes participation in public procurement contracts open to all members of society so that everyone can fairly share in government business. In some countries, such a policy in public procurement may be a reflection of a more general value adopted in those countries of equal treatment of persons by the administration.

It is important to note at this point, however, that the concept of equal treatment in public procurement may take on two different roles. Thus, it may serve as an objective of the procurement process in its own right, reflecting the notions outlined above such as the right to equal opportunities in government business.

In addition, however, it can also serve simply as a means to achieve other objectives of the public procurement system, such as value for money in

35 On the state as *commercially* distinct from other market participants, see G. Quinot, *State Commercial Activity: A Legal Framework* (Cape Town: Juta & Co., 2009), pp. 155–7, 224–9, 268–9.

36 *Ibid.*, pp. 102–4, 227–8.

37 *Ibid.*, pp. 130–1 and in particular p. 131 note 561; Arrowsmith, *The Law of Public and Utilities Procurement*, note 1 above, p. 6.

obtaining goods, works and services, preventing corruption (as will be argued below) and opening up markets to competition. Thus, holding a competition in which all interested firms have an equal opportunity to participate is often the method chosen for seeking out the best terms for the goods, works and services. Requiring that those involved in the competition are treated on an equal basis during the conduct of the competition can help ensure value for money and/or prevent corruption in the procedure in two ways – first, limiting the opportunity for the procuring entity to make discretionary decisions that could be abused to favour particular firms (for example, a firm that has paid a bribe or – from the perspective of opening up markets – a national firm); and, secondly, by encouraging firms to have confidence in the process and thus encouraging the best firms to participate in the procedure. Different systems may perceive different roles for equal treatment in this respect – but in practice this is not always articulated.

Another important, and often prominent, objective of public procurement regulation is to combat corruption. Curbing corrupt practices such as the payment of bribes in exchange for the award of contracts has become another major aim of public procurement regulation.[38]

38 See further Chapter 14 of this volume; Arrowsmith, *The Law of Public and Utilities Procurement*, note 1 above, pp. 5–6; Arrowsmith, Linarelli and Wallace, *Regulating Public Procurement*, note 1 above, pp. 32–61. See further, for example, F. Anechiarico, 'Reforms in Procurement Policy and Their Prospects' in S. Arrowsmith and M. Trybus (eds.), *Public Procurement: The Continuing Revolution* (London: Kluwer Law International, 2002), Chapter 9; F. Anechiarico and J. Jacobs, *The Pursuit of Absolute Integrity: How Corruption Control Makes Government Ineffective* (Chicago: University of Chicago Press, 1996); S. Arrowsmith, J. Linarelli and D. Wallace, *Regulating Public Procurement: National and International Perspectives* (London: Kluwer Law International, 2000), pp. 32–61; International Trade Centre UNCTAD/WTO, *A Framework for Balancing Business and Accountability within a Public Procurement System*; International Trade Centre UNCTAD/GATT, Guide No. 23, *Improving Public Procurement Systems* (1993), Chapter 1; OECD, *Bribery in Public Procurement: Methods, Actors and Counter-Measures* (OECD, 2007); OECD, *Fighting Corruption and Promoting Integrity in Public Procurement* (2005), Chapters 26–34; OECD, *Integrity in Public Procurement: Good Practice from A to Z* (OECD, 2007); S. Kelman, *Procurement and Public Management* (Washington DC: AEI Press, 1990), pp. 99–100; W. Kovacic, 'The Civil False Claims Act as a Deterrent to Participation in Government Procurement Markets' (1998) 6 *Supreme Court Economic Review* 201; J. Linarelli, 'Corruption in Developing Countries and Economies in Transition: Economic and Legal Perspectives' in S. Arrowsmith and A. Davies (eds.), *Public Procurement Global Revolution* (London: Kluwer Law International, 1998), Chapter 7; J. Linarelli, 'Corruption in Developing Countries and in Countries in Transition: Legal and Economic Perspectives' in S. Arrowsmith and A. Davies (eds.), *Public Procurement Global Revolution* (London: Kluwer Law International, 1998), Chapter 14; S. Rose-Ackerman, *Corruption and Government: Causes, Consequences and Reform* (Cambridge University

As is discussed in more detail in Chapter 14, corruption in public procurement can cover various types of practice. Many of these involve various forms of collusion between government and bidders.[39] These may include: awarding contracts on the basis of bribes; awarding contracts to firms in which one has a personal interest; awarding contracts to firms in which one's friends, family or business acquaintances have an interest; and awarding contracts to political supporters (for example, to firms which have provided financial support; or to regions which have voted for a particular political party). Such corruption can occur in the execution as well as award of contracts – for example, officials can collude with bidders to allow them to claim extra payments for non-existent work. Obviously, states need to have a clear conception of and clear rules on which practices are, and are not, acceptable. In Chapter 14, it is shown that corruption may be culturally specific, with a dichotomy between Western and non-Western notions of what constitutes corrupt practices. For example, in some countries small gifts between those in business are regarded as 'expected' rather than corrupt. It is also often said that corruption is more of a problem in public sector procurement

Press, 1999), Chapters 1–5; I. Shihata, 'Corruption: A General Review with an Emphasis on the Role of the World Bank' (1997) 15 *Dickinson Journal of International Law* 451; F. Stapenhurst and P. Langseth, 'The Role of the Public Administration in Fighting Corruption' (1997) 10 *International Journal of Public Sector Management* 311; Transparency International Sourcebook, Chapter 12 on Public Procurement, available at www.transparency.org/publications/sourcebook; P. Trepte, *Transparency and Accountability as Tools for Promoting Integrity and Preventing Corruption in Public Procurement* (2005) (paper to OECD Expert Group meeting on Integrity in Public Procurement); W. Wittig, 'A Framework for Balancing Business and Accountability within a Public Procurement System: Approaches and Practices of the United States' (2001) 10 *Public Procurement Law Review* 139; C. Yukins, 'Integrating Integrity and Procurement: The United Nations Convention against Corruption and the UNCITRAL Model Procurement Law' (2007) 36 *Public Contract Law Journal* 307.

39 Corruption in public procurement may of course also occur as a result of private sector action, without any collusion on the part of public authorities. One important practice is 'collusive tendering' by private firms. Obviously, this will prevent effective public contracting and, in particular, attainment of value for money, and states will wish to ensure that effective laws are in place to deal with this kind of problem, usually by an area of law known as competition law. Another problem is the provision of false information by contractors, for example concerning their qualifications and experience, to obtain contracts, and fraudulent practices in the execution of contracts, such as billing for services not actually provided to the public (for example, for non-existent patients under health care contracts). Procurement systems may also employ criminal sanctions as ways of addressing these private corrupt practices such as the case for example in South Africa, as discussed further in Chapter 9, setting out the procurement regime in South Africa, and Chapter 14, dealing with corruption in public procurement.

than in private sector procurement, because of factors such as (in some countries) low wages and the structure of government.[40] Given the generally low public sector wages in most African countries as well as unwieldy bureaucracy, based on these factors, one would thus expect corruption to be a particular problem in African public procurement. It is thus not surprising to find that anti-corruption objectives are universally found in the African procurement systems under review in this book, and that the anti-corruption objective is perceived as being of significant importance in African regulatory systems on public procurement.

The anti-corruption objective links the objectives of value for money and integrity and fairness. If a contract is awarded for corrupt reasons – for example, because of the payment of a bribe or in self-interest – best value for money is undermined. Corrupt practices in the award of public contracts may also do serious 'reputational' harm to a particular procurement system so that potential suppliers will be put off from bidding for future contracts leading to less competition and higher prices. However, curbing corruption is also an important part of achieving the objectives of fairness and integrity apart from any impact it may have on value for money, and also potentially an important objective for other reasons. These include to avoid supporting corrupt enterprises that could operate also in other sectors, to avoid providing financial support for criminal or other undesirable activities that may be financed through corruptly awarded government contracts, and to set an example to the private sector.

Whilst to some extent the different objectives of regulation are complementary, as is illustrated by the role of anti-corruption measures in supporting value for money, there are also situations in which achieving value for money in the goods, works or services acquired, especially if the focus is on the particular procurement in question, may come into conflict with other goals, and an appropriate balance must be drawn between them. One example that commonly occurs in practice is the case in which a procuring entity receives a bid which does not comply with some formal requirement of the tendering process – for example, is late or does not contain a bid bond in the required form, or is otherwise not in compliance with substantive or procedural requirements laid down in the bid documents. In this case, a principle of equal treatment or fairness might suggest that the bid should be rejected – but if the bid is the best one

40 See further P. Trepte, *Regulating Procurement: Understanding the Ends and Means of Public Procurement Regulation* (Oxford University Press, 2004), pp. 74–7.

submitted the principle of value for money as applied in the particular transaction might indicate that it should be accepted, as it will provide better value for the procuring entity.[41] Another potential area for conflict is with rules to prevent corruption, as is also discussed in Chapter 14 of this volume. Rules that are designed to reduce corruption by limiting the discretion of procuring entities, and hence limiting opportunities for abuse to favour a particular supplier, may also curtail discretion that could be used to obtain better value for money – a point that we will return to later below.

The tension between the various objectives outlined above, as well as within the objective of value for money internally, can also be seen when comparing actions which will achieve value for money in the short term and those based on principles that are designed to promote value for money in the longer term by encouraging suppliers to have confidence in, and participate in, the public market. An example can again be given by reference to the issue of late tenders raised above. As well as being an independent objective of the procurement process, the principle of equal treatment or fairness can also operate to support other objectives, including supporting value for money by maintaining the confidence of tenderers in the procurement process, which will encourage them to tender in the future and hence promote greater value for money. Thus, in the case of the late tender referred to above, if rejection of late tenders is considered as giving effect to equal treatment, this can be seen not merely as supporting a separate objective of equal participation or fairness in procurement but also as supporting value for money in the procurement system as a whole – rather than the individual transaction – by encouraging participation. In this case, a conflict can be seen between short-term value for money (value in the particular procurement) and value for money overall in the system. Similar conflict emerges between value for money and some horizontal policies in procurement, such as support for small or domestic suppliers, when viewed in the short or longer term, as we will discuss below.

Apart from value for money, tension can also exist between anti-corruption objectives and efficiency in procurement. Simply put, the cost of anti-corruption measures in terms of less efficient procurement

41 This example is given by Dekel, 'The Legal Theory of Competitive Bidding for Government Contracts', note 32 above. For a further discussion of the policy considerations involved in these situations, see Arrowsmith (ed.), *Public Procurement Regulation: An Introduction*, note 29 above, Chapter 3, section 3.7.

processes may overshadow the savings in corruption-free procurement. For example, the cost of vetting all bidders for potential links with firms barred from government contracts because of past corrupt practices in every procurement may simply be much more than the gain of excluding such firms from bidding.[42] The government must then ask whether the objective of preventing corruption is such an important goal in its own right and for reasons other than financial, that resources should be spent to pursue it.

Public procurement regulation is also often influenced by objectives 'external' to the procurement of goods and services itself. Public procurement has thus been used to promote what can be called 'horizontal policies',[43] as will be explained in more detail in Chapter 15. Such horizontal policies, also called 'secondary' or 'collateral' policies, may be industrial/economic, social, environmental or political in nature. For example, horizontal policy objectives in public procurement may aim at supporting small, medium and micro enterprises (SMEs) or domestic suppliers or goods to support domestic economic development. In this way, public procurement becomes a policy tool and the regulation thereof often takes this into account. In South Africa, for example, one finds prime examples of both these types of policy as key objectives of public procurement.[44] Public procurement is used as a means to support local industry in an attempt to stimulate economic growth. In addition, South African public procurement is used as a mechanism to redistribute wealth in favour of those disadvantaged by the previous apartheid system.[45] For both these policy objectives, particular rules have been created within public procurement regulation in South Africa, as is discussed in Chapter 9, dealing with public procurement regulation in South Africa, and Chapter 15, dealing with social policy objectives in procurement.

The use of public procurement as a tool of domestic policy, however, also has costs and often stands in tension with other policy objectives such as value for money and efficiency. As is the case with anti-corruption measures in procurement, outlined above, the inclusion of social policy objectives in public procurement may lead to higher prices since it may

42 On this problem, see F. Anechiarico and J. Jacobs, 'Purging Corruption from Public Contracting: The Solutions Are Now Part of the Problem' (1995) 40 *New York Law School Law Review* 143.

43 S. Arrowsmith and P. Kunzlik (eds.), *Social and Environmental Policies in EC Procurement Law: New Directives and New Directions* (Cambridge University Press, 2009), Chapter 1.

44 See Chapter 9 of this volume, setting out the public procurement regime in South Africa.

45 See Chapter 15 of this volume, dealing with social policy in procurement.

reduce the pool of competition. However, as also indicated above, value for money may in the long run benefit from certain social policy objectives, such as support for SMEs and domestic industries when the pool of competing bidders are extended by these policy objectives, leading to more competition and lower prices. There will, however, mostly be adverse cost implications in using procurement for policy purposes, if not in the form of procuring entities actually paying higher prices to targeted bidders, then at least in the form of more complex procurement procedures and more scope for supplier challenges. These specific issues are discussed in more detail in Chapter 15.

The use of public procurement for social policy purposes also often stands in conflict with a final objective in many public procurement systems, namely, to open up public markets to international trade.[46] This last objective has been a major driver of international development in public procurement regulation over the last twenty years. Both regional public procurement regimes, such as that of the EU or COMESA, and international regimes such as the WTO's Agreement on Government Procurement and the UNCITRAL Model Law on Public Procurement of 2011, have developed largely to advance this objective. While the WTO's Agreement on Government Procurement has not influenced African systems, with not a single African country being a party to that agreement, the UNCITRAL Model Law (in its 1994 version, the UNCITRAL Model Law on Procurement of Goods, Construction and Services) has been extremely influential in Africa: a large number of African procurement systems are based on that Model Law, including many of the systems reviewed in this book. This trade liberalisation objective is obviously in conflict with policy objectives aimed at supporting domestic suppliers and/or goods.

As is clear from the discussion of public procurement objectives above, the two key mechanisms to realise many of the objectives in public procurement systems are transparency[47] and competition. These are not

46 See Arrowsmith, Linarelli and Wallace, *Regulating Public Procurement*, note 1 above, pp. 310–22; P. Bolton and G. Quinot, 'Social Policies in Procurement and the Agreement on Government Procurement: A Perspective from South Africa' in Arrowsmith and Anderson, *The WTO Regime on Government Procurement*', note 3 above, p. 459.

47 See further S. Kelman, 'Remaking Federal Procurement' (2002) 31 *Public Contract Law Journal* 581; S. Kelman, *Procurement and Public Management* (Washington DC: AEI Press, 1990); Arrowsmith, Linarelli and Wallace, note 1 above, pp. 72 *et seq*; S. Arrowsmith, 'The EC Procurement Directives, National Procurement Policies and Better Governance: The Case for a New Approach' (2002) 27 *European Law Review* 3; S. Schooner, 'Commercial Purchasing: The Chasm between the United States Government's Evolving Policy and Practice' in S. Arrowsmith and M. Trybus (eds.), *Public Procurement: The Continuing*

objectives in their own right, but rather ends towards different means, namely, the objectives outlined above. As with the objectives themselves, these mechanisms may at times complement each other and at other times stand in conflict. For example, higher levels of transparency will attract more bidders and lead to higher competition; but, on the other hand, transparency rules may at times insist on the exclusion of certain bids – for example late bids or incomplete bids – or certain practices – for example extensive negotiations with bidders or high levels of discretion in the hands of contracting authorities – which may inhibit competition.

Transparency can be understood as consisting of four elements:[48]

(1) Publicity for contract opportunities.
(2) Publicity for the rules governing each procedure.
(3) A principle of rule-based decision-making that limits the discretion of procuring entities.
(4) The possibility for verification of the fact that the rules have been followed and for enforcement where they have not.

Each of these can be aligned to one or more of the objectives of public procurement regulation outlined above. For example:

- Publicity for contract opportunities obviously supports value for money by ensuring that the best suppliers know about an opportunity, and helps open up contracts to trade when publicity is required in a form accessible to foreign suppliers.
- Publicity for the rules of each procedure, such as the award criteria, helps ensure that tenderers submit tenders that best match the procuring entity's priorities, thus ensuring better value tenders.
- Limits on discretion help prevent decisions based on illegitimate considerations, such as decisions based on corrupt motives (thus

Revolution (London: Kluwer Law International, 2002), Chapter 8; S. Schooner, 'Fear of Oversight: The Fundamental Failure of Businesslike Government' (2001) 50 *American University Law Review* 627; J. Schwartz, 'Regulation and Deregulation in Public Procurement Law Reform in the United States' in G. Piga and K. Thai (eds.), *Advancing Public Procurement: Practices, Innovation and Knowledge-Sharing* (Boca Raton, FL: PrAcademics Press, 2007), Chapter 8; P. Trepte, *Transparency and Accountability as Tools for Promoting Integrity and Preventing Corruption in Public Procurement* (2005) (paper to OECD Expert Group meeting on Integrity in Public Procurement); C. Vacketta, 'Lessons from the Commercial Marketplace' (2002) 11 *Public Procurement Law Review* 126; W. Wittig, 'A Framework for Balancing Business and Accountability within a Public Procurement System: Approaches and Practices of the United States' (2001) 10 *Public Procurement Law Review* 139.

48 As outlined in Arrowsmith, Linarelli and Wallace, note 1 above, pp. 72–3.

supporting the objective of integrity) or decisions that favour national suppliers. Eliminating the possibility for decisions based on these motives will also enhance value for money. Such limits also ensure that decisions are made in accordance with the wisdom of past experience (as reflected in the rules limiting discretion on, for example, how to evaluate tenders or when to depart from competitive tendering), and help maintain the confidence of contractors in the system, thus encouraging participation – again promoting better value for money. The combination of publicity for the applicable rules and the existence of substantive limits on discretion also enhance accountability.

A key consideration of transparency as a mechanism in public procurement is the amount of discretion granted to procuring entities. Whilst limiting discretion can have the benefits outlined above, limiting discretion too much can undermine value for money since contracting authorities will not be able to freely respond in a manner most appropriate under given circumstances to achieve the best possible terms for the goods, services or works procured.[49] One of the key areas of debate in the literature on public procurement regulation is the extent to which discretion should be allowed in public procurement systems to achieve the most appropriate balance between these competing considerations.[50] As far as the benefits of limiting discretion are concerned, the importance of limitations on discretion as a means of preventing corruption has been particularly prominent. From this perspective, important factors in deciding on the level of limits on discretion will include the level of corruption within the system and the importance of anti-corruption objectives. Given the focus on corruption in many African public procurement systems, it is not surprising that limitations on discretion have often been given an important role in these systems. Thus, for example, as Chapter 12 explains, when deciding which procurement methods to choose from the variety offered by the UNCITRAL Model Law for undertaking complex procurement of goods and construction, African states using the 1994 Model Law have tended to choose those methods that involve the least discretion (in particular, two-stage tendering – or even open tendering – rather than request for proposals or competitive negotiation).[51] Limited capacity of

49 For further discussion and illustration, see Arrowsmith, 'The EC Procurement Directives, National Procurement Policies and Better Governance', note 47 above; Arrowsmith (ed.), *Public Procurement Regulation: An Introduction*, note 29 above, Chapter 1, section 1.4.8.

50 See generally the works cited in note 47 above.

51 See Chapter 12, section 3.

procurement officers to make difficult commercial judgments – another issue in African countries – is also a factor that supports limiting discretion[52] and another reason that has influenced choice of methods of procurement as set out above. On the other hand, the actual value of limiting discretion in addressing corrupt behaviour – both of itself and in relation to alternative approaches for addressing corruption – is also clearly important. Thus, if, for example, the transparency rules can easily be evaded or if sanctions for non-compliance do not actually deter corrupt behaviour because the rewards are so great or (avoidably or unavoidably) the risk of detection is low, then this may affect the balance of costs and benefits. There is, in fact, little empirical evidence on this subject[53] and further research would be useful in helping to develop sound policy on this important but contentious issue.

The second mechanism commonly used in public procurement systems, along with transparency, to achieve the regulatory objectives outlined above, is competition.[54] In public procurement regulation, this translates to rules insisting that contracts be awarded through some procedure involving multiple would-be suppliers competing for the contract, as is discussed in more detail in Chapter 12 of this volume, dealing with procurement methods. Competition is not only important for achieving value for money, but also plays an important role in ensuring integrity in the system by creating incentives for bidders to monitor compliance with rules in a given procurement. In this manner, the procurement system becomes 'self-enforcing'. However, as with everything else above, competition may also involve costs. It is thus widely accepted that a competitive procedure cannot be adopted for all forms of procurement since the cost of running a competition may simply be too high for low-value purchases. It is thus fairly common, as will also be outlined in Chapter 12, to find that, in low-value procurements, competition is either limited or dispensed with altogether.

52 On the issue of capacity, see P. Trepte, 'Building Sustainable Capacity in Public Procurement' in Arrowsmith and Anderson, *The WTO Regime on Government Procurement*', note 3 above, Chapter 12.

53 For one piece of research that throws some light on this by examining the relative importance of active waste (including corruption) and passive waste (broadly speaking, inefficiency), see O. Bandiera, A. Prat and T. Valletti, 'Active and Passive Waste in Government Spending: Evidence from a Policy Experiment' (2009) 99 *American Economic Review* 1278.

54 For detailed treatment of the mechanism of competition, see Trepte, *Regulating Procurement: Understanding the Ends and Means of Public Procurement Regulation*, note 40 above, pp. 85–9.

Finally, it needs to be observed that it is an important feature of any system of regulation that it should be as clear and simple as possible: a lack of clarity and simplicity in the rules may result in substantial costs in terms of time and staffing resources, as well as a failure to apply the rules properly, which may in turn prejudice the attainment of the substantive goals of those rules. In public procurement, where the realisation of the regulatory objectives depends on the confidence of, and participation by, the private sector, this is a matter of particular importance. (Indeed, the main way in which the UNCITRAL Model Law aims to enhance international trade is by promoting the standardisation of laws between countries, in the expectation that suppliers will be more willing to participate in a system where the regulatory rules are familiar to them.)[55] However, clarity and simplicity are not easy to achieve in any public procurement system in view of the complexity of the subject matter and the variety of goals pursued by most systems, and its attainment is a challenge for all countries.

As we will see in Chapter 11, Africa faces particular difficulties in this respect, arising from the fact that much of its procurement is funded by foreign aid, and that aid donors frequently require use of procurement rules that they themselves lay down, rather than allowing the award of contracts in accordance with the national regulatory rules of the beneficiary country. In part – although this is far from the whole picture – this situation can be attributed to different priorities between the different objectives outlined above (at the risk of simplification, it can be said, for example, that the development banks have a stronger anti-corruption focus than many regulators), or on differing views on how particular objectives are best achieved (for example, the appropriate balance between transparency and discretion), with each donor insisting on compliance with rules that reflect its own objectives and viewpoints. It goes without saying that the need to operate under a multiplicity of different procedural rules in carrying out public procurement – both national rules and those set out by a variety of different donors – is significantly detrimental to the clarity and simplicity of the system, as well as giving rise to other problems, as elaborated in Chapter 11. The resolution of this unfortunate situation is to some extent tied to the development of successful regulatory systems on a national basis, which is the main focus of the country chapters in this book, since the existence of sound national systems is an essential condition for a solution that allows use of those systems for donor-funded

55 See further S. Arrowsmith, 'Public Procurement: An Appraisal of the UNCITRAL Model Law as a Global Standard' (2004) 53 *International and Comparative Law Quarterly* 17.

procurement. However, this alone will not solve the problem, given the conflicting perspectives on the objectives of regulation and the means for achieving them, as well as other considerations discussed in Chapter 11. This is one of the major difficulties faced by African public procurement systems today. It is to be hoped that, as the internal regulation of public procurement in Africa continues to improve, some satisfactory solution will be found to this 'external' difficulty.

PART I

Country studies

2

The regulatory framework for public procurement in Botswana

REKHA A. KUMAR AND ELINOR CABORN

1. Introduction

Botswana, formerly the British protectorate known as Bechuanaland, adopted its new name upon independence in 1966. Botswana is a land-locked middle-income country in Southern Africa with a population of 2 million.[1] Four decades of uninterrupted civilian leadership, progressive social policies and significant capital investment have created one of the most dynamic economies in Africa. The inevitable consequence of British colonial rule was the legacy of a dual legal system, which is the co-existence of the received laws from the Cape as Roman-Dutch common law supplemented by Proclamations and the indigenous customary laws.[2] The post-independence legal system is dominated by the common law regime, especially in the fields of constitutional, administrative, criminal and labour laws. The customary regime, it is said, applies mostly to the rural population in civil or private law matters.[3]

It must be acknowledged that there has been a spate of law-making by the National Assembly since independence in an attempt to right some of the wrongs inflicted by colonialism. In line with targeted economic and social objectives, particularly growth in domestic capacity, the public procurement system in Botswana is providing a potentially powerful tool to enhance citizen participation in economic activities resulting in increased employment and capacity building through reserved and preferential procurement schemes.[4]

1 Central Statistics Office, *Preliminary Results Brief, 2011 Population and Housing Census* (2011).

2 See A. J. G. M. Sanders, 'Legal Dualism in Lesotho, Botswana and Swaziland – A General Survey' (1985) 1 *Lesotho Law Journal* 47; A. Molokomme, 'Reception and Development of Roman-Dutch Law in Botswana' (1985) 1 *Lesotho Law Journal* 121.

3 *Ibid.*

4 Public Procurement and Asset Disposal Act 2001 ('PPAD Act'), as amended 2008, ss. 66–67.

Alongside the empowerment of citizen contractors, the government of Botswana is also actively pursuing regional integration as a means of economic development. It is part of the Southern African Customs Union (SACU) and a member of the Southern African Development Community (SADC), which recently agreed upon the establishment of a free trade area with the Common Market for Eastern and Southern Africa (COMESA) and the East African Community (EAC).[5] While none of these regional agreements currently entails specific procurement obligations, increasing economic integration in the region is expected to bring public procurement markets to the fore in future.

The present chapter is an overview of the procurement system in Botswana. It begins with the mission and goals of procurement policy in the country, and then proceeds with a brief sketch of the nature and organisational structure of the procurement system in the country. The next part of the text outlines the main public procurement law of the country, including the methods, rules and procedures that currently govern the procurement of goods, works and services. The chapter concludes with some reflections about the overall procurement system, including some of the challenges it is currently facing.

2. Introduction to the public procurement system

2.1. Introduction

Botswana's public procurement system is centred on the Public Procurement and Asset Disposal Board (PPADB), whose mission is 'to lead the effective implementation of a devolved, efficient, cost-effective and transparent public procurement and asset disposal system through an appropriate regulatory environment'.[6]

2.2. The objectives of public procurement policy

The objectives are somewhat similar to those of most national procurement systems, seeking to attain value for money, fair treatment of contractors, accountability and integrity through the application of competitive bidding practices. Thus, open domestic bidding is the preferred method of procurement, with other methods permitted only in certain prescribed

5 See www.eac.int/tripartite-summit/tripartitie-overview.html (accessed 16 March 2012).

6 See www.ppadb.co.bw/mission_vision.htm (accessed 16 March 2012).

circumstances.[7] However, the government of Botswana also recognises procurement as an important mechanism for empowerment within the economic framework of a nation with few decades of independence. Thus, this first set of objectives is balanced against socio-economic objectives of economic empowerment, with the government permitted to introduce reserved and preferential procurement schemes.[8] These schemes are discussed in more detail in Chapter 15.

The objectives of public procurement policy are not independently stated in Botswana's public procurement law, but are indirectly established as obligations of the PPADB. Section 26 of the Public Procurement and Asset Disposal Act ('PPAD Act'), in describing the functions and powers of the Board, provides that the Board shall ensure that all public procurement entities, in making their decisions, take into account the principles of an open, competitive economy; standardisation in the interest of cost reduction, ease of maintenance and technological effectiveness; aggregation of procurement in order to benefit from economies of scale; using the most efficient and competitive methods of procurement to achieve the best value for money; fair and equitable treatment of all contractors in the interest of efficiency and the maintenance of a level playing field; accountability and transparency in the management of public procurement to promote ownership of the system and minimise challenges; and integrity, fairness of and public confidence in the procurement process.

Public procurement policy is a potentially powerful tool in influencing targeted economic development, particularly growth in domestic capacity. Thus, economic and social objectives in public procurement are addressed in detail in Part VII of the PPAD Act and policy developments in economic empowerment issues were one reason for amendment of that Act in 2008.[9] The PPAD Act differentiates between 'citizen contractors' which are wholly owned and controlled by citizens of Botswana and 'local contractors' whose operations are based in Botswana without involvement by citizens. Preference schemes must be targeted, time bound, non-discriminatory and based on competition with stated objectives against which progress can be assessed. Reservation schemes are limited to procurement of low value and complexity. Despite the

7 Part V, Public Procurement and Asset Disposal Regulations 2006 ('PPAD Regulations').

8 PPAD Act, s. 66.

9 Public Procurement and Asset Disposal (Amendment) Bill 2008, Memorandum. See also Chapter 15 of this volume.

importance of socio-economic objectives, these are balanced with the drive for regional integration. Reserved and preferential procurement schemes must be 'consistent with [the government's] external obligations and its stable, market-oriented, macro-economic framework'.[10] Further, the PPADB is charged with ensuring that procurement entities take into account 'changing external obligations in relation, generally to trade and specifically to procurement, which dynamically impact on a continual basis on domestic procurement policy and practice'.[11] The objectives of national procurement policy thus remain flexible, adapting in line with the government's developing trade policy.

2.3. Nature and organisation of public procurement

2.3.1. The Public Procurement and Asset Disposal Board

The PPADB is the central procurement office of Botswana, established by Act of Parliament as an independent authority responsible for the co-ordination and management of public procurement of public works, supplies and services for government.[12] The PPADB is a parastatal organisation, operating under the Ministry of Finance and Development Planning.[13] The PPADB's current role is principally one of vetting tender documents, adjudicating on award recommendations submitted by procuring entities and contractor registration, although tender vetting and adjudication functions are increasingly being performed by its committees under a process of gradual devolution, managed through automatic biennial increases in financial ceilings for the committees.[14] According to a 2007 assessment report, it is estimated that approximately 70 per cent of recurrent expenditure and all development expenditure goes through the public procurement system. The PPADB adjudicates about sixty submissions per week, roughly divided into 35 per cent supplies, 18.9 per cent services, 30.7 per cent works, 13.6 per cent information technology and 1.8 per cent legal issues.[15]

Three core divisions are in existence – works, services and supplies – to facilitate the implementation of section 3(c) of the PPAD Act which

10 PPAD Act, s. 66. 11 *Ibid.*, s. 26(a). 12 *Ibid.*, ss. 10–11.

13 See www.ppadb.co.bw/background.htm (accessed 16 March 2012).

14 PPAD Act, s. 65.

15 PPADB, Botswana: *Methodology for the Assessment of the Benchmarking Tool: Report of the Assessment of Public Procurement System in Botswana (for OECD-DAC Joint Venture on Procurement)*, p. 3, www.oecd.org/dataoecd/17/45/39244758.pdf (accessed 16 March 2012).

refers to the procurement of all works, services and supplies, or any combination thereof, however classified. The Board comprises the Executive Chairman, who is also the Chief Executive, three Executive Directors, each of whom heads divisions responsible for works, services and supplies, and three part-time Non-Executive Directors (from the private sector) each of whom have been assigned to work with a particular division.[16]

The PPADB is currently undertaking process re-engineering to streamline, standardise and publish its internal processes, and is investing heavily in computer systems to give greater access to government procurement activities through integrated networks, common databases and accessible websites that will provide details of government tender requirements. In addition, funds permitting, plans are underway for the PPADB to set up satellite offices in some major villages and towns around the country, so as to bring its services closer to the people.[17]

The PPADB has various powers of investigation, including powers to inspect records and summon witnesses, which it can use for tender, contract or performance audits.[18] It also provides the first level of review for procurement complaints, which is discussed in more detail in Chapter 13. As greater procurement responsibilities are devolved, the PPADB is providing an increasingly important input into legislation and regulation, policy and procedures, training and capacity building, and it is the intention of the PPADB to move over the next few years towards a regulatory, training and compliance-checking role. It will reduce its tender adjudication role by devolving increased responsibilities to procuring entities, although it will retain the adjudication of all high-value, high-profile procurement activities. The Board is increasingly providing training to procuring entities to support their devolved status, and also plans to assist contractors with training to improve their capability and capacity to participate in government procurement.[19]

2.3.2. Committees

The PPADB is required by the Act to establish various committees to which it delegates specific functions and powers in respect of public procurement.[20] These include Ministerial Tender Committees (MTCs)[21] for each central government ministry or department; and District

16 See www.ppadb.co.bw/ppadb_divisions.htm (accessed 16 March 2012).

17 The PPADB is currently located in Gaborone, the capital city. 18 PPAD Act, s. 52.

19 PPADB Executive Director: Supplies, Speech: 'PPADB Workshop for General Suppliers' (December 2009).

20 PPAD Act, Part VII. 21 *Ibid.*, s. 61.

Administration Tender Committees (DATCs)[22] which act for the decentralised offices of central government bodies. Tender Committees are also established for each local authority and parastatal organisation. Delegations are subject to financial ceilings, which are reviewed and increased by the PPADB biennially; the current ceilings (due for review in 2012) are 25 million pula (approximately £2.2 million) for MTCs; and 2 million pula (approximately £175,000) for DATCs. In addition, a Special Procurement and Asset Disposal Committee manages the procurement of highly sensitive works, supplies, services and properties.[23]

Although the requirement to 'devolve significant responsibilities' to the committees over time is mandated in the PPAD Act, the PPADB remains 'responsible and accountable for all the decisions taken', and may vary or set aside any such decision.[24] Revisions to the Act are likely to be necessary should a fully decentralised system, monitored by an independent procurement policy office be desired.

The PPAD Act establishes two committees with regulatory functions, which are independent of the PPADB. The Independent Complaints Review Committee (ICRC) is responsible for dealing with challenges by contractors, as well as various other dispute resolution functions,[25] as discussed further in section 2.4 below. The Advisory Committee on Public Procurement and Asset Disposal, which consists of thirteen members appointed by the Minister for Finance from a range of public, private and oversight bodies, is charged with reviewing the performance of the Board, its committees, procuring entities and the ICRC. It may then recommend to the minister improvements to the legal framework, procurement system, coordination of procurement policies with other public entities and standardisation between central government, local authorities and parastatals.[26] This committee was appointed for the first time in 2011.[27]

2.3.3. Procuring entities

Each procuring entity is responsible for the management of all procurement activities within its jurisdiction.[28] The accounting officer has the overall responsibility for the procurement process, with particular responsibilities for recommending to the PPADB suitably qualified and

22 *Ibid.*, s. 64. 23 *Ibid.*, s. 63. 24 *Ibid.*, ss. 62 and 50.

25 *Ibid.*, Part X. See also Chapter 13 of this volume. 26 PPAD Act, Part XI.

27 See www.ppadb.co.bw/Advisory_Committee_pressrelease.pdf (accessed 16 March 2012).

28 PPAD Regulations, reg. 6.

experienced staff to become members of the MTC, procurement planning, certifying the availability of funds prior to commencement of procurement and prior to award, and ensuring contracts are implemented in accordance with the terms and conditions of the award.[29] The PPAD Regulations also give accounting officers responsibilities for the investigation of complaints by contractors, although this is on an informal basis, as procuring entities are not an official part of the complaints system.

The accounting officer for each procuring entity must establish a procurement unit, staffed at an appropriate level by qualified persons with the requisite qualifications and experience to competently manage its activities, ranging from procurement planning through to contract management and reporting.[30]

2.3.4. Oversight institutions

The Auditor General plays a key role in providing oversight of public procurement activities. In addition to his general powers under the Finance and Audit Act, which empower him to audit procurement or contract execution at any time, the PPAD Act mandates the Auditor General to undertake an annual performance audit of the PPADB, including its committees and procuring entities.[31] The Directorate on Corruption and Economic Crime may also investigate procurement, as may the Botswana Police Service or any commission of enquiry.[32]

2.4. The legal regime on public procurement

Public procurement law in Botswana has been designed to curb fraud, waste, abuse and corruption in particular. The legal system is based on a strong perception that a clear public procurement law coupled with strong compliance measures will promote and assist national and international trade, which will attract investment and create conditions for economic development.[33]

Public procurement in Botswana is governed by the PPAD Act. For central government, this is supplemented by two sets of regulations: the Public Procurement and Asset Disposal Regulations 2006[34] ('PPAD Regulations') cover procurement methods, rules and processes, further functions of procuring entities and the handling of complaints by the PPADB; while the Independent Complaints Review Committee Regulations

29 *Ibid.*, reg. 7. 30 *Ibid.*, regs. 11–13. 31 PPAD Act, ss. 79 and 77.
32 *Ibid.*, s. 83. 33 PPADB Operations Manual, 23. 34 Issued 24 February 2006.

2006[35] ('ICRC Regulations') govern the operations and procedures of the ICRC in hearing complaints. Local authorities and parastatals follow different regulations, but are expected to progressively align with central government rules over time.

The PPAD Regulations are supported by the PPADB Operations Manual of 2008, which provides standard operations policies and procedures for public procurement.[36] The legal status of the Operations Manual is currently unclear, but it is understood that the PPADB plans to re-issue it as a circular to ensure it is legally enforceable. The PPADB also issues standardised bidding packages, containing standard bidding instructions and general conditions of contract, whose use is mandatory for all procurement.[37] The legal regime on public procurement also includes a number of government circulars prescribing preference and reservation schemes for various sectors of the economy, which are subject to frequent change; following 2008 amendments to the Act, the Minister for Finance is empowered to prescribe these schemes.[38]

The PPAD Act came into force on 2 July 2002 and was amended in 2008.[39] Procurement had previously been governed by parts of the Supplies Regulations,[40] but procurement legislation was needed for various reasons including the rapid expansion in the volume of procurement; the increase in the range and complexity of procurement; the shift in the procurement budget away from simple supplies-based contracts to technically sophisticated works and service contracts; donor-funded projects, which had created conflicting bidding practices, and complex contract documentation and specific standards, all of which contributed to excessively complicated procurement procedures; the lack of efficient involvement of citizens as beneficiaries of public procurement; and the need to promote greater transparency, public accountability and efficiency in the management of the public procurement system. In contrast to international standards such as the UNCITRAL Model Law, the PPAD Act focuses principally on the institutions to manage public procurement and mechanisms for economic empowerment; procurement rules, methods and processes are largely left to regulations, although the PPAD Act contains some surprisingly detailed provisions on contractual clauses to

35 Issued 31 March 2006. 36 PPADB Operations Manual. 37 PPAD Act, s. 29.

38 *Ibid.*, s. 72. See Chapter 15 of this volume for more discussion of preference and reservation schemes.

39 Public Procurement and Asset Disposal (Amendment) Act 2008, which came into force on 22 August 2008.

40 Supplies Regulations and Procedures 1988, Chapter 4.

be included, reflecting some of the concerns driving the introduction of the Act.

Regrettably, the time delay between the issuing of different parts of the legal and regulatory framework and the various influences discussed in section 2.5 below have resulted in a number of inconsistencies between different parts of the framework; for example, different evaluation methodologies are included in the PPAD Regulations and the standardised bidding packages. The PPAD Regulations also omit various subjects which the PPAD Act requires to be prescribed in regulations, such as PPADB Board and advisory committee procedures and a code of conduct for contractors.

The Operations Manual is a living and evolving document which will need to be constantly updated over the years. Its objective is to create a standardised national approach to public procurement activities. As a reference manual, it assists the procurement units of procuring entities with a standard set of procurement policies, procedures and practices to be used. The Operations Manual's standard operating procedures and the standard tender documents, as contained in the standardised bidding packages, cover the entire scope of procurement in procuring entities. The aim is to ensure that due care is taken in the expenditure of public funds and that the process is undertaken in an economic and efficient manner, is transparent, and offers equal opportunity for eligible competitors.[41]

In the case of a conflict between the provisions of the PPAD Act and any obligations of the Republic of Botswana arising from any treaty or other agreement to which Botswana is a party, the requirements of such treaty or agreement shall, to the extent that they conflict, prevail over the PPAD Act.[42] This provision not only allows international trade agreements to prevail over domestic law, but allows the application of alternative procurement rules where required under the terms of agreements with donors and development banks. At the moment, the country's developments in procurement are primarily funded from the national treasury without direct aid contributions incorporated into the national budget. Where development partners are involved, procurement for the relevant projects is governed by the rules prescribed by the partner, as provided for in the procurement legislation.[43] However, where the government of Botswana contributes counterpart funding, the PPAD Act requires this to be used to fund discrete activities where possible, which remain subject to the

41 PPADB Operations Manual. 42 PPAD Act, s. 4. 43 PPADB, note 15 above, p. 6.

PPAD Act.[44] Furthermore, where procurement for an external obligation 'favours an external beneficiary', such as in the context of tied aid, procurement using contributions made by Botswana is required to be undertaken through contractors registered in Botswana.[45] The influence of donors on public procurement systems is considered in more detail in Chapter 11.

Aggrieved contractors have the right to challenge procurement and registration decisions by the PPADB and its committees at any point prior to contract award,[46] provided the complaint is submitted in writing within fourteen days of the date when the contractor comes to the knowledge of the grounds for the complaint.[47] Any monetary claim for compensation must be accompanied by documentary evidence of loss.[48] While the PPAD Act places no limitations on the scope of complaints, the PPAD Regulations exclude certain types of decisions, namely, selection of procurement method, choice of evaluation procedure, decisions to reject all bids and refusal to respond to unsolicited offers,[49] mirroring exclusions found in the 1994 UNCITRAL Model Law. The PPAD Regulations further require that complaints are not based on frivolous evidence or circumstances.[50]

Botswana has a tiered system for resolution of disputes, with contractors required to first submit a written complaint to the PPADB, before having a right of appeal to the ICRC and subsequently the High Court.[51] Where procurement is delegated to one of the PPADB's committees, the complaint should first be submitted to that committee, with any appeal to the PPADB. While procuring entities have no formal role in the complaints process, in practice contractors are encouraged to contact them first in order to resolve simple errors or misunderstandings. The PPADB's role in the complaints system also lacks legal clarity, with some provisions referring to dispute resolution and attempts to reach a mutually agreed settlement, while others refer to the PPADB issuing decisions in the manner of a review body.[52] The PPADB has fourteen days to either resolve a dispute or refer it to the ICRC,[53] and contractors have a further fourteen days to lodge any appeal with the ICRC or seven days to refer the dispute to the ICRC where the PPADB fails to either issue a decision

44 PPAD Act, s. 4(3). 45 *Ibid.*, s. 5.

46 *Ibid.*, Part X; PPAD Regulations, Part IX; ICRC Regulations.

47 PPAD Regulations, reg. 78(4). 48 *Ibid.*, reg. 78(2).

49 *Ibid.*, reg. 77(2). 50 *Ibid.*, reg. 79(2).

51 PPAD Act, s. 104. The right of appeal to the High Court was added in the 2008 amendments to the Act.

52 PPAD Regulations, reg. 78(6) and (9). 53 *Ibid.*, reg. 78(6).

or itself refer the dispute to the ICRC.[54] The ICRC is required to issue its decision within thirty days.[55]

The ICRC, established by section 95 of the PPAD Act, consists of a chairperson and four members appointed by the Minister for Finance for up to five years.[56] Members are required to be of at least executive director level and to be persons of good standing, qualifications and experience drawn from commerce, industry, academia and relevant professions.[57] It is thus a non-judicial body and persons appearing before the ICRC are required to 'appear in person and not by means of legal representation'.[58] Members are required to disclose any personal interest in matters before the ICRC, with penalties of fines and/or imprisonment for failure to do this. In addition to contractor challenges to procurement and registration, the ICRC's scope of responsibilities include any disputes between procuring entities, the PPADB, its committees and contractors on interpretation of the Act; any issue related to the Act raised by public petition; conflicts between the PPADB and its employees; and appeals against disciplinary measures by the PPADB. It may recommend to the Minister any amendments to the Act which it considers necessary to prevent the recurrence of challenges or to improve the performance of the regulatory framework.[59]

Where a complaint is received prior to commencement of a contract, procurement is automatically suspended by the Board and may be suspended by the ICRC.[60] All participating bidders are informed and have a right to participate in review proceedings before the PPADB.[61] Contracts are considered irrevocable, even where the award decision remains disputable, although the execution of contracts may exceptionally be suspended by the ICRC where it is satisfied that execution of the contract may cause substantial loss to the public revenue or prejudicially affect the public interest.[62]

The ICRC may uphold or reject the PPADB's decision and may order procuring entities to do or redo an action or proceeding or cancel procurement proceedings.[63] It may levy fines on complainants to recover costs or award costs to aggrieved contractors, although these are limited to the commercial outlay for preparation of a bid.[64] Where fraud or bias is found by the ICRC in its enquiries, it may order any person found guilty

54 ICRC Regulations, reg. 9(3); PPAD Regulations, reg. 78(7).
55 ICRC Regulations, reg. 11(2). 56 PPAD Act, s. 96. 57 *Ibid.*, s. 98.
58 ICRC Regulations, reg. 11(3). 59 PPAD Act, s. 103.
60 PPAD Regulations, reg. 79(1); ICRC Regulations, reg. 12.
61 PPAD Regulations, reg. 78(5) and (8). 62 PPAD Act, s. 105.
63 ICRC Regulations, reg. 14(1). 64 PPAD Act, ss. 107–108.

to be excluded from any procurement process resulting from an order to cancel or redo proceedings, but the exclusion appears to be limited to the procurement in question.[65] It may also refer matters to the Attorney-General, the Directorate on Corruption and Economic Crime or other authority for further action.[66] The ICRC's decisions must be notified to the complainant within three days and published in the *Gazette*.[67] The ICRC is required to maintain a register of persons against whom fault was found in any inquiry, which is publically available,[68] but no exclusion from procurement or other action appears to result from inclusion on the register.

The role of the courts has so far been very limited in the development of public procurement law and, following the 2008 amendments to the PPAD Act, parties to a dispute may only refer their complaint to the High Court after completing the review procedures of the PPADB and the ICRC.[69] There are sparse cases in the decade since the formal specific law came into existence. Most of these cases related to the award of tenders, issues of the comparability of the tenders and their conformity in regard to pricing and application of administrative principles.[70] Supplier remedy systems are considered in more detail in Chapter 13.

2.5. Public procurement regulation: the context

As one of the first countries in the region to introduce public procurement legislation, Botswana had few working models as sources of inspiration, and its PPAD Act is essentially home-grown, with little influence from either neighbouring countries or international standards. Motivations for introducing public procurement legislation, as discussed in section 2.4 above, were essentially domestic, stemming from changes in the profile of public procurement and the growing importance of the economic empowerment agenda.

As an early reformer, some of Botswana's policies influenced procurement reforms in Uganda, with a two-way exchange later resulting in Uganda's regulations being used as the basis of many parts of the

65 ICRC Regulations, reg. 14(2). 66 *Ibid.*, reg. 15.

67 *Ibid.*, reg. 14(3)–(4). 68 *Ibid.*, reg. 16. 69 PPAD Act, s. 104.

70 *Public Procurement and Asset Disposal Board* v. *Researched Solutions Integrators (Pty) and Others* [2006] (1) BLR 319 (CA); *AST Botswana (Pty) Ltd* v. *Public Procurement and Asset Disposal Board and Others* [2005] 1 BLR 504 C; *Researched Solutions Integrators (Pty) Ltd (formerly known as AST Botswana (Pty) Ltd)* v. *Public Procurement and Asset Disposal Board and Others* [2005] 2 BLR 493.

2006 PPAD Regulations in Botswana. As Uganda itself used parts of the 1994 UNCITRAL Model Law, some similarities can be seen with the UNCITRAL Model Law in areas such as procurement methods, but Botswana's Act and Regulations are not closely modelled on any international standard, either in text or substance. As noted above, the Act focuses principally on institutional arrangements for public procurement and empowerment mechanisms, relegating the procurement methods and rules generally found in international agreements to secondary legislation. A few UNCITRAL-based rules are found in provisions on supplier review, but, again, in regulations rather than primary legislation.

Botswana is a member of the World Trade Organization, but is neither a member nor an observer to the Government Procurement Agreement. However, the government of Botswana is actively pursuing *regional* integration as a means of economic development. It is one of fifteen members of SADC, whose economic mission is the promotion of sustainable and equitable economic growth and socio-economic development so that the region emerges as a competitive and effective player in the world economy.[71] It is also part of the SACU, along with Lesotho, Namibia, Swaziland and the region's economic powerhouse, South Africa. Similarly to SADC, SACU is seeking regional integration and development, industrial and economic diversification, the expansion of intra-regional trade and investment, and global competitiveness.[72] Regional economic integration is expanding, with the decision in 2008 to establish a free trade area comprising SADC, COMESA and the EAC.[73]

None of these trade agreements yet includes specific procurement obligations, but the government remains conscious of its potential future obligations and has built flexibility of domestic procurement policy and practice in relation to changing external trade obligations into its procurement policy, as noted in section 2.2 above. The accelerating pace of economic integration in the region and the existence of procurement regulations within COMESA may well lead to pressure for the regulation of public procurement in future.

In 2007, Botswana was one of twenty-two countries which piloted the Methodology for Assessing Procurement Systems, developed by the OECD/DAC Joint Venture on Procurement (now Task Force on Procurement) to provide a common tool which developing countries and donors can use to assess the quality and effectiveness of procurement

71 See www.sadc.int/english/about-sadc/ (accessed 16 March 2012).

72 See www.sacu.int/about.php?id=395 (accessed 16 March 2012).

73 Note 5 above.

systems.[74] The assessment, led by the PPADB, concluded that the existing regulatory and legislative framework conforms to the criteria set out in the methodology to a large extent,[75] but that improvements to the procurement system were needed in information systems, capacity development, strengthening oversight structures and performance audit mechanisms, providing role clarity to avoid conflicts of interest and direct involvement in the execution of procurement transactions and procurement planning to inform the budgetary process; requirements in many of these areas needed to be included in legislation.[76]

3. Coverage of the public procurement rules

3.1. Procuring entities

According to the PPAD Act, procuring entity means any ministry or department duly authorised to engage in public procurement.[77] The Operations Manual further describes a procuring entity as an official body, as in a government body which has the authority to make legal decisions, to sue, and to be sued (as in a legal person). Under section 3 of the Act, its provisions originally applied to 'all entities of the central Government which are involved in public procurement . . . whether they are located abroad or within Botswana'. Following amendments to the legislation in 2008, this was extended to include all land boards and all parastatals, statutory organisations and local authorities. Where the government makes contributions to entities falling outside the scope of the Act, any procurement is to be kept discrete and identifiable as far as possible and be subject to the Act; thus any entity, including private companies, may be subject to the Act when receiving government funding.

3.2. Type of procurement subject to regulation

Public procurement has been defined in the PPAD Act as 'the acquisition in the public interest by any means, including by purchase, rental, lease, hire-purchase, licences, tenancies, franchises, etc., of any type of works, services or supplies or any combination thereof, however classified', and as

74 See www.oecd.org/document/40/0,3746,en_2649_3236398_37130152_1_1_1_1,00.html (accessed 16 March 2012).

75 PPADB, note 15 above, p. 15.

76 *Ibid.*, p. 4.

77 PPAD Act, s. 2.

including 'management, maintenance and commissioning' by a procuring entity.[78] The procurement legislation applies to works, services and supplies contracts and any combination thereof.[79]

The PPAD Act establishes the Special Procurement and Asset Disposal Committee (SPADC) to manage sensitive procurement and requires that items to be managed by the SPADC be listed in a Schedule to the Regulations. The Act also imposes confidentiality obligations on those with access to confidential or restricted communications,[80] but does not otherwise differentiate between sensitive and other procurements. The PPAD Regulations do not contain the required schedule of items, but introduce an exception to application of the Regulations for any procurement determined by the PPADB to require different procedures for purposes of national security,[81] thus appearing to leave the determination of sensitive items to be decided on an *ad hoc* basis by the PPADB.

The Regulations also provide a special procedure which allows procuring entities of the Defence Force, Police Service and other security organs of the state to conduct their procurement through an open or restricted list basis. This concept is not defined further, but is assumed to require entities to distinguish between items suitable for open publication of procurement opportunities under the usual procurement rules and those requiring alternative rules to allow direct approaches to a shortlist of potential contractors with additional confidentiality safeguards, due to the sensitive nature of the contract. Procuring entities must first commit themselves to a progressive reduction in procurement through the restricted list and obtain prior written approval of the PPADB to the procurement procedures to apply to each category of procurement activity on the restricted list. Procuring entities in the security sector must comply with the PPAD Regulations in all areas other than where alternative restricted procedures are approved.[82]

4. Public procurement procedures

4.1. Introduction

Public procurement procedures are principally covered by the PPAD Regulations, with very limited rules contained in the primary legislation.

78 *Ibid.*, s. 2. 79 *Ibid.*, s. 3(c). 80 *Ibid.*, s. 89.
81 PPAD Regulations, reg. 3(1). 82 *Ibid.*, reg. 19.

4.2. Procurement planning and registration

Effective procurement requires adequate, timely and efficient planning. While requirements for the production of an annual procurement master plan are included only at the level of the PPADB Operations Manual, the Act does require the PPADB to take into account the principles of aggregation of common items and standardisation, as discussed in section 2.2 above. Further, no procurement activity may commence without a signed certificate (warrant) verifying the availability of adequate funds or a suitable written assurance received from the Treasury that suitable funds will be made available to cover the expected expenditure of the procurement, prior to any procurement activity, or before the awarding of a contract.[83]

The PPADB is responsible for management of a contractor registration system, which includes deciding on registration or reclassification of firms and disciplining contractors who breach the code of conduct or default on awarded contracts.[84] The register of contractors is intended to provide up-to-date information on workloads and performance records, although it is not considered a pre-qualification list and registered contractors are still required to meet applicable pre-qualification criteria for any procurement.[85] Section 121 envisages fairly complex categories for registration, with classification by type of works, services and supplies, grades, type of ownership and type of business associations. Further procedures and criteria for registration are intended to be included in Regulations, along with a code of conduct for contractors,[86] but registration is not addressed in the Regulations. In practice, due to the scale of the task, the register is being gradually developed, with registration only completed for certain items, such as different grades (values) of works, certain medical supplies and ICT services. Registration is closely linked to economic empowerment initiatives, with registration required to benefit from preferential treatment or to be eligible for reserved contracts. For some items, contractors are registered as 100 per cent, majority- or minority-owned citizen companies. Registration is mandatory for contractors domiciled in Botswana and registration is only permitted for contractors licensed or incorporated under the laws of Botswana.[87] The PPADB has the power to suspend or delist contractors who fail to comply with either the code of

83 PPAD Act, s. 45; PPAD Regulations, reg. 27. 84 PPAD Act, s. 49.
85 *Ibid.*, ss. 116 and 119. 86 *Ibid.*, ss. 127 and 123. 87 *Ibid.*, ss. 118 and 117.

conduct or a contract, although complaints regarding such decisions can be submitted to the ICRC.[88]

4.3. Procurement method and procedures

The PPAD Act does not prescribe procurement methods to be used, beyond the general principle of using competitive methods to achieve value for money. The permitted methods are defined in Part V of the PPAD Regulations, all of which are applicable to the procurement of supplies, works and services. Although precise terms and definitions differ, Botswana's procurement methods are broadly based on the 1994 UNCITRAL Model Law, reflecting UNCITRAL's influence on Uganda on whose regulations the PPAD Regulations were modelled. Like the UNCITRAL Model Law, Botswana's Regulations provide for use of (open) tendering as a default, with methods similar to restricted tendering, request for quotations and single-source procurement available only in specific circumstances. Both open and restricted methods can be domestic or international, although the differences are limited to the location for publication of notices or nationality of shortlisted contractors. Botswana does not use any more flexible methods, such as request for proposals or competitive negotiation. Procurement methods permitted in Botswana are:

- Open domestic bidding, the preferred method, which is to be used unless another method is justified. Despite its name, the method is not limited to domestic companies and participation is open to all, including foreign bidders, unless otherwise restricted by registration or reservation requirements. Bid notices must be advertised in the *Government Gazette* and at least one newspaper of wide circulation in Botswana and a minimum bidding period of four weeks must be allowed prior to the deadline for submission of bids.[89] The PPADB is preparing to advertise bid notices on its website, but this function is not yet operational. As under the UNCITRAL Model Law, open domestic bidding can involve a pre-qualification process for complex or specialised purchases.[90]
- Open international bidding, which is identical to open domestic bidding with the exception that bid notices must, in addition to the *Gazette*,

88 *Ibid.*, ss. 124 and 103(1)(b).

89 PPAD Regulations, regs. 55 and 33.

90 *Ibid.*, reg. 28.

be published in appropriate international publications or trade journals with wide international circulation and the minimum bidding period is extended to six weeks. Open international bidding may be used where foreign bidders' participation would enhance competition or increase value for money or the technical complexity of the procurement requires the participation of foreign bidders.[91]

- Restricted domestic bidding, which follows the same procedures as open domestic bidding, with the exception that the invitation to bid is addressed directly to a shortlist of bidders without advertising and the minimum bidding period is reduced to two weeks. This method may be used where there are only a limited number of potential contractors; there is insufficient time for open bidding due to an emergency or in other exceptional circumstances.[92] The Regulations provide that it may also be used for values below a threshold, but no such threshold has been issued and this justification is not used in practice.
- Restricted international bidding and its conditions for use are identical to restricted domestic bidding, but the term is used whenever the shortlist includes foreign contractors.[93]
- Quotations proposals procurement is similar to the UNCITRAL Model Law's request-for-quotations method, although at least five quotations are required as far as is practicable. The method may be used where there is insufficient time for bidding procedures in an emergency, the estimated value is below a threshold (currently 100,000 pula or approximately £8,600) or in other exceptional circumstances.[94] The Regulations prohibit the splitting of requirements to avoid use of any method of procurement.[95]
- Micro procurement is used for very low values of procurement (currently less than 20,000 pula or approximately £1,700) which require a petty-cash-type procedure. No competition is required and documentation requirements are limited to an invoice or receipt, with no requirements for a written invitation, bid or contract document. Micro procurement must be reported to the relevant MTC within thirty days.[96]
- Direct procurement allows single-sourced procurement of any value where there is insufficient time for other methods in an emergency, where the supplies, works or services are only available from one contractor and in various situations relating to the extension of existing

91 *Ibid.*, regs. 56 and 33. 92 *Ibid.*, reg. 58. 93 *Ibid.*, reg. 57.
94 *Ibid.*, reg. 59. 95 *Ibid.*, reg. 24. 96 *Ibid.*, reg. 60.

contracts for purposes of compatibility or continuity, subject to value limits. There is also a catch-all condition of 'it is justified in the circumstances', although use of direct procurement requires prior approval by the PPADB. Direct procurement must follow the standard procurement rules for bidding, as far as is practicable, and written invitation and contract documents are required.[97]

Section 55 of the PPAD Act states that both electronic and paper forms of invitations to tender, bidding packages and bid submissions have legal validity. Where electronic means are used, the transmitter is responsible for the confidentiality, completeness, integrity and timeliness of the data and documents transmitted.[98] Although these provisions may enable the introduction of e-procurement in future, in practice, all procurement remains paper-based at the current time. Procurement methods are also considered in more detail in Chapter 12.

4.4. *Criteria for awarding contracts*

Section 35 of the Act requires that bidding documents must provide instructions on the evaluation methodology to be used, the criteria and the value and weights attached to each criterion. While the Act also states that 'no factor outside those explicitly stated in the bidding package shall be taken into account', this strict rule is weakened by an exception which permits the use of 'an industry standard or best practice' where there are 'extenuating reasons'.[99]

Evaluation methodologies are specified in the Regulations,[100] drawing heavily on Uganda's regulations, which themselves were based on World Bank evaluation methods. For supplies and most works, evaluation must use the least cost selection – supplies and works method, to identify the lowest priced bid which is responsive to the procuring entity's commercial and technical requirements. For consultancy services, the preferred evaluation method is quality and cost based, which may also be used for works which are difficult to define or where specific operational considerations have a significant importance in the success of the work. This method awards weighted technical and financial scores to bids in a two-stage process and recommends award to the bidder with the highest total

97 *Ibid.*, reg. 61. 98 PPAD Act, s. 56. 99 *Ibid.*, ss. 35–36.
100 PPAD Regulations, regs. 43–48, and the Fourth Schedule.

score. For consultancy services, alternative evaluation methods of quality based selection; fixed budget selection, least cost selection services and qualification selection are also available.

Negotiations are permitted, where authorised by the Board or relevant tender committee. However, for competitive methods, the scope for negotiations is strictly limited and cannot include amendments to the bid price. Contracts are awarded by means of a notice of bid acceptance, without any standstill period.[101]

5. Concluding remarks

The public procurement system in Botswana, like many national systems, is seeking to achieve value for money, fairness, integrity and accountability in its legal and regulatory framework. It is also seeking to maintain a difficult, and constantly changing, balance between support for the domestic economy and promoting international trade and integration. Its objective of devolving greater responsibility to procuring entities over time is prompting changes in the role of the PPADB, its central agency for public procurement, and may also necessitate changes to its legal and regulatory framework. Such revisions would provide the opportunity to address the anomalies in the present system identified through use of the OECD/DAC Methodology for Assessing Procurement Systems.

The devolution process, as well as the drive to increase the use of domestic contractors, requires the PPADB to implement training and education to develop capabilities and competencies among both procuring entities and contractors. Capacity development efforts must also address contract management, which has been found to be an area that needs attention as it affects the implementation of projects. Implementation of projects has been delayed and contracts cancelled for failure to deliver by suppliers. Procuring entities continue to engage contractors without comprehensive contracts or do not enforce contracts if these are in place. In addition, the training offered by the PPADB on tendering procedures has been skewed towards development of capacity in government procuring entities. Training is still to reach the private sector and civil society, and this needs attention.[102] Finally, it can be noted that capacity development practice is expected to take into account the specific mandate that the PPADB has in relation both to reservation and preferential treatment

101 *Ibid.*, regs. 51–53.

102 PPADB, note 15 above, Chapter 3.

policies on the one hand and foreign direct investment on the other. This will ensure that the procurement system in Botswana is responsive to the socio-economic needs of the country.[103] Capacity development efforts must be supported by the strengthening of monitoring and oversight structures.

103 *Ibid.*, p. 23.

3

The regulatory framework for public procurement in Ethiopia

TECLE HAGOS BAHTA*

1. Introduction

Ethiopia is the second most populous country in Africa with nearly 80 million people. It is situated in the Horn of Africa, bordering the Sudan and South Sudan in the West, Kenya in the South, Somalia and Djibouti in the East, and Eritrea in the North.

Ethiopia was not colonised except for a brief occupation of five years by the Italian invading army until the latter was defeated by the joint forces of Ethiopia and Great Britain at the end of the Second World War. Thus, until the early 1960s, Ethiopia did not subscribe to either the common law or the continental legal system. While Ethiopia was determined to abolish consular and special or mixed (Ethiopian–foreign) courts[1] that existed prior to the Italian occupation, it agreed to appoint a few British judges in the Ethiopian courts to see that the applicable Ethiopian customary rules were not contrary to the Western orientation of justice, making sure that all Europeans were treated fairly.

As part of the policy of modernisation in the 1950s, however, Ethiopia decided to adopt its own modern laws. Ethiopia thus hired some of the best contemporary comparative scholars in Europe, who, by the 1960s,

* The author gratefully acknowledges the constructive comments made by his colleague, Charra Tesfaye Tirfessa, on an earlier draft of this work.

1 According to Aberra Jembere: '[T]he former was a tribunal set up at the consulate level . . . to dispose of civil and criminal cases arising in the host country but involving exclusively foreigners, while the latter was a court in which judges of the host country and foreign judges sat together to hear and dispose of civil and criminal cases involving the nationals of the host country and foreigners.' These courts were created by treaties since 1849. Thus, until 1936, consular jurisdictions were allowed to Belgium, France, Germany, Great Britain, Italy, the United States, Egypt, Turkey and Sweden which then had diplomatic missions in Ethiopia. For more on this, see A. Jembere, *An Introduction to the Legal History of Ethiopia (1434–1974)* (Münster: LIT, 2000), pp. 121–7, 232–5.

managed to draft the Civil Code,[2] the Commercial Code, the Penal Code, the Criminal Procedure Code and the Maritime Code. These codifications classified Ethiopia into the continental legal system. However, in 1965, Ethiopia promulgated the Civil Procedure Code, which, by and large, was adapted from the Indian Civil Procedure Code, reflecting more or less common law procedural principles. Apart from this, Ethiopia has recently adopted the doctrine of *stare decisis*, or judicial precedent, in the fields of constitutional interpretation and the Federal Supreme Court's cassation decisions.

In the political field, as of 1995, the 'nations, nationalities and peoples' of Ethiopia have established a constitutionally federal Ethiopia.[3] Under the federal constitution, the federal government and the federated states have legislative, executive and judicial powers.[4] At the federal level, the task of constitutional interpretation is vested in the second chamber, the House of the Federation, which is composed of the representatives of the 'nations, nationalities, and peoples' of Ethiopia.[5] Thus, the House of the Federation is not mainly involved in the legislative processes. This is unique in the Ethiopian federation in that a political body is

2 Professor René David, a French comparative lawyer, was the draftsman of the Civil Code.

3 Constitution of the Federal Democratic Republic of Ethiopia No. 1/1995, *Federal Negarit Gazeta*, Year 1, No. 1, 21 August 1995 ('Federal Constitution'). The federation is comprised of the following nine federated states (locally referred to as '*kilil*'): (i) the State of Tigray; (ii) the State of Afar; (iii) the State of Amhara; (iv) the State of Oromia; (v) the State of Somalia; (vi) the State of Benshangul/Gumuz; (vii) the State of the Southern Nations, Nationalities and Peoples (SNNP); (viii) the State of the Gambela Peoples; and (ix) the State of the Harari People. There are also two federal enclave cities, Addis Ababa and DireDawa. The former is the seat of the federal government, the capital city of the State of Oromia, and is also referred to as 'the Capital City of Africa' as it hosts the headquarters of the African Union. The two cities are administered under their respective charters enacted by the federal legislature which enables them to enjoy some degree of autonomy in the legislative, executive and judicial powers.

4 Art. 50(2) of the Federal Constitution. The House of Peoples' Representatives and the State Councils are the highest authorities of the federal government and the federated states respectively. According to the Federal Constitution, all powers exercisable in Ethiopia are reposed in (a) the federal government where the power is *expressly* vested in it; (b) the federal government and the state governments where the power is *expressly and concurrently* vested in them; and (c) the state governments for all the *residual* powers. The federal government's legislative power is exhaustively enumerated under Arts. 51 and 55 of the Federal Constitution.

5 Each 'nation, nationality and people' is represented by at least one member in the House. For each one million of its population, it will have one additional representative in the House. See Art. 61 of the Federal Constitution.

entrusted with the power of constitutional interpretation. In this process, it is assisted by a Council of Constitutional Inquiry which comprises eleven members.[6]

For our purpose, therefore, the federal government, all the states and the two cities are vested with the legislative power of their own respective procurement and financial administration laws. It has, however, remained the tradition thus far that procurement laws at the state and city levels have mirrored whatever comes out of the federal legislature. The reasons for these similarities are: first, the states' and cities' lack of expertise in the field; secondly, financial constraints in initiating studies or research on procurement reforms; thirdly, the harmonisation efforts exerted by the federal government in the laws on procurement and financial administration; and, finally, as the procurement laws involve the spending of a substantial amount of their budget, including grants and subsidies from the federal government, officials at state level are anxious to avoid provoking a negative reaction from their party leaders at the federal level.

As of 1991, Ethiopia has, slowly but gradually, improved its performance in all political, social, diplomatic and economic aspects. It is worth mentioning that Ethiopia has consistently registered an average GDP growth of 11.2 per cent for the last six years.[7] It also has poverty-alleviation spending of more than 60 per cent of its annual budget[8] on economic, health, education and social facilities, of which the road infrastructure expansion takes the lion's share. The country spends 62 per cent of its total annual budget on procurement.[9] This comprises 15 per cent of its GDP.[10] As part of its infrastructure expansion projects, Ethiopia has just completed the construction of at least four multi-billion-dollar hydro-electric dams, and the construction of others is well underway.

6 As per Art. 82 of the Federal Constitution, the members are the President and Vice President of the Federal Supreme Court, six legal experts with proven professional competence and high moral standing who are, upon recommendation by the House of Peoples' Representatives, to be appointed by the President of the Republic, and three members of the House of the Federation. For the powers and functions of the Council of Constitutional Inquiry, see Art. 84 of the Federal Constitution.

7 Additional information is available on the National Bank of Ethiopia's website, www.nbe.gov.et (accessed 1 March 2012).

8 *Fortune*, 11 July 2010, p. 30.

9 *The Reporter*, 5 February 2010, p. 6, citing Sufian Ahmed, the Minister of Finance and Economic Development.

10 *Ibid.*

2. Introduction to the public procurement system

2.1. Introduction

To show the development of the Ethiopian procurement system briefly, it is sufficient to mention the following salient legislative features in the evolution of the federal rules on public procurement. With the promulgation of the Civil Code in 1960, Ethiopia received the French procedure of allocation of contracts by tender which formed part of the administrative contract law in Ethiopia. The Codal provisions[11] did not require use of the procedure; rather, it was set out for use by the administrative bodies whenever required by other pertinent laws or whenever they decided to use it.[12] It is submitted that Ethiopia did not have the tradition to guide the administrative authorities and, thus, it was important to 'establish a framework for administrative action'.[13] Thus, the Civil Code rules on administrative contracts[14] contained a significant number of provisions on procurement contract formation and contract administration.

The second major step towards regulating administrative actions was taken by better elaborating the procurement processes in the Federal Financial Administration Proclamation No. 57/96 and the Council of Ministers Financial Administration Regulation No. 17/97.[15] The enactment of the Federal Financial Administration Proclamation No. 57/1996 dedicated some of its provisions[16] to the regulation of, albeit insufficiently, public procurement proceedings. Similarly, some of the provisions[17] of the Federal Financial Administration Regulations No. 17/1997 also dealt with public procurement proceedings. The Ministry of Finance and Economic Development also issued Directive No. 1/1998 enunciating detailed working rules and procedures for the implementation of the aforementioned Proclamation and Regulation.

11 Arts. 3147–3169 of the Ethiopian Civil Code No. 165/1960.

12 See R. David, 'Administrative Contracts in the Ethiopian Civil Code' (1967) 4 *Journal of Ethiopian Law* 148. The draftsman also stated that the procedure reproduced the French rules which were satisfactory.

13 *Ibid.*, p. 153. The draftsman submitted that 'administrative contract law' is not dealt with in 'civil codes'.

14 Arts. 3131–3306 of the Ethiopian Civil Code.

15 See particularly Arts. 54–57 and 66–73 of this Proclamation and Regulation, respectively.

16 Federal Financial Administration Proclamation No. 57/96, Arts. 54–57.

17 *Ibid.*, Arts. 58–73.

The enactment of the Federal Public Procurement Proclamation No. 430/2005 (the '2005 Proclamation') was a landmark piece of legislation in terms of modernising Ethiopian public procurement laws and approximating them to the international standards.[18] This was a relatively modern public procurement law.[19] It heralded the establishment of a federal supervisory agency, the Public Procurement Agency (now renamed the Federal Public Procurement and Property Administration Agency), which was set up to supervise all procurement processes by public bodies, and was entrusted with carrying out procurement, contract and performance audits in addition to serving as the administrative tribunal for handling procurement complaints or protests. Pursuant to the 2005 Proclamation, the Ministry of Finance and Economic Development also issued the Public Procurement Directive No. 1/2005 which set out the detailed rules for implementing the 2005 Proclamation. The Agency also put in place standard bidding documents for the procurement of works, goods and services. The Federal Criminal Code of 2004 attempted to define the scope and nature of procurement corruptions as well.[20]

In September 2009, the federal government enacted the Federal Government Procurement and Property Administration Proclamation No. 649/2009[21] and the Federal Financial Administration Proclamation No. 648/2009.[22] With regard to procurement, the latter is relevant as it attempts to further consolidate the role of the internal auditing system[23] and establishes the detailed rules[24] on the modalities of financing and effecting payments in the procurement of goods, construction works and services. The new Procurement Proclamation (which entered into force as of 9 September 2009) entirely repealed the previous 2005 Proclamation

18 In drafting the law, the drafters relied heavily on the UNCITRAL Model Law on Procurement of Goods, Construction and Services with Guide to Enactment (1994) ('1994 UNCITRAL Model Law'). The full text of the Model Law and its accompanying Guide is available at the UNCITRAL website, www.uncitral.org (accessed 1 March 2012).

19 Federal Public Procurement Proclamation No. 430/2005, *Federal Negarit Gazeta*, Year 11, No. 15, 12 January 2005, Addis Ababa.

20 Arts. 402–419 and 427–429 of the Ethiopian Federal Criminal Code (Proclamation No. 414/2004). It entered into force on 9 May 2005.

21 The Federal Government Procurement and Property Administration Proclamation No. 649/2009, *Federal Negarit Gazeta*, Year 15, No. 60, 9 September 2009 ('the Proclamation'). This Proclamation is comprehensive in style, as it tries to cover the procurement process end-to-end: i.e. procurement planning, contract formation, contract administration, property administration, and finally disposal.

22 The Federal Government of Ethiopia Financial Administration Proclamation No. 648/2009, *Federal Negarit Gazeta*, Year 15, No. 56, 6 August 2009.

23 *Ibid.*, Art. 5(5) *cum* Art. 7.

24 *Ibid.*, Art. 33.

and all other laws, regulations, directives or practices that do not accord with it. Thus, with the recent issuance of the Federal Government Procurement Directives[25] which entered into force as of 8 June 2010, Ethiopia can be considered as one of the African countries which has successfully modernised its procurement laws.

It should be recalled, as was explained in section 1 above, that, in the Ethiopian federal setting, each state has the power to legislate and regulate its own public procurement system. Consequent to each of the aforementioned successive reforms at federal level, the states have been enacting their own respective public procurement proclamations and directives which are modelled on the federal laws. The parallel development of the states' procurement systems with that of the federal procurement system can be shown by tracing, for instance, the legislative history of the state of Tigray in the area of public procurement.[26]

2.2. The objectives of public procurement policy

It is the duty and responsibility of the government to provide public services of an essential nature to the public. In so doing, the government must acquire those facilities that are necessary for the provision of these services. Indeed, these facilities are so essential that they must be there ready for use so that essential public services must be available to the public with continuity, equality and, if need be, adaptability.[27]

These facilities are essentially goods, services and construction works. The government acquires these facilities, in the main, through contractual

25 The Federal Government Procurement Directives ('the Directives') have been enacted for the purpose of implementing the newly enacted Proclamation.

26 Thus, the following parallel legislative enactments regulating the procurement procedures of goods, works, and services by its state agencies could be noted: the Financial Administration Proclamation No. 26/1996; the Financial Administration Regulations No. 11/1997; the Public Procurement Directives No. 1/2002; the Public Procurement Proclamation No. 123/2007; the Revised Public Procurement Directives No. 1/2007; the Public Procurement Directives relating to Micro and Small-Sized Enterprises (MSEs) Set Asides and the Housing Development Agency's Special Procurement Procedure of Construction Works of February 2007; and the recent Government Procurement and Property Administration Proclamation No. 174/2010 (entered into force in March 2010). Finally, for the purpose of implementing the foregoing State Proclamation No. 174/2010, Procurement Directive No. 125/2010, which in the main is the mirror image of its federal counterpart, has been brought into force as of December 2010.

27 For more on these principles, see B. Dickson, *Introduction to French Law* (London: Longman Group Ltd, 1994), p. 70. These principles equally apply to the administration and maintenance of the public services in Ethiopia.

relationships with private contracting parties using public funds. While the government may resort, in times of military emergency, to non-contractual unilateral action to which contract principles are not applicable (i.e. by a requisitioning or seizure process),[28] it normally acquires these goods, services and works by way of contractual processes. These contractual procurement processes are regulated by law so as to achieve the following objectives: (1) value for money;[29] (2) non-discrimination among candidates on grounds of nationality or any other criteria not having to do with their qualification;[30] (3) transparency[31] and fairness of the criteria on the basis of which each decision is given in procurement proceeding;[32] (4) accountability for decisions made and measures taken with regard to procurement proceedings;[33] (5) competitiveness;[34] and (6) horizontal policies (such as industrial, environmental, social, etc.).

In principle, it is stated that no discrimination is tolerated on the basis of nationality, race or 'any other criteria not having to do with suppliers' qualifications'.[35] By way of exception, however, Article 25 of the Proclamation sets out the details for according preferential treatment in the evaluation process for goods that are produced in Ethiopia,[36] and

28 Requisition Proclamation No. 10/1942. The Proclamation grants the government the power to requisition any private property for 'public safety, national defence, military emergency or any necessary action for rescuing endangered society' against compensation. See Arts. 3–4 of the Proclamation.

29 Art. 5(1) of the Proclamation.

30 As will be discussed below, the Proclamation allows some exceptional preferential treatment.

31 The concept is enshrined in the Federal Constitution, which provides that 'the conduct of affairs of government shall be transparent'. See Art. 12(1) of the Federal Constitution.

32 Art. 5(3) of the Proclamation.

33 *Ibid.*, Art. 5(4) *cum* Art. 11.

34 See Art. 14(1) of the Proclamation wherein (as will be discussed below) the objectives of the Federal Public Procurement and Property Administration Agency (FPPA) are provided for, one of which is ensuring competitiveness.

35 Art. 24 of the Proclamation.

36 According to Art. 16.20 of the Directives (entered into force on 8 June 2010), this margin of preference is granted in the price evaluation process; hence quality will not be compromised. Accordingly, pharmaceutical products and equipment will receive 25 per cent; any other goods receive 15 per cent; and 7.5 per cent will be given to construction works and consultancy services. For this purpose, it should be noted that 'goods produced in Ethiopia' meant 'any good to which, as certified by a certified auditor, more than 35 per cent of the value added occurs in Ethiopia'. See Art. 25(4) of the Proclamation *cum* Art. 16.20.3 of the Directives.

for construction works and consultancy services rendered by Ethiopian nationals.[37] Furthermore, the Directives grant additional[38] margin of preferential treatment to micro and small-scale enterprises (MSEs) established under the relevant Ethiopian laws. In terms of the according of preferential treatments to MSEs, the practice slightly differs from one state to another.[39] Preferential procurement as a mechanism to implement social policies in public procurement is discussed further in Chapter 15 of this volume.

2.3. Nature and organisation of public procurement

Goods, works and services can be procured by any governmental department to which a budget (usually an itemised budget) is appropriated. Thus, all ministries, commissions, authorities, agencies and public enterprises (at federal, state and city levels) carry out procurement of goods, services or works within the ambit of their budget. The federal procurement system is by and large run and/or monitored by a variety of institutions, entities or persons, each of which will be discussed below.

37 Procurements of construction works and consultancy services receive the stated margin of preference only if the following requirements are cumulatively satisfied: (a) the company is incorporated and headquartered in Ethiopia; (b) more than 50 per cent of the capital of the company is owned by Ethiopians; (c) more than 50 per cent of the members of the board of directors are Ethiopians; *or* (d) at least 50 per cent of the key employees of the company are Ethiopians.

38 A price preferential margin of 3 per cent will be granted whenever MSEs compete with local suppliers. However, in an international competitive bidding, the margin of preference is limited only to what is provided for under Art. 16.20 of the Directive, i.e. as indicated in note 36 above. It is also worth noting that MSEs can participate in all federal government procurement proceedings without having to produce bid security, contract (performance) security or advance payment guarantee. Up to 30 per cent of the contract price can be advanced to suppliers and contractors by way of advance payment. It is also provided that MSEs can be issued with free copies of the bidding documents.

39 Some states give a margin of preference of up to 13 per cent. Others have set out 'set-asides' for MSEs. The State of Tigray, for example, has a significant number of 'set-aside' lists involving construction works, goods and services to MSEs where state procuring entities have to allocate them to MSEs without any competition whatsoever. See Art. 5 of State Directives on MSEs Set Asides in Government Procurement and Housing Development Agency's Procurement of Construction Works, February 2007. In a bid to further strengthen such MSEs' set-asides, a new directive was issued in November 2010, namely, the Directive relative to Procurement Set-Asides for MSEs No. 124/2010.

The first of these institutions is the Ministry of Finance and Economic Development.[40] This ministry is the ultimate organ responsible for the proper functioning of the federal system of government procurement and financial administration. To this effect, it carries out overall oversight and systemic auditing in any federal organ either through its own staff or through the reports from internal audits (who are legally required to observe procurement proceedings) of each federal organ. On this basis, the Ministry takes necessary corrective measures in respect of those federal organs whose performance in procurement and financial administration is found to be sub-standard or tainted with corrupt practices.

The overall procurement functions in individual entities that undertake procurement is carried out by the head of the procuring entity, the Procurement and Property Administration Department, the Procurement Endorsing Committee (PEC) and, if need be, an *ad hoc* evaluation committee. The head of the procuring entity is responsible, *inter alia*,[41] for adequately staffing the department, and setting up the PEC and *ad hoc* committees. The head of the procuring entity is also responsible for creating training opportunities for those involved in procurement on all aspects of the procurement system. Unlike the previous procurement laws, the new Proclamation divests the head of the procuring entity of his or her right to endorse the procurement processes. The rationale is that this will enable the head of the procuring entity to hear complaints from bidders and neutrally evaluate the proceedings rather than hearing complaints in which he or she is also implicated by having endorsed the proceeding.

The Procurement and Property Administration Department is the part of the procuring entity which actually carries out the procurement functions. It has the duties and responsibilities, *inter alia*,[42] of executing procurements in a 'perfectly ethical and skillful manner'; carrying out procurement in compliance with the Proclamation, Directives, manuals, standard bidding documents, forms and the contract; and maintaining records on all procurements as prescribed by law. The

40 See the Ministry's website, www.mofed.gov.et (accessed 1 March 2012). See also Art. 13 of the Definition of Powers and Duties of the Executives of the FDRE Proclamation No. 4/1995, *Federal Negarit Gazeta*, Year 1, No. 4, 23 August 1995.

41 Art. 8 of the Proclamation *cum* Art. 5 of the Directives enumerate the duties and responsibilities of the head of a procuring entity.

42 Art. 9 of the Proclamation *cum* Art. 6 of the Directives enumerate the duties and responsibilities of the Department.

PEC,[43] on the other hand, ensures that all procurements are effected in compliance with the procurement laws; reviews and endorses procurements; and advises the head of the procuring entity on the means and methods of achieving effective procurement. Finally, the *ad hoc* evaluation committee is set up to evaluate and endorse the procurement whenever the nature of the procurement is highly complex and requires detailed technical evaluation.

Another important institution is the Office of the Federal Auditor General. This Office is established by virtue of Proclamation No. 68/1997,[44] and is burdened with the tasks, *inter alia*, of carrying out (or causing to be carried out) a programme and efficiency audit or performance audit in order to ensure that the performance of federal government entities is consistent with the law, is economically sound and has attained the desired objectives;[45] of training internal auditors;[46] and of regulating and maintaining the competence of private auditors and accountants who provide auditing and accounting services to those entities involving the federal financial interest.[47]

Another crucial institution, the Federal Ethics and Anti-Corruption Commission,[48] was established, in the main, with the objectives of (a) striving to create an aware society where corruption will not be condoned or tolerated by promoting ethics and anti-corruption education; (b) preventing corruption offences and other improprieties; and (c) exposing, investigating and prosecuting corruption offences and impropriety. Thus, the Commission is empowered to implement the various pieces of national anti-corruption legislation, and international conventions that are ratified by Ethiopia. These include the Revised Anti-Corruption Special Procedure and Rules of Evidence Proclamation No. 434/2005, the Disclosure and Registration of Assets Proclamation

43 Art. 10 of the Proclamation *cum* Art. 7 of the Directives enumerate the duties and responsibilities of the PEC. However, the duties and responsibilities of its chairperson and the secretary are annexed to the Directives.

44 The Office of the Federal Auditor General Establishment Proclamation No. 68/1997, *Federal Negarit Gazeta*, Year 3, No. 26, 6 March 1997.

45 *Ibid.*, Art. 7(4). 46 *Ibid.*, Art. 7(9). 47 *Ibid.*, Art. 7(14).

48 The Commission is accountable to the Prime Minister. However, it is 'free from any interference or direction by any person with regard to cases under investigation or prosecution or to be investigated or prosecuted'. See Arts. 3 and 4 of the Revised Federal Ethics and Anti-Corruption Commission Establishment Proclamation No. 433/2005, www.feac.gov.et (accessed 1 March 2012).

No. 668/2010, the United Nations Convention against Corruption,[49] and the African Union Convention on the Prevention and Combating of Corruption.[50] The issue of corruption in public procurement is discussed further in Chapter 14 of this volume.

The overall administration of the federal[51] public procurement system in Ethiopia is the responsibility of the Federal Public Procurement and Property Administration Agency (FPPA or 'the Agency'). The Agency, accountable to and physically located within the premises of the federal Ministry of Finance and Economic Development, was created by virtue of the now repealed 2005 Proclamation under its former name, the Public Procurement Agency (PPA).[52] It is a small autonomous federal organ having its own juridical personality. The Agency, recently renamed the Public Procurement and Property Administration Agency, is mandated, *inter alia*, to:[53] advise the federal government on all public procurement policies, principles and implementation, and extend technical assistance to the states and city administrations;[54] review and decide on complaints submitted by procuring entities on the conduct of bidders or suppliers;[55] undertake research and surveys on public procurement implementation;[56] set up, develop, maintain and update a database that covers the entire spectrum of public procurement;[57] conduct procurement and performance audits to ensure the compliance of procurement activities with the law;[58] prepare, update and issue authorised versions of the standard bidding documents, procedural forms and any other attendant documents pertaining to procurement;[59] and initiate

49 The UN Convention against Corruption (31 October 2003), UN Doc. 58/4. The Convention entered into force in Ethiopia on 21 August 2007 by virtue of the Convention's Ratification Proclamation No. 455/2007.

50 The full text, as well as a list of African states parties to the Convention, are available online at www.africa-union.org/root/au/documents/treaties/treaties.htm (accessed 1 March 2012).

51 There are no counterpart organs in the federal states; hence, the overall administration of the states' procurement systems is the responsibility of the respective state executive organ, often called the 'Bureau of Finance and Economic Development' in some states and the 'Bureau of Finance and Planning' in others.

52 Arts. 8–16 of the 2005 Proclamation. Additional information about the Agency is also available on the website of the Ministry of Finance and Economic Development, www.ppa.mofed.gov.et/index.php (accessed 1 March 2012).

53 Arts. 14–15 of the Proclamation enumerate the objectives and functions of the Agency respectively.

54 *Ibid.*, Art. 15(1). 55 *Ibid.*, Art. 15(7). 56 *Ibid.*, Art. 15(13).

57 *Ibid.*, Art. 15(10). 58 *Ibid.*, Art. 15(9). 59 *Ibid.*, Art. 15(4).

amendments on laws and implementation system improvements.[60] Upon the request of the procuring entities, it may also permit, on sound grounds, exceptional procurement methods other than provided for under the law.[61]

Furthermore, the Agency is entrusted with the goal of ensuring the application of fair, competitive, transparent, non-discriminatory and 'value for money' principles in all federal procurement undertakings.[62] It is also mandated to strive to bring about uniformity and consistency in the procurement system at national level[63] and 'harmonize the system of public procurement with internationally recognized standards'.[64]

A further entity which is integral to the Ethiopian procurement system, is the Procurement Services Enterprise (PSE).[65] This is a state-owned enterprise established for the purposes of: (a) providing procurement services based on up-to-date national and international market information; (b) providing consultancy services relating to all aspects of international procurements; and (c) providing services relating to the preparation of procurement documents.

Another institution is the Federal Procurement and Disposal Service.[66] This governmental department was established by the Council of Ministers Regulation No. 184/2010 with the mandate to carry out high-value procurements of national significance (so-called 'strategic items'),[67] fulfil procurement requirements that are similar across various public bodies (so-called 'common-user items') and undertake the procurement of recurrent supplies (so-called 'recurrent items').[68] These methods of

60 *Ibid.*, Art. 15(2).

61 *Ibid.*, Art. 16(5). Under this legal provision, pending the enactment of detailed procedures for the procurement of public–private partnerships for infrastructure projects, it may be possible to resort to the 'competitive dialogue' method.

62 *Ibid.*, Art. 14(1). 63 *Ibid.*, Art. 14(4). 64 *Ibid.*, Art. 14(5).

65 The PSE is established pursuant to Regulation No. 46/1998. It is established for an indefinite duration and cannot be liable beyond its assets; its head office being in Addis Ababa, it may open branch offices elsewhere as necessary. See www.pse-eth.com (accessed 1 March 2012).

66 Art. 60 of the Proclamation.

67 Such purchases will definitely include essential food items (e.g. sugar and wheat) and construction materials (e.g. cement) where such items are not affordable or available on the market to the community at large due, for example, to price hikes due to high inflation or hoarding by businessmen. Such purchases have been executed by *ad hoc* committees during the last five years when such occurrences were not infrequent.

68 Art., 60 of the Proclamation *cum* Art. 4 of the Council of Ministers Regulation No. 184/2010. The duty to identify and update the types of procurements (goods and

procurement will be utilised whenever a need arises to procure goods or services of a sizable volume that ought to be procured in bulk due to 'the national significance' of that procurement, or in order to fulfil similar requirements of various public bodies.[69] The Regulation mandates the Service to supply these items on a timely basis 'in the desired quality and at prices attributable to economies of scale resulting from bulk purchases'.[70] Furthermore, the establishment of the Service is also aimed at enabling the speedy disposal (by sale) of properties of public bodies at fair prices, and assisting public enterprises in the procurement of goods and services and disposal of assets.[71] The work of this body is largely predicated on three assumptions: preventing procurement corruption, minimising procurement costs (i.e. economies of scale) and standardising goods and services that are used by federal public bodies. The Service will particularly procure the common-user items through 'framework purchasing agreements' that are to be awarded through open bidding for up to three years. Under the framework contracts, while it is possible to negotiate (between a public body and the supplier) on terms that have not been dealt with in the framework contract, the public body is not permitted 'to vary unit prices and such other fundamental terms of the framework contract when placing orders for goods and services'.[72]

Yet another important institution is the Procurement and Disposal Complaints Review Board (CRB). Complaints relating to or arising out of public procurement and disposal proceedings are vested, at first instance, in the head of the procuring entity, and go to the Complaints Review Board at an appellate level. The latter is an entity established to review and decide on complaints from candidates relating to procurements and disposal proceedings.[73] The applicant candidate or the procuring entity, against which a complaint was lodged can further appeal against the decision of the Board to the appropriate court.[74]

The Board is accountable to the Ministry of Finance and Economic Development. The Minister will appoint the members[75] of the Board

services) to be executed on account of their national significance rests on the Minister for Finance and Economic Development.

69 A procuring entity may also resort to 'framework contracting' to procure its recurring requirements for goods and services within a given period of time.

70 Art. 4(1) of Regulation No. 184/2010. 71 *Ibid.*, Art. 4(2)–(3).

72 Art. 61(3) of the Proclamation. 73 *Ibid.*, Art. 2(20) *cum* Art. 70.

74 Art. 50 of the Directives; the 'appropriate court' that will have the jurisdiction to entertain appeals from the Board is not, however, stipulated in the Directives.

75 The members, whose allowance and mode of payment also remain to be determined by the Minister, are not required to possess a particular professional and/or educational

who will be composed of representatives from the private business sector, the relevant public bodies and public enterprises.[76] The setting up of the Board and the manner of staffing is claimed to have been aimed at allaying the concerns of business who complained that the Agency sides with procuring entities. Unfortunately, the Board is left at the mercy of the FPPA for the provisions of office facilities, technical assistance and secretarial services. In carrying out its activities, the Board may 'require the production of relevant documents and the testimony of officials and employees of the concerned bodies'.[77] It may also seek professional assistance from governmental and non-governmental bodies when and if it deems it useful in reviewing and deciding on complaints. The Board, upon receipt of the complaint, is required to immediately give notice of the complaint to the concerned public body and the procurement proceeding is automatically suspended thereafter until the Board has settled the issue.

The Board has the power to adopt one or more of the following decisions:

(1) a decision prohibiting the procuring entity from acting or deciding unlawfully;
(2) an order requiring the procuring entity to proceed in a manner conforming to the laws; or
(3) annul in whole or in part an unlawful act or decision by the procuring entity.

It is provided under Article 73 of the Proclamation that a candidate is entitled to submit a complaint to the head of the public body or to the Board against an act or omission of the public body in regard

background. Their tenure of service is three years unless dismissed for 'failing to properly discharge his/her duty'. Furthermore, by virtue of Art. 72(4) of the Proclamation, the members 'should discharge their duty in a perfectly ethical manner'. Accordingly, they are duty-bound to report any potential or actual conflict of interest.

76 The Board is composed of (according to the Directives): the chairperson (as representative of the Ministry of Finance and Economic Development); and a member from each of the following institutions: the Agency, public enterprises, public bodies, and the Chamber of Commerce. The members are selected solely on the basis of knowledge and experience in procurement and property administration, discipline and ethical behaviour. Thus, this should be distinguished from a system where highly qualified and independent arbiters are elected by the parties from a roster of arbiters, such as those in Poland and Lithuania. See M. Lamke, 'The Experience of Centralized Enforcement in Poland' in S. Arrowsmith and M. Trybus (eds.), *Public Procurement: The Continuing Revolution* (London: Kluwer Law International, 2003), pp. 127–8.

77 Art. 72(1)(b) of the Proclamation.

to a public procurement or property-disposal proceedings whenever it believes that such an act or omission violates the Proclamation or the Directives. However, certain decisions have been expressly excluded from the ambit of review. These are the selection of procurement and disposal methods and the rejection of bids.[78]

The procuring entity has to observe the seven-day standstill period[79] before it signs the contract with the successful bidder after the announcement of the provisional successful bidder so that aggrieved bidders may have time to institute their complaints.[80] This is also aimed at affording a breathing space to the provisionally successful bidder to process the performance security (from banks or insurance companies) as the bidder is obliged to present the performance security at the time of signing the contract.

Once the contract is signed with the successful bidder, however, no complaint may be lodged with the head of the procuring entity or the Board in relation to acts or omissions during the procurement proceeding leading to the award.[81] Despite the time limits being very short, the timeliness rule is strictly observed by the Board; no complaints submitted out-of-time are admitted. Following the conclusion of the contract with the successful bidder, therefore, the only recourse for the complainant is to relate all information and documents evidencing the illegal acts or omissions by the procuring entity to the anti-corruption bodies which are capable of taking the case to court and eventually having it annulled. Supplier remedies are further discussed in Chapter 13 of this volume.

A procuring entity itself is required to submit a complaint in writing to the Agency whenever 'it believes that an unlawful act or an act prejudicial to its legitimate interests has been committed' by candidates or suppliers.[82] This could be, for example, partial performance or non-performance of the awarded procurement contract, violation of the 'no-bribery pledge',

78 Art. 73(2)(a)–(c) of the Proclamation.

79 Art. 45.1.a of the Directives.

80 Nor may the contract be entered into before all the unsuccessful bidders are notified of the results of the procurement proceeding.

81 While the idea incorporates the 'sacred cow' principle, it does not, however, indicate whether the complainant has the option of taking its complaint to the pertinent court. It is worthwhile to note that the complainant is entitled to invalidate the contract by virtue of Arts. 3170–3171 of the Ethiopian Civil Code on the ground of cause (cause illicit or absence of cause). However, this recourse is rarely resorted to. According to Professor René David, the doctrine of *causa* was fully incorporated into the administrative contract law in Ethiopia to 'protect the public interest against administrative carelessness and against collusion between administrators and scoundrels'. See David, 'Administrative Contracts in the Ethiopian Civil Code', note 12 above, p. 148.

82 Art. 76(1) of the Proclamation.

or any other unlawful act or omission on the part of the candidates. In resolving the complaint,[83] the Agency is empowered to summon interested parties to appear in person and give evidence on the matter.[84] The Agency is duty bound to review the complaint and deliver its decision[85] thereon within fifteen working days from the receipt of the complaint. It is not, however, clear yet as to how far due process of law applies to the candidate or supplier against whom a complaint is lodged to enable it to defend itself. Procedural and evidentiary rules that may assist the Board or the Agency in informing itself on the legal and factual contentions at hand to reach an informed decision are not put in place.

Foreign-financed procurement contracts cannot be concluded unless and until the 'no-objection notice' is issued by the lending bodies. In cases of complaints in such procurement proceedings, the lending institutions tend to encourage the complainant to submit its complaints to the available governmental forum (the Board) while at the same time urging the relevant bodies to provide a convenient forum in which complainants can have access to a fair hearing. The formal complaint investigation process, if any, is unleashed by the lending institutions when and if the complainant is still not satisfied as a result of the Board's proceedings. Thus, there is a possibility for parallel investigations of allegedly illegal acts or omissions in a foreign-financed procurement proceeding. In practice, if, for example, the World Bank Group, through its discrete investigation, is convinced that there were no procurement irregularities, the Board or Agency dismisses the case. The converse is not, however, equally true.

2.4. The legal regime on public procurement

The procurement process follows certain phases. These phases normally run through: (i) procurement planning; (ii) contract formation; and (iii) the contract administration phases. The proper management and

83 In this regard, both the Proclamation and the Directives are silent on the composition and qualification of the individuals mandated to hear the complaints. It is currently vested in the Directorate for Procurement and Disposal Complaints Review, established under the Agency where the complaints review is done within the Directorate by some of the employees of the Agency.

84 It may also seek professional assistance from any appropriate body. However, it is not clear whether the expected professional assistance is to be sought from consultants against remuneration or just by requiring procuring entities to give their opinions on the matter.

85 The penalties to be levied upon the defaulting suppliers may range from issuing a written notice of warning (Art. 48.5.3 of the Directives), suspension and debarment for up to two years (Art. 48.5.2 of the Directives), to an indefinite debarment (Art. 48.5.1 of the Directives) from all federal and state procurement transactions. See generally Art. 48 of the Directives.

administration of the property once procured and the disposal of the property on scrap-value, trade-in, transfer, land-fill, or any other means fall outside of the procurement processes.[86] While the first and second phases of the public procurement processes are regulated under the recently enacted Proclamation, the third phase (i.e. contract administration) is regulated either under the rules on public law contracts (Articles 3131–3306 of the Civil Code on administrative contract law) or under the rules of ordinary private law contracts.

Ethiopia's legal system, being dominantly of the civil law legal tradition, relies on its codified laws. The embodiment of the legal rules on administrative contract law in the Civil Code is nevertheless peculiar to Ethiopia.[87] These administrative contract law rules in the Civil Code may regulate the contract administration phase of the procurement process.[88] These codal provisions deal generally with the various prerogatives of the public bodies and compensation to suppliers. They also ensure that the balance of the contract remains fair whenever the public body resorts to these prerogatives. In particular, the administrative contracts rules have, in the general part, embodied principles[89] such as cause (illicit cause and absence of cause), the non-applicability of the theory of *exceptio non adimpleti contractus*, the right of supervision (unilateral variation rights and termination rights for the government), the doctrine of *imprévision* (unforeseen supervening events), and the doctrine of 'acts of government' (*fait du prince*). These Codal provisions also set out detailed rules on the three classical types of administrative contracts: concessions of public services;[90] public works contracts;[91] and public supplies contracts.[92] Based on the premise that the public interest should be

86 However, it was considered appropriate to incorporate the field of property administration and disposal systems within the procurement law. Hence, it was promulgated under the title of the 'Government Procurement and Property Administration Proclamation'. The manner of financing and effecting payments to public contracts is to be governed under the Federal Government Financial Administration Proclamation No. 648/2009.

87 The French draftsman of the Code, Professor René David, underscored that administrative contracts are never dealt with in the Civil Codes but that this exception or anomaly was justified, as it was necessary to set out these principles as a guide in the area in the absence of trained lawyers or of any treatises on the Ethiopian administrative law. See David, 'Administrative Contracts in the Ethiopian Civil Code', note 12 above, pp. 143–5.

88 Although there were a few provisions dealing with the contract formation phase, these had by and large fallen into desuetude due to the introduction of the modern public procurement rules in 2005.

89 For more on these principles, see J. Bell, S. Boyron and S. Whittaker, *Principles of French Law* (2nd edn, New York: Oxford University Press, 2008), Chapter 6.

90 Arts. 3207–3243 of the Ethiopian Civil Code.

91 *Ibid.*, Arts. 3244–3296.

92 *Ibid.*, Arts. 3297–3306.

weightier than private contracting parties' interests, attempts have been made at achieving the optimal preference that could be bestowed upon the public bodies without too great a burden on the individual contracting parties. While these principles of administrative law contracts developed and continue to be expounded in France by the French Conseil d'Etat (the French Supreme Administrative Court), Ethiopia has not yet established such an organ. Thus, the administrative contract laws in Ethiopia have remained stagnant and marginalised. It is, however, curious to find in practice that governmental departments continue to label their contracts as 'administrative contract' without the parties and the courts having to rely on or apply these rules on administrative contracts.

It should be underlined that the incorporation of the administrative contracts provisions into the legal system empowered government departments to choose between two types of contracts: a private law contract or a public law contract (administrative contract). Accordingly, while all contracts that are concluded by governmental departments are subject to the procurement rules in the whole process of awarding the contract, they may not necessarily be administrative contracts.[93] A government contract may qualify as an administrative contract if it satisfies one of the following criteria:

(a) [i]t is expressly qualified as such by the law or by the parties, or
(b) [i]t is connected with an activity of the public services and implies a permanent participation of the party contracting with the administrative authorities in the execution of such service, or
(c) [i]t contains one or more provisions, which could only have been inspired by urgent considerations of general interest extraneous to relations between private individuals.[94]

Apart from those contracts that satisfy one or more of the foregoing criteria, the law categorises some contracts as administrative contracts, *ipso jure*, as per Article 3132(a) of the Civil Code. These are: government concession contracts; public construction contracts (public works contracts); and government supplies contracts (public supply contracts).

Thus, Article 3131 of the Civil Code defines the scope of applicability of the administrative contract provisions. It provides that the administrative contract provisions in the Civil Code either supplement or replace the

93 This is so even though all government purchases are subject to the procurement methods described in section 4 below.
94 Art. 3132 of the Ethiopian Civil Code.

provisions relating to contracts in general or special contracts where the contract is in the nature of an administrative contract.

3. Coverage of the public procurement rules

3.1. Procuring entities

Within the ambit of the Ethiopian federal public procurement regulatory system lies any 'public body' which is partly or wholly financed by the federal government budget. These are governmental departments established by the federal laws and variously referred to as ministries, commissions, authorities, agencies, etc. It also includes the Federal Houses (the House of the Federation, and the House of Peoples' Representatives). All public higher education institutions are also covered. Public enterprises (state-owned enterprises) that are established[95] with an initially authorised capital are not expected to abide by these regulations; they can, however, voluntarily employ them with a *caveat* that a liberal application of the rules is given sufficient room in light of the flexibility needed in business decisions. Under the Civil Code, even the applicability of the contract award procedures to 'business organizations which appeal to public savings or place their shares with the public'[96] was envisaged. It was not, however, stipulated under the current public procurement regulations.

Thus, from the definitional paragraphs, it can be understood that 'public procurement' means the obtaining of goods, works, consultancy or other services through purchasing, hiring or obtaining by any other contractual means[97] by public bodies using public funds.[98]

95 A public enterprise is a wholly state-owned entity established, with an initially authorised budget (capital) to carry on, for gain, manufacturing, distribution, service rendering or other economic and related activities as per the Public Enterprises Proclamation No. 25/1992. Owing to the free market policy that the current government is pursuing, the number of public enterprises that were inherited from the defunct socialist military junta has significantly decreased.

96 Art. 3133 of Ethiopian Civil Code.

97 This is in contrast to the situations in times of military emergency, where the federal government may resort to non-contractual unilateral action to which contract principles are not applicable, i.e. by a requisitioning or seizure process.

98 According to Art. 2(7) of the Proclamation, 'public fund' is defined as 'any monetary resource appropriated to a public body from the Federal Government treasury or aid grants and credits put at the disposal of the public bodies by foreign donors through the Federal Government or internal revenue of the public body'.

3.2. Type of procurement subject to regulation

As stated above, the public procurement regulations cover goods, works and services (including consultancy services) by public bodies. It should also be mentioned that the term 'works' is defined to include the 'Build-Own-Operate', 'Build-Own-Operate-Transfer' and 'Build-Operate-Transfer' concessionary contractual modalities under public–private partnership (PPP) arrangements for the development and expansion of infrastructure projects. The Proclamation gives a modern definition to the concept of a public–private partnership. However, it leaves the rules governing the 'formation and mode of implementation' thereof to be prescribed by the minister through directives which have not yet seen the light of day.[99]

As stated above, the Proclamation applies to all federal government procurement and property administration processes. However, this general application excludes procurement involving national defence and national security interests: in the procurement processes of items with national defence and security implications under certain conditions a different procedure may be used. These are: (i) situations where the minister decides, in consultation with the heads of the relevant public bodies, whether to use a different procedure; (ii) those situations where the decision is based on the interest of national security or national defence; and (iii) the situations where procedures are defined, by the minister through directives, in order to ensure that the procedures meet the interest of economy and efficiency.

This is not a general exemption for all procurements by, for example, the Ministry of Defence, the National Defence Forces, the Federal Police Commission, or the Federal Security and Immigration Authority, etc.; rather, it is the category of materials (civil, soft defence (dual use) or hard defence materials) that is relevant for excluding the applicability of the ordinary procurement methods. The power of the minister is to be effected by enacting directives that define the applicable procurement processes and property administration procedures for these cases, which should be aimed at ensuring the 'interest of economy and efficiency' without compromising what is necessary to safeguard 'national security and defence interests'. The minister's power to issue specific directives has not yet been put into practice, however. Thus, the procurement of civil and dual-use materials is executed in the main under the general rules

99 Art. 2(27) *cum* Art. 34 of the Proclamation.

of the Proclamation and the directives. The procurement system for hard defence materials, however, is left in limbo; as yet, there is no directive on that subject.

It should also be recalled that, while the defence procurements exception has to be regulated by directives, other special procurement methods may be permitted, exceptionally and on sound grounds, by the FPPA[100] upon request by the relevant public bodies.

Furthermore, when the Proclamation conflicts with any bilateral or multilateral agreements concluded with a state or international organisation, the agreement prevails.[101] Thus, loan, credit and/or grant agreements with donor countries, the World Bank Group and other international multilateral development banks are ratified by the House of Peoples Representatives[102] and become part of domestic law[103] by being published in the *Federal Negarit Gazette.*[104] Thus, to the extent that the multilateral development banks accompany loans and credits with concomitant standard bidding documents, the public bodies are legally bound to observe their provisions in their procurement processes. It is, thus, possible that a procuring entity (i.e. the same individuals in the procurement and property administration department) would have a *smorgasbord* of standard bidding documents for it to apply depending on what the donor, lending bank or state prescribes in connection with the loan, credit or grant.

In line with this, Ethiopia also receives financial grants from various friendly countries which include tied-aid arrangements[105] whereby Ethiopia can only accept bids from nationals of the donor country for

100 Art. 16(5) of the Proclamation.

101 Art. 6(1) of the Proclamation.

102 Under the Ethiopian federal system, the federal executive has the power to negotiate and sign international agreements (bilateral, plurilateral and multilateral). However, these international agreements have to be submitted to and ratified by the Federal Parliament, House of Peoples Representatives. See Art. 55(12) of the Federal Constitution.

103 As per Art. 9(4) of the Federal Constitution, all international agreements that are ratified by Ethiopia form an integral part of the federal laws.

104 Any law that is not published under the *Federal Negarit Gazeta* is not accorded judicial notice as per Art. 2(2) of the Federal Negarit Gazeta Establishment Proclamation No. 3/1995, *Federal Negarit Gazeta*, Year 1, No. 3, 22 August 1995. This is a federal law gazette, published under the umbrella of the House of Peoples' Representatives. All federal and states' legislative, executive and judicial organs, as well as any natural and juridical person, are required to take judicial notice of the laws published in the *Gazette*. The *Gazette* is published in both Amharic and English, and, in cases of a discrepancy between the two versions, the Amharic version prevails.

105 This is a situation in which donor countries encourage or even prescribe certain rules for the receiving country to purchase goods, services or construction works for the funded project from the donor country itself.

the implementation of the infrastructure project for which the grant was given, as is generally discussed in Chapter 11 of this volume, dealing with the impact of aid-funded procurement on national procurement systems.

Ethiopia is a member of the Common Market for Eastern and Southern Africa (COMESA) free trade area. Due mainly to the direct and indirect pressures by some of the multilateral development banks (particularly the World Bank Group) to modernise its financial administration and public procurement systems, Ethiopia commenced reform of its procurement laws earlier than the COMESA Public Procurement Project in 2002 which involved Ethiopia designing its procurement laws based mainly on the UNCITRAL Model Law and, to some extent, international best practice. Thus, in Ethiopia the COMESA Public Procurement Project assisted a process of public procurement reform which had already substantially matured in its draft form and the use of the UNCITRAL Model Law cannot be seen as a direct result of COMESA's influence. However, the Project ensured that the reform benefited from COMESA's work on best practices and did not contradict COMESA's public procurement objectives. Further, since that time Ethiopia has continued through the FPPA, since its establishment in 2005, to be involved in COMESA's public procurement reform projects. Thus, in another round of further refining the procurement system (particularly to incorporate the lessons learnt from the practical implementation of the relatively modern public procurement law of 2005 and to take into account the civil service reforms under the 'Business Process Reengineering' (BPR) undertaking), attempts have been made to harmonise and integrate its new procurement law of 2009 with the COMESA directive on public procurement.

4. Public procurement procedures

The procurement methods used in Ethiopia are adapted from the 1994 UNCITRAL Model Law to achieve the stated procurement objectives in Ethiopia.[106] These are:

(1) Open tendering.[107] This is the preferred procurement method that is prescribed for use for the procurement of goods, works and services. If a procuring entity opts out of the open tendering procedure, the use

106 S. Arrowsmith, 'Public Procurement: An Appraisal of the UNCITRAL Model Law as a Global Standard' (2004) 53 *International and Comparative Law Quarterly* 17, 21 note 23.

107 Arts. 35–48 of the Proclamation.

of a different method will need to be justified. A procurement method other than open tendering may be used only if the given conditions for use of such other method are satisfied. In other words, other procedures may only be applied in special cases and the conditions for their application are defined in the Proclamation.

(2) Restricted tendering.[108] This procurement method is used in situations where the procuring entity has ascertained that the goods, works, and services can only be obtained from a limited number of suppliers, and the value of the procurement does not exceed the threshold provided in the Directives. Procuring entities may also use the method whenever, in addition to the limited suppliers criterion, a repeated advertisement of the invitation to bid fails to attract bidders.

(3) Request for quotation (RFQ) (locally referred to as 'pro forma tendering').[109] This is used, within the prescribed threshold, for the procurement of goods that are readily available or of construction works and services for which there is an established market. Procuring entities resort to the RFQ method to procure items that have not been embodied within the procurement plan and are needed for immediate use. In effecting such procurement, the procuring entity has to prepare a form detailing the quantity, quality, time and place of delivery, and other terms and requirements in which the bidders approached have to quote the price thereof.

(4) Request for proposal (RFP).[110] This is used only for the procurement of consultancy services. Thus, the RFP method is used whenever procuring entities seek to obtain consultancy services or contracts for which the component of consultancy services represents more than 50 per cent of the amount of the contract. This method is particularly used in soliciting engineering and architectural services in large infrastructure projects in Ethiopia. In an RFP method, contracts are awarded based on the most economically advantageous tender (MEAT). In so doing, procuring entities may apply differing award criteria which signify the priorities and importance they accord to each criterion. These are:[111] quality and cost based selection (QCBS), quality based selection (QBS), fixed budget based selection (FBBS), and consultant qualification based selection (CQBS). Consultancy services can only be procured through single-sourcing

108 *Ibid.*, Arts. 49–51. 109 *Ibid.*, Arts. 55–56.

110 Arts. 53–54 of the Proclamation *cum* Art. 21 of the Directives.

111 Art. 21 of the Directives.

where the conditions for the single-sourcing procurement method are satisfied.

(5) Two-stage tendering.[112] The procedures and circumstances under which two-stage tendering takes place have been entirely adopted from Articles 19 and 46 of the 1994 UNCITRAL Model Law.[113] The salient fact that needs to be pointed out, however, is that procuring entities, under exceptional circumstances, resort to the two-stage tendering method when they realise that they have an uncertain idea of what exactly they are looking to procure and, thus, cannot set out a finalised and detailed specification setting forth an exhaustive list of criteria by which tenders can be evaluated and compared. Thus, in an effort to optimise its options, the procuring entity invites tenders for technical proposal, at the first stage, from which the procuring entity augments its technical know-how to refine the required technical specification on its part. The revised technical specification is then communicated to qualified bidders to compete on the basis of a renewed proposal and price.

(6) Direct (single-source) procurement.[114] This procurement method is used primarily when there is only one supplier or contractor. It may also be used in circumstances where the need is one of pressing emergency in which delay would create serious problems and therefore be injurious to the performance of the procuring entity;[115]

112 Arts. 57–58 of the Proclamation.

113 See also S. Arrowsmith, J. Linarelli and D. Wallace, *Regulating Public Procurement: National and International Perspectives* (The Hague: Kluwer Law International, 2000), p. 513.

114 Arts. 51–52 of the Proclamation. It should also be noted that, within the category of single-sourcing procurement, one can find the 'shopping' and 'small-value (micro) procurement' procedures. 'Shopping' is used exceptionally to purchase goods that, regardless of their price, are necessary for the purposes of studying and research services where it is impractical to obtain them on the market or whenever such purchase is deemed to procure pecuniary benefit to the procuring entity. This is of significant import to the universities, particularly in the natural and applied sciences, where animals and/or plants of different species are needed for scientific research. The 'small-value procurement' procedure is limited to the situations where (i) goods or services of a maximum threshold of Birr 1,500 (at a time) which had not been pre-planned are urgently needed; or (ii) goods or services are necessary to overcome any problems or accidents encountered in field works (in each case, the total purchase cannot exceed Birr 30,000 per annum). See Art. 51(1)(g) and (2) of the Proclamation *cum* Art. 25 of the Directives. (Note that, on 1 March 2012, the exchange rate was US$1 to Birr 17.68.)

115 This shows the divergence from Art. 22(1)(b) of the 1994 UNCITRAL Model Law, which requires that the urgency be 'neither foreseeable by the procuring entity nor the result of dilatory conduct on its part'.

instances where the continuation of an already satisfactorily performed consultancy service would be in the interests of economic efficiency; instances where 'shopping' becomes necessary (as discussed below); and instances where rare opportunities of exceptionally advantageous conditions present themselves. This method cannot, however, be resorted to in an anti-competitive and discriminatory manner.

(7) The 'specially permitted procurement' procedure.[116] The use of this procedure (which may be inconsistent with the legally established procedures under the Proclamation and Directives) may be exceptionally permitted by the Agency whenever its use is justified on sound grounds by the requesting procuring entity.

In order for a candidate to participate in federal public procurement, it must demonstrate that all of the following conditions are satisfied:[117] (i) that it has the necessary professional and technical qualifications, competences, financial resources, managerial capability, experience in relation to the subject matter of the procurement, reputation and personnel to perform the contract; (ii) that it has legal capacity to enter into the contract; (iii) that it is not insolvent, in receivership, bankrupt or being wound-up, its business activities have not been suspended, and it is not the subject of legal proceedings for any of these; (iv) that it is not suspended or debarred; (v) that it is registered in the suppliers list; (vi) that it has an up-to-date trade licence and tax-clearance certificate; (vii) that it has a bank account; and (viii) in instances where the value of the procurement exceeds Birr 100,000, that it has a VAT registration certificate.[118] Items listed under (v)–(viii) are not pertinent to foreign suppliers or contractors.[119] The 'Instructions to Bidders'[120] should contain statements communicating to the potential candidates the foregoing requirements and any other additional criteria that must be complied with.

In Ethiopia, the registration of (domestic) suppliers and contractors in the suppliers list is mandatory. The registration will also be posted on the Agency's website.[121] In the states, such websites have not been fully developed; thus, each supplier is issued (by the Bureaus of Finance and

116 Art. 16(5) of the Proclamation *cum* Art. 31 of the Directives.

117 Art. 28 of the Proclamation.

118 Art. 16.4.2.b of the Directives.

119 Instead, foreign companies are required to produce a certificate of incorporation from their country of incorporation. See Art. 16.4.2.b of the Directives.

120 Art. 28(3) of the Proclamation *cum* Art. 16.4 of the Directives.

121 See www.ppa.mofed.gov.et/index.php (accessed 1 March 2012).

Economic Development) with a certificate (or ID card) of registration in the suppliers list,[122] which is renewed annually following the production of a tax-clearance certificate by the supplier. A copy of the ID card is meant to be simultaneously submitted with the tender offer to procurement entities. The ID card is revoked or suspended by the issuing authorities in the states or deleted from the Agency's website whenever any supplier is debarred by any of the states or the Agency. Such debarment applies across the country through cross-debarment. Procurement from traders or businesses outside of the suppliers list can only be permitted under the request for quotation,[123] 'shopping', 'small-value' procurement, and the 'specially permitted procurement' methods discussed above. Federal government entities may also purchase goods, works or services from suppliers not registered in the suppliers list with the *caveat* that there are no registered suppliers in the localities where the entities are situated.[124]

The manner and style of procurement advertisements differ substantially depending on whether the procurement method is national competitive bidding or international competitive bidding. The criteria[125] set out for selecting the national competitive bidding are, first, the construction works, goods and services can be locally procured from domestic suppliers and contractors and that the procurement value is below the minimum threshold for international competitive bidding.[126] Secondly, even where the procurement value lies above the minimum threshold for international competitive bidding, national competitive bidding should be used if it is established that the goods or services can only be found locally. Under internationally competitive bidding,[127] therefore, the procuring entities prepare invitations to tender and tender documents in English.

122 The supplier is registered on the suppliers list for the procurement of goods, services or works for which it is duly licensed by the business licensing and registration authorities. However, a supplier, once registered by any of the states or the federal government, can participate in procurement tenders in all the states and the federal government without having to re-register.

123 Art. 56(1) of the Proclamation.

124 See Art. 33.1.c of the Directives.

125 Art. 16.1 of the Directives.

126 Art. 59(1) of the Proclamation *cum* Art. 17 of the Directives. Art. 17(2) of the Directives particularly sets out the minimum threshold for internationally competitive bidding as follows: for construction works, Birr 50 million; for goods, Birr 10 million; for consultancy services, Birr 2.5 million; and for services, Birr 7 million.

127 However, it should be kept in mind that international (procurement) purchasing can also be effected using restricted tendering, RFP, RFQ and single-sourcing with the *proviso* that the conditions for the use of these procurement methods are present and that carrying out 'effective procurement without the participation of foreign companies

The invitation to tender is advertised in a newspaper published in English with worldwide circulation and capable of attracting foreign competition. Moreover, in instances of procurement with a value equal to or exceeding the prescribed amount,[128] it is mandatory to post these tender advertisements on the Agency's website as of the date of their publication in the newspapers. To make the procedure more competitive, the procuring entity is also given the discretion to post the invitation to tender on its website and, if need be, even inform various foreign embassies.[129] Within five days after the signing of the contract with the winning tenderer, necessary information is communicated to the public via the Agency's website.[130] Where international procurement is not the method selected, the invitation to tender[131] and all procurement proceedings are processed in the Amharic language.[132] However, exceptionally procuring entities may prepare tender documents in English and permit the submission of tenders in English (instead of or in addition to Amharic) even if only local bidders participate, provided that the use of the language expedites the procurement process without being prejudicial to fair competition.[133] The procurement of public works using specifications and/or bills of quantities and standard bidding documents are invariably in English is a practical example.

With regard to the right of rejection of some or all of the tenders, unlike the 1994 UNCITRAL Model Law,[134] the Proclamation has taken procuring entities a step forward towards accountability and transparency. It has set out an exhaustive list of reasons[135] absent which

is ascertained to be impossible'. See Art. 59(4) of the Proclamation *cum* Art. 18 of the Directives.

128 This requirement applies both to national competitive bidding and to internationally competitive bidding. As provided for under Art. 6.5 of the Directives, the prescribed amounts are as follows: for construction works, Birr 10 million; for goods, Birr 3 million; for consultancy services: above Birr 2 million; and for other services, Birr 1 million.

129 Art. 17.4.b of the Directives.

130 Art. 6.6 of the Directives.

131 The 'Invitation to Tender' is published at least once in a national newspaper that has a nationwide circulation. When the procuring entity deems it necessary, it may also advertise on national radio and television.

132 Amharic is the working language of the federal government and is widely spoken in Ethiopia. Each of the states, on the other hand, is entitled to have its own working language.

133 Art. 27(1) of the Proclamation.

134 See Art. 12 of the 1994 UNCITRAL Model Law and p. 71 of its accompanying Guide to Enactment. See also Art. 19 of the new UNCITRAL Model Law on Public Procurement (2011) ('2011 UNCITRAL Model Law').

135 Art. 30(1) of the Proclamation, which states: '(a) there is proof of error in the procurement proceeding which could affect the outcome of the bid; (b) it is ascertained that the procurement has no use in enabling the public body to obtain a better

the procuring entity should not reject tenders in whole or in part. The procuring entity has the duty to disclose forthwith the reasons for rejecting bids. However, the reasons do not have to be justified in the sense of being explained. It is also provided that the procuring entity does not incur any liability solely for rejecting the bids based on one or more of the reasons listed therein provided that it communicates the rejection to the bidders.[136] The rejection of tenders on the basis of the stated reasons can be exercised only if the right to do so has been reserved by the procuring entity in the invitations to tender. Despite the lengthy list, this aspect of the Proclamation opens the door for the bidders to be able to scrutinise whether the reasons put forward for the rejection of their tenders are included in the list and, to thereby curb rejections based on arbitrary, capricious or frivolous grounds.

Tenders are required to be in writing, signed and in a sealed envelope and deposited in a box at the place and by the deadline stated in the invitation to bid.[137] There are no e-tendering rules or practices at present. The Proclamation only envisages the use of e-tenders, upon authorisation thereof by the minister, on the condition that the overall system and capacity of the public bodies and suppliers are sufficient for this, and that the appropriate framework for the operation of electronic information exchange is put in place.[138]

Tenders are opened in public and in front of the bidders who wish to be present. Tender-opening sessions may be observed by any interested person. Although some universities claim to have made it open for representatives (of student councils) to attend entire procurement proceedings, it has seldom been a serious commitment. Unfortunately, there is no law or practice that enables civil society organisations to attend procurement proceedings in Ethiopia.

The procuring entity cannot use any criterion that has not been clearly set out in the tender documents. Procurement contracts are awarded to

technical or economic advantage as a result of a change of work plan or another alternative representing a better option to meet the requirement of the public body; (c) bidders fail to meet the minimum criteria set forth in the bid document; (d) the minimum price offered in the bid does not match with the market price circulated by the Agency and the public body expected that it can get a better price advantage by re-advertising the bid; (e) the price offered by the successful bidder exceeds the budgetary allocation made for the procurement and the public body cannot make up for the deficiency from any other source; (f) it is proved that the bidding is not sufficiently competitive as a result of connivance among candidates.'

136 Art. 30(2) and (4) of the Proclamation. 137 *Ibid.*, Art. 41.

138 *Ibid.*, Art. 31. The task of laying out the necessary infrastructure for the use of e-tendering is, however, entrusted to the Agency.

those whose tenders are found to be substantially responsive and with the lowest evaluated price.[139] The procuring entity may also award the contract, if it has so stipulated in the tender documents, to the most economically advantageous tender.[140] While the procurement of goods, construction works and services using the RFQ procurement method is awarded to the 'lowest evaluated tender',[141] consultancy services solicited through the RFP procedure are awarded to the most economically advantageous tender.[142]

The procurement contract is signed[143] with the winning tenderer within fifteen days after the award of the contract after observing a seven-day standstill period.[144]

International procurement contracts are to be concluded based on international commercial terms and conditions[145] so long as these terms

139 *Ibid.*, Art. 8(a).

140 For this purpose, the most economically advantageous tender should be 'ascertained on the basis of factors affecting the economic value of the bid which have been specified in the bidding documents, which factors shall, to the extent practicable, be objective and quantifiable, and shall be given a relative weight in the evaluation procedure or be expressed in monetary terms wherever practicable'. See Art. 8(b) of the Proclamation.

141 Art. 24.6 of the Directives.

142 Art. 54(6) of the Proclamation.

143 As per Art. 1724 of the Ethiopian Civil Code, contracts binding the government or any procuring entity should be made in writing, supported by a special document, signed by the contracting parties and attested by two witnesses, and registered with a notary. The parties need not have to satisfy the foregoing formalities only when the procuring entities resort to the 'shopping', 'small-value' and RFQ methods where, in the latter case, the price quotation by the contracting party and the purchase order by the procuring entity suffice. See Arts. 25.11 and 24.11 of the Directives, respectively.

144 Art. 16.27 of the Directives.

145 This approach unnecessarily renders the national laws amenable to what is termed 'international commercial terms and conditions'. In national and international construction contracts, the FIDIC Red Book (FIDIC Conditions of Contract for Works of Civil Engineering Construction of 1987, 4th edn) has been the model contract for all government construction contracts cumulatively because drafting such complex contracts had been beyond the capacity of the civil servants and/or (with Ethiopia being one of the largest recipients in Sub-Saharan Africa of aid and/or grant from the World Bank Group) because of the World Bank's Standard Bidding Documents which adopted the FIDIC Red Book for World-Bank-funded infrastructure projects in the developing countries. As of January 2006, the widely used standard form of construction contract is the Federal Standard Bidding Document for the Procurement of Works (issued by the FPPA) which adopted, with slight modifications, the MDB (Multilateral Development Banks) Harmonized Edition of 2006, which is used for projects funded in whole or in part by the participating bank which include the IBRD, the IADB, the EBRD, the AfDB and the Islamic Bank for Development. For more on this, see C. Murray, D. Holloway and D. Timpson-Hunt, *Schmitthoff's Export Trade: The Law and Practice of International Trade* (11th edn, London: Sweet & Maxwell, 2007), p. 598.

and conditions are not inconsistent with the Proclamation and the Directives.[146] In relation to national and international procurement of construction works, the standard forms of contract have been significantly different from domestic construction laws, particularly public works contracts governed by the administrative contracts legal regime.[147] While procuring entities in Ethiopia have invariably inserted a clause subjecting their public works contracts to administrative contract law, the rights and duties detailed therein have been seldom applied by the contracting parties. Thus, owing to the standard forms of construction contracts, the applicability of administrative law to public works contracts has been minimal, if not non-existent.[148] The problem will, however, surface more acutely when other national laws are made subservient to the so-called 'terms and conditions as are applicable to international commercial contract' as stipulated under the Directives. In this regard, the Directives make it imperative that Ethiopian laws remain the chosen applicable laws if the aforementioned international procurement contracts are made subject to the terms and conditions applicable in 'international commercial contracts', thereby ensuring the applicability of the Ethiopian mandatory rules.

5. Concluding remarks

Ethiopia has modernised its public procurement laws. The newly enacted Proclamation attempts to consolidate the end-to-end processes involving public procurement and property administration. It enshrines rules on procurement planning, procurement contract formation proceedings, contract administration, property administration, and, finally, the disposal of unserviceable, obsolete or surplus stores and equipment. Directives have also been recently issued for the proper implementation of the Proclamation. However, in spite of the relatively modern public procurement rules in Ethiopia, the lax or weak enforcement of the rules may hinder the desired effective implementation of these rules.

146 However, unless otherwise indicated, the applicable law in settling disputes arising out of or relating to such contracts is that of Ethiopia. See Art. 17.4.g and 17.4.h of the Directives.

147 See generally M. Beth Lyon, 'The Role of the Consulting Engineer in Developing Country Construction under the FIDIC Form Contract' (1994–5) 26 *Law and Policy of International Business* 273.

148 For more on this, see T. H. Bahta, 'Adjudication and Arbitrability of Government Construction Contract Disputes' (2009) 3 *Mizan Law Review* 1.

Ethiopia's public procurement system is based on the principles of: (i) value for money, i.e. ensuring economy, efficiency and effectiveness; (ii) non-discrimination, save the exceptional situations expressly provided for; (iii) transparency; (iv) accountability; and (v) assisting national producers and micro and small-sized enterprises which are considered vital for the country's economic development. Except for defence procurements, these principles apply to all federal and state government-funded public bodies and public enterprises alike. Ethiopia, however, uses standard bidding procedures adopted by international development funding agencies and donor countries whenever loans and/or grants are made that are required to be accompanied by the standard bidding documents and, at times, when it implements infrastructure projects funded under the tied-aid arrangements.

Procuring entities should advertise all procurements of goods, construction works and services, and use open procedures to award these, except when certain conditions are satisfied which allow them to resort to methods such as direct procurement, shopping, small-value procurements, and restricted tendering. Advertisements can vary depending upon whether the procurement is national or international.

Public procurement rules are enforced through a supplier remedies system that includes bid protests by candidates to the Complaints Review Board, whose decision can in turn be subjected to judicial review. The Board may grant annulment and/or re-tendering orders to the complainants, although monetary relief has not been granted. On the other hand, procuring entities submit their complaints against the defaulting suppliers or contractors to the Agency, whose decision (which is subject to judicial review) may result in debarment from all future government (federal and state) procurement contracts.

4

The regulatory framework for public procurement in Ghana

DOMINIC N. DAGBANJA

1. Introduction

The Republic of Ghana, prior to political independence on 6 March 1957 from Britain, was called the Gold Coast. Ghana is located on West Africa's Gulf of Guinea a few degrees north of the Equator.[1] It is bordered by Côte d'Ivoire to the west, Burkina Faso to the north, Togo to the east, and the Gulf of Guinea to the south.[2] The earliest Europeans to arrive in Ghana were the Portuguese in the fifteenth century. The Portuguese found so much gold in Ghana that they named it 'Da Mina', meaning 'The Mine'. Many other European traders came to the Gold Coast to trade, including the British, Danes and Swedes. In 1872, the Dutch lost interest in the region and ceded their forts to the British. The Dutch occupation of the Gold Coast lasted for about 274 years. By 1874, the British were the only Europeans in the Gold Coast, and Britain made the Gold Coast a Crown colony. After independence in 1957, Ghana spearheaded the political liberation of colonised Africa. The celebrated Dr Kwame Nkrumah, first President of Ghana, championed the cause of African unity, which led to the formation of the Organization of African Unity (OAU), now the African Union (AU).[3] Ghana has a population of about 24 million people and is a unitary republic consisting of those territories comprised in the ten administrative regions into which the country is divided, namely, the Northern, Upper East, Upper West, Volta, Eastern, Brong-Ahafo, Sekondi-Takoradi, Central, Ashanti and Greater Accra regions. Ghana has a system of local government and administration which is decentralised. At the apex of the governance and administrative structure of Ghana is the Executive, consisting of the President and

1 See www.ghanaweb.com (accessed 18 March 2012). 2 *Ibid.*
3 See www.ghana.gov.gh (accessed 18 March 2012).

Ministers of State.[4] The Legislature, namely, Parliament of the Republic of Ghana, is vested with the legislative power.[5] The Judiciary, which is vested with the judicial power, is independent and subject only to the Constitution of the Republic of Ghana 1992.[6] The institution of chieftaincy and traditional systems of administration as established by customary law and usage are also guaranteed and recognised in Ghana.[7] As a developing country, Ghana has largely relied on foreign funding from the International Bank for Reconstruction and Development or the World Bank, the International Monetary Fund and other major donors and states for most major projects. As a former British colony, Ghana has a legal system based on the common law. The Constitution of Ghana also recognises customary law, defined as rules of law which by custom are applicable to particular communities in Ghana.[8] These make the Ghana legal system dual in nature.

The Constitution of Ghana states that the sovereignty of Ghana 'resides in the people of Ghana *in whose name and for whose welfare* the powers of Government are to be exercised'[9] and that the state of Ghana 'shall take all necessary action to ensure that the national economy is managed in such a manner as to *maximise the rate of economic development and to secure the maximum welfare, freedom and happiness of every person in Ghana* and *to provide adequate means of livelihood and suitable employment and public assistance to the needy*'.[10] These provisions and the reliance of the country on foreign aid and loans with their requirement for transparency in the use of such funds and, generally, the quest for effective management of public finances have played a significant role in the development of the public procurement system in Ghana. The origin of the current procurement system can be traced to the mid-1990s financial reforms in Ghana. In order for Ghana to live up to its constitutional and foreign aid obligations and to improve how public finances were managed, there was a need for legal and institutional mechanisms which would assure judicious, economic, efficient, transparent and accountable use of public or borrowed funds. These financial reforms came about at the time when the UNCITRAL Model Law on Procurement of Goods, Construction and Services ('UNCITRAL Model Law') was just developed, giving an opportunity for Ghana to use this model law.[11]

4 Constitution of the Republic of Ghana 1992, Arts. 57, 78 and 79. 5 *Ibid.*, Art. 93.
6 *Ibid.*, Art. 125(1) and (3). 7 *Ibid.*, Art. 270. 8 *Ibid.*, Art. 11(2)–(3).
9 *Ibid.*, Art. 1(1). 10 *Ibid.*, Art. 36(1) (emphasis added).
11 The UNCITRAL Model Law of 1994 with a Guide to Enactment is available at www.uncitral.org/pdf/english/texts/procurem/ml-procurement/ml-procure.pdf (accessed 16 March 2012). A revised UNCITRAL Model Law was adopted in 2011.

This chapter serves as an introduction to the public procurement system in Ghana. It covers, in the main, the purpose, nature and scope of the procurement system from both legal and institutional perspectives, and relies on the author's recently published book, which treats the subject in greater detail.[12]

Currently, there is one instrument of primary legislation governing public procurement contracting in Ghana, which is the main subject of analysis in this chapter. This is the Public Procurement Act 2003 (Act 663) ('Public Procurement Act').

2. Introduction to the public procurement system

2.1. The objectives of public procurement policy

Public procurement in Ghana represents about 24 per cent of total imports of Ghana and, apart from personal emoluments, between 50 and 70 per cent of the national budget, and 14 per cent of GDP.[13] Given the percentage of public resources spent on procurement, an improvement in government contracting became a necessary factor as part of the public financial management improvement system in Ghana.

In the Ghanaian context, the purpose of the public procurement system is reflected in the object for the establishment of the Public Procurement Authority of Ghana. This, according to section 2 of the Public Procurement Act, is 'to harmonise the processes of public procurement in the public service to secure a judicious, economic and efficient use of state resources in public procurement and ensure that public procurement is carried out in a fair, transparent and non-discriminatory manner'.[14] A number of objectives may thus be outlined from section 2 of the Public Procurement Act as key to the public procurement system in Ghana.

First is the objective of securing 'judicious, economic and efficient use of state resources'. This objective focuses on 'best value for money' ('best value' for short). This concept requires that government money should not be wasted in procurement of goods, services or works. In

12 D. N. Dagbanja, *The Law of Public Procurement in Ghana: Law, Policy and Practice* (Saarbrücken: Lambert Academic Publishing, 2011).

13 *Ibid.*, pp. 45, 210 and 254. Indeed, indications are that the government of Ghana's spending on procurement could be higher, from 18.2 per cent to 25 per cent of the country's GDP could be said to be used for procurement. *Ibid.*, p. 210.

14 The vision of the Public Procurement Authority of Ghana is available at www.ppaghana.org (accessed 16 March 2012).

other words, government must not spend more money than necessary in procuring what is needed. The output delivered by the other contracting party to the government or its agent or procurement entity must meet the needs for which the procurement was initiated, whether in terms of quality, quantity or both or other values. The efficiency aspect of this provision means, it is submitted, that procurement must be done in a timely manner and in the most cost-effective manner by all participating in the procurement process. The idea that judicious, *economic and efficient use of state resources* ranks at the top of the list of objectives stated in section 2 of the Public Procurement Act suggests the paramount and fundamental importance attached to best value for money in the procurement system in Ghana over all other values.[15]

Secondly, fairness and non-discrimination are also objectives of the public procurement system in Ghana as reflected in the requirement to carry out procurement in a 'fair' and 'non-discriminatory' manner. The use of the verbal phrase 'carried out' which precedes 'fair' and 'non-discriminatory' and the adverb 'manner' which comes after these concepts in section 2 of the Public Procurement Act suggests that fairness and non-discrimination are *process-oriented or procedural objectives* and not ultimate or substantive goals as such. The requirements mandate how procurement must be carried out and not what it must achieve. They are necessary and required as *means* and not as *ends.* The concept of fairness appears to mean that those conducting and those participating in the procurement process must not take advantage of each other. This requires honesty, frankness, truthfulness and sincerity. Each participant in the procurement process must receive his or her due. Fairness in dealings requires that none must seek to cheat the other or take unfair advantage. Fairness also calls for the right to be heard. The requirement in the Public Procurement Act that procurement be carried out in a 'non-discriminatory . . . manner' calls for even-handedness and impartiality in the procurement process except where differential treatment is justified by the law.[16]

The third is the requirement to carry out procurement in a 'transparent . . . manner', hence the objective of transparency. This is interpreted as referring to the need for openness in procurement in Ghana; all information and opportunities in the procurement process must be made known to all participating in procurement. No secrecy, except a legally

15 Dagbanja, *The Law of Public Procurement in Ghana*, note 12 above, pp. 18–19.
16 *Ibid.*, p. 19.

justified one, is permitted. Again, it is submitted that the requirement that procurement be 'carried out' in a transparent 'manner' suggests the objective of transparency is a *process-oriented or procedural objective* and not an ultimate or substantive goal as such. It is necessary and required as a *means* and not as an *end*.

The Public Procurement Act in section 3(t) requires the Public Procurement Authority to 'assist the local business community to become competitive and efficient suppliers to the public sector', suggesting that collateral policies in procurement might be legally justified in Ghana and, as we will see below, the existing law also provides for various policies included as contract award criteria. However, these policies have not been fully pursued yet in Ghana. The use of procurement for social policy purposes is further discussed in Chapter 15 of this volume.

2.2. Nature and organisation of public procurement

Prior to the enactment of the Public Procurement Act there was no centralised procurement authority in Ghana. The Public Procurement Act provided for the establishment of the Public Procurement Authority. The functions of the Public Procurement Authority are broad and sweeping. They range from policy, adjudicatory, implementation, monitoring, advisory, coordination, capacity building and training, regulatory and data management, to environmental protection. Specifically, the functions of the Authority are to:

- Make proposals for the formulation of policies on procurement.[17]
- Ensure policy implementation and human resource development for public procurement.[18]
- Develop draft rules, instructions, other regulatory documentation on public procurement and formats for public procurement documentation.[19]
- Monitor and supervise public procurement and ensure compliance with statutory requirements.[20]
- Establish and implement any information system relating to public procurement.[21]
- Publish the *Public Procurement Bulletin* monthly containing information germane to public procurement, including proposed

17 Public Procurement Act, s. 3(a). 18 *Ibid.*, s. 3(b). 19 *Ibid.*, s. 3(c).
20 *Ibid.*, s. 3(d). 21 *Ibid.*, s. 3(f).

procurement notices, notices of invitation to tender and contract award information.[22]
- Assess the operations of the public procurement processes and submit proposals for improvement of the processes.[23]
- Present annual reports to the Minister of Finance and Economic Planning on the public procurement processes.[24]
- Facilitate the training of public officials involved in public procurement at various levels.[25]
- Develop, promote and support training and professional development of persons engaged in public procurement, and ensure adherence by the trained persons to ethical standards.[26]
- Advise government on issues relating to public procurement.[27]
- Organise and participate in the administrative review procedures.[28]
- Plan and coordinate technical assistance in the field of public procurement.[29]
- Maintain a register and the relevant data on procurement entities and contractors.[30]
- Undertake the investigation, and debar firms from procurement and maintain a list of firms that have been debarred.[31]
- Hold an annual forum for consultations on public procurement and other related issues.[32]
- Assist the local business community to become competitive and efficient suppliers to the public sector.[33]
- Perform such other functions as are incidental to the attainment of the objects of the Public Procurement Act.[34]

Sub-committees recognised under the Public Procurement Act are the Tender Committee, the Tender Evaluation Panel and the Tender Review Board.

First, each procurement entity is required to have a Tender Committee.[35] In the performance of its functions, a Tender Committee must ensure that, at every stage of the procurement activity, procedures prescribed in the Public Procurement Act are complied with.[36]

Secondly, the Public Procurement Act also requires each procurement entity to appoint a Tender Evaluation Panel with the required expertise

22 *Ibid.*, s. 3(g). 23 *Ibid.*, s. 3(h). 24 *Ibid.*, s. 3(i). 25 *Ibid.*, s. 3(j).
26 *Ibid.*, s. 3(k). 27 *Ibid.*, s. 3(l). 28 *Ibid.*, s. 3(m). 29 *Ibid.*, s. 3(n).
30 *Ibid.*, s. 3(o) and (p). 31 *Ibid.*, s. 3(q) and (r). 32 *Ibid.*, s. 3(s).
33 *Ibid.*, s. 3(t). 34 *Ibid.*, s. 3(u). 35 *Ibid.*, s. 17(1).
36 *Ibid.*, s. 17(1) and Sched. 1.

to evaluate tenders and assist the Tender Committee in its work.[37] The Tender Evaluation Panel is constituted each time there are tenders to be evaluated. Therefore, its membership is not constant.

Thirdly, the Public Procurement Act requires the establishment of a Tender Review Board, the function of which at 'each level of public procurement',[38] in relation to the particular procurement under consideration, is to review the activities at each step of the procurement cycle leading to the selection of the lowest evaluated tender or best offer by the procurement entity. The Tender Review Board is also required to ensure compliance with the provisions of the Public Procurement Act and its operating instructions and guidelines.[39] There are various Tender Review Boards which review procurement decisions and give threshold approval requests to procurement entities under their jurisdiction.

It can be suggested that, since the functions of *Tender* Committees and *Tender* Review Boards go beyond reviewing the *tender* process, their names should be changed to 'Procurement Committee' and 'Procurement Review Committee' respectively, consistent with the broader procurement functions they perform.[40]

2.3. The legal regime on public procurement

As regards the legal regime on public procurement, of primary importance is the Constitution of the Republic of Ghana 1992. Various provisions of the Constitution, such as Articles 1(1) and 36(1), require, either directly or indirectly, prudent and efficient use of state resources by imposing a duty on the government to exercise its power for the welfare of the people of Ghana and to manage the economy in such a manner as to secure the maximum welfare, freedom and happiness of the people of Ghana. These provisions provide a solid constitutional reference point for any enactment of legislation on public procurement. The Constitution is also important in the scheme of public procurement in Ghana because the Public Procurement Act, in section 93(1), requires procurement entities and participants in the procurement process in undertaking procurement activities to abide by the provisions of Article 284 of the Constitution. This states that public officers must not put themselves in a position where their personal interests conflict or will be likely to conflict with the performance of the functions of their office.

37 *Ibid.*, s. 19(1). 38 *Ibid.*, s. 20(1) and Sched. 2. 39 *Ibid.*, s. 20(2)(a).
40 Dagbanja, *The Law of Public Procurement in Ghana*, note 12 above, p. 94.

In addition to the Constitution is, as noted above, the Public Procurement Act. This is the substantive legislation on public procurement. It seeks to give effect to the constitutional requirements relating to accountability, prudence and transparency in the disbursement and use of public funds. In broad terms, the Public Procurement Act provides for public procurement methods and procedures and administrative and institutional arrangements for procurement in Ghana.

The Public Procurement Act, in section 97, empowers the Minister of Finance and Economic Planning, in consultation with the Public Procurement Authority, to make regulations by legislative instrument to give effect to the purposes of the Act in relation to procurement. Pursuant to this provision, the Minister has put in place draft regulations, yet to take effect.[41] For the most part, these draft regulations simply reproduced the contents of the Public Procurement Act rather than dealing with implementation issues that have come up or that may not have been treated in the Public Procurement Act. The Public Procurement Act, in section 93(2), also provides that an act amounts to corruption if so construed within the meaning of corruption as defined in the Criminal Offences Act 1960 (Act 29). Therefore, the Criminal Offences Act, though not primary, is also an important piece of legislation on procurement in Ghana. Corruption in public procurement is considered further in Chapter 14 of this volume. Also of importance are the Financial Administration Act 2003 (Act 654) and its accompanying regulations, which regulate transactions relating to finance and payments from public funds. In addition, there is the Contract Act 1960 (Act 25), although this deals less with procurement issues.

Apart from these substantive enactments, the Public Procurement Authority, as the regulatory and policy institution, also develops guidelines on various aspects of procurement such as framework agreements, single-source procurement and margins of preference. These are available on the website of the Public Procurement Authority.[42] Further, under section 50(1) of the Public Procurement Act, procurement entities are required to use the appropriate standard tender documents. These tender documents and the Public Procurement Act constitute the core legal regime on procurement in Ghana, from procurement planning through contract award and all phases of contract administration.

41 See www.ppaghana.org/documents/GhanaPPARegualtions.pdf (accessed 18 March 2012).

42 *Ibid.*

Above all, as a common law country, common law principles relating to contracts and international commercial law (for example, international commercial terms, or 'incoterms') have application in Ghana and may play some role in the procurement process. In this connection and in terms of litigation, there have not been many court decisions on procurement. This is mainly because not many procurement disputes have been sent to the courts. There has been a decision on single-source procurement in Ghana,[43] and there is also ongoing procurement litigation in the courts which may contribute to the body of judicial literature on procurement in Ghana. However, at present, the role of the courts in the development of procurement law in Ghana is extremely limited.

Under the Public Procurement Act, tenderers have the legal right to enforce the legal and procedural rules governing procurement before procurement entities themselves and the Public Procurement Authority. The Act entitles a tenderer that 'claims to have suffered, or that may suffer loss or injury due to a breach of a duty imposed on the procurement entity'[44] to seek redress. Complaints for redress are required to be submitted to the procurement entity concerned first, and, if the tenderer is not satisfied with the decision of the procurement entity or if a decision is not made by the procurement entity at all after the specified period, then a complaint may be lodged before the Public Procurement Authority for an administrative review. The Public Procurement Authority has the power, among others, to declare the legal rules or principles that govern the subject-matter of the procurement, revise an illegal decision and to order the payment of compensation for reasonable costs incurred by the tenderer who submitted the complaint.[45] The Public Procurement Act is silent on appeals from the decision of the Public Procurement Authority. This lacuna is addressed in Article 23 of the Constitution. This provision requires administrative officials and administrative officers to act fairly and reasonably and to comply with the requirements imposed on them

43 *The Republic* v. *Ministry of Education and Sports and Others* [Suit No. AP6/2006] High Court (decided on 18 December 2006, unreported). In this case, the plaintiff sought a declaration that the decision of the Ministry of Education and Sports to engage in single-source procurement for the procurement of textbooks and other educational materials from Macmillan Education Ltd was contrary to s. 40 of the Public Procurement Act. The plaintiff also sought a declaration that the Public Procurement Authority erred in law when it granted approval to the Ministry of Education and Sports to use single-source procurement to procure the said items. The High Court decided that the Ministry and the Public Procurement Authority had not complied with s. 40 of the Public Procurement Act and accordingly quashed the decision of the Authority.

44 Public Procurement Act, s. 78(1).

45 *Ibid.*, ss. 78–82 generally.

by law. The provision grants persons who are aggrieved by the exercise of administrative acts the right to seek redress before a court of law or other tribunal. Based on this provision, it is submitted, an appeal from the decision of the Public Procurement Authority lies to the courts or other tribunal. This position is further supported by Order 55, rule 1, of the High Court (Civil Procedure) Rules of 2004 (CI 47), which provides that an order for *mandamus*, prohibition, *certiorari*, *quo warranto* or injunction shall be made by way of an application for judicial review to the High Court.

The Public Procurement Authority, by exercising its administrative review powers under section 80 of the Public Procurement Act, has played an important role in the enforcement of the Act. The complaints that have so far been administratively resolved have included those related to:

- Alleged manipulation of specifications.
- Declaration of successful tenders at tender openings contrary to procurement rules.
- Clarification of rules on award notification and formation of contract.
- Timely release of tender security.
- Past performance as criterion for pre-qualification.
- Discrimination in the award of contracts.
- Whether a tender may be rejected if one or more of the required certificates are not submitted prior to tender submission deadline.
- Delayed communication of award of the contract.
- Violation of procedures for request for quotation and pre-qualification provisions.
- Contravention of procedure for inviting tenders or applications to pre-qualify.
- Violation of provisions relating to content of invitation to tender or to pre-qualify.
- Failure to publish notice of procurement contract award.
- Whether a tender committee has the mandate to cancel an award made after due acceptance of the evaluation report and concurrent approval by a tender review board.
- Changes to essential items required after the tender process.[46]

Supplier remedies are discussed in more detail in Chapter 13 of this volume.

46 See www.ppaghana.org/documents/appealscases.asp (accessed 18 March 2012).

2.4. *Public procurement regulation: the context*

The public procurement system in Ghana is said to be traceable back as far as the pre-independence era.[47] In the pre-independence era (before 1957), there was a public procurement policy in which public procurement was treated as part of the colonial administrative process in the British Empire.[48] The Public Works Department (PWD) was used for procurement of works, and Crown Agents were used for the procurement of goods. After Independence in 1957 and up to 1967, the government relied less frequently on Crown Agents for procurement of goods, and instead procured goods directly through ministries, departments and agencies. For procurement of works, the government set up the Ghana National Construction Corporation (GNCC) to carry out works.[49] In 1960, the government established the Ghana Supply Commission (GSC) for procurement of goods for all public institutions. In 1976, the government established the Ghana National Procurement Agency (GNPA) for procurement of bulk items such as sugar, fertilisers and auto parts for sale to both public and private sectors.[50] In 1975, the Architectural and Engineering Services Corporation (AESC) was established to carry out consulting services for works contracts.[51] Various legislation also regulated procurement in Ghana prior to the current legal framework, including the Ghana Supply Commission Act 1960, which was replaced by the Ghana Supply Commission Law 1990 (PNDCL 245), and which in turn was repealed by the Public Procurement Act 2003.[52] The National Procurement Agency Decree 1976 (SMCD 55) and the Financial Administration Decree 1977 (SMCD 221), both now repealed, also dealt with procurement issues.

These various legal and institutional mechanisms, however, were not well coordinated, leading to implementation inefficiencies and lack of attainment of best value for money. For example, a study undertaken by the government and the World Bank found substantial inefficiency in public procurement, and concluded that the principle of value for money was not being achieved. This finding was said to be true for both government-financed and donor-financed procurements. The study further found that there were slow project implementation and disbursement. These, in

47 Dagbanja, *The Law of Public Procurement in Ghana*, note 12 above, pp. 42–8.

48 World Bank and Government of Ghana, *Ghana: Country Procurement Assessment Report* (2003), vol. 2, www.procurementafrica.org/2010/12/ghana-procurement-resources.html (accessed 18 March 2012).

49 *Ibid.* 50 *Ibid.* 51 *Ibid.* 52 Public Procurement Act, s. 99.

turn, were attributed largely to inadequate procurement planning, non-transparent procurement procedures and poor contract management. A review of 132 works contracts in 2002, which constituted an important part of public expenditure, indicated that 84 per cent of the contracts incurred cost overruns of up to 30 per cent of the initial amount.[53] As part of the Public Financial Management Reform Programme, which was aimed at bringing about efficiency in financial management, procurement reform was targeted. With studies undertaken by the government of Ghana and the World Bank, this ultimately resulted in the enactment of the Public Procurement Act. The Public Procurement Act in substance follows the UNCITRAL Model Law,[54] and has been in operation since 2004. There are already ongoing efforts to amend this law. Prior to the present procurement system, the procurement process was centralised in the sense that there were in place key institutions which procured goods, services and works for the various government institutions. Under the present system, however, each procurement entity is responsible for its own procurement. The present system also, as we have seen, has a centralised regulatory and policy institution responsible for the implementation of procurement laws.

Ghana joined the General Agreement on Tariffs and Trade in October 1957, and became a founding member of the World Trade Organization (WTO) in 1995. However, it is currently not a party to the WTO's Agreement on Government Procurement. Ghana is also a party to the African Caribbean Pacific–European Commission Partnership Agreement of 2000, the Treaty establishing the Economic Community of West African States of 1975 and the Treaty Establishing the African Economic Community of 1991. All of the foregoing agreements envisage, among other objectives, trade promotion among member states. In addition, Ghana has signed bilateral investment promotion and protection agreements with a number of countries including China, Malaysia and the United Kingdom and Ireland aimed at encouraging foreign investment between the contracting parties. These trade and investment promotion and protection agreements do not affect the public procurement process in Ghana. The only case where an international obligation might affect the procurement process in Ghana is where the source of funding

53 World Bank and Government of Ghana, *Ghana: Country Procurement Assessment Report* (2003), vol. 4, www.procurementafrica.org/2010/12/ghana-procurement-resources.html (accessed 18 March 2012).

54 See note 11 above.

for an intended procurement is a grant or a concessionary loan. Under section 96 of the Public Procurement Act, any procurement with international obligations arising from a grant or concessionary loan to the government is to be carried out in accordance with the terms of the grant or loan if any such terms exist. The influence of donor funding on national procurement systems is further considered in Chapter 11 of this volume.

3. Coverage of the public procurement rules

3.1. Introduction

The long title of the Public Procurement Act shows that the scope of application of the Act is all processes, procedures, administrative and institutional mechanisms needed for the procurement of goods, services (including consultancy services) and works in Ghana. In other words, it covers all matters connected with procurement in Ghana. Specifically, the Public Procurement Act covers the following.

3.2. Procurement entities

The Public Procurement Act covers all government institutions, and any other institutions for that matter, which use public funds to procure goods, services and works. The government institutions required to comply with the procedures stipulated for procurement are called procurement entities under sections 15 and 98 of the Public Procurement Act.

Under section 14(2)(a)–(h) of the Public Procurement Act, the Act regulates the procurement activities of:

- Central management agencies.[55]
- Government ministries, departments and agencies.
- Subvented agencies.[56]
- Governance institutions.[57]
- State-owned enterprises to the extent that they utilise public funds;
- Public universities.

55 Public Procurement Act, s. 98. These institutions refer to the Public Services Commission, the Office of the President and the Office of the Head of Civil Service.

56 Public Procurement Act, s. 98. These institutions refer to agencies set up by government to provide public service and financed from public funds allocated by Parliament in the annual appropriation.

57 *Ibid.*, s. 98. These institutions include regional coordinating councils, district assemblies, metropolitan and municipal assemblies.

- Public schools, colleges and hospitals.
- The Bank of Ghana and financial institutions such as public trusts, pension funds, insurance companies and building societies which are wholly owned by the state or in which the state has a majority interest.
- Institutions established by government for the general welfare of the public or community.

These institutions are the procurement entities and are responsible for carrying out procurement.[58] They are public institutions or institutions that use public funds to acquire goods, services and works.

It should be added that the Public Procurement Act is silent on the involvement of civil society in procurement. Rights and remedies in procurement are available only to suppliers or tenderers who have actually taken part in procurement.

3.3. *Type of procurement subject to regulation*

The Public Procurement Act and its regulations regulate:

- The procurement of goods, services and works financed in whole or in part from 'public funds'.[59]
- Functions that pertain to procurement of goods, works and services, including the description of requirements and invitation of sources, preparation, selection and award of contract.
- Contract administration.[60]
- The disposal of public stores and equipment.[61]

58 Public Procurement Act, ss. 15 and 98.

59 *Ibid.*, s. 14(1)(a). 'Public funds' are defined under s. 98 of the Act as including 'the Consolidated Fund, the Contingency Fund and such other public funds as may be established by Parliament'. The Consolidated Fund contains 'all revenues or other moneys raised or received for the purposes of, or on behalf of, the Government and any other moneys raised or received in trust for, or on behalf of, the Government'. The Contingency Fund contains moneys voted by Parliament for the purpose of urgent or unforeseen need for which no other provision exists to meet the need. Public funds include loans raised or received for the purposes of or on behalf of government or loans raised or received in trust for, or on behalf of, the government. Constitution of Ghana, Arts. 176(1) and (2) and 177(1).

60 Public Procurement Act, s. 14(1)(b). Although the Act claims to cover all phases of contract administration, in substance the Act has very limited provisions dealing with contract administration.

61 *Ibid.*, s. 14(1)(c).

The Public Procurement Act also covers procurement with 'funds or loans taken or guaranteed by the State and foreign aid funds except where the applicable loan agreement, guarantee contract or foreign aid agreement provides the procedure for the use of the funds'.[62] Further, under section 96 of the Public Procurement Act, procurement 'with international obligations arising from any grant or concessionary loan to the government shall be in accordance with the terms of the grant or loan'. This means, for example, that, when the government of Ghana borrows money from the World Bank or another lender, the Bank's Guidelines: Procurement of Goods, Works, and Non-Consulting Services under IBRD Loans and IDA Credits and Grants or the procurement rules of the lender concerned may apply in Ghana instead of the Public Procurement Act. The implication of this is that Ghana, like many developing countries that are heavy borrowers, has multiple systems of procurement: local legislation on procurement to be used when the funds are public in nature and what may be described as 'lender procurement systems', that is, the system of law to govern procurement as may be required by the lending institutions. These procurements are usually undertaken by the same procurement entities irrespective of the source of the funds, whether public or borrowed. The influence of aid funding on national procurement systems is considered further in Chapter 11 of this volume.

3.4. Exceptions

Under section 16(2) of the Public Procurement Act, a procurement entity may undertake procurement in accordance with 'established private sector or commercial practices if (a) the procurement entity is legally and financially autonomous and operates under commercial law; (b) it is beyond contention that public sector procurement procedures are not suitable, considering the strategic nature of the procurement; and (c) the proposed procurement method will ensure value for money, provide competition and transparency to the extent possible'.[63] These four elements must be met before a procurement entity can undertake procurement in accordance with established private sector or commercial practices. The phrase 'established private sector or commercial practices' is not defined in the Public Procurement Act. However, this has been interpreted to refer to 'established ways [in which] individuals or businesses usually

62 *Ibid.*
63 Dagbanja, *The Law of Public Procurement in Ghana*, note 12 above, pp. 54–7.

create contracts'. This might include 'hire purchase agreements, public private partnerships, common law contracts and laws governing the sale of goods'.[64] Since the key phrase to this exception to the application of the Public Procurement Act is not defined, there could be controversy as to its meaning and scope. No such controversy has arisen yet.

The Public Procurement Act also does not apply where the Minister of Finance and Economic Planning decides that it 'is in the national interest to use a different procedure'.[65] Where the Minister so decides, 'the Minister shall define and publish in the *Gazette* the method of procurement to be followed in order to serve the interest of the economy'.[66] It is submitted that all procurements in Ghana, including military procurements, must follow the procedures laid down in the Public Procurement Act except where these exceptions apply, since there is no separate legislation governing military procurements in Ghana.

4. Public procurement procedures

4.1. Procurement procedures

The Public Procurement Act requires the use of various procurement methods in the procurement of goods, non-consultancy services and works. These methods are:

- competitive tendering;
- two-stage tendering;
- restricted tendering;
- single-source procurement; and
- request for quotations.

All of these methods are based very closely on the methods that are provided under the 1994 UNCITRAL Model Law, which is discussed further in Chapter 12 of this volume, dealing with procurement methods. Each of these is examined briefly.

The default method for procurement in Ghana is competitive tendering. This involves a general requirement that participation in procurement proceedings should be based on competition[67] in the sense that the procurement proceedings must be open for participation by every eligible prospective tenderer.[68]

64 *Ibid.*, pp. 55 and 54. 65 Public Procurement Act, s. 14(1).
66 *Ibid.*, s. 14(3). 67 *Ibid.*, s. 25. 68 *Ibid.*, s. 35(1).

The two-stage tendering method is appropriate where it is not feasible to formulate detailed specifications for the goods or works or, in the case of services, to identify their characteristics or where the character of the goods or works are subject to rapid technological advances.[69] The two-stage tendering technique is also appropriate for contracts for research, experiments, study or development.[70]

The use of restricted tendering is conditioned upon: (1) goods, works or services being available only from a limited number of prospective tenderers;[71] or (2) the time and cost required for examining and evaluating a large number of tenders being disproportionate to the value of the goods, works or services to be procured.[72] The primary aim of this method is to save the transaction costs associated with procurement. The use of this method requires the approval of the Public Procurement Authority.[73]

The use of single-source procurement means that procurement will be made from only one prospective tenderer. To use single-source procurement, the approval of the Public Procurement Authority is required.[74] Among others, single-source procurement is justified where any of the following is established:

- Where goods, works or services are only available from a particular prospective tenderer.
- If a particular supplier or contractor has exclusive rights in respect of the goods, works or services, and no reasonable alternative or substitute exists.[75]
- Where there is an emergency or catastrophic event.[76]
- For purposes of standardisation,[77] compatibility with existing goods, equipment and technology.[78]
- Where the proposed procurement is limited in comparison with the original procurement.[79]
- For research and development contracts.[80]
- For national security reasons.[81]

Requests for quotations are used for readily available goods or technical services that are not specially produced or provided to the particular specifications of the procurement entity.[82] This method is also used for

69 *Ibid.*, s. 36(1)(a). 70 *Ibid.*, s. 36(1)(b). 71 *Ibid.*, s. 38(a).
72 *Ibid.*, s. 38(b). 73 *Ibid.*, s. 38. 74 *Ibid.*, s. 40. 75 *Ibid.*, s. 40(1)(a).
76 *Ibid.*, s. 40(1)(c). 77 *Ibid.*, s. 40(1)(d)(i). 78 *Ibid.*, s. 40(1)(d)(ii).
79 *Ibid.*, s. 40(1)(d)(iii). 80 *Ibid.*, s. 40(1)(e). 81 *Ibid.*, s. 40(1)(f).
82 *Ibid.*, s. 42(a).

goods when there is an established market and the estimated value of the procurement contract is less than specified amounts.[83] Requests for quotations are to be made from as many suppliers or contractors as practicable, and from at least three different sources.[84]

The foregoing methods are used for procurement of goods, services (other than consultancy services) and works. In the case of procurement of consultancy services,[85] the methods for engagement of consultants include:

- The selection procedure where price is a factor.
- The selection procedure where price is not a factor.
- Quality based and quality cost based selection.
- Fixed budget and least-cost selections.[86]

Community participation in procurement as a method is not known under the Public Procurement Act, whether the procurement is in relation to goods, services or works.

4.2. Advertising contracts

In the procurement of goods, non-consultancy services and works, there are various procedures for inviting tenders under the procurement methods described above, varying according to whether competition will be achieved through invitation of national tenderers only, or through invitation of both national and international tenderers. The two tendering

83 *Ibid.*, s. 42(b). 84 *Ibid.*, s. 43(1).

85 The Public Procurement Act makes a distinction between services generally and consultancy services. The Act defines 'service' in s. 98 as 'the furnishing of labour, time, or effort not involving the delivery of a specific end product other than reports, which are merely incidental to the required performance; and includes consulting, professional and technical services but does not include employment agreements or collective bargaining agreements'. Again in s. 98 of the Act, 'consultancy services' are defined as 'services which are of an intellectual and advisory nature provided by firms or individuals using their professional skills to study, design and organise specific projects, advise clients, conduct training or transfer knowledge'. As 'services' other than 'consultancy services' are defined as including 'consulting, professional and technical services', the distinction between services generally and consultancy services is quite blurred. However, the methods for the procurement of goods and works are the same for the procurement of services other than consultancy services, whereas the methods for the procurement of consultancy services are distinct from those for the procurement of goods, services and works. Unless the context otherwise requires, 'services' when used without qualification is used to refer to services generally as distinct from consultancy services.

86 Public Procurement Act, ss. 72, 75 and 76.

techniques used to invite tenders on the basis of nationality are nationality competitive tendering[87] and international competitive tendering.[88] Which is to be used depends on the value of the procurement in terms of money (threshold) as defined in Schedule 3 to the Public Procurement Act. A procurement entity is required to invite tenders, or, where applicable, applications to pre-qualify, by issuing an invitation to tender or an invitation to pre-qualify, to be published in the *Public Procurement Bulletin* and in at least two newspapers of wide national circulation.[89] The invitation may also be published in a newspaper of wide international circulation, in a relevant trade publication or technical or professional journal of wide international circulation.[90] The *Public Procurement Bulletin* and the various tender documents are available on the Public Procurement Authority's website.

In the case of contracts for consultancy services, procurement entities are required to invite for consulting services by issuing notice seeking expression of interest in submitting a proposal to be published in the *Public Procurement Bulletin* for consultancy contracts above specified thresholds.[91] Upon shortlisting of candidates to participate in the selection process, the procurement entity must provide the invitation for proposals to the shortlisted consultants selected on the basis of quality and to the most qualified or single-sourced consultant selected on the basis of the consultant's qualifications.[92]

4.3. *Supplier lists and responsibility determinations*

The Public Procurement Act is silent on the maintenance of closed lists of qualified contractors by procurement entities themselves. The Public Procurement Act, in section 3(p), requires the Public Procurement Authority to 'maintain a database of suppliers, contractors and consultants and a record of prices to assist in the work of procurement entities'. Clearly, this provision requires the Public Procurement Authority itself and not procurement entities to maintain a database on contractors. It might be argued that the Public Procurement Authority could rely on this provision and order procurement entities to maintain a closed list of qualified contractors for procurement decisions in the future. On the basis of having gone through the various procedures required for procurement and

87 *Ibid.*, s. 44. 88 *Ibid.*, s. 45. 89 *Ibid.*, s. 47(1) and (2).
90 *Ibid.*, s. 47(1) and (3). 91 *Ibid.*, s. 66(1). 92 *Ibid.*, s. 67(3) and (4).

previous engagement with contractors, procurement entities often maintain supplier lists in Ghana. Procurement entities often rely on supplier lists when any of the non-competitive methods of procurement are used. The use of closed lists is not envisaged when the competitive methods of procurement are used. This position in Ghana is similar to the position under the 1994 UNCITRAL Model Law.

Pre-qualification and repeat tender qualifications are recognised in Ghana.[93] Pre-qualification and repeat qualification of tenderers and the contractor qualification criteria[94] are the bases on which the capacity of a contractor to perform a contract is determined. Qualification criteria include those dealing with professional and technical qualifications and competence, possession of financial resources, equipment and other physical facilities, managerial capability, legal capacity to contract and fulfilment of tax and social security obligations.

4.4. Contract award criteria

The provisions in the law on award criteria, like those on methods of procurement, are based very closely on those of the 1994 UNCITRAL Model Law. In the procurement of goods and works, the successful tender is measured in terms of the 'lowest evaluated tender price . . . on the basis of criteria specified in the invitation documents'.[95] The criteria in the invitation documents must be objective, quantifiable and given relative weight in the evaluation procedure or expressed in monetary terms where practicable and stipulated in the invitation documents.[96] The successful tender is the tender with the lowest evaluated tender price.[97] The lowest evaluated tender is determined based on the following, as chosen by the procurement entity in each case:

- The tender price (subject to any margin of preference).[98]
- The cost of operating, maintaining and repairing the goods or works.[99]
- The time for delivery of the goods, completion of works or provisions of the services.[100]
- The functional characteristics of the goods or works, the terms of payment and of guarantees in respect of the goods, works or services.[101]
- The effect the acceptance of the tender will have on:

93 *Ibid.*, ss. 23 and 63. 94 *Ibid.*, s. 22. 95 *Ibid.*, s. 59(3)(a) and (b).
96 *Ibid.*, s. 59(3)(b). 97 *Ibid.*, s. 59(3)(a). 98 *Ibid.*, s. 59(4)(a).
99 *Ibid.*, s. 59(4)(b). 100 *Ibid.*, s. 59(4)(b). 101 *Ibid.*, s. 59(4)(b).

- the balance of payments position and foreign exchange reserves of Ghana;[102]
- the countertrade arrangements offered by suppliers or contractors;[103]
- the extent of local content, including manufacturer, labour and materials, in goods, works or services being offered by suppliers or contractors;[104]
- the economic development potential offered by tenders, including domestic investment or other business activity;[105]
- the encouragement of employment, the reservation of certain production for domestic suppliers;[106]
- the transfer of technology;[107]
- the development of managerial, scientific and operational skills;[108] and
- national security considerations.[109]

The lowest evaluated tender, then, may not be given an award or be declared the successful tender merely on price and price only. Some form of trade-off decision would have to be made in arriving at the *lowest evaluated tender*. In other words, in deciding on the lowest evaluated tender the focus is not just on the tender with the lowest evaluated *price*, but the tender that meets the criterion or criteria the procurement entity considers most important in meeting its needs. Thus, the lowest evaluated tender may be determined by using a combination of the various award criteria listed above in addition to price ranked in order of their importance in meeting the needs of the procurement entity. For example, where time is more important than price, the procurement entity may award the contract to the tenderer with the highest price but with the most suitable time of delivery rather than the tenderer with the lowest price with the most unsuitable delivery schedule. The 'lowest evaluated *tender*' is, therefore, different from the tender with the 'lowest evaluated tender price', price being only one of the evaluation factors. However, if the tender with the lowest price also happens to be the lowest in terms of the criterion or criteria the procurement entity considers most important in meeting its needs, then preference is to be given to this tender.

Notice of acceptance of a successful tender must be given to the tenderer submitting the successful tender within thirty days of acceptance of the

102 *Ibid.*, s. 59(4)(c)(i). 103 *Ibid.*, s. 59(4)(c)(ii). 104 *Ibid.*, s. 59(4)(c)(iii).
105 *Ibid.*, s. 59(4)(c)(iv). 106 *Ibid.*, s. 59(4)(c)(v). 107 *Ibid.*, s. 59(4)(c)(vi).
108 *Ibid.*, s. 59(4)(c)(vii). 109 *Ibid.*, s. 59(4)(d).

tender.[110] A notice of the decision is to be given to the unsuccessful tenderers, although the Public Procurement Act appears to be silent on the time frame within which such notice is to be given.[111] The rule with regard to non-disclosure of tender evaluation details in the procurement of goods and works is that information relating to the examination, clarification, evaluation and comparison of tenders is not to be disclosed to tenderers or third parties except as specified by law or as ordered by a court.[112] In the procurement of consultancy services, procurement entities are to treat proposals and negotiations as confidential and are to avoid the disclosure of the contents of proposals and negotiations to competing consultants.[113] Parties to negotiations are also not to reveal to any other person information relating to the negotiations without the consent of the other party.[114]

5. Concluding remarks

During the colonial and post-colonial period up to 2003, the legal and institutional frameworks for public procurement in Ghana were numerous and varied. There were different legal frameworks and institutional structures. It is of particular significance to note that there were centralised institutions that were mandated to procure on behalf of and for the various government procurement entities. The procurement system as it existed then, however, did not seem to have guaranteed best value for money, and efforts at reform resulted in the enactment of the Public Procurement Act which came into force on 31 December 2003. The Public Procurement Act is the main legal regime on procurement in Ghana. Under this law, the objectives of the public procurement system are best value for money, fairness, transparency and non-discrimination. Given the structure and language of the law and the history of the procurement system which was erected against the backdrop of financial reforms in Ghana, it can be emphasised, as we have seen, that best value for money is an overriding objective in Ghana's procurement system.

In terms of scope, the Public Procurement Act covers procurements undertaken mainly by government institutions using public funds or foreign aid funds or loans advanced to or guaranteed by the government of Ghana. In the case of procurements undertaken with foreign aid or loans borrowed or guaranteed by the state, where the applicable foreign

110 *Ibid.*, s. 65(1). 111 *Ibid.*, s. 65(9). 112 *Ibid.*, ss. 63 and 28.
113 *Ibid.*, s. 77(1). 114 *Ibid.*, s. 77(2).

aid or loan agreement or guarantee contract provides for a different procurement or method to govern the use of the funds, the Public Procurement Act does not apply. Further, in terms of subject-matter, the Public Procurement Act covers the procurement of goods, services (including consultancy services) and works.

The Public Procurement Act has decentralised the procurement system in line with the decentralisation requirements of the Constitution of Ghana so that various procurement entities can now undertake their own procurements by themselves. The Public Procurement Act, nevertheless, made provision for the establishment of the Public Procurement Authority as the central policy and regulatory institution responsible for ensuring the effective implementation of the law. The methods and procedures for procurement in Ghana follow those of the UNCITRAL Model Law, which has since been revised. Also, the Public Procurement Act has been in operation for quite some time now. It is therefore time to begin to question empirically what impact its implementation has had for the quest for best value for money in Ghana.

5

The regulatory framework for public procurement in Kenya

KINGSLEY TOCHI UDEH

1. Introduction

Kenya is a country located on the east coast of Africa, with Nairobi as its capital. It has an estimated population of 38.53 million people.[1] Kenya, a republic, is a constitutional democracy with a unitary system of government headed by the President;[2] local administration is divided into sixty-nine rural districts, each headed by a commissioner appointed by the President. Consequently, there is a single public procurement regime that applies to all the tiers of government in Kenya; unlike in a federal government, where there are usually separate public procurement regimes for the federal government and the federating states. The Kenyan legislature, the National Assembly, makes laws for the country. However, subsidiary legislation forms part of the legal system. According to the Kenyan Constitution, the National Assembly, through the yearly Appropriation Act and other Acts of Parliament, authorises withdrawal of money from the consolidated fund and other government funds.[3] This is the foundation upon which the public procurement regulatory framework of Kenya rests. Kenyan law is interpreted by its High Court and the Court of Appeal, whose practice and procedure are offshoots of the common law.

With a GDP of US$34.51 billion, a gross national per capita income of US$770 and an annual growth rate of 3.6 per cent, Kenya, still a developing country, is the leading economy in East Africa.[4] As at March 2012, the World Bank's aid portfolio in Kenya consists of twenty-four active

1 World Bank, *World Development Indicators 2009.*

2 Constitution of the Republic of Kenya, ss. 1, 1A, 4, 23 and 52.

3 Constitution, s. 99: '"Consolidated fund" is defined as the fund where all revenue or other money raised or received for the purpose of the Government of Kenya shall be paid into.'

4 World Development Indicators database, 2009.

operations and six proposed projects, with total investment of US$7.070 billion.[5] The World Bank, in conjunction with the Kenyan government, in the late 1990s initiated a procurement reform process that resulted in the current public procurement regulatory framework of Kenya.[6] One of the objectives of the Bank-initiated procurement reforms was to align Kenya's procedures for procurement with international standards, particularly the UNCITRAL Model Law on the Procurement of Goods, Construction and Services ('UNCITRAL Model Law'),[7] and the current public procurement regulatory framework of Kenya is in fact based on the UNCITRAL Model Law of 1994.[8] Kenya is a signatory to a Customs Union established under the East African Community,[9] which partly entails that certain goods are exclusively imported or procured from member states.[10] In addition, Kenya is one of the nineteen member states of the Common Market for Eastern and Southern Africa (COMESA), a trade bloc established in 1994 to replace the Preferential Trade Area (PTA) which had been in existence since 1981. As will be seen later in this chapter, COMESA has to an extent influenced the emergence of the current public procurement system in Kenya. It is noteworthy that about 60 per cent of Kenyan government revenue in the fiscal year 2008/9 was spent on public procurement.[11]

This chapter presents an outline of the Kenyan public procurement system with a focus on its legal and organisational framework.

5 See http://web.worldbank.org/WBSITE/EXTERNAL/COUNTRIES/AFRICAEXT/KENYAEXTN/0,,menuPK:356516~pagePK:141159~piPK:141110~theSitePK:356509,00.html (accessed 20 March 2012); the figures stated above are particularly displayed under 'Country Portfolio' on the webpage.

6 W. Odhiambo and P. Kamau, 'Public Procurement: Lessons from Kenya, Tanzania and Uganda', OECD Working Paper 208 (2003), p. 20.

7 *Ibid.*, p. 37.

8 Kenya is listed on the UNCITRAL website as one of the countries whose public procurement legislative texts are based on or largely inspired by the UNCITRAL Model Law: see www.uncitral.org/uncitral/en/uncitral_texts/procurement_infrastructure/1994Model_status.html (accessed 25 March 2012). See also J. M. Migai Akech, 'Development Partners and Governance of Public Procurement in Kenya: Enhancing Democracy in the Administration of Aid' (2006) 37 *International Law and Politics* 829, 846 and 852.

9 The East African Community (EAC) is a regional intergovernmental organisation whose membership consists of Burundi, Kenya, Rwanda, Tanzania and Uganda.

10 East African Community, *The East African Community Trade Report 2007* (2008), p. 56. These goods, termed 'sensitive goods', include sugar, milk, wheat flour, maize, rice, palm oil and textiles.

11 Economic Affairs Department in the Office of the Deputy Prime Minister and Ministry of Finance, Republic of Kenya, *Statistical Annex to the Budget Speech for Financial Year 2009/2010* (2009), Chart 4B.

2. Introduction to the public procurement system

2.1. The objectives of public procurement policy

Kenya's public procurement policy is mainly discoverable from and founded upon the Kenya Public Procurement and Disposal Act 2005 (the 'Procurement Act'). Section 2 of the Procurement Act provides that the purpose of Kenya's public procurement policy is to establish procurement procedures for its public entities to achieve set objectives. These objectives correspond with those stipulated under the UNCITRAL Model Law and those of most national procurement systems, which are:

- value for money;
- integrity;
- accountability to the public;
- ensuring that markets are open to competition and trade partners;
- support of economic and social objectives; and
- efficiency.

There is an emphasis on promoting economic and social objectives in the recent public procurement policy of Kenya as established by the Procurement Act, compared with what obtained previously under the now-defunct Kenya Exchequer and Audit (Public Procurement) Regulations 2001.[12] Unlike the Regulations of 2001, the Procurement Act specifically provides, in section 2, that procurement shall be used to facilitate the promotion of local industry and economic development. To promote local industries, a prescribed margin of preference may be given during the evaluation of bids to suppliers offering goods manufactured, extracted or grown in Kenya. In addition, exclusive preference is given to Kenyan citizens over procurements below certain monetary thresholds funded wholly by the Kenyan government.[13] The thresholds below which exclusive preference shall be given to Kenyan citizens are: Ksh50 million (approximately US$745,700) for procurement of goods or services, and Ksh200 million (approximately US$2,983,000) for procurements in respect of works.[14] Furthermore, the Procurement Act provides that international tendering shall be resorted to only when supply from local industries will be inadequate or inefficient.[15] However, when international tendering is used,

12 Hereinafter the '2001 Regulations'.

13 Procurement Act, s. 39(8).

14 Public Procurement Oversight Authority, *Assessment of the Procurement System in Kenya* (2007), p. 11.

15 Ss. 71 and 86.

the inference is that foreign suppliers invited to bid will enjoy the same rights as local suppliers in accordance with fair treatment of competitors enunciated by the Procurement Act.[16] Also, the Procurement Act empowers the Minister of Finance to prescribe procurement preferences and reservations targeted at disadvantaged groups, identified regions, and micro, small and medium enterprises in Kenya, with the intention of enhancing their economic and social capacity.[17] The use of public procurement to promote social policy in Kenya is analysed in more detail in Chapter 15 of this volume.[18]

Another policy thrust is to stem corruption in Kenya. Consequently, Kenya's Procurement regime now strongly emphasises integrity in procurement, to the extent that certain breaches of procurement rules attract criminal sanctions.[19] Corruption in public procurement is further discussed in Chapter 14 of this volume.

2.2. *The nature and organisation of public procurement*

The size of Kenya's public procurement market is estimated to be approximately 11 per cent of its GDP.[20] This market size is enhanced by the fact that all public entities in Kenya, including those in the local administration, are empowered to procure for their needs in accordance with the annual budget and the Procurement Act. Also, procurements for some aid-funded projects in Kenya are undertaken by the Kenyan government through its procurement system.[21] However, the market access and size of the procurement system is constrained by the excessively high thresholds, mentioned above, in respect of procurements below which exclusive preference is given to Kenyan citizens. This actually debars competitive non-citizens from participating in viable procurements below the thresholds. Another major constraint is the registration threshold for competing for large-scale government contracts. In effect, only a small number of companies registered can bid for major government contracts. For example, only 4.7 per cent of the Contractors on the Register of Approved

16 K. T. Udeh, 'A Critical Analysis of the Legal Framework for Supplier Remedies System of Kenya in the Light of International Standards' (unpublished LLM dissertation, University of Nottingham, 2008), p. 7.

17 S. 39(2)(4). 18 See, in particular, Chapter 15, section 4.1, of this volume.

19 Ss. 135–137. 20 Government of Kenya, *Economic Surveys* (2001).

21 This is usually where the Kenyan government is to make a contribution towards the aid-funded project: Procurement Act, s. 6(3). On the impact of aid-funded procurement on national procurement systems, see Chapter 11 of this volume.

Building Contractors (June 2007) are listed in the top category (category A), and therefore only this 4.7 per cent may compete for large-scale building contracts.[22]

In each public entity, no single office is allowed to handle all aspects of procurement. Instead, each entity's Tender Committee, Evaluation Committee, and Inspection and Acceptance Committee, handle tendering processes, evaluation of tenders, and receipt of procured items, respectively. The members of each of these committees are prescribed in the Procurement Act and Regulations.[23] The Ministry of Health, the Kenya Medical Supplies Agency, Ministries of Education, Energy and Roads, and the Office of the President, are the six high-spending procuring entities of Kenya;[24] and at the local administration level, it is the Nairobi City Council and the Municipal Council of Thika.[25] As a major purchaser, the Ministry of Health and its medical supplies procurement and delivery body, the Kenya Medical Supplies Agency, have been identified as being particularly susceptible to waste, fraud and abuse throughout the procurement and delivery process.[26] Generally, public procurement accounts for 80 per cent of corruption in Kenya, according to the Kenya Anti-Corruption Commission.[27] This Commission, established under the Kenya Anti-Corruption and Economic Crimes Act 2003, assists the Kenyan Public Procurement Oversight Authority (PPOA) in enforcing compliance with the procurement rules by prosecuting suppliers or procurement officers found to have acted corruptly in the public procurement process. The PPOA, which is Kenya's main procurement oversight body, conducts investigations on any complaint of non-compliance with the procurement rules, and makes its recommendations to the Anti-Corruption Commission. Working also in the area of ensuring transparency and compliance to procurement rules in Kenya are the Kenya

22 Public Procurement Oversight Authority, *Assessment of the Procurement System in Kenya* (2007), p. 17.

23 Kenya Public Procurement and Disposal Regulations 2006, regs. 11–17; Procurement Act, s. 26.

24 Kenya Public Procurement Oversight Authority (PPOA), *Procurement Review Report*, 1 July 2007–30 June 2008 (2009), p. 6.

25 Public Procurement Oversight Authority, *Assessment of the Procurement System in Kenya* (2007), p. 4.

26 Millennium Challenge Corporation, *Report on Kenya*.

27 World Bank, http://web.worldbank.org/WBSITE/EXTERNAL/COUNTRIES/AFRICAEXT/KENYAEXTN/0,,contentMDK:21713760~menuPK:356529~pagePK:2865066~piPK:2865079~theSitePK:356509,00.html (accessed 25 March 2012).

National Audit Office (KENAO) and the Internal Auditor-General (IAG). The IAG is responsible for the internal audit function across government, especially in the area of procurement. This internal audit, governed by the Public Financial Management Act 2003, is carried out on an ongoing basis throughout the fiscal year and in accordance with the required annual work plan, thus providing the basis for a sound internal audit mechanism. External auditing, including that of procurement, is carried out on an annual basis by the KENAO. The mandate of the KENAO is derived from the Constitution and is further governed by the Public Audit Act 2003. The KENAO reports to the Public Accounts Committee of the Parliament; the Parliament then makes recommendations which are passed on to the Treasury for issuance of a Memorandum, the instrument upon which implementation of the KENAO recommendations are based.[28]

There appears to be a duplication of the audit function relating to procurement, as the Procurement Act[29] also mandates the PPOA to inspect and audit procurement contracts, but did not confine this function to the PPOA. What this has led to is that none of the institutions concerned sees procurement audit as their clear-cut mandate, thereby creating a serious gap in conducting regular procurement audits.[30]

It is the exclusive function of the PPOA to prepare and distribute manuals and standard documents for use in connection with procurement by public entities, to issue written directions to public entities with respect to procurement and to monitor the public procurement system and report on its overall functioning to the appropriate minister.[31] Other important functions of the PPOA include ensuring compliance with the Procurement Act, initiating public procurement policy and proposing amendments to the Procurement Act and its Regulations, and developing, promoting and supporting the training and professional development of procurement officers.[32] It is noteworthy that the PPOA does not procure for any public entity, since the Kenya public procurement system is fully decentralised.

The PPOA is a body corporate established under section 8 of the Procurement Act. It has a Director-General (DG), appointed by the

28 Public Procurement Oversight Authority, *Assessment of the Procurement System in Kenya* (2007), pp. 18–19.
29 Ss. 9(b) and 49.
30 Public Procurement Oversight Authority, *Assessment of the Procurement System in Kenya* (2007), p. 19.
31 Public Procurement Act, s. 9(b) and (c).
32 *Ibid.*, s. 9(a), (c)(iii) and (d).

Public Procurement Oversight Advisory Board ('Advisory Board') with the approval of Parliament, as its chief executive officer.[33] In some national procurement systems, the chief executive of the procurement oversight body is appointed solely by the President.[34] The procedure and bodies involved in the appointment of the DG of the PPOA enhance the chances of appointing a person of eminent qualifications and character, as well as exempting the DG and the PPOA from subservience to any person or any particular arm of government.

The Advisory Board is an unincorporated body established under section 21 of the Procurement Act. It is composed of the DG of the PPOA and nine members appointed by the Minister of Finance and approved by Parliament, from persons nominated by fourteen prescribed civil society and professional organisations.[35] The inclusion of members of civil society and professional organisations in the Advisory Board is one important formal mechanism for involving civil society in Kenya's public procurement. The Advisory Board's main function is to render advisory services to the PPOA. In addition, it appoints the DG of the PPOA, determines the DG's terms of service and terminates the DG's appointment on certain grounds before the expiration of the DG's single or dual five-year term.[36] The PPOA provides the secretariat to the Advisory Board and also the Public Procurement Administrative Review Board ('Review Board'). The Review Board is the administrative tribunal that adjudicates on complaints from aggrieved bidders. Its composition is the only other known formal mechanism for involving civil society in Kenya's public procurement. Six of the nine members of the Review Board appointed by the Minister are nominees and members of fourteen prescribed civil society/professional organisations.[37] One of the two nominees that each of the fourteen civil society organisations may submit to the Minister for appointment must be a woman.[38] The chairman of the Review Board must be one of the persons appointed from civil society. These civil society members have a term of three years on the Review Board, and may be reappointed for one further term of three years.[39]

Critical to the effectiveness of the Kenyan public procurement legal framework are the functions of the Review Board. These are discussed below.

33 *Ibid.*, s. 10(2). 34 Nigeria is an example: see Chapter 7 of this volume.
35 2006 Regulations, reg. 5(1). 36 Public Procurement Act, ss. 13 and 23.
37 2006 Regulations, reg. 68(1). 38 *Ibid.*, reg. 68(2). 39 *Ibid.*, reg. 67(1).

2.3. *The legal regime on public procurement*

It is the Procurement Act, with its Regulations, that regulates all aspects of the procurement process until an enforceable contract has come into being. But the execution of the contract awarded is governed by the common law principles of contract, enforceable at the regular courts of Kenya. Nevertheless, the Procurement Act empowers the PPOA to debar suppliers that default in the execution of procurement contracts.[40] All other laws of Kenya, such as the Anti-Corruption Act and the Financial Management Act, whose relevant provisions were discussed above, are ancillary to procurement regulation. In all matters of procurement (pre-execution of the contract stages) in Kenya, the Procurement Act and its Regulations override every other law, including international agreements and treaties to which Kenya is a signatory.[41] But note the exception to this rule in the case of international loan agreements, discussed in section 3.2 below.

The Procurement Act covers in detail all aspects of procurement in Kenya, and its Regulations provide further details. The Procurement Act stipulates the procurement policy objectives of Kenya, establishes procurement regulatory bodies, specifies general procurement rules, provides a default procurement method and the alternatives thereto, establishes a procurement challenge mechanism, provides compliance measures, including investigation, debarment and criminalisation of breaches, and also stipulates procedures for disposal of the government's properties. To supplement the Procurement Act there are the Regulations, guidelines, circulars, manuals and standard tender documents issued by the PPOA, as well as decided cases arising from reviews/appeals of public procurement decisions.

Owing to detailed regulatory control of all aspects of procurement, procuring entities are allowed minimal discretion. Furthermore, the regulatory control is enhanced by the right of suppliers under the Procurement Act to legally challenge any breach of the procurement rules by a procuring entity. It is exclusively vested in suppliers that participated in the procurement proceedings complained about.[42] This right of procurement review is exercisable, first, at the Review Board. Its jurisdiction does not extend to concluded contracts, and it cannot award

40 S. 115(1)(c). 41 Ss. 5 and 6.

42 Procurement Act, s. 93(1); see s. 3, which defines 'candidate'.

compensational damages.[43] The remedies that the Review Board may grant a bidder-complainant include: annulling the offending procurement action or proceedings; directing the procuring entity to do or redo a particular thing in the procurement proceedings; making decision(s) that substitutes the decision(s) of the procuring entity; and awarding trial costs.[44] The Review Board usually suspends the procurement proceedings complained about until the complaint is determined, as held in *Belra Chord Investments* v. *Postal Corporation of Kenya.*[45] This is because, if the proceedings are not suspended, the procuring entity concerned may carry on to the signing of the contract, at which point the matter will arguably be outside the Review Board's jurisdiction.[46] Its decisions are binding and final, except when appealed within the prescribed time.[47] An appeal from the Review Board lies to and ends at the High Court.[48] This right of review/appeal has increasingly been exercised by suppliers,[49] and the consequent decisions of the Review Board and courts have contributed to developing Kenya's procurement law. For instance, the Review Board, in *Mits Electrical Company Ltd* v. *Office of the President and Ministry of Lands and Housing,*[50] closed a gap in Kenya's procurement law when it held that the fourteen-day period of standstill between the award of a procurement contract and the signing thereof, within which suppliers are allowed to request a review, begins to run on receipt of notice of award by suppliers and not on issuance of the notice. Supplier remedies are further discussed in Chapter 13 of this volume.

Apart from the supplier remedies discussed above, bidders, procuring entities and even interested members of the public can request the Director-General of the PPOA to order an investigation of procurement proceedings to determine whether there has been a breach of the

43 *Ibid.*, s. 93(2)(c), *Republic* v. *Public Procurement Complaint, Review and Appeal Board and 2 Others, ex parte Apex Security Services Ltd* [2007] eKLR. In *Jambo World Ltd* v. *City Council* (2006) eKLR, the High Court's decision therein suggests that it may entertain a direct procurement complaint where a contract is already concluded, by way of judicial review.

44 Procurement Act, s. 98.

45 Review Board, *Application No. 1/2005 of 26th January, 2005*; see also s. 94 of the Procurement Act.

46 *Republic* v. *Public Procurement Complaint, Review and Appeal Board and 2 Others, ex parte Apex Security Services Ltd* [2007] eKLR.

47 Procurement Act, s. 100(1) and (2).

48 *Ibid.*, ss. 100(2) and 112.

49 The number of cases heard by the Review Board in 2004–7 was as follows: 2004, forty-six; 2005, fifty-two; 2006, fifty-eight; and 2007, seventy. See the PPOA's website, www.ppoa.go.ke.

50 *Applications No. 3 and 6/2005 of 2nd and 9th 2005.*

Procurement Act.[51] Where the investigation reveals that there has been a breach, the Director-General may: order the procuring entity to take actions necessary to rectify the contravention; cancel the procurement contract (if concluded) and terminate the procurement proceedings; and report findings and recommendations to the procuring entity and the Kenya Anti-Corruption Commission.[52] This power is subject to a fair hearing of concerned parties.[53] Parties may appeal the Director-General's decision(s) before the Review Board.[54] A final appeal can be made to the High Court.[55]

2.4. Public procurement regulation: the context

Before Kenya adopted this modern procurement regime, it had, until the early 1970s, made all its procurement using external entities such as the British Crown Agents. By 1974, Kenya established an elaborate procurement system wherein supplies offices within ministries and departments procured for their respective ministries and departments.[56] However, the Treasury was charged with the overall responsibility of regulating public procurement, which it performed by issuing numerous regulations and guidelines in the form of circulars to procurement officers in the ministries and local authorities.[57] These circulars were unenforceable, and breaching them did not attract legal sanctions. The principal instrument under that regime was the Government Financial Regulations and Procedures, which dealt with administration of government finances, including procurement. In 2001, Kenya promulgated the Exchequer and Audit (Public Procurement) Regulations. This Regulation governed Kenya's public procurement until 31 December 2006. Notwithstanding that it was in 2005 that the Procurement Act was enacted, followed by its Regulations in 2006, it was not until 1 January 2007 that the Procurement Act and its Regulations became operational, thereby replacing the 2001 Regulations as the main procurement law of Kenya. Indeed, the Procurement Act borrowed heavily from the 2001 Regulations. Nevertheless, the Procurement Act introduced some major changes, mentioned herein, in Kenya's Public Procurement system.

51 Procurement Act, Part VIII, particularly s. 102. 52 *Ibid.*, s. 105(1).
53 *Ibid.*, s. 105(2). 54 *Ibid.*, s. 106. 55 *Ibid.*, s. 112.
56 Odhiambo and Kamau, 'Public Procurement: Lessons from Kenya, Tanzania and Uganda', note 6 above, p. 16.
57 *Ibid.*

It was stakeholders in Kenyan procurement, especially donor agencies such as the World Bank, who called for reforms to harmonise Kenya's procurement system with internationally accepted standards. This call eventually led to the enactment of the 2001 Regulations and ultimately the Procurement Act.[58] It is noteworthy that the World Bank posted one of its top procurement officers, Robert Hunja, a Kenyan national, to serve as the pioneer head of the PPOA. Also, the United States influenced Kenya's procurement system when it signed an agreement in March 2007 with the government of Kenya to launch a US$12.7 million threshold programme designed to reduce public sector corruption by overhauling the public procurement system, with a particular concern for health care procurement.

Although the reforms in Kenya's procurement system were initiated by development partners, mainly the World Bank, COMESA has contributed to this process through its procurement reform project that commenced in May 2002.[59] A core aspect of COMESA's reform project was to familiarise member states, including Kenya, with international procurement standards, and to direct them to adopt a comprehensive procurement Act based on the UNCITRAL Model Law.[60] However, it should be noted that the UNCITRAL Model Law had already been used by Kenya as a basis for its procurement regulation before the commencement of the COMESA reform project. Thus, Kenya's Exchequer and Audit (Public Procurement) Regulations 2001, which was the country's main procurement regulatory framework until the enactment of its Procurement Act, was based on the UNCITRAL Model Law.[61] It is to be expected that Kenya's procurement system will be significantly affected in the near future by COMESA's Public Procurement Regulations 2009,[62] which primarily provide for 'regional competitive bidding' to give contractors/suppliers from member states access to other member states' procurement contracts within prescribed

58 Odhiambo and Kamau, 'Public Procurement: Lessons from Kenya, Tanzania and Uganda', note 6 above, p. 17.

59 See S. R. Karangizi, 'The COMESA Public Procurement Reform Initiative' (2005) 14 *Public Procurement Law Review* NA51, for more on the COMESA procurement reform project.

60 African Development Bank Group, *COMESA Public Procurement Reform and Capacity Building Projects: Project Performance Evaluation Report* (February 2012), pp. 3 and 10.

61 Akech, 'Development Partners and Governance of Public Procurement in Kenya', note 8 above, p. 846.

62 Legal Notice No. 3 of 2009. It is provided in Art. 38 that the Regulations shall come into force on the date of their publication in the *Official Gazette of the Common Market*; the Regulations were so published by order of the Council and Authority on 9 June 2009.

thresholds.[63] At present, the monetary thresholds are to be variously set by member states in their domestic procurement legislation; COMESA's Secretary General is to be notified and the thresholds are to be posted on respective member states' national procurement websites.[64] However, within five years of the adoption of the Regulations, a common financial threshold for regional competitive bidding is to be adopted by the COMESA Council.[65]

3. Coverage of the public procurement rules

3.1. Procuring entities

All public entities in Kenya are designated as procuring entities to which the Procurement Act and its Regulations apply.[66] The Procurement Act defines 'public entity' as including:[67]

- the government or any department of government;
- state corporations (enterprises);
- cooperative societies and commissions;
- local authorities;
- the courts;
- commissions;
- public schools;
- public universities; and
- colleges or other educational institutions maintained or assisted by public funds.

In addition to the above entities, section 3(2) of the Procurement Act provides that any entity may be designated as a 'public entity' for the purpose of the Procurement Act. Following this, the PPOA issued a gazette in January 2007 which included 'voluntary organisations/institutions' as procuring entities to which the Procurement Act applies.[68] It could be inferred from the Procurement Act that, if an entity uses public funds, which includes aid grants and credits, to finance its procurement, then the

63 COMESA Public Procurement Regulations 2009, Art. 2.

64 *Ibid.*, Art. 6(1)–(4). Not much appears to have been done by Kenya towards implementing the COMESA Public Procurement Regulations on setting a regional threshold, since no such threshold has been prescribed in Kenya's public procurement legislation or posted on Kenya's PPOA website.

65 *Ibid.*, Art. 6(5). 66 Procurement Act, s. 4(1)(a).

67 *Ibid.*, s. 3(1). 68 Gazette Notice No. 719.

Procurement Act and Regulations will apply to that entity. This inference is informed by the combined reading of the definition of 'public entity', 'procuring entity' and 'public funds' under the Procurement Act.

These procuring entities, following the Procurement Act and Regulations, may undertake certain types of procurement contract, as discussed below.

3.2. *Type of procurement subject to regulation*

Goods, works and services are specifically mentioned and uniformly covered under the Procurement Act. However, the Procurement Act recognises certain procurement methods that may be used for only specific items of procurement. For example, the Procurement Act provides that a '[r]equest for quotations' shall be used for procuring '*goods* that are readily available and . . . [for which] there is [an] established market' and a '[r]equest for proposals' is for 'the procurement . . . of *services or a combination of goods and services* and the services to be procured are advisory or otherwise of a predominantly intellectual nature'.[69]

It is noteworthy that the Act does not leave open for argument the issue of whether selling and letting of public assets fall within the definition of 'procurement' for the purpose of applying the procurement rules, as Part X of the Act specifically deals with selling and letting of public assets, referred to in the Act as 'disposal of stores and equipments'. In fact, section 4(1)(d) provides that 'this Act applies . . . to disposal by a public entity of stores and equipment that are unserviceable, obsolete or surplus'; and section 4(3)(a) emphatically states: 'For greater certainty . . . this Act applies [to] the renting of premises.'

Unlike the 2001 Regulations, the Procurement Act covers a substantial part of defence procurement. Section 133(1) emphasises that, '[f]or the avoidance of doubt, defence and national security organs shall comply with this Act'. Indeed, the objectives of public procurement law are best served by the widest possible application of the law, defence procurement included, as is now provided by the 2011 UNCITRAL Model Law on Public Procurement.[70] The defence and national security organs to which this section applies are the following:

69 See ss. 88 and 76(1) respectively (emphasis added).

70 Art. 1, changing the rule provided in Art. 1(2)(a) of the 1994 Model Law, which *prima facie* excluded 'procurement involving national defence and security'.

(1) the armed forces;
(2) the Kenyan police force;
(3) the National Security Intelligence Service;
(4) the Kenya Prisons Service;
(5) the Administration Police;
(6) the Kenya Wildlife Service; and
(7) such other institution as may be prescribed.

The only exception reserved for defence procurement in the Act is that the defence/security organs are permitted, in conjunction with the PPOA, annually to make two lists of forthcoming procurements: first, a list of those procurements to be done through restricted/alternative procurement methods; and, secondly, a list of those procurements to be done through the open tendering method.[71] This provision, permitting the defence/security organs to decide which procurement methods to use for various procurement items, supersedes the general provisions of the Act relating to the choice of which procurement method to use. This is because section 133(1) of the Act, which mandates the defence/security organs to comply with the Act, is stated to be subject to section 133(2) and (3) that empower the defence/security organs to decide which method to use. By implication, the defence/security organs are not bound to satisfy the preceding conditions for using the various restricted procurement methods. The PPOA is meant to act as a check on this wide discretion of the defence/security organs, since the Act enjoins those organs to agree with the PPOA in deciding, each year, which items are to be procured using the various restricted procurement methods. However, procurement reviews undertaken by the PPOA have revealed that the defence/security entity under review had not, in the years under review, consulted with the PPOA in deciding which procurement methods to use and had not developed the aforementioned two lists for its procurements.[72] This failure to draft the two lists and the absence of consultation with the PPOA make it impracticable for the PPOA to moderate and ensure transparency in the exercise of the wide discretionary power of the defence/security organs in choosing the procurement methods to use. In the circumstances, the defence/security organs may be inclined to use restricted methods of procurement, even when unwarranted. Nevertheless, the country's Auditor-General is empowered to carry out classified audits of the defence

71 S. 133(2)–(4). 72 PPOA, *Procurement Review Report*, pp. 24–5.

procurements undertaken by restricted procedures as provided by section 133(4) of the Act. However, in the absence of the PPOA's involvement, it is doubtful whether the classified audit will act as a check on the unfettered discretion to use restricted procurement procedures by defence/security organs. An unfettered use of restricted procurement procedures may stifle competition and transparency in defence/security procurement.

Regarding contracts funded by international development agencies, it should be noted that Kenya is a beneficiary of substantial aid from development agencies. Recognising that 'he who pays the piper calls the tune', the Procurement Act provides that the Act shall not prevail where there is any conflict between the Act and the terms of an international agreement on negotiated loan or grant to which Kenya is a party.[73] Consequently, in Kenya, if an international development agency, by virtue of the applicable loan/grant agreement, provides that its funded projects/contracts are to be subject to rules other than those provided by the Act, then such rules will apply. There is no evidence that the Kenyan judiciary or the Review Board has interpreted this enabling provision of the Act, for instance, to determine the extent to which it applies in practice. However, it could be argued that the Act and its Regulations may apply, where appropriate, to supplement the rules of the international financing institution. Where a bidder has a complaint, the World Bank, which is a major development partner of Kenya, enjoins aggrieved bidders in the Bank-financed procurement to lay their complaints first to the borrowing country.[74] To make such a complaint in Kenya, the aggrieved bidder, it appears, would necessarily follow the procurement review/complaint mechanism provided under the Act. In addition, aggrieved bidders may copy or complain directly to the Bank, especially where the borrowing country does not respond promptly.[75] The borrowing country also submits its decision on such complaints to the Bank for reviews and comments.[76]

However, if Kenya makes any contribution towards loan-financed-projects carried out within Kenya, the part of the projects/contracts funded by Kenya's contribution are subject to the provisions of the Act.[77]

73 S. 6(1).

74 World Bank's Guidelines on Procurement of Goods, Works and Non-Consulting Services under the IBRD Loans and IDA Credits and Grants 2011, Appendix 1, para. 2(e), and Appendix 3, paras. 11–14.

75 *Ibid.*, Appendix 3, para. 11.

76 *Ibid.*, Appendix 1, para. 2(e), and Appendix 3, para. 11. For more discussion on such dual systems of remedies, see Chapter 13, section 3, of this volume.

77 S. 6(3).

This to an extent appears acceptable to the World Bank, whose position is that '[f]or the procurement of those contracts for goods, works, and non-consulting services not financed in whole or in part from a Bank loan, but included in the project scope of the loan agreement, the Borrower may adopt other rules and procedures'.[78] In addition, it is the Act that applies for disposal of assets accruing to Kenya by virtue of aid-funded projects/contracts.[79]

Generally, there is no evidence suggesting that procurement under the Act and under international loan agreements is undertaken by separate Kenyan state officials.

The impact of aid-funded procurement on national procurement systems is discussed further in Chapter 11 of this volume.

4. Public procurement procedures

The rules on procurement methods and their conditions of use as provided by the Procurement Act are substantially modelled on the provisions of the 1994 UNCITRAL Model Law. Following the example of the Model Law, the procurement methods provided in the Act are generally used for goods, works and services. However, two methods, namely, competitive negotiation and two-stage tendering, which are provided in the Model Law, do not appear in the Act. Apparently, this omission is in response to a recommendation made in the Guide to Enactment of the UNCITRAL Model Law, that the enacting state need not necessarily provide for the two omitted methods, provided that it also provides for the request for proposals method, since the three methods share common circumstances, and uncertainties are likely to be encountered by procuring entities in trying to determine the most appropriate method from among two or three similar methods.[80] Furthermore, although the Model Law and Kenya's Procurement Act prescribe similar circumstances where single-sourcing may be used, nevertheless, the Model Law provides for other circumstances where single-sourcing may be used, which are not found in the Act.[81] For instance, the Model Law permits the use of sole-sourcing 'for the purpose of research, experiment, study or development, except where

78 World Bank's Guidelines on Procurement of Goods, Works and Non-Consulting Services 2011, para. 1.5.

79 S. 6(4).

80 Section 1, para. 19, of the Guide. Kenya's Public Procurement Act, s. 76, provides for request for proposal.

81 See UNCITRAL Model Law 1994, Art. 22; and Kenya's Public Procurement Act, s. 74.

Table 5.1 *Kenya, levels of usage of procurement methods*

Procurement method	Level of usage
Open tendering	37.8%
Restricted tendering	35.7%
Direct tendering	2.4%
Request for proposal	0.5%
Request for quotations	23.6%

the contract includes the production of goods in quantities to establish their commercial viability or to recover research and development costs', but the Act does not include these circumstances.

Similar to many modern national regulatory frameworks on procurement and to the UNCITRAL Model Law, Kenya's Procurement Act provides for 'open tendering' as the default procurement method.[82] The main alternative procurement methods include restricted tendering, direct procurement, request for proposals and request for quotations. These alternatives only apply under prescribed circumstances.[83] However compliance and performance indicators surveys carried out by the PPOA in 2007 and 2009 reveal a low level of usage (at 37.8 per cent) of open tendering in Kenya compared to the OECD's recommended level of about 60 per cent (see Table 5.1 for more detail).[84] Apart from the aforementioned alternative procurement procedures, the PPOA may permit special procurement procedures, such as concessioning and design competition.[85] However, community participation is not mentioned by the Act as a method of procurement in Kenya.

Table 5.1 illustrates the percentage (in contract/monetary value) of procurement methods used for procurement of works, goods and services during the fiscal year 2007, from a procurement budget of approximately Ksh40 billion, of seven procuring entities assessed.[86]

A limitation to the enforcement of the Act's stipulation on appropriate use of procurement methods is that procuring entities' choice of procurement method is exempted from challenge. This follows the rule in the 1994 version of the UNCITRAL Model Law, which commentators had

82 S. 29(1). 83 S. 29(2).

84 See PPOA, note 24 above, p. 24; and PPOA, note 14 above, pp. 11 and 12.

85 Procurement Act, s. 92. 86 PPOA, note 14 above, pp. 11 and 12.

criticised and advised that national procurement laws should not follow and which has now been changed under the 2011 Model Law so that the decision on which procurement method to use is not excluded from being challenged.[87] Nonetheless, an aggrieved person may petition the PPOA to investigate and review a choice of procurement method by a procuring entity, where there is evidence that the procurement method used is inappropriate for the circumstances.[88]

A feature common to open tendering and request for proposals under the Act is advertising of the procurement. These advertisements are mainly placed by procuring entities in daily newspapers of nationwide circulation. In addition, where the Act requires the engagement of competitors outside Kenya, the procurement shall also be advertised in one or more English-language newspapers or other publications with sufficient international circulation.[89] Furthermore, the advertisement is posted on the procuring entity's website (if it has one), and also posted at any conspicuous place reserved for this purpose on the premises of the procuring entity. The advertisement must identify the procuring entity, describe the contract, and inform on when and how to participate in the procurement process.[90] There is no central national portal for advertising procurement, since the PPOA (which might have provided such a portal) does not have such a mandate; however, its website publishes notices of contracts awarded by procuring entities.

A wide discretion is granted to procuring entities by Kenya's Procurement Act to use closed lists of qualified suppliers. These supplier lists are to be maintained by the procurement unit of each of the procuring entities;[91] although, as at October 2007, it was still primarily the Kenya Ministry of Public Works that registered contractors for various categories of government procurements.[92] Also, the PPOA keeps a register of suppliers. However, neither the Procurement Act nor the Regulations expressly mandate suppliers to be registered in these lists before they can participate in procurements. However, the Regulations, by implication, make it compulsory for suppliers interested in being selected for a request for quotation and restricted tendering to register in the lists, since, as discussed in detail below, only suppliers on the lists may be selected for

87 J. Myers, 'Commentary on the UNCITRAL Model Law on Procurement' (1994) 22 *International Business Lawyer* 253, 255.

88 Procurement Act, s. 102.

89 *Ibid.*, ss. 54(2), 71(b) and 78(3).

90 *Ibid.*, ss. 51 and 78(2).

91 Procurement Regulations, reg. 8(3)(a).

92 PPOA, note 14 above, p. 10.

a request for quotation[93] and a type of restricted tendering.[94] Also, in practice, registration is mandatory for contractors wishing to work for the Ministry of Public Works and other public entities.[95] The Kenyan procurement regulatory framework does not provide the conditions for registering on the lists. Stipulating these conditions is therefore left to the discretion of procuring entities. However, entities are to be guided by the provisions of the Act[96] on general qualifications for an award of contract which include the legal capacity to enter into contracts, and that the supplier is not debarred from participating in procurement proceedings pursuant to the Act. To regulate the use of these lists and for the sake of competition, the Regulations enjoin procuring entities to update the lists annually.[97] How they are to be updated is not clearly stated by the regulatory framework. However, the usual practice is that, in each financial year, suppliers wishing to tender, following a pre-qualification or tender advertisement, are permitted to register or renew their registration. Another control over the use of the lists is that the Tender Committee of the procuring entities, which is separate from and autonomous to the procuring unit, must approve the lists before they may be used for requesting quotations and for restricted tendering.[98] The Tender Committee may, with stated reasons, reject the list submitted.[99] Apart from those discussed above, no other known rules are provided to control the use of the lists.

Section 32 of the Act provides that '[t]o identify qualified persons a procuring entity may use a pre-qualification procedure or may use the results of a pre-qualification procedure used by another public entity'. Hence, a pre-qualification list could be used for any form and method of procurement, arguably even for open tendering, as an entity could advertise the procurement, noting that only those earlier pre-qualified may tender. But this argument that the pre-qualification list may apply to open tendering is not based on evidence. The Act leaves it to the entities to decide when and how to use pre-qualification and whether to use pre-qualification lists of previous financial years or to renew the lists in each financial year.

In the 2006 Regulations, it is provided that, in selecting suppliers to be asked for quotations among those pre-qualified, the procuring entity shall

93 Procurement Regulations, reg. 59(2)(a). 94 *Ibid.*, reg. 54(3).

95 PPOA, note 14 above, p. 10. 96 Procurement Act, s. 31.

97 Procurement Regulations, reg. 8(3)(a).

98 *Ibid.*, reg. 10(i) and (k). 99 *Ibid.*, reg. 11.

ensure a 'fair and equal rotation'.[100] The pre-qualified suppliers here refer to suppliers drawn from standing lists of registered tenderers maintained by the procuring entity, also relying on its own knowledge of the market.[101] However, the concept of 'fair and equal rotation' is not given adequate interpretation to provide a clear and measurable direction to the entities on this. The only direction on this provided in the Regulations is that, where the procurement unit is of the view that the successful quotation is higher than the prevailing market price, the procurement unit shall reject the quotations and repeat the process, by giving a fresh request for quotations to a set of new suppliers in the list approved by the Tender Committee.[102] The requirement to ensure a 'fair and equitable rotation' in selecting from the list only applies to request for quotation. Nonetheless, a clear rule exists on how suppliers are to be selected from the lists where the restricted tendering method is used in a particular circumstance. The rule is that, where the time and cost required to examine and evaluate a large number of tenders would be disproportionate to the value of the goods, works or services to be procured, the procuring entity shall invite tenders from at least ten suppliers selected from the list.[103] Apart from the aforementioned, there are no rules on selecting suppliers from the lists for the other procurement methods.

It appears that, in all the above procedures for determining qualification of suppliers, reliance is placed on documents submitted by suppliers as evidence of the claims relating to qualification and capacity, but procuring entities may inspect a contractor's equipment and facilities before awarding a contract.[104]

In line with the Kenyan public procurement objective of value for money, government contracts are generally awarded to a supplier whose tender has the 'lowest evaluated price'.[105] A tender with the 'lowest evaluated price' is one that represents goods or services or works that meet the desired specifications and quality, which will be supplied or undertaken for the lowest price compared with the other bids. Apart from the criteria of the price and the quality of goods/services to be supplied, other criteria, including any prescribed margin of preference to suppliers offering goods manufactured, extracted or grown in Kenya, may be used in evaluating the tenders.[106] Any criterion to be used for evaluation must be

100 *Ibid.*, reg. 59(2)(c). 101 *Ibid.*, regs. 8(3)(a) and 59(2)(a).
102 *Ibid.*, reg. 61(2). 103 *Ibid.*, reg. 54(3); Procurement Act, s. 73(2)(b).
104 Procurement Act, s. 31(1)(a). 105 *Ibid.*, s. 66(4).
106 Preferences to local goods are further discussed in Chapter 15 of this volume.

clearly set out in the advertised tender solicitation documents and be, to the greatest extent possible, objective and quantifiable.[107] A tender must be 'responsive' before it can be considered under the lowest evaluated price criterion. 'Responsive' means that the tender conforms to all the mandatory requirements in the tender solicitation documents.[108]

Though it is not expressly provided in the Act that the criteria discussed above will apply to the alternative methods of procurement, it is reasonable to presume that these criteria will also apply to those alternative methods. This of course exempts direct procurement. Furthermore, for request for proposals, especially for intellectual services, considerations of technical qualification/capacity are as weighty as or weightier than price consideration.[109] However, there is a lack of clear procedures governing the use of technical qualification/capacity in the Act and Regulations; this engenders some confusion as to when and how to apply technical capacity as a key criterion.[110]

An express reference made in the Kenyan Procurement Act to the use of an electronic medium in public procurement is the placing of an advertisement calling for tenders on the website of the procuring entity (if the entity has a website).[111] No specific means of communication is stipulated for the giving of notices under the Act and Regulations, which makes it reasonable to assume that electronic communication (for instance, via website, email or SMS) could be used if practicable and acceptable. In fact, the PPOA publishes on its website notices of contracts awarded by Kenya's procuring entities and decisions of the Review Board. Also, forms (such as forms for procurement challenge) and documents relating to Kenyan public procurement are downloadable from the PPOA website. Furthermore, the mention of 'bids as may be submitted through the electronic system' in section 135(1) makes it apparent that electronic submission of bids is allowed under the Act. However, at the time of writing, there appears to be no adequate capacity or regulatory provisions for the Kenyan public procurement system to support complex electronic procurement such as electronic auctions.

There is also no evidence that community participation as a method of procurement is practised in Kenya.

To maintain the highest possible level of integrity in public procurement, the Kenyan Procurement Act provides for the debarment of any

107 Procurement Act, s. 66(2) and (3). 108 *Ibid.*, s. 64(1).
109 *Ibid.*, ss. 80 and 82(5). 110 PPOA, note 14 above, p. 10.
111 Procurement Act, s. 135(1), also makes reference to 'bids as may be submitted through the electronic system'.

person from participating in procurement proceedings on grounds that the person has committed an offence under the Procurement Act or an offence relating to procurement under any other Act, breached a public procurement contract, misrepresented his qualifications in a procurement proceeding and, having submitted a successful bid, refused to sign the contract.[112] Debarments last for not less than five years. The Director-General of the PPOA, with the approval of the Advisory Board, imposes debarments. A person is given a fair hearing before he is debarred and a debarment can be appealed before the Review Board.[113] In addition to debarment, a person is held guilty of an offence under the Act if the person obstructs or hinders or knowingly misleads a person carrying out a duty or function or exercising a power under the Act, unduly influences an official of a procuring entity to favour a particular bidder, or opens or divulges the contents of any sealed bid or document before the appointed time for the public opening.[114] Also, it is an offence to contravene the orders of the Review Board or of the Director-General made according to the Act.[115] Punishment for an offence under the Act is a fine or term of imprisonment not exceeding ten years.[116] Indeed, debarment and penal sanctions provided by the Act, if enforced, have the capacity to deter contravention of the Kenyan procurement rules. Corruption in public procurement is further considered in Chapter 14 of this volume.

5. Concluding remarks

This chapter has highlighted the key areas of Kenya's public procurement regulatory and institutional frameworks. Having reviewed the Kenyan procurement system from Kenyan independence to the present, it can be concluded that substantial progress has been made towards aligning the system with international standard practices. Indeed, Kenya's regulatory development from mere issuance of unenforceable government circulars to the current regime founded on an Act of Parliament, the Procurement Act of 2005, with enforceable provisions that are largely modelled after international regulatory standards, is remarkable. It has been noted that the coverage of the regulatory framework is quite extensive, covering even defence procurement, and the procurement procedures provided do not fall short of international best practices. Also, the procurement oversight and review institutions have become properly structured and strengthened by the enabling provisions of the Act and its Regulations. In turn,

112 *Ibid.*, ss. 35 and 115. 113 *Ibid.*, ss. 116–123.
114 *Ibid.*, s. 135. 115 *Ibid.*, s. 136. 116 *Ibid.*, s. 137.

these institutions have contributed to the development of procurement regulations in Kenya. Indeed, the Review Board/High Court's interpretations of the procurement rules in the course of adjudicating over procurement complaints have enhanced the understanding and application of the procurement rules.

Notwithstanding the progress made in the Kenyan procurement system, there is still, however, a need to address the identified areas that fall short of international standards. It may be advised that legislation should provide reasonable limits for the application of preferences favouring Kenyan citizens and products instead of leaving it to the unfettered discretion of the Minister. Furthermore, Kenya could start developing its procurement regulations and institutions to provide for and take advantage of electronic procurement. Indeed, the system must continue to develop for it to match the ever-evolving public procurement practices and challenges.

6

The regulatory framework for public procurement in Namibia

SAMUEL KWESI AMOO AND SCOTT DICKEN

1. Introduction

Namibia was the name officially adopted by the United Nations in 1968 to replace the territory's former colonial name of South West Africa. Namibia became an independent sovereign state in March 1990 after being placed under German and apartheid South African colonial administrations.[1] It is situated in the southwestern part of Africa, bordered by Angola to the north, South Africa to the south and Botswana to the east. It occupies a land area of 823,144 square kilometres, with about 1,300 kilometres of coastline and is occupied by about 2 million people.[2]

The country has one of the most unequal economic structures in the world,[3] as evidenced with a gini coefficient of 0.6,[4] and a 51 per cent[5] unemployment rate. Whites, who constitute about 7 per cent of the population, may control up to 70 per cent of the economy. Nearly half of

1 South West Africa, as Namibia was known before independence in 1990, was colonised by the German imperial government after the declaration of the territory as a German protectorate in 1884 and a Crown Colony in 1890. The territory remained a German colony until 1915 when South African troops invaded and occupied it. However, after the occupation of the territory by the South African troops in 1915, German law remained in force except for such laws as were found necessary to be repealed under martial law. At the end of the First World War, South West Africa was placed under the League of Nations mandate system as 'C' mandate. The King of Great Britain accepted and delegated the mandate to the government of the Union of South Africa to exercise it under the supervision of the League of Nations. Art. 2 of the mandate agreement gave the mandatory all powers of administration and legislation over the mandated territory as an integral part of the Union and authorised the mandatory to apply the laws of the Union to the territory.

2 CIA World Factbook: Namibia People 2011, www.cia.gov/library/publications/the-world-factbook/geos/wa.html (accessed 29 March 2012).

3 K. Schade, 'Poverty' in H. Melber (ed.), *Namibia: A Decade of Independence 1990–2000* (Windhoek: Namibian Economic Policy Research Unit (NEPRU), 2000), pp. 111–24.

4 World Bank, *Namibia: Country Brief* (2008).

5 World Bank, *World Development Indicators* (2008).

Namibia's blacks live at the subsistence level in rural poverty on an income of US$200 per capita per year or less. The economy is heavily dependent on the extraction and processing of minerals for export. Mining accounts for 8 per cent of GDP, but provides more than 50 per cent of foreign exchange earnings. Namibia is the fourth largest exporter of non-fuel minerals in Africa, the world's fifth largest producer of uranium and a producer of large quantities of lead, zinc, tin, silver and tungsten. The mining sector employs only about three per cent of the population while about half of the population depends on subsistence agriculture for its livelihood, and, despite a high per capita GDP, Namibia has one of the world's most unequal income distributions,[6] a fact that has necessitated the formulation of various government economic strategies, including the Poverty Reduction Strategy (PRP) in 1998 and the use of public procurement to redress such imbalances. Namibia's economic growth has foreign investment as a crucial source of infusion of capital and employment creation. The realisation of the role of foreign investment in stimulating economic growth and employment has led to the promulgation of the Foreign Investments Act 27 of 1990 which governs the foreign investment regime. The foreign investment laws guarantee equal treatment for foreign investors and Namibian firms. These include provisions for international arbitration of disputes between investors and the government, the right to remit profits and access to foreign exchange.

The Namibian legal system is historically linked to the South African legal system. The nucleus of the South African legal system is the element of Roman-Dutch law which constitutes the common law of South Africa. In so far as South West Africa was concerned, Roman-Dutch law was formally introduced as the common law of the territory by Proclamation 21 of 1919,[7] which provided, inter alia, that Roman-Dutch law was to be applied in the territory 'as existing and applied in the Province of the Cape of Good Hope', and the Proclamation remained the legal basis for the application of the common law of the Cape as a source of the law of South West Africa until the promulgation of the Namibian Constitution in 1990. Article 66(1) of the Constitution stipulates that the common law of Namibia in force on the date of independence shall remain valid to the extent to which such common law does not conflict with the Constitution. It must also be added that, since 1959, after the amalgamation of the judiciary of the territory into that of South Africa, which was effected

6 CIA World Factbook: Namibia Economy 2010.
7 *South West Africa Gazette*, No. 25 of 1919.

by the Supreme Court Act[8] resulting in the High Court of South West Africa being made a division of the Supreme Court of South Africa, the courts of the territory were bound by the decisions of the Supreme Court of South Africa. To this extent, the Roman-Dutch law that was developed by the South African courts as the common law of South Africa was binding on Namibian courts. Furthermore, as a consequence of English colonial administration over the Cape of Good Hope, English common law was introduced into the Cape, and, by virtue of the application of Proclamation 21 of 1919, English law that applied in the province of the Cape of Good Hope applied in South West Africa or Namibia. The attainment of the status of an independent sovereign state in 1990 ushered in a new constitutional dispensation embodying a Bill of Rights premised on the principles of constitutionalism and accountability.

2. Introduction to the public procurement system

2.1. The objectives of public procurement policy

One of the primary objectives of the liberation struggle against South African rule in Namibia was the overthrow of the apartheid system which had marginalised the indigenous non-white community of the country. Consequently, the new dispensation seeks to correct this malaise by introducing various economic and political empowerment programmes. For legitimacy, these empowerment, or affirmative action, programmes are grounded in positive constitutional and legislative sources. Article 23(1) of the Namibian Constitution prohibits the practice of racial discrimination and the practices and ideology of apartheid. Article 23(2) legitimises the promulgation of Parliamentary enactments providing, directly or indirectly, for the advancement of persons within Namibia who have been socially, economically or educationally disadvantaged by past discriminatory laws or practices or for the implementation of policies and programmes aimed at redressing social, economic and educational imbalances in the Namibian society arising out of past discriminatory laws or practices, or for achieving a balanced structuring of society. Public procurement is generally recognised as one such empowerment strategy and a means of sustaining entrepreneurship.[9] Accordingly, when evaluating

8 Act 59 of 1959.

9 S. 15(5) of the Tender Board of Namibia Act of 1996 provides that, in comparing tenders, the Tender Board shall give effect to the price preference policy of the government to redress social, economic and educational imbalances. The Act is supported by several regulations

tenders, the Namibian Tender Board is required to apply mandated price preferences aimed at benefiting disadvantaged Namibian groups during the award process.[10] Preference schemes in public procurement are further discussed in Chapter 15 of this volume, dealing with social policy in public procurement.

While not expressly recognised in the Tender Board of Namibia Act, other common procurement regulatory system objectives, including those of the UNCITRAL Model Law on the Procurement of Goods, Construction and Services ('UNCITRAL Model Law'), are recognisable in the provisions of both the Act and the regulations passed under the Act; including the Tender Board Regulations 1996 and the Tender Board of Namibia Code of Procedures 1997. In particular, the *de facto* standard of competitive open tendering, supported by a public invitation to bid,[11] should be seen as an attempt to achieve economy and integrity in the procurement process.[12]

In addition, the prevention of corruption; and the perception thereof, continue to be a clear objective of the regulatory system.[13] Corruption in public procurement is further discussed in Chapter 13 of this volume.

2.2. *Nature and organisation of public procurement*

The statutorily mandated authority that has jurisdiction over the procurement regime in Namibia is the Tender Board of Namibia established under section 2(1) of the Tender Board of Namibia Act.[14] It is responsible for regulating and overseeing the procurement function of the government of Namibia. It replaces the erstwhile South West Africa Tender Board established under section 26A of the Finance and Audit Ordinance 1 of 1926.[15] The Board resides under the Directorate of Administration of the Ministry of Finance. It functions as a division with a separate budget

passed under it, one of which is the Tender Board of Namibia: Preferences, Government Notice 160 of 1992, *Government Gazette*, No. 551.

10 Reg. 7 and Annexure A of the Tender Board Regulations 1996. See also section 2.4 below on legislative amendments currently being considered that will strengthen this social policy dimension of procurement, and section 4 below on price preferences.

11 Tender Board of Namibia Act, s. 11, subject to the provisions of s. 17.

12 Although exemption provisions under s. 17 of the Act leave room for potential abuse.

13 For example, Tender Board of Namibia Regulations 1996, reg. 13, provides for the withdrawal of tenders or cancellation of contracts for reasons of fraudulent behaviour and bribery. In addition, s. 6(1)(3) provides for imprisonment for any Tender Board member found guilty of failure to disclose personal interest in a tender or agreement.

14 Tender Board of Namibia Act.

15 Tender Board of Namibia Act, s. 2(2).

and provides administrative, secretarial and support services to all line ministries, regional and local authorities, the business community and the broader public. It is responsible for the procurement of goods and services for the government and for the arrangement of the letting or hiring of anything or the acquisition or granting of any right for or on behalf of the government, and for the disposal of government property.[16] The roles and responsibilities of the Board are articulated in various publications of the Board, and include the empowerment of previously disadvantaged groups, small and medium-sized enterprises (SMEs) and the promotion of local enterprises. The Board further strives to carry out its mandate in an effective manner so as to ensure that the government gets value for money while socio-economic goals are achieved in the execution of the government's procurement services.[17] In furtherance of this general objective, the Board is empowered on behalf of the government to conclude an agreement with any person within or outside Namibia for the furnishing of goods and services. The membership of the Tender Board of Namibia comprises the accounting officers of government ministries, offices and agencies as the main members, while each main member has an alternate member. The chairmanship rests with the Accounting Officer of the Ministry of Finance.

The Tender Board procures all goods and services centrally, and there is an overarching supervisory mandate vested in the Minister of Finance to ensure compliance with these rules, while the Minister in turn is accountable to Parliament with respect to the exercise of the mandate of the Board.

The Anti-Corruption Commission (ACC) is mandated to combat and prevent corruption through law enforcement.[18] Under the Anti-Corruption Act 2003,[19] the ACC has a statutory function to investigate matters that raise suspicion that conduct constituting, or prone to, corruption has occurred, or is about to occur. Section 37 of the Anti-Corruption Act provides specifically for corrupt behaviours in relation to public tenders. This, together with the Tender Board Regulations (in particular regulation 13 thereof), empowers the ACC to conduct investigations in cases of public procurement corruption. In addition to the ACC, the Auditor-General and the Ombudsman play a role in ensuring accountability of the public regulatory system.

16 *Ibid.*, s. 7(1). 17 Tender Board of Namibia, *Annual Report 2006/7*.

18 Anti-Corruption Commission, Mandate, www.accnamibia.org (accessed 29 March 2012).

19 Anti-Corruption Act 2003 (Act No. 8 of 2003).

The procurement system has also been influenced by ILO Convention No. 94 which is enshrined in the Constitution under Article 95(d). It is for this reason that preference is allowed within the tendering process to companies implementing affirmative action policies. The preference standards also ensure fundamental rights and protection so that child labour,[20] forced labour,[21] discrimination[22] and sexual harassment at work are all prohibited by law.[23] In line with the Constitution, the Labour Act 2007 also provides for freedom of association and the right to collective bargaining.

2.3. *The legal regime on public procurement*

The primary sources of procurement law in Namibia include:

- the Constitution of Namibia, in so far as it relates to the administrative actions by respective decision-making bodies;
- the Tender Board of Namibia Act 16 of 1996;
- the Tender Board Regulations 1996;
- the Tender Board of Namibia Code of Procedure 191 of 1997;
- the Regional Council Tender Board Regulations;[24]
- the Local Authority Tender Board Regulations;[25] and
- the common law.

The laws and regulations contained therein cumulatively prescribe a rule-based transparent system geared towards the implementation of the development agenda of the government.[26] These include provisions relating to disclosure of interests,[27] and invitation for tenders.[28]

Article 18 of the Constitution provides that:

> All administrative bodies and administrative officials shall act fairly and reasonably and comply with the requirements imposed upon such bodies and officials by common law and any relevant legislation.

Applied to procurement procedures, Article 18 implies, despite the lack of provision of a challenge mechanism in procurement regulation, that all

20 Art. 15(2)–(4) of the Constitution; s. 3 of the Labour Act 2007 (Act No. 11 of 2007).
21 Art. 9 of the Constitution; s. 4 of the Labour Act.
22 Art. 10(2) of the Constitution; s. 5 of the Labour Act.
23 S. 5 of the Labour Act.
24 *Government Gazette*, No. 2492 of 2001.
25 *Government Gazette*, No. 2486 of 2001.
26 Tender Board of Namibia, *Annual Report 2005/2006*.
27 S. 6 of the Tender Board of Namibia Act.
28 *Ibid.*, s. 7(1)(b); and reg. 16(1) of the Regulations.

administrative actions pertaining to procurement within Namibia should be conducted fairly, reasonably and lawfully. These principles are applicable to administrative decisions concerning tenders made by the government and its agencies but are also extended to procurement bodies at local government level and state-owned enterprises whose procurement procedures are ultimately subject to the Constitution. Thus, the public procurement process in its entirety, that is, the evaluation of tenders and the award of contracts, are subject to the constitutional principle of administrative justice and administrative rule of law. It follows that any aggrieved party, namely, an unsuccessful bidder, has the right to seek redress from the High Court on grounds of fairness, reasonableness and lawfulness by way of judicial review. In this regard, decisions by officials in the tendering process, and even the Tender Board itself, have been subjected to judicial review.[29] However, there are not as many cases on procurement as with other areas of law such that the courts have had no opportunity to develop their own principles to control procurement.

The rules and procedures for procurement by the state, its organs and other entities such as local government and parastatals are governed by legislation. The Tender Board Act 16 of 1996 governs the procurement process at central government level, while the Regional Council Act and the Local Authorities Act govern their respective bodies. The process of tendering in parastatals is governed by their own constitutions, rules and regulations. While the regulatory frameworks are not the same, these instruments govern the same scope (that is, the process of disclosure of interest and invitation to tenders and even the granting of tenders) but do not provide for the position following the award of tenders. Therefore, once a tender has been awarded in compliance with the statutory provisions, all remedies sought thereafter are governed by delict (tort) and/or contract law. Here, too, there are not many cases decided by the courts that have established principles on procurement.[30]

29 See *Herald J. Coetzee* v. *Tender Board and Others* (Case No. 01/05/A19/C); *Nampharm (Pty) Ltd* v. *Ministry of Finance and Ministry of Health and Social Services* (Case No. 844/09/A18/N); *AFS Group Namibia (Pty) Ltd* v. *Chairperson of the Tender Board of Namibia* (A55/2011) 2011 NAHC 184 (1 July 2011); *Disposable Medical Products (Pty) Ltd* v. *Tender Board of Namibia* 1997 NR 129 (HC); *Kerry McNamara Architects Inc.* v. *Minister of Works, Transport and Communication* 2000 NR 1 (HC); *RBH Construction* v. *Windhoek Municipal Council* 2002 NR 443 (HC); *Shetu Trading CC* v. *Chairperson of the Tender Board of Namibia* 2011 JDR 0761 (Nm); *Skeleton Coast Safaris* v. *Namibia Tender Board* 1993 NR 288 (HC); *United Africa Group (Pty) Ltd* v. *Chairperson of the Tender Board of Namibia* 2011 JDR 0738 (Nm).

30 See *Serenity Manufacturers* v. *Minister of Health and Social Services* 2007 (2) NR 756 (SC).

2.4. Public procurement regulation: the context

Unlike neighbouring South Africa, whose public procurement is regulated by the Preferential Procurement Policy Framework Act[31] to provide a framework for the implementation of preferential procurement policies, Namibia does not have any such framework. The primary statutory instrument regulating procurement is the Tender Board Act. As noted above, the 1996 Tender Board Act replaced the South West Africa Tender Board established under section 26A of the Finance and Audit Ordinance 1 of 1926. However, the current legislation is regarded as relatively primitive and woefully inadequate in the face of the increasingly sophisticated nature of public procurement needs, pressures and requirements, as well as the increasing move towards greater democratisation of economic processes in the context of an interconnected global economy.[32]

A Tender Board Bill is currently being considered that is aimed at bringing the Tender Board Act into line with the aim of the government to promote economic development and bring about economic growth through local enterprise development and economic empowerment. In this regard, it has been recognised that the current system of price preferences in the Tender Board Act is not favourable to the small and medium-sized enterprise (SME) sector, and therefore the Bill aims to give preference to tender bids by SMEs and previously disadvantaged groups, including youth and women.[33] Considerations in this regard will be made to the objectives of the government's Black Economic Empowerment (BEE) policy and the existing Namibian Financial Services Charter. Moreover, state-owned enterprises would have to align their procurement processes to the Tender Board to effect development in the local economy. Preferential procurement is considered further in Chapter 15 of this volume, dealing with social policy in public procurement.

Another significant change proposed in the Bill pertains to the awarding of tenders so that not only the lowest bids are accepted. The changes also include the restructuring of the Tender Board to ensure the expansion of the Board's duties from solely administrative to one that supports the development of an appropriate procurement framework.[34] There is also

31 Act No. 5 of 2000.

32 F. Links and C. Daniels, 'The Tender Board: Need for Root and Branch Reform', Institute for Public Policy Research, Anti-Corruption Research Programme, Paper 3 (September 2011), p. 1.

33 J. Duddy, 'Changes in Tender Act More SME Friendly', *The Namibian*, 21 July 2009.

34 B. Weidlich, 'Government Changes Tender Board Law', *The Namibian*, 17 February 2010.

a proposal that, as a quality control strategy, the Board will be vested with the jurisdiction to verify the tender process and the approval of the award but the line ministries will be responsible for entering into contracts with tenderers. Finally, the Bill intends to introduce a provision which empowers the withdrawal of tenders from a tenderer who has been found guilty of corrupt practices as defined in the Anti-Corruption Act. Exemptions to tenders shall also not be negotiated or granted without the approval of the Treasury.

While Namibia is party to various trade agreements, such as the Southern African Customs Union (SACU), the SADC Trade Protocol and Mercado Comun del Cono Sur (Southern Cone Common Market), none of these have any procurement-specific obligations that may especially impact Namibia's use of procurement for domestic policy purposes.[35]

3. Coverage of the public procurement rules

3.1. Procuring entities

3.1.1. Introduction

Procuring entities in Namibia may be classified into five categories, namely: central government, regional councils, local authorities, statutory bodies and state-owned enterprises. The classification of central government, regional councils and local authorities into distinct and separate categories in public procurement is consistent with the decentralisation principle as enshrined in Chapter 12 of the Namibian Constitution. Under Article 102 of the Constitution, the government is divided into regional and local government, which shall consist of regional and local authorities.[36] Consistent with decentralisation, the procurement rules and procedures are regulated independently. It follows that the rules and procedures governing procurement are provided for separately for each of these levels of government.

35 As noted in Chapters 2 and 5 of this volume, the recent free trade agreement between the SACU, the SADC, the Common Market for Eastern and Southern Africa (COMESA) and the East African Community (EAC) may bring the opening up of procurement markets to the fore in the near future, especially when viewed against the 2009 COMESA Procurement Regulations, which prescribes 'regional competitive bidding' to facilitate broader access to the procurement markets of member states.

36 This decentralisation is provided for in the Decentralisation Enabling Act No. 33 of 2000.

3.1.2. Central government

The Tender Board Act provides in section 3 for the composition of the Tender Board to include, *inter alia*, government ministries and agencies. In reading this provision, it becomes apparent that it provides only for procurement by central government. It follows that statutory bodies, local authorities and regional councils are not covered.[37] State-owned enterprises have their own procurement rules and policies, although the principles of the Tender Board Act apply to them too.[38]

3.1.3. Regional councils and local authorities

The procurement of goods and services for regional councils is specifically regulated by the Tender Board Regulation[39] established under section 44B of the Regional Council Act 22 of 1992, while that of local authorities is regulated by the Local Authorities Tender Board Regulation[40] established under section 94A of the Local Authorities Act 23 of 1992. In terms of these regulations the regional and local tender boards are established for each of these regional and local authority councils in Namibia to provide tender services to them. The respective regulations elaborate the services as those that include the obligation to invite tenders for the procurement of goods and services for the local authority council. Every regional council or municipality therefore has a tender board established specifically for itself.

The general purpose of the Tender Board Regulations is to ensure good governance in the field of procurement policies and procedures. Priority is accorded to fair dealing and equitable relationships among parties to municipal contracts by interposing a local tender board between the council of a local authority and those it may wish to contract with for the procurement of goods and services, the letting and hiring of anything, the acquisition or granting of certain rights or the disposal of property. They seek to eliminate patronage or worse in the awarding of contracts, to provide members of the public with opportunities to tender to fulfil provincial needs, and to ensure the fair, impartial and independent exercise of the power to award provincial contracts.[41] The power to procure goods and services for regional councils or local authorities is therefore vested by regulation in the regional or local tender board.

37 Trade Policy Review, WT/TPR/222/NAM, p. 228. 38 *Ibid.*

39 GN 43/2001 *Government Gazette*, No. 2492.

40 GN 30/2001 *Government Gazette*, No. 2486.

41 *RBH Construction* v. *Windhoek Municipal Council* 2002 NR 443 (HC).

3.1.4. State-owned enterprises

Statutory bodies and state-owned enterprises are also not provided for under the rules and regulations for central, regional or local government. Thus, they too each have their own policies and regulations concerning procurement. However, the guiding legislation for all the different procurement entities is the Tender Board Act. The Act does not bind parastatals but most, if not all, parastatals have adopted the preferential procurement system in accordance with the Tender Board Act.[42]

3.2. Type of procurement subject to regulation

3.2.1. The acquisition, selling and letting of goods or services

Section 14 of the Tender Board Act specifically provides for the procurement of goods and services, the letting and hiring of things, the acquisition or granting of rights, and the disposal of property for or on behalf of government. While the Act does not elaborate on the goods, services, things and rights, it has been accepted that the scope of procurement includes:

- goods, that is, raw materials, products, equipment and other physical objects in any state or form, including utilities;
- services, that is, tasks to be performed by the consultant under a service contract such as studies, designs, provision of technical assistance and training; and
- works, that is, design/construction, rehabilitation, maintenance and repair of buildings, factories, roads, plants, bridges and other works related to construction.[43]

It must be noted that the Act does not specifically provide for works. However, in practice there has been procurement of works, and it can be implied that works may be classified under services. Important also to note is the inclusion of rights and property as falling under specific types of procurement contracts.

Similar wording provides for the type of procurement at local government level so that it involves the selling of goods and services, the letting

42 For instance, Namibia Wildlife Resorts, a tourism parastatal, has adopted the preferential procurement system in accordance with the National Tourism Policy that recognises this system of procurement.

43 S. Sankwasa, 'Tender Procedures Presentation', paper presented at an international forum on Corporate Governance and Transparency, Windhoek, 2010, http://unpan1.un.org/intradoc/groups/public/documents/cpsi/unpan043414.pdf (accessed 29 March 2012).

or hiring of things, the acquisition or granting of rights or the disposal of property.[44] It follows that the nature of the contracts are similar to those of central government.

Since the procurement rules and procedures of state-owned enterprises are not regulated by statute, the types of procurement are provided for in their individual rules and procedures. However, it can be inferred from the nature of the contracts provided for by central and local government that the type of procurement is similar, that is, it covers services, goods and works.

3.2.2. Defence procurement

Section 21 of the Tender Board Act exempts the Namibian Defence Force and the Namibia Security Intelligence Agency from the provisions of the Act when they are procuring security related goods, services and property.

3.2.3. Contracts funded by international development agencies

The Tender Board Act does not draw a distinction between contracts funded by international agencies and other government procurement contracts. Consequently, it can be concluded that such contracts are subject to the rules and procedures of the Act, unless otherwise agreed. Such opting-out of the Namibian procurement rules seems to be fairly common. The 2011 OECD/DAC survey on implementing the Paris Declaration shows that only 14 per cent of aid reported for the government sector used Namibian procurement systems.[45] It is suggested that the same inference be made of the local government procurement contracts that are internationally funded. However, the position is different with state-owned enterprises. In a number of parastatals, where there is outside funding, the international funding organisation will require a certain degree of compliance with its own procurement system. The impact of aid-funded procurement on national procurement systems is further discussed in Chapter 11 of this volume.

44 Reg. 14 of the Regional Council Tender Board Regulations; reg. 14 of the Local Authorities Tender Board Regulations.

45 OECD/DAC, *Aid Effectiveness 2005–10: Progress in Implementing the Paris Declaration* (Paris: OECD, 2011), pp. 124–5.

3.2.4. Other potential exemptions from the Tender Board Act

In 2011, Namibia adopted the Targeted Intervention Programme for Employment and Economic Growth (TIPEEG)[46] due to concerns regarding high unemployment rates, particularly within the unskilled sector. TIPEEG is designed to stimulate economic growth and create employment opportunities, and focuses on the agriculture, transport, tourism and housing and sanitation sectors. In light of TIPEEG's objectives, procurement under the TIPEEG has been exempted from the public procurement procedures contained in the Tender Board Act. The TIPEEG Implementation Committee will recommend the most effective procurement procedures to be utilised under this initiative, and thus an estimated N$9.1 billion (excluding public works and state-owned enterprise investment) of public procurement funding will be exempted from the Tender Board Act.

4. Public procurement procedures

Namibia has a free market system, and therefore allows any prospective tenderers to participate. The primary aim of the Tender Board is to ensure that tenders are awarded to the best bid in an open or competitive bidding process.[47] To this extent, the provision of open tendering as the *de facto* standard follows the UNCITRAL Model Law.

Exemptions to open tender procedures are provided for in section 17 of the Act. In this respect, procurement is exempt from open tender procedures where:

- the estimated value does not exceed N$10,000;
- the respective party to an agreement is a statutory body, local authority or regional council in Namibia which has been approved by the Minister of Finance;
- the respective party to an agreement is a government, statutory body, local authority or regional council in a country other than Namibia approved by the Minister of Finance; or
- where the Board has 'good cause' to deem open tender impractical or inappropriate.

46 National Planning Commission, *Targeted Intervention Programme for Employment and Economic Growth* (2011).

47 S. 15(7) of the Tender Board Act.

The latter exemption in particular has resulted in widespread accusations of shortcomings in the legislative framework resulting from widespread exemptions to open tender procedures.[48] Beyond the procedures for open tender, the regulatory system provides little guidance on alternative methods of procurement and therefore remains open to potential abuse, and harm to the integrity of the public procurement system.

The particularly low threshold of N$10,000 for exemption also results in considerable disadvantage to the efficiency and economy of the procurement regulatory system. While offices, ministries and agencies may have capable personnel to conduct otherwise relatively low-value procurement, once the threshold is exceeded procurement must pass through the Tender Board. Given the low threshold value, a substantial amount of low-value tenders pass through the Tender Board; which again is harmful to both efficiency and economy.

In addition, there is no procurement threshold matrix that separately addresses goods, works and services procurement; the low threshold applies to all categories. With no systematic procurement planning, the potential to secure economies of scale in procurement currently remains under-exploited.[49]

Under section 11 of the Tender Board Act, invitations to tender are published in the *Government Gazette* and at least once in each of the newspapers contracted by the government. Unfortunately, in practice, the *Government Gazette* only publishes the tender notices after the tenders have expired, thereby defeating the purpose of such a publication.[50] It is important to note that there is no centrally located source of government tender advertisements, with the result that tenders are primarily published in local newspapers. Currently, the *New Era*, a government-owned newspaper, is contracted to publish a weekly list of central government tenders.[51] The Ministry of Finance's website also publishes these tenders once a week. Parastatals publish their tenders in local newspapers and some through their own website as well.

Once published, tenderers are required to collect and pay for tender documents themselves. Tenders are *not* made available for download on the Ministry of Finance's website. While this could promote

48 Links and Daniels, 'The Tender Board: Need for Root and Branch Reform', note 32 above.

49 European Network on Debt and Development, *Targeting Development? Procurement, Tied Aid and the Use of Country Systems in Namibia* (2010), http://eurodad.org/?p=4021 (accessed 29 March 2012).

50 M. Townsend, 'Tendering in Namibia', *Tenderscan*, November 2008.

51 *Ibid.*

the government's objectives of 'Namibianisation', it does have significant drawbacks:

- cost considerations in the requirement to purchase tender documents could prohibit some companies from seeking to participate, particularly SME's; and
- requiring tender documents to be collected in Windhoek essentially prohibits many regional and international companies from participation. Again, while this may go some way in assisting the horizontal policy objectives of the government, it may hinder overall achievement of economy.

Submission of tenders is to be done within twenty-one days from the date of the last publication of the invitation.[52] At present, there is no system for the electronic submission of tenders.[53]

The Board may request a tenderer to clarify its bid at any time in order to assist in the evaluation of the tender. A tender shall not be considered in cases where the tender does not comply with the characteristics, terms, conditions and other requirements of the invitation unless the Board, in its opinion, deems the deviation to be immaterial.[54] In this regard, there appears to be little or no guidance on what may be considered an immaterial deviation; thus, this remains an area for potential abuse.

During evaluation, the Board may disqualify a tenderer if that tenderer does not 'qualify' in regard to the conditions set out in the invitation, or if, in the opinion of the Board, the tenderer has engaged in corrupt practices with a view to influencing the Board.[55]

When conducting an evaluation, consideration is required to be given to the capacity, experience, integrity and financial status of the tenderer,[56] and to apply price preferences.

Having opened the tenders, the Board submits the tenders to the procuring office, ministry or agency, which is required to make its recommendation. Where the lowest offer is not recommended, the relevant permanent secretary is required to certify that the recommendation is in the best interest of the government and represents best value to the government.[57]

52 Reg. 6 of the Tender Board Regulations.
53 Townsend, 'Tendering in Namibia', note 50 above.
54 Tender Board of Namibia Act, s. 15(2). 55 *Ibid.*, s. 15(3). 56 *Ibid.*, s. 15(4).
57 Tender Board of Namibia, *Code of Procedure* (1997), Art. 19.

Once tenders are submitted in accordance with the prescribed procedures,[58] there are evaluation criteria or grids that must be developed to identify the best technical quality and more economical (price) tender.[59] Tailor-made evaluation grids are developed for each evaluation, which entails the weighing of the technical quality of a tender against the price at a ratio of 80 per cent for the technical tender and 20 per cent for the price tender. These evaluations are considered on a case-by-case basis and require approximately one week in order to give the assessors time to scrutinise the tender documents and for the Tender Board to sit.[60]

Awards for tenders are given to the tenderer who receives the highest composite score on its technical and price tenders against the qualifying criteria. For works and supplies contracts, the tender is awarded to the tenderer who offered the most advantageous tender as assessed on the basis of: the price, operating and maintenance costs, quality of the technical tender, guarantees offered by the tenderer, conditions and time limits for performing the contract, responsiveness to Namibian procurement policies, and responsiveness to local conditions. For service contracts, the tender is awarded to the tenderer who offers the most advantageous tender, taking into account: price, technical quality of the tender, the organisation and methodology proposed for the provision of the services, proven track record in the relevant field, educational/academic qualifications and availability of the proposed personnel.

The lowest and best bid is determined by factors such as the expertise proposed, the methodology and the technical means to execute the contract. The technical evaluation of supplies tenders focuses more on quantities and compliance with the technical specifications and tenderers' proposals for after-sales service. The three main technical criteria are: (1) experience, past performance and resources of the bidding company/firm; (2) qualifications and experience of the proposed personnel; and (3) understanding of the assignment and methodology.[61]

In furtherance of the objective of redressing past discriminatory policies, as outlined above, the Act, in its regulations, provides for price preferences according to certain socio-economic goals and strategies.[62] The

58 Tender Board of Namibia Act, s. 6. 59 *Ibid.*, s. 15(4).

60 Sankwasa, 'Tender Procedures Presentation', note 43 above, p. 27. See also Regional Councils Procurement Policy 2007.

61 Sankwasa, 'Tender Procedures Presentation', note 43 above, p. 32.

62 Tender Board of Namibia Act, s. 15(5).

Tender Board is required to apply mandated price preferences aimed at benefiting disadvantaged groups during the award process.[63] These price preferences support the furtherance of the Affirmative Action Act 29 of 1998 through preferences for 'implementing affirmative action policies and programmes to redress social, economic or educational imbalances in a democratic society'. The Tender Board may grant a price preference of 2–3 per cent on the merits of each particular case, based on factors such as structured training programmes, apprenticeship courses of approved standards for labour, technical staff and managerial cadre, substantial employment of women and disabled persons, and other programmes or activities benefiting disadvantaged groups, using a formula provided for in the Tender Board Regulation to calculate the extent of preference to be granted.[64] While there are a number of preference criteria, the main preference is for consultants and contractors domiciled in Namibia. Another important criterion is that a bidder may obtain extra preferential points if the bidder has Namibian domicile, the methodology proposed will employ a number of people in small local industries, people in the communal areas or in notified under-developed areas, or (as mentioned earlier) if the bidder implements the Namibian government affirmative action policy.[65] To obtain preferential recognition, tenderers are required to register on Namibian government service providers' databases. Preferential procurement is also discussed in Chapter 15 of this volume, dealing with social policy in public procurement.

On completion of the evaluation process, the Board must notify the tenderers concerned, in writing, of the acceptance or rejection of their tenders.[66] On the written request of a tenderer, the Board shall give the reasons for the rejection of his or her bid. Within thirty days of notification and acceptance by the tenderer, the Board is required to enter into a written agreement with the tenderer. This period may be extended at the discretion of the Board. If a written agreement is not required, the agreement will come into force from the date of acceptance by the tenderer. If the tenderer fails to enter into an agreement within the required period or if it fails to provide the required security for the performance of the agreement, the Board may withdraw its acceptance of the tender and accept any other tender from among the tenders submitted to it or invite fresh tenders.

63 Reg. 7 and Annexure A of the Tender Board Regulations 1996.

64 *Ibid.*, reg. 7(2). 65 TenderNews.com, 'Tendering in Namibia' (2009).

66 Tender Board of Namibia Act, s. 16.

5. Concluding remarks

There are a number of identified limitations to the efficiency of the current procurement system in Namibia. One of the major challenges is the limited capacity and professional skills of the tender board staff.[67] Half of the established posts are vacant, and there is a heavy workload as a result of the low threshold (N$10,000) for the issue of tenders.[68] Secondly, the Tender Board processes and records are not computerised, limiting the efficiency of the process.[69] There is a need for line ministries to have their procurement guidelines strengthened and capacity building for developing expertise on how to qualify and evaluate bids and make recommendations.[70] Concern has been raised over the performance of the awarded tenders. It is reported that the performance of awarded tenders is not being monitored on a sufficiently regular basis, and that there are a number of cases where tenders have not been awarded to the successful bidder and ministries have chosen to obtain goods and services from other suppliers.[71] These occurrences could be as a result of the existence of discretion in the process. These discrepancies are exacerbated by the lack of sufficient sanctions and penalties for non-compliance.[72]

Despite the principles of integrity, good governance and accountability upon which tendering has been regulated, public procurement in Namibia remains vulnerable to corruption. In addition, the failure in the current legislation to provide one framework for central government, local government and state-owned enterprises tends to compromise the entire process. The procurement system and the Tender Board of Namibia are currently being reviewed in order to increase the efficacy of the system. It is anticipated that the amendments will assist in bringing Namibia's procurement regulatory system into line with international standards.

67 International Monetary Fund, Fiscal Affairs Department, 'Namibia: Report on Observance of Standards and Codes – Fiscal Transparency Module', *IMF Country Report No. 08/184* (June 2008), p. 24.

68 *Ibid.* 69 *Ibid.* 70 *Ibid.* 71 *Ibid.* 72 *Ibid.*

7

The regulatory framework for public procurement in Nigeria

KINGSLEY TOCHI UDEH AND M. L. AHMADU

1. Introduction

Nigeria is a federal republic in West Africa. It occupies a total area of 923,768 square kilometres, of which 909,890 square kilometres is land mass and 13,878 square kilometres is under water. With a population of 158 million people, Nigeria is the largest country in Africa and accounts for 47 per cent of West Africa's population.[1] It is also the biggest oil exporter in Africa, with the largest natural gas reserves in the continent. Nonetheless, Nigeria is still a recipient of international aid, in the form of grants and loans, among others. With a total investment of US$13,157 billion in the country, the World Bank is one of Nigeria's most important international development partners.[2] There are currently twenty-eight active and seven proposed Bank projects in Nigeria. The World Bank has also influenced the emergence of Nigeria's current public procurement regime; it funded the production of Nigeria's 'Country Procurement Assessment Report' (CPAR) 2000. The CPAR laid the groundwork for the enactment of Nigeria's Public Procurement Act 2007, which is based on the 1994 UNCITRAL Model Law,[3] as recommended by the CPAR.[4]

1 According to the World Bank's estimate as at September 2011. These figures are available on the World Bank's website, http://web.worldbank.org/WBSITE/EXTERNAL/COUNTRIES/AFRICAEXT/NIGERIAEXTN/0,,menuPK:368906~pagePK:141132~piPK:141107~theSitePK:368896,00.html (accessed 13 March 2012). The 2006 national population census put Nigeria's population at 140 million persons.

2 See http://web.worldbank.org/WBSITE/EXTERNAL/COUNTRIES/AFRICAEXT/NIGERIAEXTN/0,,menuPK:368902~pagePK:141159~piPK:141110~theSitePK:368896,00.html (accessed 28 March 2012); see particularly, 'Country Portfolio' on the webpage. The World Bank began a partnership with Nigeria in 1958, and after Nigeria's independence (October 1960) resumed the partnership in November 1961.

3 UNCITRAL Model Law on Procurement of Goods, Construction and Services with Guide to Enactment (1994) ('1994 UNCITRAL Model Law').

4 World Bank, *Nigeria Country Procurement Assessment Report*, vol. 1 (2000), p. 6; Nigeria is listed on the UNCITRAL website as one of the countries whose public procurement

Nigeria's administrative capital is Abuja. Nigeria is a member of the Economic Community of West African States (ECOWAS), which is a regional group of fifteen countries founded in 1975, with the mission to promote economic integration among member states. The ECOWAS Treaty 1993[5] could be regarded as a trade agreement between the member states, especially as it indicates the eventual establishment of a common market and an economic union as part of the aims of ECOWAS.[6] There have been progressive efforts by ECOWAS towards promoting trade among member states, to achieve the aforementioned aims.[7] However, it does not appear that ECOWAS presently has any rule or project relating to member states' public procurement regimes.[8] Abuja hosts the headquarters of ECOWAS – an indication of the economic and political importance of Nigeria in West Africa, and indeed in the whole of Africa.

Nigeria has thirty-six politically and fiscally autonomous federating states. Both the federal and state governments run democratically elected governments. The elected President is the executive head of the federal government; while each state has an elected governor. The federal and state governments have separate legislatures, composed of elected members from various constituencies/districts delineated in the states. There is a bicameral legislature at the federal level, called the National Assembly, comprising the Senate and House of Representatives; while each of the states has a unicameral legislature, called the State House of Assembly. Most of the laws made by the National Assembly apply to the whole federation.[9] Both the federal and states legislatures have oversight powers, which entail investigating the affairs of relevant authorities, government ministries, departments and agencies (MDAs) that are within their legislative competencies.[10] This is intended to enable the legislatures to make laws with respect to any matter within their legislative competences and correct any defects in existing laws. This power is also meant to expose

legislative texts are based on or largely inspired by the UNCITRAL Model Law: www.uncitral.org/uncitral/en/uncitral_texts/procurement_infrastructure/1994Model_status.html (accessed 25 March 2012).

5 The Treaty establishing the ECOWAS was signed in Lagos, Nigeria, on 28 May 1975.

6 ECOWAS Treaty, Art. 3(2)(d) and (e).

7 To a large extent, there has been a free movement of citizens of member states within the ECOWAS territory.

8 Also, Nigeria is a member of the World Trade Organization (WTO), but not a party to the WTO's Agreement on Government Procurement.

9 The Constitution of the Federal Republic of Nigeria, 1999 (amended), s. 4(1)–(5) (the 'Constitution').

10 *Ibid.*, ss. 88 and 128.

corruption, inefficiency or waste in the execution or administration of laws within the legislative competences of the respective legislatures and in the disbursement or administration of funds appropriated by them. The states, Abuja and the federation have separate High Courts. Appeals from these High Courts go to the Court of Appeal, and then to the Supreme Court of Nigeria.[11] The Nigerian judiciary is an offshoot of the English common law, which is part of Nigeria's colonial heritage.

The Nigerian Constitution vests the federal and the state governments with power and control over public funds accruing to them.[12] Expenditures from public funds by the governments of the federation and states are provided for in their separate annual budgets, authorised by means of an Appropriation Act or Law. Consequently, there are separate public procurement regimes for the federal government and the states. However, the public procurement regime at the federal level overshadows the procurement regimes in the states, owing to the larger size of the federal revenue and the existence of federal agencies in all the states. Moreover, the procurement legal frameworks in practically all the states are largely an adaptation of the past or present federal procurement regimes. This is as a result of a deliberate national policy to harmonise public expenditure management in Nigeria and also because all the states depend for their sustenance on the Federation Account,[13] funded mainly by oil revenues controlled by the federal government.

This chapter will focus on the public procurement regime of Nigeria's federal government, but will also make reference to the procurement regimes in the states where appropriate.

2. Introduction to the public procurement system

2.1. The objectives of public procurement policy

The public procurement policy objectives of Nigeria can be gleaned from the Public Procurement Act 2007 (PPA). The Act does not expressly state what its objectives are, but section 16 (entitled 'Fundamental Principles for Procurements') contains what could reasonably be assumed to be the policy objectives. It states that 'all public procurement shall be conducted . . . in a manner which is transparent, timely, equitable for ensuring accountability and conformity with this Act and regulations

11 There are other courts in Nigeria apart from those mentioned herein.

12 Constitution, ss. 80–83 and 120–123.

13 *Ibid.*, s. 162.

deriving therefrom; with the aim of achieving value for money and fitness for purpose; in a manner which promotes competition, economy and efficiency'.[14] These largely correspond with the procurement objectives suggested by the 1994 UNCITRAL Model Law, which are adopted by most national procurement systems.

At present, transparency has become a weighty matter in Nigeria's public procurement policy. This is owing to the government's drive to achieve value for money and stem corrupt practices in public procurement – perceived to be high and debilitating to the Nigerian economy.[15] President Goodluck Jonathan succinctly captured the situation thus:

> We must look at our procurement process if we must move fast, because whenever I travel out of this country to another and I happen to see some infrastructural development, I always ask about the cost of execution. And sometimes the cost I am told is three times less of what we are charged in this country . . . [M]oney that will give us three times the price of something, but ended up giving us only one. For instance, money that will give us three vehicles, we end up getting one; money that will give us three dams, we are getting one. Money that will give us 30 kilometres of road we are getting 10. Then our visioning will not materialize.[16]

In furtherance of the policy of stemming corruption and enhancing value for money in public procurement through transparency, civil society organisations (CSOs) have been vested with the right to participate in procurement proceedings as observers to monitor compliance with procurement rules.[17] The role of CSOs as procurement observers in Nigeria entails having access to and analysing solicitation and bidding documents; being present to observe procurement proceedings; and gaining access to procurement records and information.[18] The CSOs do not have the right to interfere directly with the procurement proceedings, but they can send a report of their observations to the relevant regulatory or anti-corruption agencies for further action.[19] To the credit of the CSO observers, some

14 *Ibid.*, s. 16(1)(d)–(f).

15 Transparency International, *Country Study Report on Nigeria* (2004), pp. 20 and 53–6.

16 President G. Jonathan, speaking at the first Presidential Retreat on the Implementation Plan for Vision 20:2020 and Public Private Partnership Framework for Infrastructure Development in Nigeria at the Banquet Hall, Presidential Villa, Abuja, 14 June 2010, as reported by *ThisDay Newspaper*, 15 June 2010, p. 1 (captioned 'Corruption – Jonathan Warns Contractors, Public Servants').

17 PPA, s. 19(b).

18 This right, created by the PPA, has been further strengthened by the Freedom of Information Act 2011.

19 PPA, s. 19(b)(ii).

cases of breach of public procurement rules have been identified and reported to appropriate quarters and corrective actions initiated. Nevertheless, it has been identified that procuring entities in practice invite or permit CSO observers only during the opening of bids and exclude them from other stages of the procurement processes. This is despite the fact that the Act expressly states that CSO observers shall be invited in 'every procurement process', not just bid opening. In fact, the marginal note and title of section 19 of the Act, where the role of observers is provided for, is entitled 'Procurement Implementation', whereas it is section 30 that deals with 'Bid Opening'. Indeed, these observers have the right to monitor and access information on all aspects of public procurement. The only lawful restriction to this right is the restriction on the time for accessing information provided by section 32(8) of the Act, which states that after the opening of bids, information relating to the examination, clarification and evaluation of bids and recommendations concerning award shall not be disclosed to bidders or to persons not officially concerned with the evaluation process until the successful bidder is notified of the award. Another formal involvement of CSOs in Nigeria's public procurement is their inclusion in the membership of the National Council on Public Procurement (discussed below). Other measures introduced by the PPA to enhance integrity and transparency in public procurement include: granting interested members of the public access to unclassified procurement records;[20] providing for supplier remedies; conferring procurement oversight power to the Bureau of Public Procurement (BPP); and providing for offences and punishment for contravention of procurement rules. These are further discussed below. It should be noted that, before the adoption of the Act, regulations on public procurement in Nigeria did not provide for any of the integrity and transparency measures above.

To protect Nigerian local industries, margins of preferences during evaluation of tender are provided in favour of local bidders and locally manufactured goods competing with foreign bidders or goods.[21] However, it is interesting that the domestic preferences are hardly ever applied in practice. In fact, the limits and formulae for the computation of margins of preference and determination of eligibility are yet to be prescribed by the BPP. It could therefore be concluded that the government is not yet keen on pursuing the policy of promoting local industries through the application of domestic preferences. Preferential procurement is further

20 *Ibid.*, s. 38(2)(a). 21 *Ibid.*, s. 34(1).

discussed in Chapter 15 of this volume, dealing with social policy in public procurement.

2.2. The nature and organisation of public procurement

Nigeria's government procurement market, in the context of Africa, is comparatively large. There are separate public procurement markets for the federal government and the thirty-six states, since the states purchase for themselves. Both local and foreign contractors participate actively in the states and federal procurement markets. In particular, foreign companies have a significant presence in Nigeria's huge oil and gas subsector. The procurement systems at the federal and state levels are largely decentralised; that is, the respective governments' MDAs, including government corporations, are vested with power to procure goods, works and services for their own use. However, in the states, procurements of works contracts are mostly awarded or supervised by the Ministry of Works. In the last five years, the largest federal capital expenditures have been by MDAs responsible for transport, energy, agriculture and water resources, education, and health. It is noteworthy that the legislature and the judiciary in both the federal and state levels receive direct budgetary allocations for their expenditure (largely for administration purposes) and they conduct their own procurement through their respective administrative structures. For example, at the federal level, the National Assembly conducts its procurement through the National Assembly Management, composed of civil servants headed by the Clerk of the National Assembly.

Apart from the procurement funded by Nigeria government revenues, aid-funded projects at the federal and state levels also form part of the Nigerian procurement market. International development agencies that have developmental projects in Nigeria include the United Nations Development Programme, the United Nations Children's Fund (UNICEF) and the European Union, among others. As at September 2010, the World Bank had approved over 130 International Bank for Reconstruction and Development (IBRD) loans and International Development Association (IDA) credits to Nigeria for a total amount of more than US$10.5 billion.[22] The impact of aid-funded procurement on national procurement systems is further considered in Chapter 11 of this volume.

22 See the World Bank's website for further details, http://web.worldbank.org/WBSITE/EXTERNAL/COUNTRIES/AFRICAEXT/NIGERIAEXTN/0,,menuPK:368902~pagePK:141159~piPK:141110~theSitePK:368896,00.html (accessed 13 March 2012).

In Nigeria, public procurement is conducted by designated public officers in the various MDAs, under the supervision of the MDAs' respective accounting officers. The accounting officer of a procuring entity shall be the person charged with line supervision of the conduct of all procurement processes; in the case of ministries, it is the Permanent Secretary, and, in the case of extra-ministerial departments and corporations, it is the Director-General or officer of corporate responsibility.[23] At the federal level, these public officers are formed into the MDA's Tenders Board, Procurement Planning Committee, and Evaluation Sub-committee. This is intended to depersonalise the procurement process. The Tenders Board is the approving authority for the conduct of procurement within the respective MDAs; it is also responsible for the award of contracts.[24] A Procurement Planning Committee undertakes procurement planning in the MDAs, such as preparing needs assessment and evaluation, identifying the items required and carrying out market surveys. The Evaluation Sub-committee evaluates the bids. Notwithstanding this, political office-holders such as federal ministers and state commissioners, still become involved in the procurement process either formally or informally. In particular, at the federal level, their formal involvement entails presenting the budgets of their respective MDAs to the Federal Executive Council for adoption and subsequent presentation to the legislature. They also implement the procurement decisions of their MDAs.[25] Their informal involvement is in the form of influence on the procurement process, since they would, following civil service practice, be consulted (and probably deferred to) before major contract awards are made.

However, it is the accounting officer of each federal MDA that is responsible for ensuring compliance with the provisions of the Act by his entity. He is liable in person for a breach of the Act or its derivative regulations, whether or not the act or omission was carried out by him personally or by any of his subordinates.[26] One could argue that the liability of these accounting officers is predicated on the fact that they are the highest-ranked civil servants in their respective MDAs, and are signatories to their MDAs' accounts. Furthermore, being largely civil servants, with security of tenure and ideally being apolitical, it is assumed that they will contextually act as checks to the political heads of the MDAs and that the procurement process will to an extent be protected from being used for politicking. In *Economic and Financial Crimes Commission* v. *Dimeji*

23 PPA, s. 20(1). 24 *Ibid.*, s. 22(3). 25 *Ibid.*, s. 22(5).
26 *Ibid.*, ss. 16(22) and 20(1)–(2).

Bankole and Another (2012),[27] the High Court of the Federal Capital Territory, Abuja, absolved the accused persons, who were the former Speaker and Deputy Speaker of the Nigeria House of Representatives, of breach of trust in the procurement of a N40 billion loan for the 'running cost' of the House during their leadership. The reasoning of the court was that the Clerk of the National Assembly and other top civil servants/management staff of the National Assembly were the accounting officer of the House and signatories to the House Account respectively, not the accused persons (who were politicians), and therefore that the accused persons were neither responsible nor liable for approving the loan.

The body exercising regulatory oversight over the implementation of procurement policies by federal procuring entities is the Bureau of Public Procurement (BPP). The BPP was established by the PPA as a body corporate with perpetual succession.[28] Its functions include monitoring of public procurement, formulating procurement policies, setting standards, and developing the legal framework and professional capacity for public procurement in Nigeria, among others. The President of Nigeria appoints a Director-General, with certain qualifications, to head the BPP for a fixed four-year term, renewable for another four years.[29] The BPP enjoys a level of financial autonomy, since its funds are appropriated directly to it by the National Assembly. It is noteworthy that the BPP is not directly involved in carrying out procurement transactions; and is not represented in any entity's Tenders Board or Tender Evaluation Subcommittee. However, it can procure for its own administration.[30] This separation of functions is aimed at avoiding any conflict of interest in the discharge of its duties. However, the BPP's Director-General regularly attends the Federal Executive Council (FEC) meetings, and the BPP is officially presented as an agency under the Presidency. The FEC is a body of federal ministers, presided over by the President or the Vice-President.[31] The FEC is currently the approving authority for the award of contracts valued at N1 billion and above. It has been argued that the BPP Director-General's attendance of FEC meetings may subject him to political influence.[32] However, an argument to the contrary is that it gives a high standing to the Director-General to enable him to perform his functions.[33]

27 Unreported as at the time of writing. 28 PPA, s. 3.

29 *Ibid.*, s. 7. 30 *Ibid.*, s. 3(2)(c). 31 Constitution, ss. 144(5) and 148.

32 Public and Private Development Centre (PPDC), *Implementing the Nigerian Procurement Law: Compliance with the Public Procurement Act 2007* (PPDC, 2011), p. 85.

33 *Ibid.*

Another body, the National Council on Public Procurement (NCPP), is established by the Act and is responsible mainly for: approving policies and regulations on public procurement; recommending the appointment of the Director-General of the BPP, and approving the appointment of the directors of the BPP.[34] The Act[35] prescribes that the NCPP shall be composed of twelve members; out of which six are specified government officials (including the Minister of Finance as chairman, and the Director-General of the BPP as the secretary); and the other six shall be representatives of specified civil society/professional organisations.[36] This is another formal mechanism to involve civil society and the private sector in Nigeria's public procurement process to enhance integrity through social audit and control. However, the NCPP has not been inaugurated to commence its functions. This has been so since the coming into force of the PPA, notwithstanding mounting pressures from several quarters for its inauguration. Indeed, this is a grave oversight that threatens the Nigerian public procurement system with illegality. The aforementioned functions of the NCPP, which are critical to the sustenance of the procurement system of Nigeria, have either been left unattended to or performed illegally, since the NCPP has not been inaugurated. For instance, the BPP in fact has a Director-General and directors, but their appointments have not been recommended or approved by the NCPP as required by the Act. Further, if the relevant provisions of the PPA are interpreted strictly, one would regard the procurement policies and regulations made by the BPP after the commencement of the Act as inchoate, at best, since they have not been approved by the NCPP, in accordance with the law.

Playing a pivotal role in the public procurement system of Nigeria is the Economic and Financial Crimes Commission (EFCC), established by the Economic and Financial Crimes Commission (Establishment) Act 2004. It is charged with the investigation and prosecution of financial and economic crimes in both private and public sectors of the whole federation.[37] There is also the Anti-Corruption Commission,[38] whose

34 PPA, ss. 2 and 7(1). For a critical analysis of the current position, as outlined below, see A. J. Osuntogun, 'Procurement Law in Nigeria: Challenges in Attaining Its Objectives' (2012) 21 *Public Procurement Law Review* (forthcoming).

35 PPA, s. 1(2).

36 These include the Nigerian Bar Association; the Nigerian Institute of Purchasing and Supply Management; the Nigeria Association of Chambers of Commerce, Industry, Mines and Agriculture; the Nigeria Society of Engineers; civil society (understood as referring to non-governmental organisations in the narrow sense); and the media.

37 Economic and Financial Crimes Commission (Establishment) Act, s. 6.

38 Established by the Corrupt Practices and other Related Offences Act 2003.

powers are mainly focused on corruption in the civil/public service; however, its operations are not as active as those of the EFCC. The EFCC has prosecuted, or facilitated the prosecution of, some procurement-related cases, the two most famous being *Economic and Financial Crimes Commission* v. *Dimeji Bankole*,[39] and *Federal Republic of Nigeria* v. *Chief Olabode George and Others*.[40] Although the offences for which the accused persons in Olabode George's case were charged were not founded on the PPA, since the offending procurement actions occurred before the Act commenced, the prosecution succeeded in securing their conviction for abuse of office in the form of splitting of contracts (contrary to section 104 of the Criminal Code Act). This demonstrates that previously existing laws could have been relied upon to tackle corruption in government procurement prior to the PPA, if government had had the will. Indeed, the Criminal Code Act and the Penal Code Act, which apply to the various states of the federation directly or by re-enactment, sufficiently provide for offences and punishments for corrupt practices in the public service that have a direct bearing on public procurement.[41]

Apart from the roles played by the institutions mentioned above in public procurement regulation, the BPP has other specific functions that touch on enforcement of public procurement rules, which are presented below.

2.3. The legal regime on public procurement

The PPA is the main legal instrument that currently regulates public procurement conducted by the Nigerian federal government. As noted earlier, this legislative instrument does not apply to the states, since they have their own public procurement regimes, although the PPA is increasingly being adopted through enactment by the states. The Act contains sixty-one sections divided into thirteen parts, and is supplemented by the Regulations issued from time to time by the BPP. The provisions of the PPA cover the steps in the procurement process from procurement

39 Another aspect of this case directly relating to the contravention of the PPA (namely, the inflation of the prices of goods purchased for members of the House of Representatives) is still pending before the Federal High Court, Abuja.

40 Suit No. LD/71C/2008, High Court of Lagos State.

41 The Criminal Code Act applies to states in the southern part of Nigeria, while the Penal Code Act applies to states in the northern parts. Both Acts were enacted before Nigeria's political independence.

planning to contract award and disposal of properties, but do not cover budgeting processes and the performance of contracts.

The budgeting and financial management practices of the federation are regulated by the Nigerian Constitution and the Finance (Control and Management) Act, in addition to government circulars in that regard. The performance of the procurement contracts awarded is governed by common law principles. Some of the common law principles of contract have been codified or modified by some extant legislation in the federation and states.[42] Contractual rights and obligations involving the government, are protected or enforced in the regular courts of Nigeria, and there is a plethora of decided cases on this. As was held by the Nigerian Court of Appeal in *Bamidele* v. *Commissioner for Local Government and Community Development, Lagos State*,[43] every right founded on contract (whether or not the government is involved) is a private right conferring sufficient interest on a party to seek redress in the courts in order to protect the contractual relationship or enforce the contractual obligations. However, it can be noted that the PPA provides that all procurement contracts shall contain provisions for arbitral proceedings as the primary form of dispute resolution.[44] Noteworthy also is that the PPA provides for payment of mobilisation fees and prompt payment for contracts, which concern the performance of contracts.[45]

The PPA is quite detailed in providing for procurement rules. Procurement and disposal decisions of procuring entities must be carried out with strict adherence to the provisions of the Act and its derivative regulations.[46] Only very minimal discretion is allowed to procuring entities. Instances where a procuring entity's discretion is allowed include: deciding what documentary evidence or other information it may require bidders to provide as proof that they are qualified in accordance with the PPA and the solicitation documents; deciding whether to reject all bids at any time prior to the acceptance of a bid; and deciding whether to pay a mobilisation fee to the bidder awarded the contract.

The procurement rules established by the PPA are enforceable. The enforcement may occur by way of: supplier remedies arising from procurement reviews;[47] debarment by BPP of any contractor or supplier

42 An example is the Law Reform (Contracts) Act 1961, which deals mainly on frustration and enforcement of contract.

43 [1994] 2 NWLR (PT. 328) 568 (per Uwaifo JCA).

44 PPA, s. 16(26).

45 *Ibid.*, ss. 35(2) and 37.

46 *Ibid.*, s. 16(23).

47 *Ibid.*, s. 54.

that contravenes the procurement rules;[48] the BPP investigating, and, if satisfied, nullifying a procurement proceedings or cancelling a contract awarded or performed in breach of the Act;[49] and criminal prosecution of any person that contravenes any provision of the PPA by relevant authorities, such as the EFCC.[50]

A bidder may seek administrative review for any breach of procurement rules by a procuring entity. The complaint must be made first, in writing, to the accounting officer of the procuring entity within fifteen working days from the date the bidder first became or should have become aware of the breach. The accounting officer has fifteen days to make a decision indicating the corrective action to be taken, if any. Where he fails to make a decision or the decision made is not satisfactory to the bidder, the bidder may file a complaint to the BPP within ten working days of receiving the decision. The BPP must give its written decision within twenty-one working days of receiving the complaint. The remedies it may grant the complainant-bidder include:

(a) prohibiting the procuring entity from taking any further action;
(b) nullifying the unlawful procurement act or decision;
(c) revising an improper decision by the procuring entity or substitute its own decision for such a decision.

However, the BPP has no power to grant compensation.

There are indications that bidders have taken advantage of the review process, but the BPP does not publish the complaints and its related decisions.

It is noteworthy that the BPP does not constitute any panel to hear complaints. Rather, it considers the written complaint and then simply writes to the procuring entity concerned to obtain its written response before making a decision on the complaint.

The bidder may appeal the decision of the BPP or its lack of decision within the stipulated time to the Federal High Court, within thirty days of receipt of the decision, or the expiration of the stipulated time. The PPA neither states that the decision of the Federal High Court may be appealed, nor that it is final. It is therefore assumed that the decision of the Federal High Court may be appealed to the higher courts, by virtue of the inherent jurisdiction of those courts. If this is so, it may result in prolonged litigation that may derail or frustrate procurement processes that should ordinarily have been concluded within a financial year. It is

48 *Ibid.*, s. 6(1)(e). 49 *Ibid.*, s. 53. 50 *Ibid.*, s. 58.

advised that an amendment of the PPA making the Federal High Court's decision final on procurement reviews be considered.[51]

In *AC Egbe Nig Ltd* v. *Director-General of Bureau of Public Procurement and Others*,[52] the Federal High Court held that the court will not entertain any suit challenging a procurement decision of an entity unless a complaint has first been made to the accounting officer concerned and to the BPP. This decision has helped to settle the rule that the administrative remedies provided in the PPA must be exhausted before embarking on actual litigation in court.

It is to be noted that procurement-based litigation is only beginning to arise in the Nigerian courts. However, the decisions of the courts on the few instances that public procurement rules were considered have thrown more light on the PPA.

Remedies systems in procurement in Africa are considered in more detail in Chapter 13 of this volume.

2.4. *Public procurement regulation: the context*

Prior to the PPA, public procurement at the federal and state levels was regulated simply by Financial Regulations and official circulars issued respectively by the federal Minister of Finance and the various states' Commissioners of Finance. The provisions of these federal and state regulations and the circulars were generally unenforceable by private persons; but, where a public servant violates their provisions, he can be prosecuted and convicted for abuse of office or other offences contained in the Penal Code or Criminal Code, as was the case in *Federal Republic of Nigeria* v. *Chief Olabode George*.[53] The use of financial regulations and circulars to regulate public procurement is a practice rooted in Nigeria's colonial heritage, consolidated by the still extant Finance (Control and Management) Act 1958, which was enacted two years before Nigeria's independence. However, in 2000, the federal government partnered with the World Bank to conduct a nationwide assessment of public procurement regulations and practices. This was a first step to introducing acceptable international standard practices and regulations for public procurement in Nigeria. The result of that assessment was Nigeria's 'Country Procurement Assessment

51 This is the case in Kenya. See the Kenya Public Procurement and Disposal Act 2005, s. 100(2). The Kenyan public procurement regime is discussed in more detail in Chapter 5 of this volume.

52 Suit No. FHC/B/CS/116/2010, Federal High Court.

53 Note 40 above.

Report' (CPAR),[54] which formed the basis of the Public Procurement Bill later sent to the National Assembly, which was revised and enacted as the Public Procurement Act. Also in response to the CPAR, the federal government established the Budget Monitoring and Price Intelligence Unit (BMPIU) in June 2003 as the procurement regulatory body. The structure and staff of the now-defunct BMPIU were later inherited by the BPP following the enactment of the PPA.

There are reports on the assessment of the levels of compliance of the federal MDAs and the National Assembly with the provisions of the PPA, conducted by a Nigerian CSO[55] with the support of the United Nations Democracy Fund in 2011 and 2012 respectively. There have also been assessments of the procurement systems of some states in Nigeria conducted in conjunction with EU/UNICEF in 2011, which have galvanised some of the states to adopt by enactment the PPA as their procurement regulations. The compliance assessment reports on the federal entities suggest that there is still only partial compliance with the PPA; however, there has been a reduction of the impropriety in contract award processes following the enactment of the PPA.

3. Coverage of the public procurement rules

3.1. Procuring entities

The provisions of the PPA apply to all procurement carried out by the federal government of Nigeria and all federal public bodies, including ministries, extra-ministerial offices, government agencies, parastatals and corporations.[56] In addition, where a particular procurement conducted by any entity other than those just mentioned is funded by a contribution of at least 35 per cent from the federal government, this procurement must be regulated by the PPA.[57] For instance, procurement activities of the federal government joint venture partners in the oil sector come within this definition, although there is no evidence that the provisions of the Act are being applied to them. In addition, water supply agencies of states which receive a percentage of their funds from the federal government for certain projects under the Water Supply and Sanitation Sector Reform

54 See World Bank, *Nigeria Country Procurement Assessment Report*, vol. 1, *Summary of Findings and Recommendations* (30 June 2000); and World Bank, *Nigeria Country Procurement Assessment Report*, vol. 2, *Main Text and Annexes* (30 June 2000).

55 The Public and Private Development Centre (PPDC).

56 PPA, ss. 15 and 60.

57 *Ibid.*, s. 15(1)(b).

Programme (WSSSRP) are required to apply the provisions of the PPA to procurements for such projects.

These procuring entities may undertake the types of procurement contracts discussed below.

3.2. Type of procurement subject to regulation

Procurement of goods, works and services by the procuring entities are covered by the PPA. The rules under the PPA apply uniformly to all these types of procurement. However, a separate part of the PPA deals with the procurement of consultancy services. It is only under this part of the PPA that request for proposal is mentioned as a procurement method. This part of the PPA provides criteria for the evaluation of proposals which are different to the evaluation criteria for other forms of bids/tenders.[58]

The Act does not leave open for argument the issue of whether the selling and letting of public assets fall within the application of the procurement rules. Part X of the Act specifically deals with the selling and letting of public assets (referred to in the Act as 'disposal of public property'). In fact, section 55(2) of the Act provides that '[f]or the purposes of this Act every procuring entity shall also be a disposing entity'.

For defence procurement, section 15(2) of the Act states that '[t]he provisions of this Act shall not apply to the procurement of *special* goods, works and services involving national defence or national security, unless the President's express approval has been first sought and obtained'.[59] What constitutes 'special' is not defined in the Act. However, it could be argued that 'special' refers to those goods, works and services for national defence/security whose procurement ought not to be made public so as to protect national defence/security interests or secrets; or those that the President, as Commander-in-Chief of the Nigerian armed forces, declares as 'special'. These may include arms and ammunition, and security/defence intelligence services. Note that defence and security is within the exclusive legislative competence of the National Assembly.[60] In practice, defence and security agencies use the competitive procedures provided by the PPA to conduct a significant proportion of their procurement, since they are not 'special'. In fact, President Yar'adua was reported to

58 *Ibid.*, ss. 32 and 49–52. 59 Emphasis added.
60 Constitution, 2nd Schedule, Part 1, Items 17 and 45.

have approved the application of the Act to all federal government procurement without exception, and there is no evidence of a reversal of this approval by the current administration.[61]

For contracts funded by international development agencies, the agencies may impose their own procurement rules. An example is the European Development Fund (EDF) projects in Nigeria's water and sanitation sector, for which the EU's Procurement Guidelines and templates for aid-funded projects are used. Also, for public projects in Nigeria funded by the World Bank, the Bank's Procurement Guidelines apply. Notwithstanding, there is no provision in the PPA that is akin to Article 3 of the 1994 UNCITRAL Model Law. Article 3 suggests that, where the national procurement law conflicts with the requirement of a treaty between the government and an intergovernmental international finance institution, the treaty requirement shall prevail. As already alluded to above, the direction of Article 3 is followed in practice in Nigeria. However, almost all the projects funded or co-funded by these international agencies in Nigeria usually rely on the established procurement structures and personnel in the government institutions involved in the projects. Also, the PPA may apply to supplement the rules of the international development/financing institutions. For instance, the Act was applied as a supplementary regulatory instrument in the WSSSRP projects co-funded by UNICEF/EU and other contributors, including the federal government. The World Bank, which is a major development partner of Nigeria, enjoins aggrieved bidders in Bank-financed procurement to lay their complaints first to the borrowing country.[62] To make such a complaint in Nigeria, the aggrieved bidder, it appears, would be required to follow the procurement review/complaint mechanism provided under the Act. In addition, aggrieved bidders may copy or complain directly to the Bank. The borrowing country also submits its decision on such complaints to the Bank for reviews and comments.[63] The issue of multiple remedies regimes as a result of foreign aid procurement is further discussed in Chapter 13 of this volume, and the impact of aid-funded procurement on national procurement systems generally is analysed in Chapter 11.

61 Public and Private Development Centre, note 32 above, p. 23.

62 International Bank for Reconstruction and Development and the World Bank, *Guidelines on Procurement of Goods, Works and Non-Consulting Services under the IBRD Loans and IDA Credits and Grants* (January 2011), Appendix I, para. 2(e), and Appendix III, paras. 11–14.

63 *Ibid.*, Appendix I, para. 2(e), and Appendix III, para. 11.

4. Public procurement procedures

The rules on procurement methods and the conditions for their use provided by Nigeria's Public Procurement Act are substantially modelled on the provisions of the 1994 UNCITRAL Model Law on this subject, which are examined further in Chapter 12 of this volume, dealing with procurement methods. Similar to the Model Law, the PPA provisions cover the procurement of goods, works and services. However, as is also the case in the Model Law, certain procurement methods are to be used only for the procurement of goods and works. For instance, open competitive bidding,[64] in both the PPA and the Model Law is to be used as the default method for goods and works, but not services.[65] Unlike the Model Law, the request for proposal method under the PPA is specifically limited to the procurement of services, particularly consultants.[66] The PPA does not include competitive negotiation, contained in the Model Law, as a procurement method.[67] This, apparently, is in response to the advice contained in the Guide to Enactment of the Model Law 1994, that, where request for proposal and or two-stage tendering are provided for, competitive negotiation need not be provided since the three methods could be used in similar circumstances, and uncertainty is likely to be encountered by procuring entities in trying to discern the most appropriate method from among the two or three similar methods.[68] Generally, the conditions for the use of the procurement methods are virtually the same as those contained in the Model Law, as set out in Chapter 12 of this volume.[69]

The main procurement methods prescribed by the PPA include open competitive tendering, two-stage tendering, restricted tendering, request for quotations, and direct procurement. Community participation as a form of procurement method is not provided under the PPA. The PPA provides that all procurement of goods and works by all procuring entities shall be conducted by open competitive bidding, except where the Act states otherwise. The circumstances in which other less competitive

64 These are referred to as 'tendering proceedings' in the Model Law.

65 See UNCITRAL Model Law 1994, Art. 18(1); and the Nigerian PPA, s. 24(1). This is unlike Kenya's PPA, s. 51(c), that includes services as part of what shall be procured by open competitive bidding: see Chapter 5 of this volume.

66 See UNCITRAL Arts. 3(c) and 4(b); and PPA, Part VIII generally.

67 See UNCITRAL Model Law 1994, Arts. 19 and 49.

68 Para. 19 of section 1 of the Guide to Enactment.

69 See Chapter 12, sections 3 and 5, below.

methods may be used are clearly specified by the PPA and, as we have stated, are similar to those prescribed by the Model Law. The restricted methods are used subject to prescribed monetary thresholds, and some cases require the approval of the BPP. For instance, contracts of less than N5 million may be awarded by restricted tendering. Splitting of contracts to evade the use of the appropriate procurement method is prohibited and punishable.[70]

Apart from the above procurement methods, the federal government may also grant a concession to any duly pre-qualified project proponent in the private sector for the financing, construction, operation or maintenance of any infrastructure or development facility owned by the federal government that is financially viable. Concession contracts are awarded by way of open competitive bid to a contractor who submits the most technically and economically responsive bid. Infrastructure/project concession is regulated by the Infrastructure Concession Regulatory Commission (Establishment, etc.) Act of 2005. Approvals to undertake a project by concession are granted by the Federal Executive Council. The Infrastructure Concession Regulatory Commission supervises the execution of concession agreements.

The choice of procurement methods used by procuring entities is not exempted from procurement review. It is noteworthy that the PPA provided for this even though it was enacted during the tenure of the 1994 UNCITRAL Model Law that exempted the choice of procurement methods from procurement review. In fact, there have been instances of procurement review in Nigeria arising from improper use of procurement methods prescribed by the Act. However, the level of compliance with use of appropriate procurement methods is still not high in many MDAs, according to recent assessments.[71]

Advertisement of procurement opportunities in Nigeria is mainly by publication in at least two national daily newspapers, particularly for open competitive bidding and requests for proposals. Where international competitive bidding is used, the procuring entities are required additionally to advertise in one relevant internationally recognised publication.[72] Other media used for bid advertisement include the notice board and any official website of the procuring entity and the *Procurement Journal* published by the BPP (which is yet to serve this purpose). There is a popular publication

70 PPA, ss. 58(4)(d) and 20(2)(e).

71 Public and Private Development Centre, note 32 above, p. 50.

72 PPA, s. 25(2).

of the federal Ministry of Information called the *Federal Tenders Journal* which is used exclusively to advertise federal, and occasionally state, procurement opportunities. At least sixty days from the date of advertisement is allowed for submission of bids; and at least thirty days from the date of advertisement of notice/request is allowed for submission of request for proposals.[73] The BPP has established a single Internet portal intended to serve as the main source of all federal government procurement information in accordance with the PPA;[74] however, the portal is yet to really serve as a source of bid advertisement.

To determine whether bidders are qualified, procuring entities require bidders to provide documentary evidence or other information they consider necessary as proof that the bidders are qualified in accordance with the Act and the solicitation documents. Also, pre-qualification of bidders is usually conducted before the bidding proper. The PPA does not provide or permit that suppliers must register on any supplier list to be allowed to participate in procurement. However, many procuring entities in Nigeria require bidders to pay and register for various categories of contracts before they can bid for them. This is actually more or less targeted at revenue generation and not at ascertaining the qualifications/capabilities possessed by contractors, since what gets contractors registered in a particular category is the payment of the sum stipulated for the category and nothing more. Furthermore, the registration is almost always done when a bid advertisement has been placed so that any contractor interested in bidding may register. The BPP has frowned on this practice. Although this practice is not expressly prohibited by the PPA, it may be viewed as inconsistent with the intention of the Act, considering that sums of money are paid, while the Act directs that the only money to be paid for bidding to procuring entities, if any, shall be the purchase price for tender/pre-qualification documents, which shall only cover the cost of printing and providing the documents.[75]

The contract is awarded after evaluation to the contractor who submitted the lowest cost bid out of the bidders whose bids conformed to all the mandatory requirements in the bid solicitation. All factors (such as deviations, preferences, etc.) to be considered for the purpose of bid evaluation must be calculated in monetary terms to determine the lowest cost.[76] The PPA directs that the evaluation and award criteria shall be contained in the bid solicitation.[77] However, the procuring entity may

73 *Ibid.*, ss. 24(2) and 48(1). 74 *Ibid.*, s. 5(r). 75 *Ibid.*, s. 23(2).
76 *Ibid.*, s. 32(5). 77 *Ibid.*, s. 32(1).

refrain from awarding the contract to the bidder with the lowest cost if the entity can show good grounds derived from the provisions of the Act to that effect. Such a ground may be that during post-qualification, conducted after evaluation, the bidder in question could not demonstrate a current ability to perform the contract.[78] The above award criteria apply to all types of procurement and disposal, except for procurement of consultancy services where price is not a deciding factor but the rating of the consultants – in these cases, the procuring entity negotiates with the best rated participating consultant for an acceptable price, failing which it moves to negotiate with the next highest rated.[79] By implication, where direct procurement is used, the award is not based on the above criterion of lowest responsive bidder.

Every procuring entity is required to maintain file and electronic records of all procurement proceedings made within each financial year.[80] The keeping of electronic records of procurement and the publication of procurement advertisement on procuring entities' websites are the only forms of electronic procurement provided in the PPA. However, findings show that many federal procuring entities rarely keep electronic records of all procurement proceedings made, nor do these entities publish procurement adverts on websites as an established practice. A reason for this may be that bidders are usually not required to submit electronic copies of their bids, which leaves the procuring entities with only hard copies that would be expensive to convert into electronic format through scanning, etc. Again, some procuring entities do not have functional websites, and some that have do not consistently update them. In addition, it is yet to become a common practice for Nigerian contractors to search procuring entities' websites for opportunities, except where publications (which they usually rely on) direct them there for further information.

It is noteworthy that the BPP has recently reviewed and published standard bidding/contract documents (SBDs) which incorporate relevant clauses that meet the requirements of the PPA on issues relating to instructions to bidders, bid opening, bid evaluation, contract award and aspects of contract administration. However, there is still a need to train the procuring entities on how to adapt these SBDs in carrying out their procurements, since it appears that there is a minimal use of the SBDs. The BPP presented a letter from the World Bank indicating that the documents may be used in the Bank's funded projects. These SBDs

78 See generally *ibid.*, s. 32(3). 79 *Ibid.*, s. 52. 80 *Ibid.*, s. 16(12).

are intended to act as tools for implementing procurement in Nigeria according to the provisions of the PPA and best international practices.

5. Concluding remarks

This chapter has presented the main features of the regulatory and institutional framework for public procurement in Nigeria. On the whole, it is reasonable to hold that Nigerian federal public procurement law is consistent with accepted international standards, especially as captured by the UNCITRAL Model Law. The extent to which the procuring entities and procurement processes are regulated by the procurement regulatory framework could be said to be adequate. However, the existence of an adequate public procurement regulation in Nigeria is yet to translate into a fully efficient and transparent public procurement system. More concerted efforts ought to be made towards enforcing the procurement rules and reorienting all stakeholders to support the creation of a procurement market known for integrity and efficiency.

8

The regulatory framework for public procurement in Rwanda

IVAN RUGEMA

1. Introduction

The Republic of Rwanda is a small, landlocked country located a few degrees below the Equator in the Central Africa region. Despite its small geographical size, Rwanda has a relatively large population, estimated at 10.4 million, which makes it one of the most densely populated countries in the world.[1] The United Nations, the World Trade Organization, and the World Bank all consistently list Rwanda as a least developed country (LDC). Rwanda is a constitutional democracy and has a three-tier system of government consisting of national, provincial and local levels of government. Its legal system is based largely on the German and Belgian civil law systems. However, there has been an increasing influence of the common law which is moving Rwanda closer to being a mixed jurisdiction. Despite well-documented efforts to reduce aid-dependency,[2] Rwanda remains significantly dependent on foreign aid with just under 50 per cent of its national budget financed by donors.[3]

In the recent past, Rwanda has exhibited characteristics of a 'transitional economy' in that it has engaged in a process of liberalisation, ensuring macroeconomic stability, and of carrying out legal and

1 National Institute of Statistics of Rwanda, *Rwanda Statistical Yearbook 2011*, http://statistics.gov.rw/images/PDF/Rwanda_Statistical_Year_Book_2011.pdf (accessed 16 January 2012).

2 The President of Rwanda, Paul Kagame, has been at the forefront of well-documented efforts to reduce aid-dependency on the African continent. See, for example, P. Kagame, 'Africa Has to Find Its Own Way to Prosperity', *Financial Times*, 7 May 2009; P. Kagame, 'Making Aid Work for Africa', Brenthurs Discussion Paper 7/2007 (2007). The views of Rwanda's President have also been the subject of debate amongst leading economists such as Jeffery Sachs, Dambisa Moyo and William Easterly.

3 Africa Economic Outlook, *Rwanda 2011: Overview*, www.africaneconomicoutlook.org/fileadmin/uploads/aeo/Country_Notes/2011/Full/Rwanda.pdf (accessed 16 January 2012).

institutional reforms.[4] These reform measures, which were necessitated by the collapse of Rwanda's economy after the genocide against Tutsis that took place in the country in 1994,[5] have had a significant impact on the procurement system of Rwanda which, in the years after the genocide, was unregulated and disorganised.[6]

The aim of this chapter is to provide a general survey of the regulatory framework for public procurement in Rwanda. Though not exhaustive, this chapter serves as an important building block for future study of the public procurement system in Rwanda where, to date, very little scholarly work has been carried out.[7] The chapter will be structured as follows: the next section contains an introduction to the public procurement system. It will discuss, among other things, the objectives of public procurement policy, the nature and organisation of public procurement, and the legal regime governing the system. Section 3 will look at the coverage of public procurement rules, and section 4 will consider public procurement procedures. The final section will contain a snap-shot summary of the entire system.

2. Introduction to the public procurement system

2.1. The objectives of public procurement policy

Indicative of the influence of other national and international regimes on the procurement system of Rwanda, the objectives of Rwanda's procurement regime are similar to those of most national procurement systems. Article 4 of the statute governing public procurement in Rwanda (the Procurement Act)[8] stipulates that public procurement shall be governed by transparency, competition, economy, efficiency, fairness and accountability.

4 Rwanda was recently recognised by the World Bank's annual *Doing Business Report* as the world's top reformer for the year 2009, and it has remained among the top reformers in subsequent years. This report measures issues such as the ease of starting a business, registering property, paying taxes, enforcing contracts and getting credit. See www.doingbusiness.org.

5 In 1994, Rwanda experienced one of the worst genocides in human history. It is estimated that between 800,000 and 1 million people lost their lives in a period of 100 days. In addition to the massive loss of life, Rwanda's economy and physical infrastructure were also severely affected.

6 World Bank, *Rwanda: Country Procurement Issues Paper* (24 June 2004), p. 6.

7 A single example of scholarly treatment of public procurement law in Rwanda is F. Zigirinshuti, 'Rwanda' in R. Noguellou and U. Stelkens (eds.), *Droit Comparé des Contrats Publics/Comparative Law on Public Contracts* (Brussels: Bruylant, 2010), p. 858.

8 Law No. 12/2007 of 27 March 2007 on Public Procurement (as amended).

Even though not mentioned in the same breath as the objectives listed above, the promotion of local and regional industry is also an important objective of the procurement system. The Procurement Act makes provision for local preference where tenders involve parties from other countries. Local preference is granted to companies registered in Rwanda or to nationals and bidders in regional economic integration bodies of which Rwanda is a part.[9] In terms of procurement regulations (discussed below), when bidding documents make provision for local preference, then, once all bids have been received and it has been determined which bids meet the qualification requirements, bids are divided into two categories, namely: bids with local preference (category A) and other bids (category B). Bids placed in category B then have 10 per cent added to the price of their bid and an award is then made on that basis.[10]

In instances where contracts have the potential to contribute to the economy, create employment, or enhance the involvement of a particular community, provision is also made for the awarding of a procurement contract to such a community in order to achieve these important objectives.[11] The use of procurement for social policy purposes is further discussed in Chapter 15 of this volume.

2.2. *The nature and organisation of public procurement*

Rwanda's public procurement market is estimated to account for approximately 18 per cent of the country's GDP.[12] Exact figures on key purchasers in the Rwandan economy are hard to come by, but the government's most recent budget execution report provides an indication of the key spenders. In terms of this report, spending in the education sector, which accounted for the largest share, was estimated at 18.5 per cent of the government's

9 Rwanda is a member of the East African Community (EAC), the Nile Basin Initiative (NBI), the Economic Community for the Great Lakes Region (CEPLG) and the Common Market for Eastern and Southern Africa (COMESA). The favouring of regional industry can also be attributed to the fact that Rwanda is bound by the Protocol on the Establishment of the East African Community Common Market which prevents partner states from 'discriminating against suppliers, products, or services originating from other Partner States, for purposes of achieving the benefits of free competition in the field of public procurement' (Art. 35).

10 Art. 14 of Ministerial Order No. 1/08/10/MIN of 16 January 2008 Establishing Regulations on Public Procurement and Standard Bidding Documents.

11 This method of procurement is discussed in more detail in section 4 below.

12 National Institute of Statistics of Rwanda, *Rwanda Statistical Yearbook 2009*, www.statistics.gov.rw/images/PDF/rstyb%202009_correctv_.pdf (accessed 28 April 2010).

total expenditure.[13] Even though some of the activities for which these funds were spent cannot be classified as procurement *per se*, the report indicates that spending for books and other essential materials (including computers), construction of new schools, maintenance and repairs, as well as the provision of foodstuffs, took a large percentage of the education sector's expenditure. Other major expenses during this financial year (2009) included the printing of new identification documents and drivers' licences, as well as the funding of different infrastructure projects under the ministries of internal security and infrastructure, respectively. Defence spending, at 11 per cent, also accounted for a relatively significant portion of the total expenditure.

The organ responsible for oversight of these procurement activities is the Rwanda Public Procurement Agency (RPPA). The RPPA was established in 2007 to replace the National Tender Board (NTB) which was a centralised body responsible for all procurement that took place in Rwanda. The move from the NTB to the RPPA did not just involve a change in name, but, rather, a shift in the way public procurement was organised in Rwanda. During evaluations conducted to determine where reforms to the system were to be targeted, it was discovered that it had become difficult for a centralised body like the NTB to balance its operational duties, such as the evaluation of tenders, with its policy-making, oversight and capacity building roles.[14] In other words, it was felt that procurement in Rwanda had become too centralised. The creation of the RPPA was geared towards addressing this problem by assigning to this new body an oversight and policy-making role while gradually decentralising operational duties.

A second reason behind the decentralisation of the NTB's powers was that, as part of the government's larger programme, it had decided to embark on a policy of decentralisation which, it was hoped, would empower 'all Rwandan people at all levels to actively participate in the political, economic, and social transformation of Rwanda'.[15] Part of this decentralisation policy involved fiscal decentralisation which was

13 Ministry of Finance, Government of Rwanda, *Government Execution Report for the First Half of 2009* (September 2009).

14 World Bank, note 6 above, p. 7. An assessment of Rwanda's procurement system was carried out by the World Bank. The assessment resulted in the *Country Procurement Issues Paper* and eventually in the drafting of the Procurement Act, which was drafted by the Bank's experts.

15 Ministry of Local Government, Community Development, and Social Affairs, *Rwanda Five Year Decentralization Implementation Programme* (March 2004), p. 4.

intended to empower local government authorities, state-owned enterprises and parastatals to raise revenue as well as to decide how their money would be spent.[16]

This objective of decentralising procurement seems to have been achieved if one has regard to the responsibilities of the RPPA which are set out in Article 3 of Law No. 63/2007 which establishes and determines the organisation of the RPPA. This Article lists the responsibilities of the RPPA as including: ensuring organisation of public procurement; analysing and supervising public procurement matters; advising government and other procurement organs on policies and strategies in matters related to the organisation of public procurement; developing human resource professionalism in public procurement; developing teaching materials and organising training; setting requirements to be fulfilled by members of staff dealing with public procurement; and raising public awareness of matters related to public procurement.

Operational duties are now the responsibility of what the Procurement Act refers to as procurement units.[17] The Act provides that these units are to be established by each procurement entity and are to be responsible for the procurement process from planning to contract execution. If one has regard to the definition of a procurement entity in Article 1 of the Procurement Act (which will be discussed in some detail below), it would seem that there exists a procurement unit in every central and local government authority, public institution, commission and parastatal in the country. In other words, the bodies responsible for actual procurement exist at various levels and institutions across the country.

Each procurement entity is also required to establish a 'tender committee' from amongst its staff.[18] The responsibilities of this tender committee include conducting the opening, evaluation and recommendation of bids for award. In carrying out their functions, members of a tender committee are authorised to seek the assistance of consultants, provided that those consultants do not have any interest, directly or indirectly, in the tender concerned.

In summary, the procurement unit is responsible for planning, preparing bidding documents, the publication and distribution of invitations to bid, the receipt and safekeeping of bids, the preparation of notification of

16 *Ibid.*, p. 23. 17 Art. 22 of the Procurement Act.

18 The Act, however, prohibits persons who are the head of a public body, chief budget managers, heads of finance units, internal auditors, and legal advisors from being part of a tender committee.

award and ensuring adequate contract execution. The tender committee is responsible for the decision to award the tender, whereas the RPPA is responsible for overall oversight.

In addition to the above-mentioned bodies, the Office of the Ombudsman of Rwanda has a significant influence on the public procurement system of Rwanda. The Ombudsman's office was created to, among other things, fight corruption in the public administration.[19] One of the ways in which it does this is by requiring those responsible for public tenders or anybody controlling public finance or property, to annually declare their wealth. By doing this, the Ombudsman's office plays a central role in ensuring that the objective of accountability is achieved. Corruption in public procurement is further considered in Chapter 14 of this volume.

2.3. *The legal regime on public procurement*

2.3.1. Primary sources of procurement law

Prior to 1994, public procurement in Rwanda took place under an outdated legal framework which had remained largely unchanged since 1959.[20] In the immediate years after the 1994 genocide, public procurement was carried out in a pragmatic manner, that is, without reference to any discernible legal framework.[21] In an effort to remedy this, the Procurement Act was passed to serve as an anchor for the procurement system as far as the legislative framework was concerned. Linked to this law were its accompanying regulations, which set out important details which were not fleshed out in the main statute.[22] Some of the important information contained in the regulations includes *pro forma* standard bidding documents, specific threshold amounts, and various formulae used to calculate issues such as price adjustments. Any reading of the main statue cannot be carried out without reference to its accompanying regulations.

Drawing on Rwanda's civil law tradition, the Procurement Act and its regulations are extremely comprehensive and cover in detail the entire

19 Law No. 17/2005 of 18 August 2005 Modifying and Complementing Law No. 25/2003 of 15 August 2003 Establishing the Organisation and the Functioning of the Office of the Ombudsman.

20 In the period leading up to 1994, public procurement was governed by the Royal Decree of 25 February 1959 on tenders for works, supplies and transportation.

21 World Bank, note 6 above, p. 3.

22 Ministerial Order No. 001/08/10/MIN of 16 January 2008 Establishing Regulations on Public Procurement and Standard Bidding Document.

procurement process from planning through execution. Little discretionary room is left for members of procurement units and tender committees in their decision-making. A more detailed discussion of the contents of this statute and its accompanying regulations will be carried out in the following sections. However, it is important to note at this juncture that one of the most important contributions of this law was that it created a singular source for the core rules and regulations on public procurement. Previously, one had to look through the NTB's guidelines on procurement and various Ministerial Orders in order to discern what the rules governing government procurement were.

2.3.2. Secondary sources of procurement law

Law No. 23/2003 of 7 August 2003 relating to prevention, repression and punishment of corruption and related offences also has relevance to government procurement in Rwanda. In particular, Article 18 of this law provides that any public servant who, in whatever form or for whatever motive, without authorisation by law, delivers public goods or services without compensation[23] or at an unsuitable price shall be sentenced to a term of imprisonment of between two and five years and a fine ranging from two to ten times the value of the illicit profit received. Such stringent measures are obviously important in deterring corruption in the public procurement system which had been plagued by corrupt activities. Related to this, corruption in the procurement system can also be punished under the provisions governing corruption that can be found in Rwanda's Penal Code.[24]

In addition to the above-mentioned laws, there are other statutes which are not specifically targeted towards the procurement system, but which nonetheless have an impact on the system. One such law is Organic Law No. 37/2006 of 12 September 2006 on State Finances and Property. This law was brought into place to establish principles and modalities for sound management of the budget and other state financial resources.[25] It sets efficiency, optimal uses, transparency and accountability as guidelines for the use of state finances.[26]

23 The Act does not explain what is meant by delivering public goods or services without compensation, and it is not immediately clear from the context what this phrase means.

24 See Law No. 21/77 of 18 August 1977 Establishing the Penal Code. See also Chapter 14 of this volume for further discussion of corruption in public procurement.

25 Art. 1 of the State Finances and Property Act.

26 *Ibid.*, Art. 4.

2.3.3. Bodies responsible for implementation of procurement laws

The bodies responsible for the implementation of these rules are the various procurement entities and the Independent Review Panels (IRPs). In addition to their other duties discussed above, procurement entities can review decisions taken by a tender committee. Procurement entities are empowered to review any conduct in procurement proceedings that contravenes the Procurement Act or any other procurement regulations. If a bidder does not receive the desired relief having appealed to a procurement entity, they can appeal to an IRP at their administrative level which is the second body responsible for implementing and interpreting procurement rules. Decisions of IRPs at the district level can be appealed to the national IRP which is a single body that hears final appeals. The national IRP is composed of five members taken from public service, the private sector and civil society. It is significant to note that civil society has been given the opportunity to play a meaningful role in the procurement process by way of the seat reserved for their members on the IRP. Although the Act does not explicitly state that decisions of the IRP can be appealed to the courts, Article 71 does state that decisions of the IRP at the national level shall be final *unless judicial proceedings are initiated.* Since the coming into effect of the new Act, there have been four decisions which have moved from the IRP to the national courts.

The IRPs have been the bodies most responsible for the development of public procurement law. This is because, to date, very few cases have made it past the IRPs to the formal court system. The majority of procurement cases which the courts have considered have dealt with corruption, and, as such, the courts have not played an important role in the development of procurement law. However, it is important to keep in mind that the procurement regime in Rwanda is only in its infancy, having only been reformed as recently as 2007; therefore, the role of the courts in the development of procurement law is likely to increase. Supplier remedies are further discussed in Chapter 13 of this volume.

3. Coverage of public procurement rules

3.1. Introduction

One of the main features of the Procurement Act is that it was heavily influenced by the 1994 UNCITRAL Model Law on the Procurement of Goods, Construction and Services ('UNCITRAL Model Law'). This is understandable in light of the fact that the UNCITRAL Model Law was enacted to 'serve as a model for States for the evaluation and modernization of their procurement laws and practices and the establishment of procurement legislation where none presently exist', and Rwanda was such a country.[27] In its Guide to Implementing the UNCITRAL Model Law on Procurement, relating to the 1994 Model Law, it was indicated that 'the objectives of the model law are best served by the widest possible application of the model law'.[28] The Guide further suggests that any limitations on the scope of application should be kept to a minimum. The scope of application of Rwanda's law seems to have followed UNCITRAL's guidelines. Article 2 of the Procurement Act provides that the public procurement law shall apply to the 'procurement of works, goods, consulting services or other services carried out by the procuring entity'.

3.2. *Procuring entities*

The procurement entities covered by the Procurement Act are: all central government authorities; local government authorities; and public institutions, commissions, government projects, parastatals, agencies or any other specialised institution engaged in contracts with successful bidders. This coverage is fairly comprehensive as it covers government bodies at all three levels of government, such as public universities and hospitals, the national post office, and the power and water utility companies (which are transitioning to private ownership) as well as *ad hoc* specialised institutions.

3.3. *Type of procurement subject to regulation*

The type of procurement subject to regulation is limited to three particular areas, namely, goods, works and consulting services. Works are defined as activities related to the 'realisation of building or engineering works'.[29] This can be taken to mean infrastructure-related activities such as the building of roads, airports and storied buildings. The Act defines consulting services as activities of an intellectual or intangible nature.[30] Goods on the other hand are defined as including raw materials,

27 S. Arrowsmith, J. Linarelli and D. Wallace, *Regulating Public Procurement: National and International Perspectives* (The Hague: Kluwer Law International, 2000), p. 88.

28 UNCITRAL, *Guide to Implementing the UNCITRAL Model Law on Procurement*, p. 323.

29 Art. 1(20) of the Procurement Act. 30 *Ibid.*, Art. 1(7).

equipment in solid, liquid or gaseous form, as well as services linked to the supply of these goods.[31]

Even though the scope of application of Rwanda's law is wide, if one has regard to the procurement laws of some the countries in the same regional trade area as Rwanda, it can be argued that perhaps the scope of application of Rwanda's law could have been widened or, at least, drafted with more clarity. The scope of Uganda's procurement law, for example, provides that:

> This Act shall apply to all public procurement and disposal activities and in particular shall apply to –
> (a) all public finances –
> (i) originating from the Consolidated Fund and related special finances expended through the capital or recurrent budgets, whatever form these may take;
> (ii) that may be earmarked for external obligation purposes, except those resources that may be earmarked for payments of membership subscriptions and contributions; and
> (iii) of a procuring and disposing entity;
> (b) resources in the form of counterpart transfers or co-financing or any finances of a similar nature within the context of development cooperation agreements for the implementation of national programmes; and
> (c) procurement or disposal of works, services, supplies or any combination however classified by –
> (i) entities of government within and outside Uganda; and
> (ii) entities, not of government, but which benefit from any type of specific public funds specified in paragraph (a) of this subsection.[32]

Rwanda's membership in the East African Community (EAC) might lead to a change in the breadth of the scope of its procurement law. This is because the EAC has recently embarked on an effort to harmonise the procurement systems of EAC member states.[33]

Article 2 must also be read together with Article 3 which contains exclusions from the scope of application. The two exclusions made to the scope are for national defence and security and for rules of multilateral or bilateral treaties to the extent that there is a clash with the rules of Rwanda's procurement law. In deciding to apply the usual procurement rules to

31 *Ibid.*, Art. 1(12).
32 The Public Procurement and Disposal of Public Assets Act 1 of 2003 (Uganda), s. 2(1).
33 B. Namata, 'East Africa: EAC to Harmonise Procurement System', *The New Times*, http://allafrica.com/stories/printable/200806120596.html (accessed 11 August 2009).

defence procurement, as a general rule, Rwanda follows the approach of the 1994 UNCITRAL Model Law, but it should be noted that the 2011 UNCITRAL Model Law now takes the approach that the general procurement rules should apply to defence procurement. Where a clash between multilateral or bilateral treaties and the Procurement Act exists, the former takes precedence. At present, this latter exclusion remains uncontroversial because Rwanda has not signed up to any regional and international treaties that touch on procurement. However, as mentioned above, this position might change in the near future.

4. Public procurement procedures

4.1. Introduction

Article 23 of Rwanda's procurement law makes open competitive bidding the preferred method of procurement. Article 23 provides that, except where provided otherwise, procuring entities shall apply open competitive bidding. Once again, this seems to be in line with the UNCITRAL Model Law which advocates the use of open competitive bidding because of its ability to maximise economy and efficiency which, as was noted above, are among the guiding principles of Rwanda's procurement law.[34] The other methods of procurement provided for in Rwanda's procurement law are:

- two-stage tendering, which is to be used when tendering proceedings have been engaged but no tenders are submitted or, where those that are, have been rejected, and also when it is not feasible for the procuring entity to formulate detailed specifications;
- restricted tendering, which is used when dealing with bids that are highly complex or specialised or when the time and cost required to evaluate a large number of bids would be disproportionate to the value of the goods being procured;
- request for quotation, which is to be used mainly for goods and services of low value; and
- single-source procurement, which can be used, among other situations, for procurement related to items available from a monopolist.

Another important method of procurement that is provided for by Rwanda's procurement law and which requires special mention is

34 UNCITRAL, note 28 above, p. 330.

community participation. Article 58 of the Procurement Act provides that this method, which envisions the participation of communities in the delivery of services, is to be used under circumstances to be defined by regulations accompanying the Act. According to the regulations, community participation in procurement may be used where it is established that it will contribute to the economy, create employment and enhance the community's involvement in the activities of which they are beneficiaries. This is done by an award of a procurement contract to the beneficiary community by the procuring entity, a contract which specifies the obligations of each party. The beneficiary community is required to form two separate committees. The first committee, referred to as the execution committee, is, in terms of the regulations, responsible for signing the procurement contract on behalf of the beneficiary community. The second committee, the inspection committee, is responsible for ensuring that the terms of the contract are properly implemented. These committees act on behalf of the entire community and there is therefore no need for competition.

The regulations set the ceiling amount for the use of community participation at RF20 million (approximately US$30,000). However, if the contract entered into by a community is for making terraces, anti-soil erosion trenches or for planting trees, then the regulations allow for the ceiling value to be exceeded. It therefore seems that, in addition to the economic benefits that are targeted by this method of procurement, there is also a focus on encouraging the community to take responsibility for the sustainability of the environment.

4.2. Qualification and participation

According to the guide to implementing the UNCITRAL Model Law, the provisions regarding qualification and participation are there to ensure that the suppliers and contractors with whom the procuring entity contracts are qualified to perform the procurement contracts awarded to them and that a procedural climate conducive to fairness and participation is maintained.[35] Rwanda's Procurement Act tries to achieve these goals by providing in Article 37 that a bidder is qualified to be awarded a tender only if he or she has the qualified personnel, equipment, experience and financial capacity to provide what is being procured. Other factors which are looked at in determining qualification are the legal capacity to

35 *Ibid.*, p. 324.

enter into a procurement contract, that the bidder is not insolvent, and that he or she has not been debarred from participating in procurement proceedings.[36] The Act provides a closed list of grounds on which a bidder may be debarred from bidding. These grounds include providing false information in the process of submitting a bid or pre-qualification application; collusion between the bidder and a public official concerning the formulation of terms of reference or the bidding document; fraudulent price fixing; breach of any laws in order to obtain a contract; and poor or non-performance of a procurement contract.

In addition to the above-mentioned qualification requirements, the procuring entity can also develop specific qualification requirements in the bidding document, which must be complied with before a bidder qualifies to take part in the procurement process.[37]

In order to verify that the above factors have been met, procuring entities may require a bidder to provide evidence in this regard. It is therefore conceivable that bids will be accompanied by financial statements, particulars of contracts awarded to them in the past, or a brief description of the qualifications of the members of the bidder.

4.3. Award criteria and preferences

Once bidders have met the qualification requirements, determining to whom the tender will be awarded is done by the tender committee. In order to make this determination, the Procurement Act separates the rules for goods and services from those related to consultants. With respect to goods and services, the Procurement Act provides, first, that the bid will be evaluated based only on the procedures and criteria set out in the bidding document.[38] In other words, the tender committee is not allowed to take into account any factors that were not stipulated in the call to tender. The successful bidder is then selected based on the party who has met all the qualification requirements and who has submitted the lowest monetary bid.[39] The lowest bid therefore seems to be the main criterion on which contracts are awarded.

Where there is procurement of consultancy services, the Act spells out more detailed requirements for the manner in which the successful bidder is to be chosen. The Act sets quality and cost based selection as the default method. The regulations accompanying the Act provide a

36 Art. 37(3), (4) and (5) of the Procurement Act.

37 *Ibid.*, Art. 37(5). 38 *Ibid.*, Art. 39. 39 *Ibid.*

detailed formula that is to be used when following the quality and cost based method. The following is the formula used to award a tender for procurement services. The 'combined score' (S) is calculated as follows:

$$S = (TS \times Tw) + (FS \times Fw)$$

where:

TS = technical score
FS = financial score
Tw = weight of technical score, expressed as a percentage between 70 per cent and 90 per cent
Fw = weight of financial score, expressed as a percentage between 10 per cent and 30 per cent

Note that:

$$Tw + Fw = 1$$

The financial score of each bidder is determined according to the following formula:

$$FS = (LF \times 100)/Fi$$

where:

LF = the lowest proposal;
Fi = the proposal to be evaluated

Procedurally, the procuring entity is required simultaneously to inform both the successful and the unsuccessful bidders of the provisional outcome of the bid evaluation. This notification should also make it known that information regarding the manner in which the successful bidder was selected can be made available upon request to all bidders and that unsuccessful bidders have seven days in which to lodge any protest.

4.4. Enforcement mechanism and remedies

In order to ensure that there is compliance with procurement rules, the Act and its accompanying regulations contain penalties applicable in case of breach of public procurement rules. The enforcement rules contained in the Act first and foremost make reference to the general penal code, as well as to other pieces of legislation that were mentioned in section 2.3 above. These laws include the law aimed at the prevention, suppression and punishment of corruption and related offences, and the general statute governing civil servants, including the code of ethics for civil servants.

Aside from these general provisions, the Act also sets out specific provisions enforcing procurement rules. For example, contravening rules of the Procurement Act makes the offender liable to imprisonment of between six and twelve months. Actions such as the splitting of tenders and influence peddling also attract similar penalties.

Rwanda's law on public procurement gives aggrieved bidders wide-ranging opportunities to seek review of procurement decisions. As noted earlier, the Act allows a prospective or actual bidder to apply for review, at any stage of the procurement proceedings, to an IRP. A bidder who feels aggrieved applies in writing to an IRP within his district and the IRP is authorised to order a number of wide-ranging remedies. These remedies include: requiring the procuring entity that has acted in a manner contrary to the provisions of the Act to act consistently with them; annulling in whole or in part decisions of procuring entities that are contrary to the law; substituting the decision of a procuring entity with its own; ordering the re-evaluation of a bid; ordering the payment of reasonable costs incurred in participating in the bidding process when a contract had been awarded which in the opinion of the panel should not have been awarded; and ordering that the procurement proceeding be terminated. A perusal of the 2010–11 report of the IRP indicates that it received a total of seventy-nine appeals, the majority of which (58 per cent) were rejected because of procedural defects.[40] Supplier remedies are discussed further in Chapter 13 of this volume.

5. Concluding remarks

One of the main features of Rwanda's procurement system is that it is still in its infancy. A new legal framework came into effect only in 2010. This new legal framework, which was heavily influenced by international organisations such as the World Bank, still needs to take root. Part of this 'taking root' involves developing the necessary human-resource capacity to properly apply these new and sometimes complex rules. This is especially important in light of the fact that procurement in Rwanda has now been decentralised and persons at all levels of government need to properly understand how the system should function. Also, because the current

40 Annual Activity Report of the National Independent Review Panel for the Fiscal Year 2010/2011 (July 2010–June 2011).

legal framework is one that borrows heavily from other national and international procurement regimes, it is envisioned that Rwanda's procurement system will continue to undergo reforms as it adapts to Rwanda's systems and structures. It is encouraging, however, that Rwanda's system now mirrors elements of international best practice and can be counted among one of the better procurement systems in Africa.

9

The regulatory framework for public procurement in South Africa

PHOEBE BOLTON*

1. Introduction

South Africa, more accurately referred to as the Republic of South Africa, is located at the southern tip of Africa with a population of around 50 million. Even though South Africa is, compared to other African countries, sometimes regarded and referred to as a developed country, it remains in many respects a developing country.[1] This author would be more comfortable with referring to South Africa as a 'newly industrialised country' – it has a more advanced economy than other developing countries, but at the same time it has not yet fully demonstrated the signs of a 'developed country'. South Africa is a constitutional democracy and has a three-tier system of government consisting of national, provincial and local levels of government. It has an independent judiciary and the legal system is based on Roman-Dutch law and English common law. South Africa's public procurement system, in particular, is governed by public law or administrative law rules as well as private law rules. South Africa's history of discriminatory policies and practices has further had a major impact on the public procurement system currently in place. As will be explained below, the contracting power of the government is currently used as an empowerment tool, with the primary aim to address past discriminatory policies and practices. This aspect of public procurement regulation in South Africa is further analysed in more detail in Chapter 15 of this volume, dealing with social policy in public procurement.

* The law is stated as at 13 March 2012.

1 South Africa is, for example, a founding member of the WTO and is classified as a developed country in the WTO. It is, however, also on the list of emerging and developing economies of the International Monetary Fund's *World Economic Outlook Report* (October 2009), www.imf.org/external/pubs/ft/weo/2009/02/weodata/groups.htm#oem (accessed 13 March 2012). Other African countries on the list include, *inter alia*, Botswana, Namibia, Nigeria and Ghana.

It is the aim of this chapter to provide an overview of the regulatory framework for public procurement in South Africa. First, attention is given to the procurement system in place, with particular reference to the objectives of public procurement policy and the nature and organisation of public procurement. Next, the legal regime is canvassed, including the coverage of public procurement rules and the procedures used for the procurement of goods and services. It must be emphasised that this chapter is simply an outline of South Africa's public procurement system and is intended to be accessible to those with no prior knowledge of the system. For more detailed discussion and analysis, readers are referred to the author's own work[2] and those of other writers.[3]

2. Introduction to the public procurement system

2.1. The objectives of public procurement policy

The objectives of public procurement policy in South Africa are largely the same as they are for most national procurement systems. The South African Constitution,[4] in section 217(1), stipulates that organs of state (referred to broadly here) must contract for goods or services in accordance with a system which is fair, equitable, transparent, competitive and cost-effective. Constitutional importance is therefore given to the objectives of value for money, integrity in public spending practices, accountability to the public, and efficiency in the procedure for procurement.

In recognition of South Africa's history of discriminatory policies and practices, however, section 217 (also) makes provision for organs of state to use their contracting power for empowerment purposes. Section 217(2) stipulates that organs of state are not prevented from implementing a procurement policy that provides for categories of preference in the allocation of contracts and the protection or advancement of persons or categories of persons disadvantaged by unfair discrimination. Such use of procurement must, in terms of section 217(3), take place in accordance with national legislation. The Preferential Procurement Policy Framework Act

2 P. Bolton, *The Law of Government Procurement in South Africa* (Durban: LexisNexis Butterworths South Africa, 2007).

3 See, in particular, G. Penfold and P. Reyburn, 'Public Procurement' in S. Woolman, T. Roux and M. Bishop (eds.), *Constitutional Law of South Africa* (2nd edn, Cape Town: Juta & Co., 2002), p. 25-7; S. De la Harpe, 'Public Procurement Law: A Comparative Analysis' (unpublished doctoral thesis, University of South Africa, 2009).

4 Constitution of the Republic of South Africa, 1996 (the 'Constitution').

(the 'Procurement Act')[5] was enacted in 2000, and provides a framework for the implementation of preferential procurement policies. Regulations to the Act further flesh out the use of procurement as an empowerment tool.[6] In June 2011, new Regulations were enacted and became effective on 7 December 2011.[7] The Regulations were redrafted to bring them more in line with South Africa's Broad-Based Black Economic Empowerment Act, enacted in 2003.[8] The aim of the latter Act is, *inter alia*, to establish a legislative framework for the promotion of black economic empowerment (BEE) in South Africa.[9] The Act is aimed at the adoption of a uniform approach to BEE in South Africa, and this includes procurement practices by organs of state. More attention is given to the revision of the Procurement Act and Regulations and the impact on trade relations in Chapter 15 of this volume, dealing with social policy in public procurement.

South Africa is a party to a number of trade agreements, including the Southern African Customs Union (SACU) and the SADC Trade Protocol, but none of these has any procurement-specific obligations that may especially impact on South Africa's use of procurement for domestic policy purposes.[10] However, it has been suggested that South Africa's preferential procurement remains an obstacle in free trade negotiations with trade partners such as the EU[11] and the United States.[12]

2.2. The nature and organisation of public procurement

South Africa's public procurement market is estimated to account for approximately 21.77 per cent of the country's gross domestic product

5 Act 5 of 2000.

6 Preferential Procurement Regulations, *Government Gazette*, No. 22549 of 10 August 2001 ('2001 Procurement Regulations').

7 Preferential Procurement Regulations, *Government Gazette*, No. 34350 of 8 June 2011 ('2011 Procurement Regulations').

8 Act 53 of 2003.

9 See the Preamble to the Act.

10 As noted in Chapters 2 and 5 of this volume, the recent free trade agreement between SACU, SADC, the Common Market for Eastern and Southern Africa (COMESA) and the East African Community may bring the opening up of procurement markets to the fore in the near future, especially when viewed against the 2009 COMESA Procurement Regulations, which prescribe 'regional competitive bidding' to facilitate broader access to the procurement markets of member states.

11 See e.g. S. van den Bosch, 'A Region of Winners and Losers, Not Partners', Inter Press Service, 28 February 2011; M. Khor, 'A Rethinking Is Needed on Africa's EPAs with the EU', *South Centre*, 30 November 2010.

12 See e.g. D. Langton, CRS Report for Congress: United States-Southern African Customs Union (SACU) Free Trade Agreement Negotiations: Background and Potential Issues (2008), pp. 2, 5; C. McCrudden, *Buying Social Justice* (Oxford University Press, 2007), p. 275.

(GDP).[13] In recognition of its economic and political importance, a vast array of legislation governs public procurement procedures and, as will be explained below,[14] different rules apply to national, provincial and local government levels. The common feature of the primary or dedicated procurement legislation, however, is the decentralisation of procurement powers and functions. Prior to the constitutionalisation of public procurement in South Africa, the State Tender Board Act[15] governed procurement at national and provincial government level, while various provincial ordinances were in place to govern the procurement of goods and services at local government level. From an organisational point of view, organs of state were required to conduct procurement only via the State Tender Board and they had no authority to make *ad hoc* procurement decisions.

The Regulations to the State Tender Board Act have, however, been amended.[16] The Regulations now allow accounting officers/authorities to procure goods and services either through the State Tender Board or alternatively in terms of specifically enacted legislation which allows for the establishment of supply chain management policies and units within government departments which comply with national legislative frameworks.[17] The aim is for all organs of state to have supply chain management policies and units in place, and for accounting officers/authorities to be responsible and accountable for procurement-related functions. There is, in other words, a move towards the granting of more autonomy to organs of state in the procurement of goods and services within the framework of national legislation. The 'dual system' (procurement through the State Tender Board or the specifically enacted legislation) is intended to be available until such time that the State Tender Board Act is repealed.

At provincial government level, most if not all Tender Board Acts have been repealed and the various provincial tender boards have been dismantled. The State Tender Board Act itself remains to be repealed. This, however, will first require an amendment of the legislation allowing for the dual system currently in place, and talks with a senior government

13 D. Audet, 'Government Procurement: A Synthesis Report' (2002) 2 *OECD Journal on Budgeting* 1, 180.

14 See section 2.3 below.

15 Act 86 of 1968.

16 State Tender Board Act 1968 (Act 86 of 1968): Amendment to Regulations of the State Tender Board Act in terms of Section 13, *Government Gazette*, No. 25766 of 5 December 2003.

17 For more discussion on the legislation, see section 2.3 below.

official have revealed that this is due to take place in the near future.[18]

The National Treasury, as part of its role of managing and overseeing government expenditure, exercises overall responsibility for public procurement policy at all three levels of government (national, provincial and local).[19] The 'Specialist Functions Division' of the National Treasury, in particular, is responsible for the issuing of practice notes, guidelines and circulars on procurement policy. These range from, *inter alia*: general conditions of contract and standardised bidding documents; the appointment of consultants; codes of conduct for supply chain management practitioners; and threshold values for the invitation of price quotations and competitive bids.[20]

Where appropriate, provincial treasuries may issue complementary guidelines within the parameters set by the National Treasury provided that they do not jeopardise national objectives. A provincial treasury must also submit to the National Treasury such supply chain management information as the National Treasury may require.

At local government level, the municipal council is the highest authority within a municipality or municipal entity, and it is vested with significant powers of approval and oversight. In the light hereof, councillors are prohibited from being members of municipal bid committees or any other committees evaluating or approving bids, quotations, contracts or other bids. Councillors are also prohibited from attending meetings as observers. Accounting officers, in turn, are fully responsible and accountable for expenditures relating to supply chain management, and charged with implementing the supply chain management policy adopted by the council. Use may be made of consultants or advisors to assist in the execution of the supply chain management function. Structures are further in place for the training of supply chain management practitioners.[21]

18 Conversation with K. Naik, the Director: Supply Chain Training in the National Treasury on 17 November 2010.

19 See generally the National Treasury's website, www.treasury.gov.za (accessed 13 March 2012).

20 Consult the National Treasury's website, www.treasury.gov.za/divisions/sf/sc/default.aspx (accessed 13 March 2012).

21 National Treasury, *Policy Strategy to Guide Uniformity in Government Procurement Reform Processes in Government* (7 April 2003), www.treasury.gov.za/divisions/sf/sc/policy.pdf (accessed 13 March 2012).

2.3. The legal regime on public procurement

As is the position in other common law countries, the law that applies to the entire process of public procurement in South Africa is, in principle, the private law of contract. The private law of contract is, however, modified in its application to organs of state. Special public law rules exist to take account of the distinct needs and responsibilities of organs of state. Principles of both the law of contract (private law) and administrative law (public law) influence public procurement in South Africa. As a general rule, administrative law governs the pre-award period of the procurement process, and the private law of contract and the private law of delict/tort govern the post-award period.

Section 33 of the Constitution mandates administrative procedures that are lawful, reasonable and procedurally fair, and provides for the giving of written reasons to affected parties. It further mandates the enactment of national legislation to provide for the review of administrative procedures by the courts. The courts have held that the conduct of the public procurement process, the evaluation of tenders and the award of a contract to a successful bidder attract administrative law rules. When an organ of state calls for tenders, evaluates tenders and awards a contract to a winning bidder, it is bound by section 33 of the Constitution and the national legislation enacted thereunder – the Promotion of Administrative Justice Act.[22] An unsuccessful bidder has standing to challenge public procurement decisions by means of an application for judicial review. An unsuccessful bidder can challenge public procurement decisions on the grounds of lawfulness, reasonableness and procedural fairness. An unsuccessful bidder can also challenge public procurement decisions on the basis of the reasons given for such decisions.

A number of remedies are available in review proceedings. Aggrieved bidders may, for example, be able to obtain an interdict to halt the conclusion of a contract or an order setting aside the decision to award a contract. In exceptional cases, compensation may also be awarded to an aggrieved bidder. Procuring entities themselves may further apply for an order setting aside the award of a contract. Bidders may also be excluded or debarred from a particular and/or future procurement processes in the event of, for example, the commission of fraud or corruption in relation to the particular procurement, the non-payment of taxes, and/or a failure to perform under a previous government contract.

22 Act 3 of 2000.

In practice, the remedies available in review proceedings are frequently relied upon and very often their effect is the setting aside of contract awards. This unfortunately often leads to a delay in the procurement of goods and services and, in turn, extra costs to the taxpayer. Winning bidders are moreover not adequately protected since the setting aside of a contract only in very limited instances entitles them to redress in the form of compensation under the Promotion of Administrative Justice Act. As noted below, an award of delictual damages is generally also only available where fraud was present.[23]

As noted, it is primarily private law that governs the post-award period. It is only in very exceptional cases that administrative law rules may find application, arguably where an organ of state wants to cancel a contract in the public interest because it fetters the future exercise of discretion.[24] The remedies available in private law include in the main contractual and/or delictual damages. Contractual damages may be claimed by either party for general breach of the concluded contract. Delictual damages, on the other hand, may be claimed by an unsuccessful bidder if it can prove that fraud resulted in the non-award of the contract to it. Supplier remedies are considered further in Chapter 13 of this volume.

There are, in South Africa, also various express legislative provisions regulating the way in which specific powers must be exercised. Of particular importance to the subject of public procurement is the Constitution, the most important provisions being: section 217 which, as noted, provides for a contracting system which is fair, equitable, transparent, competitive and cost-effective, and the use of procurement as an empowerment tool; section 9 which provides for the right to equality; and section 33 which, as noted, deals with the review of administrative procedures. Of particular significance also is the Promotion of Access to Information Act,[25] which gives effect to the constitutional right of access to information,[26] and the Prevention and Combating of Corrupt Activities Act,[27] which creates offences in respect of corrupt activities relating to contracts, and offences in respect of corrupt activities relating to the procuring and withdrawal of tenders.

23 For a more detailed discussion and analysis, see G. Quinot, 'Worse Than Losing a Government Tender: Winning It' (2008) 19 *Stellenbosch Law Review* 68.

24 P. Bolton, 'Government Contracts and the Fettering of Discretion – A Question of Validity' (2004) 19 *South African Public Law* 90.

25 Act 2 of 2000. 26 S. 32 of the Constitution. 27 Act 12 of 2004.

Furthermore, Parliament has established a legislative regime for the procurement procedures and decisions of organs of state in order to reflect the constitutional status of public procurement in South Africa. The relevant legislation can be referred to as primary or dedicated legislation.

The most important pieces of legislation include the Procurement Act and the Regulations thereto which, as noted, provide for the use of procurement as a tool to correct the imbalances caused by South Africa's history of discriminatory policies and practices.

In addition, at national and provincial government level, the Public Finance Management Act[28] regulates financial management in the national and provincial governments. Regulations have further been enacted that deal specifically with supply chain management and the conclusion of public–private partnerships.[29] Very detailed rules apply to the use of competition in procurement and the procedures that should be followed for different types of procurement. At local government level, the Municipal Systems Act[30] enables municipalities to provide for municipal services by way of service delivery agreements, the selection of service providers then having to be done through specified selection and pre-qualification processes. The Municipal Finance Management Act[31] further aims '[t]o secure sound and sustainable management of the financial affairs of municipalities and other institutions in the local sphere of government'.[32] Here, too, Regulations have been enacted that deal specifically with supply chain management and the conclusion of public–private partnerships.[33] As is the case at national and provincial government level, detailed rules apply to the use of competition and the procedures that should be followed for different types of procurement. The primary legislation further empowers the National Treasury to issue guidelines and instructions or practice notes on various issues relating to procurement

28 Act 1 of 1999 (as amended by the Public Finance Management Amendment Act 29 of 1999).

29 National Treasury: Regulations for Departments, Trading Entities, Constitutional Institutions and Public Entities: Issued in terms of the Public Finance Management Act 1999, *Government Gazette*, No. 27388 of 15 March 2005.

30 Act 32 of 2000 (as amended by the Local Government: Municipal Systems Amendment Act 44 of 2003).

31 Act 56 of 2003.

32 See the Preamble to the Act.

33 Local Government: Municipal Finance Management Act 2003: Municipal Public–Private Partnership Regulations, *Government Gazette*, No. 27431 of 1 April 2005; Local Government: Municipal Finance Management Act 2003: Municipal Supply Chain Management Regulations, *Government Gazette*, No. 27636 of 30 May 2005.

with the aim to ensure uniform minimum norms and standards within government.

In general, the primary legislation governing public procurement is very detailed and leaves little discretion to procuring entities when procuring goods or services. Aggrieved parties are further able to enforce public procurement rules in the ordinary courts, and, as noted, remedies are then available in either (or both) public law and private law. It is worth adding that, since the constitutionalisation of public procurement, first in 1993 and subsequently in the final Constitution in 1996, there has been a spate of court cases dealing with public procurement.[34]

As is clear from the discussion above, public procurement regulation is fully 'home-grown' in South Africa and there has been very little external influence on the development of the law. In particular, unlike most other African countries considered in this book, the UNCITRAL Model Law on Procurement of Goods, Construction and Services (1994) ('1994 UNCITRAL Model Law') has not had any noticeable influence. As a result, key aspects of the South African public procurement regulatory regime, such as procurement methods and remedies, differ markedly from those found in other African systems, as is further discussed in Chapters 12 and 13 of this volume, which provide a comparative perspective on procurement methods and remedies regimes respectively.

3. Coverage of public procurement rules

3.1. Introduction

In South Africa, there is a lack of coherence in the scope of application of the primary procurement legislation. Of particular note is the difference in the scope of application of section 217 of the Constitution and the Procurement Act and Regulations. In the next few paragraphs, specific attention is given to the procuring entities included under section 217 of the Constitution and those included under the Procurement Act and Regulations. The type of procurement that is subject to regulation in South Africa is also examined.

34 For quarterly updates, see G. Quinot, 'Public Procurement' in *Juta's Quarterly Review of South African Law*. These updates are also available on the website of the African Public Procurement Regulation Research Unit at Stellenbosch University, www.sun.ac.za/procurementlaw (accessed 13 March 2012).

3.2. Procuring entities

3.2.1. Procuring entities under section 217 of the Constitution

Section 217 of the Constitution applies first to 'organs of state in the national, provincial or local sphere of government' and secondly to 'any other institution identified in national legislation'.[35] Organs of state in the national, provincial or local sphere of government would, with reference to section 239 of the Constitution, which defines an 'organ of state', include any department of state or administration in one of the three spheres of government.[36] Institutions identified in national legislation, on the other hand, would refer to those institutions that are specifically identified as institutions to which section 217 applies. All those institutions that are governed by the Public Finance Management Act, the Municipal Finance Management Act, the Municipal Systems Act and the Procurement Act therefore fall within the ambit of section 217.[37] Entities bound by section 217 are, accordingly:

- departments of state or administration;
- trading entities;[38]
- constitutional institutions (e.g. the Public Protector, the Independent Electoral Commission and the Independent Communications Authority of South Africa);[39]
- major public entities (also sometimes referred to as parastatals or state-owned enterprises) (e.g. ESKOM, Telkom and Transnet);[40]
- national public entities (e.g. the Accounting Standards Board, the Construction Industry Development Board and South African Revenue Services);[41]
- national government business enterprises (e.g. SA Rail Commuter Corporation Ltd);[42]
- provincial public entities (e.g. the Eastern Cape Liquor Board);[43]

35 S. 217(1) of the Constitution. 36 See, in particular, s. 239(a).

37 See ss. 38(1)(a)(iii) and 51(1)(a)(iii) of the Public Finance Management Act; and s. 111, read with s. 112, of the Municipal Finance Management Act. See also Penfold and Reyburn, 'Public Procurement', note 3 above, pp. 25–7.

38 In s. 1 of the Public Finance Management Act, a trading entity is defined as 'an entity operating within the administration of a department for the provision or sale of goods or services, and established (a) in the case of a national department, with the approval of the National Treasury; or (b) in the case of a provincial department, with the approval of the relevant provincial treasury acting within a prescribed framework'.

39 Public Finance Management Act, Sched. 1.

40 *Ibid.*, Sched. 2. 41 *Ibid.*, Sched. 3A. 42 *Ibid.*, Sched. 3B. 43 *Ibid.*, Sched. 3C.

- provincial government business enterprises (e.g. the East London Industrial Development Zone Corporation);[44]
- municipalities; and
- municipal entities.[45]

It would appear that entities that exercise 'public' powers or perform 'public' functions in terms of any legislation, even though they are included in the definition of 'organ of state' under section 239 of the Constitution,[46] are not organs of state for the purposes of section 217 of the Constitution. This is because they are not organs of state 'in the national, provincial or local sphere of government'.[47] Accordingly, entities like universities would not be organs of state for the purposes of section 217.

3.2.2. Procuring entities under the Procurement Act and Regulations

The Procurement Act applies to all organs of state that are specifically defined therein, i.e. a national or provincial department as defined in the Public Finance Management Act; a municipality as contemplated in the Constitution; a constitutional institution as defined in the Public Finance Management Act; Parliament; a provincial legislature; and any other institution or category of institution included in the definition of 'organ of state' in the Constitution and recognised by the Minister of Finance by way of notice in the *Government Gazette* as an institution or category of institutions to which the Procurement Act applies.[48]

One difficulty with this definition is that, even though the Minister is given the power to recognise 'other' institutions included in the Constitution by means of a notice in the *Government Gazette*, this was only done recently with the release of the new 2011 Regulations to the Procurement Act.[49] Prior to the release of the 2011 Regulations, therefore, an 'organ of

44 *Ibid.*, Sched. 3D.

45 In s. 1 of the Municipal Systems Act (as amended by the Local Government: Municipal Systems Amendment Act 44 of 2003), a municipal entity is defined as '(a) a private company [established by one or more municipalities or in which one or more municipalities have acquired or hold an interest]; (b) a service utility; or (c) a multi-jurisdictional service utility'. A service utility, in turn, refers to a body established under s. 86H of the Act and a multi-jurisdictional service utility refers to a body established under s. 87 of the Act. The notion of ownership control by the state therefore appears to be the overriding criterion.

46 See, in particular, s. 239(b)(ii) of the Constitution.

47 See s. 217(1) of the Constitution.

48 S. 1(iii) of the Procurement Act.

49 This is based on a search conducted on LexisNexis Butterworths' Internet database, http://butterworths.uwc.ac.za (accessed 13 March 2012).

state' as defined in the Procurement Act did not include all those institutions that are bound by section 217 of the Constitution. In particular, institutions like municipal entities and major public entities were, strictly speaking, excluded from the operation of the Procurement Act and Regulations. Thus, even though municipal entities and major public entities are bound to contract in accordance with section 217, they did not fall within the ambit of the Procurement Act and Regulations. The reasoning behind the exclusion of public entities, and in particular major public entities, had been that they are involved with strategic developmental delivery and that this should not be impeded; they need flexibility in the implementation of their preferential procurement programmes.[50]

However, as noted above, the new 2011 Procurement Regulations include all public entities and municipal entities within their scope of application.[51] This inclusion is currently giving rise to much controversy. Major public entities, in particular, are arguing that their inclusion in the scope of application of the new Regulations unduly limits their freedom to use procurement for empowerment purposes.[52]

3.3. *Type of procurement subject to regulation*

3.3.1. The acquisition, selling and letting of goods or services

Section 217(1) of the Constitution only refers to organs of state contracting for 'goods or services'. No reference is made to the contracting for 'works'. In the South African context, therefore, it would appear that 'works' are regarded as synonymous with 'services'.[53]

More importantly, however, is that different views have been expressed on the scope of application of section 217. It has been argued, for example, that the word 'contracts' as used in section 217(1) of the Constitution refers only to the acquisition of goods or services and not also to the

50 Parliamentary Monitoring Group, *Minutes of the Joint Meeting of the Finance Portfolio Committee and the Finance Select Committee to discuss the Preferential Procurement Policy Framework Bill* (12 January 2000), also available on the Parliamentary Monitoring Group's website, www.pmg.org.za (accessed 13 March 2012).

51 2011 Procurement Regulations, reg. 2(1).

52 It is ostensibly for this reason that the application of the 2011 Procurement Regulations to these entities has been postponed to 7 December 2012. For more on this, see Chapter 15 of this volume.

53 See, however, the new 2011 Preferential Procurement Regulations, which refer to 'goods, works or services'.

selling and letting of assets.[54] The argument is that this interpretation is consistent with the heading of section 217 of the Constitution, i.e. 'Procurement'. Article 2 of the 1994 UNCITRAL Model Law further defines 'procurement' as the acquisition of goods, construction or services.

It is this author's view that the word 'contracts' in section 217(1) refers to instances when an organ of state contracts for the acquisition of goods or services *and* when it contracts for the sale and letting of assets. This view is also supported by Watermeyer,[55] a South African writer, who defines procurement as:

> [T]he process which creates, manages and fulfils contracts relating to the provision of supplies, services or engineering and construction works, the hiring of anything, disposals and the acquisition or granting of any rights and concessions.[56]

It is this author's view that the non-application of the principles of fairness, equity, transparency and, in particular, competitiveness and cost-effectiveness as contained in section 217(1) of the Constitution to the sale and letting of government assets would not be warranted by logic. The whole rationale for prescribing a contracting system that complies with these principles would be defeated if they were to apply only to instances when organs of state contract for the acquisition of goods and services. The non-application of the principles to the sale and letting of government assets would be an unfortunate exclusion. The public, as taxpayers, have a right to contracting procedures that comply with the principles in section 217(1) whenever the state contracts, whether for the acquisition of goods and services or the sale and letting of assets.

Due to South Africa's history of discriminatory policies and practices, organs of state also historically contracted with large and usually

54 Penfold and Reyburn, 'Public Procurement', note 3 above, pp. 25–7 to 25–8. See also G. Quinot, 'The Law of Government Procurement in South Africa, Phoebe Bolton' (2007) 16 *Public Procurement Law Review* 464, 466 (book review).

55 R. B. Watermeyer, 'Project Synthesis Report: Unpacking Transparency in Government Procurement – Rethinking WTO Government Procurement Agreements' in CUTS Centre for International Trade, Economics and Environment, *Unpacking Transparency in Government Procurement* (Jaipur: Consumer Unity & Trust Society (CUTS), 2004), also available at the CUTS' website, http://cuts-international.org/pdf/synthesis-report.pdf (accessed 13 March 2012).

56 Watermeyer, 'Project Synthesis Report: Unpacking Transparency in Government Procurement', note 55 above, p. 3. See also De la Harpe, 'Public Procurement Law: A Comparative Analysis', note 3 above, pp. 26–8.

white-owned businesses.[57] As is evident from section 217(2) and 217(3) of the Constitution, as well as the use of the word 'equitable' in section 217(1), the current aim is to use the contracting power of the state as an instrument to remedy past injustices. Therefore, even though section 217 is headed 'Procurement', the term should be given a wide interpretation and should be read as referring both to instances when an organ of state contracts for the acquisition of goods or services *and* when it contracts for the sale and letting of assets. It is further noteworthy that, during the process of drafting section 217, the clause was headed 'Contracts for Goods or Services' and not 'Procurement'.[58] It is unfortunate that this heading was not retained in its final form, particularly in light of the fact that no clear reason could be found for the change. If section 217 was headed 'Contracts for Goods or Services' in its final form, it would have made it clearer that section 217 does not apply only to the acquisition of goods and services, but also to the sale and letting of assets. It is so that the status of headings to the chapters and sections of the Constitution as interpretive aids derive:

> from the assumption that the constitutional legislature will give due consideration to the systematic division of the constitution and to the headings used in order to introduce the various subdivisions. The headings will moreover be included as part of the text of the constitution agreed on and passed by the constitution-making body.[59]

However, ultimately the primary aim of section 217 is to regulate how organs of state do business.[60] It is submitted, therefore, in view of the arguments already noted, that, whenever organs of state in South Africa contract, whether to acquire goods or services or to sell and let assets, they should comply with section 217. It is also noteworthy that most of the principles in section 217(1) of the Constitution are repeated in

57 It is estimated that, prior to 1994, around 95 per cent of state contracts were awarded to white-owned businesses: S. Gounden, 'The Impact of the Affirmative Procurement Policy on Affirmable Business Enterprises in the South African Construction Industry' (unpublished PhD thesis, University of Natal, 2000), para. 3.11.

58 See the Fourth Working Draft of the New Constitution, 25 March 1996, available from the Constitutional Assembly Database (also on file with the author).

59 L. M. du Plessis and J. R. de Ville, 'Bill of Rights Interpretation in the South African Context (3): Comparative Perspectives and Future Prospects' (1993) 4 *Stellenbosch Law Review* 356, 371.

60 S. 217 is located in Chapter 13 of the Constitution, which deals with the general financial matters of the state.

section 14(5) of the Municipal Finance Management Act with regard to the disposal of capital assets. Further support for this reading of section 217, and in particular the words 'procurement' and 'contracts' in section 217(1), may be found in the Procurement Act and 2001 Procurement Regulations. Even though the Act and Regulations regulate the 'procurement' of goods and services which is, as noted, traditionally understood as the 'acquisition' of goods and services, provision is made in the Regulations for the award of preference also when organs of state sell and let assets.[61] It is unfortunate that the new 2011 Regulations do not similarly include the selling and letting of assets within their scope of application. The application of a preference point system to the selling and letting of assets is omitted in the 2011 Regulations.

3.3.2. Defence procurement

In recent years, South African academics have increasingly focused their attention on the legal and policy rules that apply to the procurement functions of the state.[62] However, to date very little academic attention has focused on the legal and policy side of defence procurement. What is evident is that South Africa does not have legislation or a binding set of rules that specifically applies to defence procurement. Subject to a few exceptions, the same legislation and rules apply to civil goods and services; dual-use or grey-area goods and services; and hard-defence goods and services. This state of affairs is open to critique.

3.3.3. Contracts with other organs of state

Organs of state must comply with section 217 of the Constitution when they contract for their own purposes and when they contract for goods or services on their behalf. Organs of state at local government level, however, need not comply with section 217 when they specifically contract with other organs of state for the delivery of municipal services.[63] The reason for this may be that all organs of state are entities exercising powers on behalf of the state. When a municipality contracts with another organ of state for the delivery of a municipal service, the service will still be provided by the state and there is, accordingly, no need for there to be compliance with section 217. It is this author's view, however, that the requirement of transparency should, as a general rule, always be complied with. The

61 See, in particular, 2001 Procurement Regulations, regs. 5 and 6.

62 For the most comprehensive literature, see the works cited in notes 2 and 3 above.

63 See the wording of s. 80(1) of the Municipal Systems Act.

public has a right to public contracting procedures that are open and transparent irrespective whether a municipality contracts with a private party or another organ of state. Where an organ of state in the local government sphere does not specifically contract with another organ of state for the delivery of a municipal service, and/or contracts for goods or services in general, section 217 must be complied with.

Recently, the Supreme Court of Appeal further implied that section 217 of the Constitution applies to inter-organ of state contracting.[64] However, the judgment of the court is unsatisfactory in a number of respects, which for reasons of space cannot be canvassed here. In brief, the court did not deal with the application of section 217 to inter-organ of state contracting head-on. The court was of the view that whether or not section 217 is applicable is 'beside the point' and that the question is rather whether legislation, which in fact aims to give effect to section 217 of the Constitution, is of application. The court found that, under the circumstances, the rules for deviating from the prescribed competitive bidding process as prescribed by the legislation had been complied with, and that the inter-organ of state agreement in question should accordingly stand.

3.3.4. Contracts that involve outside funding

There are exceptions to the application of the general procurement procedures in the case of contracts that involve outside funding. In 1998, the Reconstruction and Development Programme Fund Act[65] was amended.[66] In short, the Act provides for the establishment of a Reconstruction and Development Programme (RDP) Fund, which may be credited with, *inter alia*, 'domestic and foreign grants'.[67] Monies in the fund 'shall be utilised (a) to finance [RDP] programmes authorised by the Cabinet; (aA) in accordance with a technical assistance agreement; and (b) for the defraying of costs incidental to the administration of this Act'.[68] Section 4 then provides for the opening of a bank account with the South African Reserve Bank '(a) into which all money received for the benefit of the fund shall be deposited; (b) from which transfers shall be made for the financing of the [RDP] projects and programmes . . . and (c) *from*

64 *Chief Executive Officer of the South African Social Security Agency NO* v. *Cash Paymaster Services (Pty) Ltd* [2011] 3 All SA 233 (SCA).

65 Act 7 of 1994.

66 See the Reconstruction and Development Programme Fund Amendment Act 79 of 1998. In particular, s. 4, which amends s. 4 of the 1994 Act.

67 Reconstruction and Development Programme Fund Act, s. 2(b).

68 *Ibid.*, s. 3.

which transfers shall be made to a spending agency in accordance with the relevant technical assistance agreement'.[69]

In section 1 of the Act, a 'technical assistance agreement' is defined as 'an international agreement ... in terms of which a foreign state or international organisation grants development aid to the Republic'. Section 4(c) therefore allows procurement carried out using foreign assistance not to use South African procurement procedures, but instead those procedures stipulated in any agreement between South Africa and the donors. However, if a technical assistance agreement does not prescribe the procurement procedures that should be followed, the prescripts of the Procurement Act and Regulations must be adhered to.[70] Furthermore, '[i]f a project is partially financed from donor funds in accordance with a technical assistance agreement and the remainder is funded by the spending agency itself, the prescripts of the [Procurement Act] and its Regulations will be applicable for the funds provided by the government institution'.[71]

It is not clear whether issues pertaining to alleged violations of legal rules in a financed procurement ever arise in practice. From the foregoing, however, it is clear that national supplier remedies would be available where a technical assistance agreement does not prescribe the procurement procedures that should be followed. This issue is further discussed in Chapter 13 of this volume, dealing with supplier remedies as well as Chapter 11, discussing the impact of aid-funded procurement on national procurement systems.

3.3.5. Applications for exemptions from procurement regulation

Section 3(b) of the Procurement Act provides that an organ of the state, which is bound by the provisions in the Act, is entitled to request the Minister of Finance to be exempted from the application of the Act. However, this may only be done if it is in the interests of national security, it is in the public interest, or the likely bidders are international

69 Emphasis added.

70 National Treasury, Supply Chain Management Office, Practice Note No. SCM 3 of 2005, 'Projects/Services Funded by Grants in Accordance with Technical Assistance Agreements and Appointment of Transaction Advisors to Assist with Public Private Partnerships' (21 September 2005), para. 1.

71 *Ibid.*

suppliers.[72] More recently, recognition was also given to the fact that multinational companies should not be treated the same as domestic firms when measuring BEE credentials. As noted, BEE plays an important role in public procurement in South Africa, and a multinational company's BEE credentials would hence be relevant when competing for a contract from an organ of state.[73]

4. Public procurement procedures

Section 217 of the Constitution does not make any reference to the use of a particular procurement method. On a plain reading of section 217, it thus appears as though organs of state have a broad discretion regarding the choice of procurement method. However, this discretion is significantly structured by legislation and government documents. As noted above, due to the lack of external influences on the development of public procurement rules in South Africa, the procurement methods differ markedly from those found in many other systems discussed in this volume.[74] Many of these other systems have been significantly influenced in this respect by the 1994 UNCITRAL Model Law, as is discussed in more detail in Chapter 12 of this volume, dealing with procurement methods.

A distinction is generally drawn between four types of procurement: petty cash purchases, verbal or written quotations, written price quotations and competitive bidding.[75] No provision is made for community

72 *Ibid.* The Practice Note provides that such applications will be dealt with individually, and on merit. Accounting officers/authorities are, however, encouraged to convince donors to use the prescripts of the Procurement Act and Regulations (para. 1).

73 See Broad-Based Black Economic Empowerment Act: S. 9(3): Codes of Good Practice: Code 100: Measurement of the Ownership Element of Broad-Based Black Economic Empowerment, Statement 103: The Recognition of Ownership Contributions made by Multinational Companies, www.thedti.gov.za/economic_empowerment/docs/2nd_phase/Code100Statement103.pdf (accessed 13 March 2012).

74 For example, no distinction is made in South Africa between international open bidding and national open bidding, which is commonly found in many of the other systems reviewed in this book, probably influenced by the distinction between International Competitive Bidding and National Competitive Bidding in the World Bank Guidelines for Procurement of Goods, Works and Non-Consulting Services as argued in Chapter 12 of this volume.

75 National Treasury, Practice Note No. 8 of 2007/2008, 'Supply Chain Management, Threshold Values for the Procurement of Goods, Works and Services by Means of Petty Cash, Verbal/Written Price Quotations or Competitive Bids', www.treasury.gov.za/divisions/sf/sc/practicenotes/Practice%20note%20SCM%208%20of%202007_8.pdf (accessed 13 March 2012) ('Practice Note No. 8 of 2007/2008'). See also the Municipal Finance

participation as a procurement method or any formal mechanisms for the involvement of civil society in procurement at national and provincial government level.

Petty cash purchases are prescribed for contracts up to R2,000; written or verbal quotations for contracts over R2,000 and up to R10,000; written price quotations should be obtained for contracts over R10,000 and up to R500,000; and open tendering should be used for contracts over R500,000. At local government level the procurement methods are the same except that written price quotations should be obtained for contracts over R10,000 and up to R200,000; and open tendering should be used for contracts over R200,000.[76]

At national and provincial government level, contractors can apply to be listed as prospective suppliers for contracts up to R500,000 and at local government level for contracts up to R200,000.[77] The requirements for inclusion on these lists are generally determined by the respective procuring entities. However, legislation does stipulate that suppliers must be afforded sufficient opportunities to apply for registration. Moreover, the criteria for inclusion on a particular list are required to be advertised and administrative law rules would allow suppliers to request reasons in the event of registration on a particular list being denied. In the construction industry, very specific rules apply to the award of contracts. In essence, contractors apply to be 'graded' for specific types of construction contracts and, once they are graded, they only qualify for contracts falling within the particular grading category.

At local government level, provision is made for a two-stage bidding process for large complex projects; projects where it may be undesirable to prepare complete detailed technical specifications; or long-term projects with a duration period exceeding three years.[78] Strict rules on competition apply in the context of municipal service delivery by an external provider

Management Act 2003: Municipal Supply Chain Management Regulations, *Government Gazette*, No. 27636 of 30 May 2005.

76 Provision is made for the lowering but not the increase of threshold values. See Practice Note No. 8 of 2007/2008, note 75 above, para. 4; Municipal Finance Management Act 2003: Municipal Supply Chain Management Regulations, *Government Gazette*, No. 27636 of 30 May 2005, reg. 12(2)(a).

77 Practice Note No. 8 of 2007/2008, note 75 above, para. 5; Municipal Finance Management Act 2003: Municipal Supply Chain Management Regulations, *Government Gazette*, No. 27636 of 30 May 2005, reg. 14.

78 Municipal Finance Management Act 2003: Municipal Supply Chain Management Regulations, *Government Gazette*, No. 27636 of 30 May 2005, reg. 25(1).

or through a public–private partnership.[79] If a municipality decides to make use of an external provider for the delivery of a municipal service, a competitive procurement process must take place.[80] The Municipal Systems Act also proceeds on the basis that procurement takes place by way of tendering.[81]

Provision is made for exceptions to the prescribed use of tendering.[82] Organs of state may, for example, do away with tender procedures if calling for tenders is impractical; or if they are faced with emergencies; or the goods or services in question are only available from a sole supplier. At local government level, a municipality does not need to make use of competition or tender procedures where it contracts with another organ of state for the delivery of a municipal service. As noted, the service in this instance will still be provided by the state, hence the non-use of competition or tender procedures.

The National Treasury further facilitates the arrangement of contracts, referred to as 'transversal term contracts', for the procurement of goods and services required by more than one government department provided that the arrangement of such contracts is cost-effective and in the national interest.[83] If an organ of state participates in a transversal term contract facilitated by the relevant treasury, it may not call for tenders for the same or similar product or service during the existence of the transversal term contract.[84] An organ of state may also partake in any contract arranged by means of a tender process by any other organ of state, subject to the written approval of such organ of state and the relevant contractors.[85]

79 S. 15 of the Municipal Systems Act; s. 120 of the Municipal Finance Management Act; and Chapter 8 of the Municipal Systems Act.

80 Ss. 111 and 112 of the Municipal Finance Management Act.

81 See the heading of Part 3 in the Act and the heading of s. 83.

82 Municipal Finance Management Act 2003: Municipal Supply Chain Management Regulations, *Government Gazette*, No. 27636 of 30 May 2005, reg. 36(1)(a); Practice Note No. 8 of 2007/2008, note 75 above, para. 3.4.3.

83 National Treasury, *Overview: Promulgation of a Framework for Supply Chain Management* (2003), clause 2.7. This document is also available on the National Treasury's website, www.treasury.gov.za/divisions/sf/sc/Guidelines/overview.pdf (accessed 23 March 2012).

84 National Treasury: Regulations for Departments, Trading Entities, Constitutional Institutions and Public Entities: Issued in terms of the Public Finance Management Act 1999, *Government Gazette*, No. 27388 of 15 March 2005, reg. 16A6.5.

85 National Treasury: Regulations for Departments, Trading Entities, Constitutional Institutions and Public Entities: Issued in terms of the Public Finance Management Act 1999, *Government Gazette*, No. 27388 of 15 March 2005, reg. 16A6.6.

There is thus no need for an organ of state to conduct its own tender procedures.

As a general rule, contracts must be advertised in at least the *Government Tender Bulletin*.[86] Organs of state must disclose upfront the criteria that will be applied in the selection and evaluation process and bids may not be evaluated based on undisclosed criteria. Electronic procurement is not widely used in the public sector. In fact, no provision is made in the applicable legislation for this vehicle to procure goods or services. It is, however, standard practice for organs of state to communicate tender opportunities by electronic means – in the *Government Tender Bulletin* and often on the entity's own website. The submission of tenders, however, is still by and large in hard copy form. As a rule, tender documents must be 'dropped off' in an allocated tender box at a specified date and time. Electronic auctions are not provided for in the South African system.

5. Concluding remarks

South Africa's public procurement system is designed to ensure compliance with internationally accepted procurement practice, i.e. value for money, integrity, accountability to the public and efficiency in procurement procedures. Due to South Africa's history of discriminatory policies and practices, the contracting power of the state is also utilised as an empowerment tool. An array of legislation applies to the procurement powers and functions of the state, and aggrieved bidders are able to enforce public procurement rules in the ordinary courts. Remedies are available in both public law and private law. The remedies available in review proceedings include, *inter alia*, an interdict to prevent the conclusion of a contract, the setting aside of an award decision or in exceptional cases an award of compensation. Other primary remedies include damages in delict/tort and/or contractual damages.

The procurement legislation generally applies to all organs of state, for example, departments, constitutional institutions and public entities, though there is still a lack of coherence in the implementation of preference methods in public entities. Defence procurement is not governed by a binding set of legislation or rules that specifically applies to it. Subject to a few exceptions, the existing procurement legislation applies to

86 Available on the National Treasury website, www.treasury.gov.za (accessed 13 March 2012) and the website of the South African government, www.info.gov.za/documents/tenders/index.htm (accessed 13 March 2012).

all procurement. Contracts that involve outside funding may escape the application of the general procurement rules and instead be subject to procedures laid down by the funding agency. The delivery of a municipal service by another organ of state is also not subject to the general procurement rules, but the procedures followed must be transparent.

The procurement methods used in South Africa are generally determined by the size or value of a contract. For high-value contracts, formal procedures are prescribed (for example, open tendering), and for low-value contracts the procedures are less formal (for example, a call for quotations). Contract opportunities are often communicated to interested parties in electronic form (for example, on the relevant state entity's website), but submissions of bids as a rule do not take place electronically. Bidders are generally required to submit their completed bids in a tender box on a certain date and time. Bidders are further entitled to know upfront the criteria that will be applied in the selection and evaluation process and under no circumstances are organs of state allowed to apply undisclosed criteria.

10

The regulatory framework for public procurement in Zimbabwe

JOEL ZOWA, NAISON MACHINGAUTA AND PHOEBE BOLTON

1. Introduction

The Republic of Zimbabwe succeeded the colonial state of Rhodesia upon its independence on 18 April 1980. Geographically it occupies the plateau between the rivers Zambezi and Limpopo in southeast Africa. It is bordered by South Africa to the south, Botswana to the southwest, Zambia to the northwest and Mozambique to the east. English is the official language. According to the most recent census, which was conducted in 2002, Zimbabwe had a population of 12 million people, of which 52 per cent were women. The population growth rate is estimated at 3 per cent per annum. Zimbabwe suffered severe economic hardships from about 2001 to 2009, years that were characterised by hyper-inflation and reduced public spending by the government. The need to restore the infrastructure to its previous state has increased procurement activity. Since February 2009, Zimbabwe has not had a domestic currency as the local currency had become worthless due to hyper-inflation. Under the new system, Zimbabwe uses a variety of currencies, including the United States dollar, the South African rand, the British pound and the Botswanan pula.

The budgeted government expenditure for 2012 is US$3.4 billion.[1] Of this amount, an estimated US$800 million has been set aside for capital development projects and programmes. US$61.9 million has been allocated to water and sewerage infrastructure rehabilitation and upgrading, US$50.9 million towards dam projects, US$53 million towards road works, US$20 million for the improvement of the rail network, US$84 million towards the rehabilitation of infrastructure at educational institutions and US$63.4 million for infrastructure rehabilitation, equipment and vehicles in the health sector.[2]

1 Ministry of Finance, *Bluebook* (2012).
2 Ministry of Finance, *2012 National Budget Statement*, paras. 502–612.

Harare, the capital city, has approved a budget of US$418 million for 2012, of which US$146 million is for capital expenditure.

The public procurement system in Zimbabwe is governed in the main by the Procurement Act (Chapter 22:14)[3] which regulates procurement by the state and state enterprises and by bodies corporate which are wholly owned or controlled by the state. A body corporate which is wholly owned or controlled by the state does not fall under the Act unless the Minister so declares in regulations.[4] Procurement by local authorities is regulated by their constitutive Acts, namely, the Urban Councils Act (Chapter 29:15) and the Rural District Councils Act (Chapter 29:13). The provisions of the Procurement Act promote fair and impartial treatment of contractors as well as the procurement of goods and services at the lowest possible price. The Procurement Act is administered by the Minister of Finance who has, in terms of the Act, made the Procurement Regulations[5] and the Procurement (Administration Fees) Regulations 2010.[6] These regulations provide for matters relating to procurement by the various entities of the state. The Act empowers the Minister to prescribe requirements in the regulations by reference to the 1994 UNCITRAL Model Law on Procurement of Goods, Construction and Services ('1994 UNCITRAL Model Law'). The Minister has used this power to include in regulation 33 of the Procurement Regulations a provision that mandates the State Procurement Board to 'take into consideration the provisions of the UNCITRAL Model Law on Procurement of Goods and Construction . . . when inviting and adjudicating tenders' (see further section 2.3 below).

2. Introduction to the public procurement system

2.1. The objectives of public procurement policy

The Procurement Act regulating central government entities requires that invitations to suppliers to tender be made available to the public and that the invitations contain comprehensive information as to the nature, quantity and quality of goods or services to be effected, the criteria and procedures by which the successful tender will be determined, and the

3 Act No. 2 of 1999. It was last amended by the General Laws Amendment Act 2011 (No. 5 of 2011).

4 S. 1(2) of the Procurement Act.

5 Procurement Regulations 2010, Statutory Instrument 171 of 2002 as amended.

6 Procurement (Administration Fees) Regulations 2010, Statutory Instrument 171A of 2010.

date, time and place for the opening of the tenders. Of note is the requirement that suppliers must be treated fairly and impartially.[7] Further, a procuring entity is obliged to accept whichever valid tender offers the lowest price unless other criteria are specified in the tender documents.[8] These considerations represent an attempt to ensure integrity and fairness in the procurement process while at the same time ensuring that goods and services are procured at the lowest possible price. Little specific mention is, however, made of internationally accepted objectives for public procurement such as openness and transparency and the attainment of value for money.

The Procurement Regulations under that Act require procuring entities to give a 10 per cent preference on the purchase price or contract price to locally based contractors over external or foreign contractors and a 10 per cent preference to previously economically disadvantaged contractors,[9] indicating the use of procurement for social policy purposes. The Procurement Act further stipulates that the Minister can make regulations authorising the restriction of participation in public procurement processes to persons who are citizens of or ordinarily resident in Zimbabwe.[10] It is also worth noting that Zimbabwe has recently enacted the Indigenisation and Economic Empowerment Act (Chapter 14:33)[11] which requires that at least 51 per cent of the shares of all businesses operating in Zimbabwe should be owned by indigenous Zimbabweans. This Act furthermore provides that the government shall ensure that 'all Government departments, statutory bodies and local authorities and all companies shall procure at least fifty per centum of their goods and services required to be procured in terms of the Procurement Act . . . from businesses in which a controlling interest is held by indigenous Zimbabweans'.[12] The use of procurement for social policy purposes is further investigated in Chapter 15 of this volume.

At the local government level, local authorities are responsible for arranging tenders for the procurement of any goods, materials and services. The Minister of Local Government prescribes the amount above which local authorities are required to call for tenders.[13] The council of a local authority is not bound to accept the lowest tender but is required to 'accept wholly or partly the tender which in all the circumstances appears

7 Ss. 31(2) and 32(2) of the Procurement Act.
8 *Ibid.*, s. 31(1)(m).
9 Reg. 19(2) of the Procurement Regulations.
10 S. 34(2) of the Procurement Act.
11 Act 14 of 2007.
12 *Ibid.*, s. 3(1)(f).
13 S. 211 of the Urban Councils Act; and s. 79 of the Rural District Councils Act.

to it to be the most advantageous'. When any tender, other than the lowest tender, is accepted, the local authority is required to record the reason for its decision in the minutes of its proceedings.[14]

2.2. The nature and organisation of public procurement

The Procurement Act establishes a State Procurement Board which is appointed by the President.[15] The Board is charged with ensuring that procurement by government departments and state-owned enterprises is conducted in terms of the Act. The Act requires that the Board itself must conduct procurement on behalf of procurement entities where the procurement is of 'a class prescribed in regulations'.[16] Procurement which does not fall under that class is the responsibility of the procurement entity but remains subject to the supervision of the Board to ensure compliance with the provisions of the Act.

The decisions of the Board are taken by a majority vote in meetings of the Board. The chairperson of the Board cannot engage in any other occupation or employment for remuneration without the consent of the President. All issues attended to by the chairperson of the Board in terms of the Act must be brought to the attention of the Board at its next meeting.[17] The Board employs a principal officer and other staff necessary for the proper exercise of its functions.

At the local government level, the Urban Councils Act provides for the establishment of a procurement board for each municipality which is responsible for arranging tenders and for making recommendations to the council in regard to the acceptance of tenders and the procurement of goods and services. The procurement board must have not less than five and not more than seven members. A municipal council is prohibited from procuring any goods, materials or services unless its procurement board has made recommendations to the council thereon and the council has considered such recommendations. Rural district councils can contract for goods, materials and services in terms of section 79 of the Rural District Councils Act. Unlike urban councils, however, there is no requirement that rural councils have to establish procurement boards.

14 S. 211(7) of the Urban Councils Act; and s. 79(7) of the Rural District Councils Act.

15 S. 4 of the Procurement Act.

16 *Ibid.*, s. 5.

17 Reg. 5(6) of the Procurement Regulations.

2.3. The legal regime on public procurement

The Procurement Act makes broad provision for the establishment, functions and composition of the Board, the financial provisions of the Board, the form of procurement proceedings, the eligibility of suppliers and the right of appeal to the Administrative Court. Acting in terms of the Act, the Minister has, after consulting the Board, made regulations providing for the procedure for the invitation of tenders, the opening of tenders, the comparison of tenders and preferences, the procedure where no tenders are received, specifications and samples, contracts, securities and deliveries, standard terms and conditions and the fees and charges payable by suppliers and other persons in respect of procurement proceedings.[18] As stated above, the Procurement Regulations also provide that, when inviting and adjudicating tenders, the Board may take into consideration the provisions of the 1994 UNCITRAL Model Law.[19] This power allows the Board to rely on the Model Law in resolving questions that are not dealt with in domestic procurement rules. One example relates to the issue of whether a tender is non-responsive when it deviates from the specifications in a particular case. In such an instance, the Board can resort to Article 34(2)(b) of the Model Law in deciding whether the tender is indeed responsive despite minor deviations from the tender specifications.

The First Schedule to the Regulations sets out the terms and conditions that entities are expected to include in drafting procurement contracts. These include patent rights, performance security, inspections and tests, packing, delivery and transfer of risk, insurance, transportation, warranty, method of payment, non-variation of prices, delays in the supplier's performance, contract amendments, damages, termination for default, *force majeure*, insolvency, taxes and duties, applicable law and the resolution of disputes.

An important piece of legislation is the Administrative Court Act (Chapter 9:16) in terms of which the Administrative Court is established. In terms of the Procurement Act,[20] any person who is aggrieved by a decision of the Board or of any other entity that procures in terms of the Act, can appeal to the Administrative Court. The decisions that may be appealed against relate to any decision by the procuring entities in any procurement proceedings. The appeal can also be against a decision

18 Procurement Regulations, note 5 above; and Procurement (Administration Fees) Regulations, note 6 above.

19 Reg. 33 of the Procurement Regulations.

20 Procurement Act, s. 43.

made in terms of section 41 of the Procurement Act which provides for the debarment or exclusion of contractors from future contract awards.[21] The Court has the power to confirm, vary or set aside the decision appealed against or to take such other decisions as in its opinion the Board ought to have taken. Where an appeal has been noted, the procurement proceedings concerned are automatically suspended for a period of seven days unless the Court considers that the appeal is frivolous or vexatious or that public interest considerations require the procurement to proceed.[22] The Administrative Court is presided over by a President who is assisted by two assessors.

The Administrative Court has considered public procurement disputes in a number of instances and granted orders that included invalidating tenders and ordering the procurement procedure to be restarted. The following are examples of such judgments illustrating the role of the Administrative Court in the public procurement context.

In *Oswell Security (Pvt) Ltd* v. *State Procurement Board and Others*,[23] the applicant sought an order suspending the conclusion and operation of service contracts between the respondents until the propriety of the contracts had been determined by the Court. The Board had awarded contracts for the provision of security services for an entity to a number of tenderers. The applicant, who was a losing tenderer, submitted that the charges which the winning companies had quoted were below the minimum charges which they were required to charge in terms of the regulations in force in their particular industry. The Court was satisfied that, in prescribing the minimum charges for the industry, the law-maker was concerned with the guards being exploited by being required to work for very little remuneration. It found that the winning companies had tendered illegal bids 'in the sense that the bids are below the legally permissible minimum amounts payable for security services'. It ordered that the tender be floated afresh.

In *Galeb Electronic Systems (Pvt) Ltd* v. *State Procurement Board and Another*,[24] the appellant was the only company which submitted a bid in response to a tender. After evaluation of the tender, the Board resolved to cancel the tender on the ground that the sole bidder had failed to meet the material requirements for the tender. The Court held that the argument by the appellant that a sole tenderer should win the tender is 'clearly

21 *Ibid.*, s. 41(1). 22 *Ibid.*, s. 44. 23 Case No. P100/11.
24 Case No. P63/2010.

misdirected at law'. The Court further agreed with the Board's finding that the appellant did not have the capacity to do the work concerned.

In *Electoral Commission* v. *State Procurement Board and Another*,[25] the appellant, the Electoral Commission, had appealed against the decision of the Board to award a tender to a company other than the one that the Commission had recommended. The Court dismissed the appeal, and held that, although the preferred company had the lowest bid, it had not complied with the technical requirements. The Court also had to deal with two noteworthy issues *in limine*. The first was whether the Commission, a state entity, had the *locus standi* to sue the Board. The second was whether a decision to cancel a tender without awarding it to a particular bidder was appealable. On the first question, the Court found in favour of the appellant on the ground that, as a procuring entity, the appellant was 'so directly involved in the procurement process that it must fall within the category of persons who might be aggrieved by a decision of the State Procurement Board as envisaged in section 43(1) of the Act'. The appellant was therefore entitled to appeal to the Court against the Board's decision. On the second question, the Court found that, when the Board met and 'deliberated and came to the conclusion that none of the tenderers had met tender requirements, and that consequently the tender was to be cancelled, that outcome was a Board decision falling within the ambit of the very wide unqualified phrase *a decision* used by the legislature in section 43 of the Act'.

Online Security and Others v. *State Procurement Board and Others*[26] was an appeal against the Board's decision awarding security services tenders. It was argued for the appellant that the winning tenderers had not quoted their bids in accordance with the gazetted rates for the industry as specified in the tender documents and ought therefore to have been disqualified. The tender specification had stated that 'the prices must be quoted using the Security Association of Zimbabwe rates ruling as at the time of the tender'. The disqualification clause stated that 'failure to quote using the Security Association of Zimbabwe rates . . . as at 30 April 2009' would lead to 'automatic dismissal'. The winning tenderers quoted their prices using the SAZ rates, but then went on to separately indicate a discount at a flat rate of 15 per cent. For the tenderers it was argued that it could not be said that by offering a discount they had quoted below the SAZ rates. The Board had rejected the secretariat's recommendation to it that the tender be cancelled due to technical irregularities in the tender documents

25 Case No. P56/2009. 26 Case No. P57/09.

and the fact that some bidders had offered discounts contrary to tender instructions. In its discussions, the Board decided that it was not illegal for bidders to offer discounts. The Court held that the Board had misdirected itself when it gave instructions for the tender process to continue. The disqualification clause bolstered the instruction to quote using SAZ rates by rendering automatically disqualified all bids not complying with the requirement. The instruction therefore prohibited the discounting of bids. By effecting a discount on their bids, the tenderers had charged below the stipulated rates and contrary to specifications. The award of the tender was set aside and the Board was directed to re-advertise and reconsider all competing tenders. The Court expressed its dissatisfaction with the conduct of the Board by making an award of costs against it. It was undesirable that the Board had chosen to involve itself and defend the merits of its own flawed decision. It ought always to consider the degree of its participation in matters of this nature instead of throwing itself into the arena. A noteworthy point *in limine* which the Court had to consider was whether it had the competence to determine allegations of corruption or other impropriety which were not brought to the attention of the Board at the time of the adjudication of the tenders. The Court held that, as a creature of statute, its powers were restricted to scrutinising, first, decisions of the Board or of any procuring entity in relation to procurement proceedings in terms of section 43 of the Act, and, secondly, any decision to disbar a tenderer made in terms of section 41 of the Act. It was not a court of first instance. Since the Court was an appeal court only on decisions of the Board or a procuring entity, it could not entertain allegations of corruption and impropriety which were never put before or determined by the Board.

Supplier remedies are considered in further detail in Chapter 13 of this volume.

In addition to supplier remedies, the Procurement Act also provides for penalties for certain types of non-compliance with procurement rules. Any supplier who knowingly misrepresents any material fact in a tender or enters or attempts to enter into a collusive agreement with any other supplier commits an offence and is liable to a fine or to imprisonment for a period not exceeding two years or to both such fine and imprisonment.[27]

A procurement contract is void between the procuring entity and the supplier if, after the contract has been signed, it is proved that the supplier gave or offered to give any consideration to an employee or agent of the

27 Procurement Act, s. 48.

supplier in contravention of the laws against bribery and corruption. A procuring entity is further required to reject any bid if it is satisfied that the supplier has given or offered to give any consideration to an employee or agent of the supplier, has knowingly misrepresented material facts in a tender, or has attempted to or entered into a collusive arrangement with any other supplier.[28]

If the Board is satisfied that a contractor has acted in a fraudulent manner or has executed a contract in an unsatisfactory manner or offered consideration to any government officer, it can direct that no tender from that person shall be considered for a period of five years. Before making that decision, the Board is required to ensure that the supplier is given an opportunity to make representations on the matter.

The Procurement (Administration Fees) Regulations also prescribe penalties for certain acts. Each of the following acts by a procuring entity attracts a penalty of US$800: unauthorised extension of a contract; failure to follow tender procedures; application to cancel tender procedures; and the late submission of an evaluation report.[29]

Both the Urban Councils Act and the Rural District Councils Act contain provision for the suspension and dismissal of councillors who are found to have acted corruptly or abused their office.[30] Corruption in procurement is further considered in Chapter 14 of this volume.

3. Coverage of the public procurement rules

3.1. Procuring entities

Government departments and all bodies which are created by statute, including the State Procurement Board, are entities whose procurement is governed by the Act. The Minister can declare a corporate body which is wholly owned by the state to be an entity whose procurement is governed by the Act. In terms of the regulations, a number of private companies which are wholly owned by the state have been declared to be procurement entities, including Air Zimbabwe and the Zimbabwe Electricity Supply Authority.[31]

A local authority can, with its consent, be declared by the Minister to be a procurement entity in which event it would thereafter be bound by the provisions of the Procurement Act.[32]

28 *Ibid.*, s. 39. 29 Schedule to Procurement (Administration Fees) Regulations 2010.
30 S. 114 of the Urban Councils Act; and s. 157 of the Rural District Councils Act.
31 Second Schedule to the Procurement Regulations. 32 S. 1(2) of the Procurement Act.

3.2. *Type of procurement subject to regulation*

The Procurement Act prescribes the procedure for the procurement of goods, construction work and services.[33] Construction work is defined as meaning all work associated with the construction, reconstruction, demolition, repair or renovation of any building or infrastructure. Goods, on the other hand, are defined as including: raw materials, products and equipment; electricity; immovable property; services incidental to the supply of the goods and where the value of the service does not exceed that of the goods.[34]

Services are defined as any object of procurement that does not qualify as goods or construction work.[35] The term accordingly includes the sale and letting of assets. The Procurement Act further applies to build-own-operate-transfer (BOOT) and build-operate-transfer (BOT) contracts under which a supplier undertakes to construct an item of infrastructure for an entity in consideration for the right to operate or control it for a specified period, after which period the supplier will transfer or restore ownership to the entity.[36]

For local authorities, the requirement is simply that, before entering into a contract for the execution of any work for the council or the supply of any goods or materials to the council which involves payment by the council of an amount exceeding such sum or sums as may be prescribed, the local authority must proceed to tender.[37] The Minister of Local Government has prescribed the relevant sum to be the equivalent of the sum prescribed by the Minister of Finance in terms of section 4 of the Procurement Regulations, which is presently set at US$50,000.[38] Contracts by councils for the provision of professional services are exempted from procurement rules.[39]

3.3. *Contracts with other organs of state and contracts involving outside funding*

Local authorities are exempted from following the procurement procedures where they enter into agreements with the state, a statutory body or another local authority.[40]

33 *Ibid.*, s. 30(1)(a) and (b). 34 *Ibid.*, s. 2. 35 *Ibid.* 36 *Ibid.*, s. 49.
37 S. 211(2) of the Urban Councils Act; s. 79(2)(a) of the Rural District Councils Act.
38 Urban Councils (Tenders) Regulations 2008, Statutory Instrument 77 of 2008.
39 S. 211(10) of the Urban Councils Act; and s. 79(3)(c)(ii)(e) of the Rural District Councils Act.
40 *Ibid.*

Unlike the Urban Councils Act and the Rural District Councils Act, the Procurement Act does not exempt organs of the state who seek to enter into contracts with other organs of the state for the supply of goods and services from complying with its requirements. The Act accordingly obliges state entities to comply with its procedures regardless of the identity of the person from whom goods and services are sought. It is submitted that the provisions of the Procurement Act are clear that, for as long as a state entity seeks to procure goods and services, it is obliged to do so in accordance with the Act. Any proposals to deviate from the tender procedures must be approved by the Board in terms of the provisions of the Act. The fact that the funds have been donated or are in the form of a loan should not be of any relevance.

4. Procurement procedures

4.1. Overview

Generally, tender conditions must state the following: that the lowest evaluated tender to specification shall be accepted; that offers must hold good for thirty days; that the country of origin and manufacture of the goods must be identified as well as the profile of tenderers; and that certified financial statements must be provided. The solicitation documents must also contain comprehensive information on the nature and quality of the work required, the manner in which and time at which tenders are to be formulated and expressed, any tender security required, the date and place for the opening of tenders and the procedure to be followed at such opening, and any right on the part of the procuring entity to reject all tenders. Any modification of a solicitation document or the deadline, within which tenders must be submitted, is to be communicated to all suppliers who have received the document. Where the Board requires samples from tenderers, tenderers furnish them at their own risk and cost.[41]

Any tender that is received after the deadline for submission is not to be opened but must be returned to the supplier concerned. All the suppliers that have submitted tenders are permitted to witness their opening and have the right to be informed of the price and other salient terms of each tender.

Tender security, where it has to be provided by successful tenderers, must be in the form of a guarantee by a bank representing 10 per cent of the value of the contract.[42]

41 Reg. 24 of the Procurement Regulations.

42 *Ibid.*, reg. 27.

No member of the public shall be furnished with the names of persons who have applied for or taken out tender documents.

The procuring entity is obliged to accept whatever valid tender offers the lowest price unless other criteria are specified in the solicitation documents. No negotiations are permitted between the procuring entity and a supplier with respect to the submitted tender.

An entity cannot enter into an agreement to vary the contract with the successful tenderer without the consent of the Board.[43] A procuring entity is required to keep a record of procurement proceedings containing the following information: a brief description of the goods, construction work or services which were sought to be procured; the names and addresses of suppliers that participated in pre-qualification proceedings; suppliers that submitted tenders, and information relating to the qualifications, or lack of qualifications, of those suppliers; the basis for determining the price, and a summary of the other principal terms and conditions of each tender that was submitted in relation to the procurement contract; the name and address of the supplier with whom the procurement contract was entered into, and the contract price; and a summary of the procuring entity's evaluation and comparison of the tenders that were submitted in relation to the procurement contract.[44]

Tenders are classified as formal, informal, competitive quotations, special-formal and public interest, with a particular procurement method for each type.[45] Procurement methods are also discussed in Chapter 12 of this volume.

4.2. Formal tenders

The formal tenders procedure applies where the proposed procurement is of a value above US$50,000. In that case, the Board itself, and not the entity which seeks the goods or services, will invite the tenders. The entity on whose behalf the invitation is made is required to supply details of the supplies or services required, the address where the tender documents will be available, the fee payable for the documents, the closing date for receipt of the tenders by the Board and the names of newspapers in which it is proposed to advertise the tender.[46] Notice of the tender is then published in the *Gazette* and in the specified newspapers by the principal officer of the Board. Where proposals are invited from suppliers who are not residents of Zimbabwe, the notice must also be published 'in a newspaper

43 *Ibid.*, reg. 26. 44 S. 35 of the Procurement Act.
45 Regs. 5, 6, 7 and 8 of the Procurement Regulations. 46 *Ibid.*, reg. 8.

of wide international circulation or in a relevant trade or technical or professional journal of wide international circulation'.[47]

This method is an open procedure in the sense that all interested tenderers may put in a bid. The Act, however, also provides for pre-qualification.[48] In this respect, the Act requires that an invitation to pre-qualify be published in the same manner as notices of tender, and that in addition information be provided as to the manner in which pre-qualification documents may be obtained and their price and the deadline for the submission of the pre-qualification documents.[49] Since the Act is silent on the purpose of pre-qualification, this is another example where the Board relies on the UNCITRAL Model Law in implementing domestic procurement rules and in particular on Article 7 of the Model Law dealing with pre-qualification proceedings.

Formal tenders are opened by the principal officer in the presence of the chairperson or a person so delegated by the chairperson. The tenders are then forwarded to the responsible entity for examination by its procurement committee. The head of the entity will return the documents to the principal officer within fifteen working days from the date of receipt together with a comparative schedule of the tenders showing prices, a summary of recommendations, a statement as to the sufficiency of any security or guarantees required and a note of any points in respect of which conditions have not been complied with.[50] The entity must furnish to the Board its reasons for rejecting or accepting tenders. In evaluating tenders, the entity is required to consider matters relating to the supplier, which include the capability to supply and perform the contract satisfactorily, the capabilities of the personnel involved, the capabilities of the equipment to be used, the financial position and any litigation history.[51]

After considering the entity's recommendations, the Board directs which tender is to be accepted. The Board is required to advise the entity of its decision within ten working days of receipt of the entity's recommendations. The entity will thereafter enter into the necessary formal procuring contract with the successful tenderer.

4.3. Informal tender procedure

An entity which seeks to procure a value less than US$50,000 but greater than US$10,000 is required to follow the informal tender procedure.[52]

47 S. 32(1)(a)(iii) of the Procurement Act. 48 *Ibid.*, s. 31(1)(c).
49 *Ibid.* 50 Reg. 16 of the Procurement Regulations.
51 *Ibid.*, reg. 19. 52 *Ibid.*, regs. 4(2) and 6.

The entity concerned must invite tenderers through newspaper advertisements. Such a call for tenders may be an open one or may be restricted to suppliers listed on the list of approved tenderers.[53] The tenders are then entered on a comparative schedule prepared by the relevant accounting officer, who in the case of a government department is the permanent secretary of the ministry in question. The accounting officer will enter his decision on the schedule, a copy of which he will then submit to the Board.

4.4. *Competitive quotation procedure*

Where the procurement is of a value less than US$10,000, the entity concerned need not follow the formal or informal procedure. Instead, the entity can obtain three competitive quotations from suppliers and then proceed to consider the bids in the same manner as for the informal tender procedure above.

4.5. *Public interest procedure*

An entity which considers that it would not be in the public interest to call for tenders in any particular instance must seek the approval of the Board giving full reasons justifying its application. For a value above US$10,000, but below US$50,000 the chairperson of the Board in consultation with three other members of the Board is authorised to approve such an application. Where the estimated value of the procurement exceeds US$50,000, the approval must be given by the Board.[54] If the approval is denied, the entity is required to follow the normal tender procedures.[55]

4.6. *Special-formal tender procedure*

Using the special-formal tender procedure, the Board can, instead of calling for formal tenders, invite tenderers on the approved list to submit their tenders.[56] This procedure is available, subject to the Board's approval, in the following cases: in respect of requirements of a proprietary nature where names of likely suppliers are known; following formal tenders to which there has been no response; and for services of a specialist nature and services which in the opinion of the Board concern national security.

53 *Ibid.*, reg. 25(4). See also section 4.7 below. 54 *Ibid.*, regs. 5(3) and (4) and 7.
55 *Ibid.*, reg. 5(5). 56 *Ibid.*, reg. 25.

The chairperson is also authorised to approve this procedure in respect of urgent requirements where time does not permit the invitation of tenders by advertisement in the *Gazette*.[57]

4.7. Lists of approved tenderers

The Regulations authorise the Board to compile and publish in the *Gazette* a list of approved tenderers in respect of specific goods and services. Before drawing up the list, the Board is required to publish a notice in the *Gazette* inviting tenderers to submit applications to be included on the list. To be included on the list, which is published annually, a fee of US$80 is payable by local companies, whilst foreign companies pay US$2,000. Some of the lists which have been published are of suppliers of stationery, suppliers of fresh fruit and vegetables, suppliers of treated wood poles, suppliers of tyres, and tubes and providers of property valuation and real estate services.[58]

Companies which do not appear on the lists are not allowed to tender under the informal, special-formal procedure or competitive procedure discussed above.

4.8. Procurement by local authorities

For all procurement at local government level of a value exceeding the prescribed amount, a call for tenders shall be posted at the office of the council and advertised in two issues of a newspaper. The notice must give details of the nature of the proposed contract and the desirable particulars thereof, together with the closing time and date for the receipt of tenders, which must be not less than twenty-eight days after the date of the first publication of the notice in the newspaper. Tenders are opened in public on the closing date and immediately after the closing time. The procurement board is required to consider the tenders without delay and submit its recommendations to the council. As stated above, the council is not bound to accept the lowest tender. If any tender, other than the lowest tender, is accepted the council must cause the reasons for its decisions to be recorded in the minutes of its proceedings. In most cases, tenders invited by local authorities will be open to all interested bidders.

57 *Ibid.*, reg. 7.

58 General Notices 45–113 of 2012, published in *Government Gazette*, vol. XC, No. 12, 2 March 2012.

The council can by resolution declare that it would be against the best interests of the municipality to invite tenders in any particular case and thereafter proceed to procure without calling for tenders.

As regards construction work, councils may, in accordance with a scheme approved by the Minister, compile a register of building and engineering contractors graded into categories according to the type and value of work for which they may be permitted to tender. Thereafter, the council can call for tenders for work from the contractors registered in any appropriate category.

In the case of rural district councils, there is, as noted above, no requirement to establish procurement boards. Before a rural district council can enter into a contract of a value which exceeds the prescribed amount, the council is required to call for tenders by notice posted at the office of the council and advertised in two issues of a newspaper. All tenders received shall be opened in public and the council is obliged to advise every tenderer whether or not its tender was accepted. In the event that the council has accepted any tender other than the lowest tender, the council shall cause its reasons for such to be recorded in its minutes of proceedings.

5. Concluding remarks

The legislative framework on public procurement in Zimbabwe seeks to promote openness and transparency. The separation of local authorities from the operations of the Procurement Act has enabled local authorities to make decisions at the local level where the inhabitants are able to judge for themselves the effectiveness of their decisions. Local authority meetings are open to members, whilst the minutes of their proceedings are also open to inspection by members of the public.

The public procurement rules in Zimbabwe promote the fair and impartial treatment of contractors by procuring entities as well as the procuring of goods and services at the lowest possible price. Due to Zimbabwe's history of racial discrimination and the unequal distribution of wealth between races, the contracting power of public bodies is used to correct these imbalances of the past.

The designation of the Administrative Court as the appeal court has meant that appeals are speedily disposed of. The Court has not hesitated to nullify tenders which in its opinion have been awarded irregularly.

A number of state entities have, however, complained at the delays in finalising tenders which are occasioned by procedures set out in the Act, more particularly, the role that the State Procurement Board plays in the procurement process. Questions have also arisen whether it is proper for the Board to act as procurer on the one hand and to be the supervisor of procurement by entities on the other.

A sound framework for any future reform is now well established.

PART II

Themes in public procurement regulation in Africa

11

Donors' influence on developing countries' procurement systems, rules and markets: a critical analysis

ANNAMARIA LA CHIMIA

1. Introduction

Developing countries' reliance on development aid resources to fulfil their basic needs, from building infrastructure to financing the health or education sectors, has allowed multilateral and bilateral donors to exercise a significant influence on recipient countries' political, social and economic policies. Thus, donors have used – directly and indirectly, formally and informally – aid resources to promote all sorts of policies in developing countries. For instance, donors have used aid conditionality – that is, making the disbursement of aid money subject to the recipient country implementing donors' conditions – as a direct and formal means to require structural reforms, to require reorganisation of recipients' legal and judicial systems, to require opening up of trade to international competition, to require protection of human rights, to implement environmental policies and to require purchase of donors' goods. Even when aid is not subject to any specific conditions, donors' decisions to fund one project or sector rather than another can have a significant impact on the pace and course of recipient countries' development.

Critics argue that donors' influence (or interference, as some say) in developing countries' economic, social or structural/legal policies risks undermining recipients' sovereignty rights,[1] is ineffective and encourages ill-suited reforms in recipient countries. There is a contrary view that instead supports donors' direct interventions in developing countries, arguing that donors have been instrumental in the implementation of important reforms which have led to progress in many countries. In

1 See G. Mohan, *Structural Adjustment: Theory, Practice and Impacts* (London: Routledge, 2000).

addition, supporters believe donors have the right to influence the way aid is spent on the basis that donors spend their taxpayers' money and are accountable to their voters.

The criticism raised against donors' influence in developing countries reflects the broader criticism raised against aid in general. Critics remain divided on the role that aid resources have played and can play in the future as a development instrument and on whether and how aid effectiveness can (if at all) be improved. A large part of the literature on foreign aid shows that the neediest countries do not receive the most aid and that a large portion of foreign aid is wasted and only increases unproductive public consumption.[2] The literature is divided on the development value and impact of aid. One approach, referred to as the public interest theory group, maintains that aid is necessary to 'fill a financing or investment gap'[3] in developing countries and is optimistic on the assessment of the role aid can play in the future.[4] Authors supporting this approach also believe that, despite the errors of the past, granting aid can help eradicate poverty if funds are made available.[5] A contrasting theory, the so-called public choice perspective, reflects a more sceptical approach,[6] and maintains that aid 'is ineffective and possibly damaging for developing

2 A. Alesina and D. Dollar, 'Who Gives Foreign Aid to Whom and Why?' (2000) 5 *Journal of Economic Growth* 33–63; L. Dudley and C. Montmarquette, 'A Model of the Supply of Bilateral Foreign Aid' (1976) 64 *American Economic Review* 132–42; A. Maizels and M. K. Nissanke, 'Motivations for Aid to Developing Countries' (1984) 12 *World Development* 879–900; R. D. McKinlay and R. Little, 'A Foreign Policy Model of US Bilateral Aid Allocations' (1977) 30 *World Politics* 58–86, cited in H. V. Milner, 'Why Delegate the Allocation of Foreign Aid to Multilateral Organizations? Principal–Agent Problems and Multilateralism', University of Southern California (2003), usccis.org/tools/software/original/public/fileforward.php?Id=3224. (accessed 1 March 2012).

3 For a discussion of the contraposition between the public interest theory group and the public choice perspective, see C. R. Williamson, 'Exploring the Failure of Foreign Aid: The Role of Incentives and Information' (2010) 23 *Review of Austrian Economics* 17.

4 J. Sachs, *The End of Poverty: Economic Possibilities for Our Time* (New York: Penguin Press, 2005).

5 *Ibid.*; and T. Pogge, *World Poverty and Human Rights: Cosmopolitan Responsibilities and Reforms* (2nd edn, Cambridge: Polity Press, 2008). See also T. Pogge (ed.), *Freedom from Poverty as a Human Right (Who Owes What to the Very Poor?)* (Oxford University Press, 2007).

6 W. Easterly, *The White Man's Burden: Why the West's Efforts to Aid the Rest Have Done So Much Ill and So Little Good* (New York: Penguin Press, 2006); W. Easterly, 'Can the West Save Africa?' (2009) 47 *Journal of Economic Literature* 373.

countries'.[7] The Achilles' heel for foreign aid, critics argue, lies in the fact that:

> proponents of aid argue that it can deliver widespread prosperity, not marginal successes. Therefore, when foreign aid's goals are compared with its achievements, the results are extremely disappointing.[8]

However, as Deaton argues, although 'few academic economists or political scientists agree with Sachs' view, there is a wide range of intermediate positions'.[9] These include the position of those authors who have adopted a constructive critical approach,[10] and, while exploring what went wrong in the past with aid disbursement and how aid can be improved, have suggested that aid can have a positive effect on growth when combined with the right policies and the appropriate institutional environment.[11] Dollar and Levin show that 'the success of aid-sponsored programmes depends primarily on the quality of institutions in the recipient country'[12] with both the rule of law and democracy significantly predicting the success of an aid project in a country.[13] Even the harshest critics agree that, on a

7 Williamson, 'Exploring the Failure of Foreign Aid', note 3 above, p. 18. Further down this sceptical road, others (Moyo), adopting a deconstructive approach, advocate the suspension of all aid projects. According to this latter current of thought, aid only generates dependency in recipient countries and is a breeding ground for corruption. See D. Moyo, *Dead Aid: Why Aid Is Not Working and How There Is a Better Way for Africa* (New York: Farrar, Straus and Giroux, 2009); and Easterly, *The White Man's Burden*, note 6 above. The literature on foreign aid is divided on the development value and impact of aid; the harshest critics have called for the abolition of aid altogether. See also 'Foreign Aid: Missing the Point', *The Economist*, 14 March 2002.

8 Williamson, 'Exploring the Failure of Foreign Aid', note 3 above, p. 18.

9 A. Deaton, 'Instruments, Randomization and Learning about Development' (2010) 148 *Journal of Economic Literature* 424, 425. The author considers Easterly a proponent of such an intermediate view. See also W. Easterly (ed.), *Reinventing Foreign Aid* (Cambridge, MA, and London: MIT Press, 2008).

10 R. C. Riddell, *Does Foreign Aid Really Work?* (Oxford University Press, 2007); and to some extent also Easterly, albeit with some fiercer criticism in terms of the future of aid policies.

11 A very interesting perspective by Leeson shows that, where foreign aid is needed, countries do not have the right institutions and environment to take advantage of it; on the contrary, countries with the appropriate institutions and environment do not need aid. See P. T. Leeson, 'Escaping Poverty: Foreign Aid, Private Poverty, and Economic Development' (2008) 23 *Journal of Private Enterprise* 39, cited in Williamson, 'Exploring the Failure of Foreign Aid', note 3 above, p. 18.

12 D. Dollar and V. Levin, *Sowing and Reaping: Institutional Quality and Project Outcomes in Developing Countries*, World Bank Policy Research Working Paper 3524 (2005).

13 See also M. S. Winters, 'Accountability, Participation and Foreign Aid Effectiveness' (2010) 12 *International Studies Review* 218, 227, 238.

micro level, aid can offer successful stories, for example increasing literacy in Africa.[14]

The debate on the role aid plays to enhance development is set to continue in the future so long as aid continues to be granted. The criticism of foreign aid has not remained unheard by the international community. As a chameleon fighting for its life, the international aid community has internalised much of the criticism against aid and has recognised the problems linked to the aid system. The aid community (of international organisations, donors and recipient countries) is now talking, in a loud voice, about enhancing aid effectiveness. Indeed, the past decade has witnessed an array of initiatives which have put development aid at the centre of the debate in the development discourse. The international community has intensified its efforts to enhance aid effectiveness, and aid actors have agreed to ensure that development assistance is well spent, setting targets for monitoring and measuring aid effectiveness. The Rome forum on harmonisation of donors' practices in 2003, the Paris Declaration on aid effectiveness in 2005, and the High Level Forum on Aid Effectiveness in Accra in 2008, are the most significant examples of donors' and recipients' joint actions towards fostering aid success.[15]

Donors have acknowledged (at least in theory) the weaknesses of a system of aid governance that does not place aid recipients at the centre of the development discourse. Hence the quest, emphasised in recent years, to align donors' policies to recipient countries' national development strategies; to guarantee true partnership between donors and recipients when aid is disbursed; and to ensure ownership by the recipient of the aid donated. This has been done with the twofold aim of guaranteeing a new, more democratic, system of governance for aid policies, and to foster aid success. Have these goals been achieved? A review of the literature on development aid reveals that, while critics generally agree that a much better use of aid resources should be made, a 'theoretical consensus surrounding the effectiveness of aid'[16] and the success of the new initiatives to foster aid success is lacking.

This chapter focuses on the influence donors exercise on recipient countries' public procurement systems; by focusing attention on aid

14 Williamson, 'Exploring the Failure of Foreign Aid', note 3 above.

15 Further information is available on the Organization for Economic Co-operation and Development's (OECD) website, www.oecd.org/document/31/0,3343,en_2649_34487_41165727_1_1_1_1,00.html (accessed 13 March 2012).

16 Williamson, 'Exploring the Failure of Foreign Aid', note 3 above, p. 17.

procurement it will shed light on the efficiencies and inefficiencies of aid procurement mechanisms and, in so doing, contribute to the wider development discourse on the role donors play in developing countries via the means of development aid. Aid procurement systems of both donor and recipient countries are characterised by many inconsistencies and inefficiencies that significantly influence the success of aid projects. Strengthening government procurement practices in the delivery of aid money can drastically increase aid effectiveness.[17] This is because an overwhelming proportion of aid is delivered through the public contracting process.[18] Donors finance a substantial portion of government expenditures in developing countries:[19] 10–20 per cent is not uncommon for low-income developing countries.[20] This percentage can reach higher levels; for instance, in Samoa it is 27 per cent; in São Tomé and Príncipe, it reaches 55.9 per cent;[21] and, in Ghana, official development assistance (ODA) accounts for 42 per cent of the national budget.[22]

Procurement is now considered a strategic aid management function and central to aid effectiveness.[23] 'Small improvements in procurement

17 Department of International Development (DFID), *Procurement Capacity Building: Applying Lessons Learned Elsewhere* (Paris: OECD, 22–23 January 2003), p. 4. This document was presented at the Joint DAC/World Bank Round Table on Strengthening Procurement Capacities in Developing Countries.

18 OECD, *Harmonising Donor Practices for Effective Aid Delivery*, DAC Guidelines and Reference Series (Paris: OECD, 2003).

19 As Evenett has noted, 'developing nations tend to have a sizeable proportion . . . of their non-defense government budgets funded by aid, loans, or grants'. See S. J. Evenett, *Can Developing Countries Benefit from Negotiations on Transparency in Government Procurement in the Doha Round?*, Task Force 9 (Open, Rule-Based Trading System) of the United Nations Millennium Project (2003), p. 1, www.alexandria.unisg.ch/Publikationen/22164 (accessed 13 March 2012).

20 S. J. Evenett and B. Hoekman, *International Cooperation and the Reform of Public Procurement Policies*, World Bank Policy Research Working Paper 3720 (September 2005), p. 7. Evenett and Hoekman point out that '[a]vailable data on the relative importance of aid flows as a share of government expenditure suggest that aid finances a significant share of total purchases of goods and services by developing country governments. The ratio of official aid flows (bi- and multilateral) to total expenditure was equivalent to 35 percent of total expenditures on goods and services for low-income countries in the early 1990s. For lower middle-income nations, total aid accounted for 16 percent of expenditures; for upper middle-income economies the figure dropped to 6 percent.'

21 See the World Bank data in T. Mkandawire, 'Aid, Accountability, and Democracy in Africa' (2010) 77 *Social Research* 1149.

22 European Network on Debt and Development (Eurodad), *For Whose Gain? Procurement, Tied Aid and the Use of Country Systems in Ghana* (2010).

23 OECD/DAC Guidelines, note 18 above.

policy would have large aid-equivalent in payoffs.'[24] Sound procurement practices in the delivery of aid projects and in the spending of aid money are necessary to ensure sustainable development and social and economic objectives. Hence, enhancing the efficiency of development aid procurement[25] is now a top priority for donor and recipient countries.

This chapter will first look into donors' aid procurement practices that have an impact on recipient countries' systems and that influence recipients' procurement markets and the way in which procurement is carried out in these countries. It will look at the international initiatives undertaken to reform donors' aid procurement systems, and it will assess whether donors have been successful in implementing such reforms. The chapter will then investigate donors' role in promoting procurement reforms in developing countries, and will ask whether and how development aid has been used to encourage procurement reforms in developing countries. The analysis ultimately aims at identifying areas where development aid procurement practices could be improved to accelerate progress towards an effective aid procurement market in both recipient and donor countries. It will do this by identifying the main problems that arise in development aid procurement practices and by pointing out the limits of current international initiatives undertaken to solve them.

The chapter is divided as follows. First, after a brief introduction on donors' aid to Africa (section 2), the chapter will analyse donors' aid procurement practices and systems which have a direct influence on recipient countries' procurement systems and discuss what initiatives have been undertaken, under the shield of aid effectiveness, to improve the way aid money is spent (section 3). The chapter continues by investigating what part donors play in supporting procurement reforms in developing countries and how they use development aid to this end (section 4). The chapter will highlight a profound contradiction in donors' behaviour, namely, while donors have both direct and indirect ways of using aid as an incentive for encouraging procurement reforms in developing

24 S. Evenett, 'Size of National Procurement Markets' (University of St Gallen).

25 The term 'development aid procurement' is used here to indicate the purchasing of goods and services required to implement development aid projects financed by government bodies. Although development aid procurement should not be treated differently from other procurement activities of government bodies (and hence should be considered within the realms of general public procurement), in practice procurement practices connected with the purchase of goods needed for the implementation of aid projects seem not to benefit from any of the current features of modern government procurement systems.

countries, they are then reluctant to actually let recipient countries use their reformed systems when it comes to spending the aid money they provide. A final section concludes (section 5).

2. Aid to Africa

Over the past fifty years, aid resources have played an important role in financing development initiatives and projects in developing countries, especially in Africa. Since 1960, Africa has received US$580 billion in aid.[26] Many lament that the conspicuous amount of money disbursed to Africa has little to show by way of results.[27] Africa remains the only continent where none of the Millennium Development Goals will be achieved by 2015, and the lack of substantial progress on development targets has prompted critics to question the value of aid resources and to maintain the argument that aid hinders rather than fosters development.[28] Yet very few authors would argue for the total abolition of foreign aid to the African continent.[29] This is because the continent lacks sufficient domestic resources to achieve an annual growth rate sufficient to attain development objectives, including the Millennium Development Goals.[30] In fact, many call for an increase in the aid donated.[31] Many believe that the lack of success of aid projects is only partly due to ineffective utilisation of aid resources and that the real problem of aid is linked to lack of sufficient resources. It has been suggested that Africa will need to fill an annual resource gap of US$64 billion (equivalent to 12 per cent of GDP), most

26 United Nations Conference on Trade and Development, *Economic Development in Africa Doubling Aid: Making the 'Big Push' Work* (New York and Geneva: United Nations, 2006), www.unctad.org/en/docs/gdsafrica20061_en.pdf (accessed 17 March 2012), p. 14.

27 Williamson, 'Exploring the Failure of Foreign Aid', note 3 above. Even worse, some authors sustain that aid to Africa has only led to corruption and aid dependency: see Moyo, *Dead Aid: Why Aid Is Not Working and How There Is a Better Way for Africa*, note 7 above.

28 See Moyo, *Dead Aid: Why Aid Is Not Working and How There Is a Better Way for Africa*, note 7 above.

29 See the criticism raised against Moyo, *Dead Aid: Why Aid Is Not Working and How There Is a Better Way for Africa*, note 7 above.

30 *Ibid.*, p. 24. Here it is reported that an annual growth rate of 8 per cent is necessary to achieve the Millennium Development Goals in Africa.

31 According to the World Bank an additional US$40–60 billion a year is needed to meet the Millennium Development Goals by 2015. S. Devarajan, M. Miller and E. V. Swanson, 'Development Goals: History, Prospects and Costs', World Bank Policy Research Working Paper No. 2819 (2002), http://papers.ssrn.com/sol3/papers.cfm?abstract_id=636102 (accessed 7 July 2009).

of which will have to come from abroad, in order to achieve development targets.[32]

Aid is the largest source of external financing in many African countries. This is especially the case in countries where other forms of financing are scarce[33] – for example in countries with low tax revenues or remittances, in countries that do not attract private financing or which attract 'predatory' private financing (where transnational corporations mostly exploit developing countries' natural and human resources[34]). Undoubtedly, some countries, especially in Africa, would struggle to survive without donors' aid.

Aid as a percentage of GDP is higher in Africa than in other developing countries, with peaks of 36.4 per cent in 1985–1994, and an average of 24.3 per cent of GDP between 1960–2004; this is 13 points greater than the average registered by developing countries in the same period.[35] Although the level of aid to Africa as a percentage of GDP helps illustrate the key role aid plays in the African continent, this is not to say that Africa is the continent which has received the most aid. In fact, despite the dire needs of the African continent, 'aid to Africa (in current prices) has generally been much lower than that to Asia. Between 1960 and 2004, Asia received some $40 billion more in aid than Africa'.[36]

Aid to Africa was essentially stagnant until the early 1970s and only started to increase due to Cold War tensions. Northern African countries received more aid. Aid to Africa, and to Sub-Sahara Africa in particular, continued to increase in the 1980s, but it suffered a severe downturn in the 1990s up until 2002 when an increase of aid to Africa was registered again.[37] Since 2002, aid to Africa has significantly increased, reaching, in 2009, a total of US$47,609 million. However, as Tables 11.1 and 11.2 show, donors are still a long way from fulfilling the promises made at the

32 NEPAD framework document, reported in United Nations Conference on Trade and Development', note 26 above, p. 24.

33 *Ibid.*

34 The literature on this issue is vast and the cases of exploitation by transnational corporation often attract the media's attention. There could be many reasons why some developing countries are unable to agree favourable terms of investments, for example lack of negotiating power or skills by developing countries' officials, corruption, the lack of an adequate international law framework capable of balancing the business interests of transnational corporations and human rights, and development issues in developing countries.

35 Data reported by Table 3 in United Nations Conference on Trade and Development', note 26 above.

36 *Ibid.*, p. 16. 37 *Ibid.*

Table 11.1 *Aid to Africa by DAC donors, 2002–2009 (US$ million)*

	2002	2003	2004	2005	2006	2007	2008	2009
ODA total, gross disbursements (i.e. the sum of grants, capital subscriptions and gross loans)	15,009.83	21,036.87	22,404.99	27,932.78	34,917.98	27,314.78	30,496.24	31,893.67
ODA total, net disbursements (i.e. the sum of grants, capital subscriptions and net loans (loans extended minus repayments of loan principal and offsetting entries for debt relief))	13,372.2	19,160.54	19,362.21	24,628	31,537.88	24,601.37	27,313.22	28,155.79
ODA total excluding debt (i.e. net ODA disbursements minus net debt relief)	10,284.31	12,482.18	15,032.99	15,759.99	17,035.2	20,931.09	25,340.41	24,265.25
ODA grants, disbursements (this category includes grants and capital subscriptions on a deposit basis to multilateral organisations)	13,770.52	19,575.67	20,274.14	25,984.64	33,049.94	25,063.55	27,758.93	27,103.32
ODA loans gross disbursements	1,239.31	1,461.2	2,130.85	1,948.14	1,868.04	2,251.23	2,737.31	4,790.35

(*cont.*)

Table 11.1 (*cont.*)

	2002	2003	2004	2005	2006	2007	2008	2009
Net debt relief (comprises grants for forgiveness of ODA, OOF or private claims; other action on debt such as debt conversions, debt buybacks or service payments to third parties; and new ODA resulting from concessional rescheduling operations; net of offsetting entries for the cancellation of any ODA principal involved)	3,087.89	6,678.36	4,329.22	8,868.01	14,502.68	3,670.28	1,972.81	3,890.54
ODA grants, commitments (this category includes grants and capital subscriptions on a deposit basis to multilateral organisations)	13,489.39	18,934.4	20,167.31	26,463.9	34,386.88	27,575.57	31,751.12	31,746.25

Note: data extracted on 5 October 2011 from the OECD.StatExtracts website (http://stats.oecd.org/Index.aspx?DatasetCode/ODA_RECIP (last accessed 5 March 2013).

Table 11.2 *Total ODA net disbursed to Africa, by DAC and non-DAC countries, multilateral donors and private donors, 2002–2009*

		2002	2003	2004	2005	2006	2007	2008	2009
All donors, total		21,299.61	27,347.41	29,865.57	35,703.61	43,962.75	39,305.29	43,926.40	47,609.88
All donors, total	DAC countries, total	13,372.2	19,160.54	19,362.21	24,628	31,537.88	24,601.37	27,313.22	28,155.79
	Multilateral, total	7,826.35	7,955.48	10,332.78	10,741.83	11,953.44	14,182.72	16,113.53	19,161.23
	Non-DAC countries, total	101.06	231.39	170.58	333.78	471.43	521.2	499.65	292.86
	Bill and Melinda Gates Foundation	–	–	–	–	–	–	–	624.12
DAC EU Members plus EU institutions, total		10,517.21	14,898.05	16,313.25	20,855.83	25,032.72	20,397.98	21,443.85	21,670.05

Note: data extracted on 5 October 2011 from the OECD.StatExtracts website (http://stats.oecd.org/Index.aspx?DatasetCode/ODA_RECIP (last accessed on 13 March 2012)).

Gleneagles Summit in 2005, when G8 leaders agreed to increase ODA to Africa by 35 per cent over the period from 2005 to 2010, doubling the aid levels compared with those of 2004. This should have led to an increase in official development assistance to Africa of US$25 billion a year by 2010 (again compared with 2004 levels[38]). G8 leaders also promised to eliminate outstanding debts of the poorest countries. However, as a recent report from the Organization of Economic Co-operation and Development (OECD) made clear, several large donors have failed to adhere to their commitments.[39] In 2009, Development Assistance Committee (DAC) countries reduced the volume of aid donated bilaterally compared to the record levels registered in 2006,[40] consideration of the level of aid donated in 2004 reveals that aid to Africa has not doubled as promised.[41]

The vast majority of aid to Africa comes from bilateral donors. In 2009, the level of ODA disbursed bilaterally by OECD/DAC countries[42] reached US$28,155 million.[43] Non-DAC countries donated US$292 million, the Bill and Melinda Gates Foundation gave US$624 million, while multilateral donors granted US$19,161 million (see Table 11.2).

It is worth noting that, although the volume of aid donated by multilateral organisations remains lower than aid donated bilaterally, it has registered significant growth since 2002 (growing in both 2006 and 2009).

38 See www.unmillenniumproject.org/documents/Gleneagles2005_ChairmanSum.pdf (accessed 13 March 2012).

39 OECD, 'Donors' Mixed Aid Performance for 2010 Sparks Concern' (17 February 2010), www.oecd.org/document/20/0,3746,en_2649_34447_44617556_1_1_1_1,00.html (accessed 13 March 2012).

40 Considering that DAC donors are major contributors of multilateral aid agencies, the lower amount of aid donated bilaterally might simply represent a shift of preference by DAC donors in favour of multilateral aid. It is, however, impossible to be sure whether the increase of multilateral aid to Africa is due to more resources being available to multilateral institutions or simply to a shift of funds from one region to the other decided by the multilateral institutions themselves, regardless of the level of funds donated multilaterally by DAC donors.

41 See www.economicsummits.info/2010/03/the-g8-and-international-aid-some-forgotten-promises (accessed 13 March 2012).

42 That is to say, countries members of the Development Assistance Committee (DAC) within the OECD. DAC members are: Australia, Austria, Belgium, Canada, Denmark, Finland, France, Germany, Greece, Ireland, Italy, Japan, Korea, Luxembourg, Netherlands, New Zealand, Norway, Portugal, Spain, Sweden, Switzerland, the United Kingdom, the United States and the European Union.

43 In ODA net disbursements (i.e. the sum of grants, capital subscriptions and loans). ODA gross disbursements (i.e. the sum of grants, capital subscriptions and gross loans) was US$31,893.67 million, http://stats.oecd.org/Index.aspx?DatasetCode=ODA_RECIP.

A look at the 2009 aid disbursement levels also reveals another major problem linked to aid to Africa, namely, aid predictability and the gap between commitments of aid (i.e. donors' promises of aid they will donate) and actual disbursements of aid (i.e. the aid actually given). Table 11.2 offers a detailed account of the various components of aid to Africa by DAC donors (DAC donors are also members of the G8).[44] The data show that in 2009 aid by DAC donors fell more than US$7 million short of the original US$35,930 million aid commitments. The reduction in the volume of aid is probably due to the 2008 financial crisis and the negative effects it had on donors' economic budgets. Some donors, such as Italy, cut their aid budgets as soon as the crisis was felt by their economies, and others (the United States) are now evaluating the possibility of reducing aid volumes. This is alarming considering, on the one hand, economists' forecast that the current state of the world's economy will not register significant improvements in the near future and, on the other, Africa's reliance on aid for its public expenditures. The aid landscape could be drastically different in forthcoming years.[45] Hence, aid agencies are pushed to devise strategies that support broad-based cost-effective development objectives to make shrinking budgets meet growing demands.

3. Donors' aid procurement (mal)practices and their impact on recipient countries' procurement systems and markets

3.1. Introduction

In the aid-effectiveness discourse, great emphasis has been placed on ensuring donors' 'effective expenditures'. This involves efficiency in the aid procurement systems. The following pages will address the issue of how donors' aid practices have influenced recipient countries' procurement systems and markets. It will be shown that major weaknesses linked to donors' aid procurement practices can be found in the donor–recipient aid relationship.

44 Both the data and the legend have been extracted from the OECD website, http://stats.oecd.org/Index.aspx?DatasetCode=ODA_RECIP (accessed 13 March 2012).

45 In the current economic crisis, aid plays a vital role, since access to other forms of financing such as loans and private investment is difficult (private investments are low and partnership with the private sector is difficult). See OECD, 3rd High-Level Forum on Aid Effectiveness (Accra, 2–4 September 2008), www.oecd.org/document/20/0,3343,en_2649_3236398_41201108_1_1_1_1,00.html (accessed 10 March 2012).

Five main areas of analysis are identified, namely, donors' institutional structures, donors' procurement rules, donors' coordination of aid policies and rules (including procurement rules), and donors' imposition of environmental and tied aid conditionality. A final paragraph will deal with current initiatives to achieve aid harmonisation and to phase out tied aid.

It is argued that donors' practices that impose burdens on the aid management capacities of partner countries need to be detected and, at best, reduced to guarantee the success of aid policies.

3.2. Donors' institutional aid structures

Donors are subject to criticism for their complex and bureaucratic aid systems, for the many different typologies of aid projects implemented,[46] and the diversity of agencies and government bodies involved in the decision-making and implementation process of development cooperation policies. Aid policies are often agreed *in concerto* between two or more government departments, and the implementation of aid projects is dislocated between a myriad of aid agencies, some of which work directly from the recipient country in a non-transparent system, operating without clear and common development objectives. This situation is complicated further by the fact that sometimes donors delegate the implementation of aid projects to private entities such as NGOs or delegate the purchase of aid goods to private procurement agencies.

This is the case for many donors' development cooperation systems. For example, the Italian development cooperation system has an intricate administrative structure. The Ministry of Foreign Affairs is responsible for the administration and implementation of aid projects, but it is not solely responsible for deciding what aid projects are to be financed. The procedure for deciding what projects to implement is complex. The Ministry of Foreign Affairs' Technical Units, operating from the recipient country, and the Ministry's Administrative Units, based in Rome, propose which projects to implement; then once a proposal is approved by the Ministry's headquarters level, the project proposal is passed to the Ministry of Finance. The decision to fund a specific project is taken by the

46 In Italy, for instance, bilateral cooperation can be financed through pure grants and soft credits (*interventi a dono* and *crediti di aiuto*). Other forms of bilateral intervention are *fondi in loco*, ODA to NGOs, and debt forgiveness. A critique of the Italian cooperation system can be found at OECD, *Italy: Development Assistance Committee (DAC) Peer Review* (Paris: OECD Publishing, 2000), www.oecd.org (accessed 13 March 2012) which stated that reforms are 'urgently needed'.

Minister of Foreign Affairs together with the Ministry of Finance and with the Inter-ministerial Committee for Economic Planning. Aid disbursements and commitments need to be included in the Financial Law which has to be approved annually by the Parliament. Although the Ministry of Finance does not directly participate in the procurement procedure for selecting the supplier who will perform the aid contract, the actual disbursement of the aid money is only made after the Ministry of Finance approves the aid contract concluded by the procurement agency and the supplier who has been awarded the contracts.[47] This can cause delays in both the implementation of the aid contract and the actual payment to the supplier. This situation is not much different to other donor countries. The United States, for example, has twenty-seven different government agencies dealing with development aid.[48] Similarly, for France, the multiplicity of government departments and agencies involved in development cooperation has been the subject of harsh criticism.[49]

One problem is that the multiplicity of donors' aid agencies drains recipients' administrative capacities. Recipients will need to report to many different aid agencies and will often need to understand and apply different procurement procedures according to the agencies involved.

> Thousands of quarterly project reports are submitted to multiple oversight agencies. Hundreds of missions monitor and evaluate these projects... and each mission expects to meet with recipients' officials.[50]

For example, between 1998 and 2008, Uganda signed grant agreements with fifty-eight donors in total;[51] if every donor had more than one aid

47 The Ministry of Finance also takes care of the relationships with the banks and multilateral funds. The organisational chart of the Ministry of Foreign Affairs is made up of a number of internal units divided according to geographic and thematic scope; adjunct to the internal units are technical units based in recipient countries. The units based at headquarter level need to coordinate their work with the technical units based in the recipient countries. Each unit has a *responsabile di progetto* in charge of monitoring and supervising the aid project. The *responsabile di progetto* coordinates his work with the recipient country.

48 P. Bigart, K. Ejlskov-Jensen and R. Roos, *Strengthening Country Procurement Systems: Results and Opportunities: Report for the OECD/DAC Task Force on Procurement* (forthcoming).

49 See OECD, *France: Development Assistance Committee (DAC) Peer Review* (Paris: OECD Publishing, 2004), www.oecd.org (accessed 13 March 2012).

50 S. Knack and A. Rahman, 'Donor Fragmentation' in W. Easterly (ed.), *Reinventing Foreign Aid* (Cambridge, MA, London: MIT Press, 2008), p. 334.

51 B. Ellmers (Eurodad), *Tapping the Potential? Procurement, Tied Aid and the Use of Country Systems in Uganda* (April 2010).

agency (or twenty-seven agencies, as in the case of the United States), and if they all had a small project in Uganda, the country would have had to deal with as many as 1,566 agencies.[52] In Lesotho in 1981, there were sixty-one donors financing 321 projects. In 2002, there were twenty-five bilateral and nineteen multilateral donors and about 350 NGOs operating in Vietnam, for over 8,000 projects.[53]

The problems seen by the recipient country are also encountered by suppliers based in recipient countries; their capacity to participate in aid procurement opportunities will be significantly undermined by the multiplicity of aid agencies operating in their country. Local suppliers will not be able to familiarise themselves with the different agencies and rules involved and will be at a disadvantage compared to suppliers based in donor countries. If there are too many agencies implementing aid projects, it will be difficult for suppliers willing to participate in aid procurement opportunities to find out, in due time, the basic facts of the aid projects (which are the aid projects funded and where) and of the procurement process (information on opportunities, tender procedures, award notices, etc.).

Donors' complex development cooperation systems hamper the possibility of establishing a sound procurement environment where international, regional and local competition can take place. One can also argue that, if suppliers based in recipient countries are denied the possibility of participating in aid procurement opportunities, they will then be less competitive on the market and will be less capable of taking advantage of the non-aid-financed public procurement market in their own country. Considering that 10–20 per cent of developing countries' GDP is financed by aid, arguably, if the aid rules are not transparent, recipient countries' industries will have a 10–20 per cent smaller procurement market of which they can take advantage.

Furthermore, as Williamson argues, the multiplicity of donors' agencies can breed corruption, as the greater the number of actors involved in the implementation of an aid project the more difficult will it be to hold

52 Although not all of a donor's agencies would be involved in one country at the same time, it is not uncommon for two or more agencies from the same donor to implement projects in the same country at the same time. Over a long period of time (as in our case of ten years), it would not be unrealistic to find that several agencies from the same donor have implemented projects in the same country.

53 The Lesotho and Vietnam examples are both cited in Knack and Rahman, 'Donor Fragmentation', note 50 above, p. 334.

anyone accountable for failures.[54] Corrupted mechanisms developed in the aid sector can easily spread to other procurement activities.

3.3. Donors' aid procurement rules

The problems seen above in respect of donors' institutional structures are magnified by the lack of general rules regulating the aid procurement process. There are no standard rules or practices for determining who will carry out the procurement process – that is, whether the recipient country or the donor (this often varies from donor to donor, and, even within the same donor, there can be differences from project to project) – or for ascertaining what procurement rules will be applied. The situation often changes from donor to donor and from project to project. Even more problematic is the fact that, even within the same donor, a multiplicity of rules and procedures are applied.

As regards the procurement rules applied, donors often insist that developing countries procure aid goods and services following international competitive bidding (ICB) (a procedure involving international advertising in a language widely used, with participation open to both local and international suppliers) or require the use of their own (donors') procurement rules.[55] The latter option is particularly burdensome for the recipient[56] (especially when a multiplicity of donors is involved in the same country). It is often the case that the same donor has different procurement rules according to what type of project is being implemented. Even within the same type of project, there can be variations according to whether the project is financed by one donor or by a multiplicity of donors. Thus, Collier reports:

> Donors often trip over each other and fail to coordinate. I came across one case where three donor agencies each wanted to build a hospital in the same place. They agreed to coordinate, which doesn't always happen, but then faced the problem of having three incompatible sets of rules for how the work should be commissioned. It took them two years to reach a compromise, which was that each agency should build one floor of the

54 Williamson, 'Exploring the Failure of Foreign Aid', note 3 above. See also Knack and Rahman, 'Donor Fragmentation', note 50 above.

55 This is, for example, the case with Italy.

56 Against the use of donor rules and in favour of the use of country systems, see O. McDonald (Christian Aid), *Buying Power: Aid, Governance and Public Procurement* (February 2008).

> hospital under its own rules. You can imagine how efficient that was likely to be.[57]

The World Bank, one of the major multilateral donors, leaves the responsibility for carrying out the procurement process using the Bank's funds to the recipient of those funds[58] (i.e. responsibility for the implementation of the project, award and administration of contracts).[59] However, when carrying out the procurement process, the borrower will have to follow the Bank's Guidelines[60] (which contain a set of principles and rules) as per the loan agreement between the Bank and the borrower.[61] 'The Bank's procurement guidelines are intended to ensure that procurements on Bank-financed projects are carried out efficiently and without corruption.'[62] The Bank will supervise the procedure via its *ex ante*, *in itinere* and *ex post* reviews of the aid project; the detailed Guidelines which the borrowers will have to follow and the thorough controls to which they

57 P. Collier, *The Bottom Billion: Why the Poorest Countries Are Failing and What to Do about It* (Oxford University Press, 2007).

58 On the Wold Bank's procedures, see S. Arrowsmith, J. Linarelli and D. Wallace, *Regulating Public Procurement: National and International Perspectives* (The Hague: Kluwer Law International, 2000). See also T. Tucker, 'A Critical Analysis of the Procurement Procedures of the World Bank' in S. Arrowsmith and A. Davies (eds.), *Public Procurement: Global Revolution* (London: Kluwer Law International, 1998), Chapter 8; J. Verdeaux, 'The World Bank and Public Procurement: Improving Aid Effectiveness and Addressing Corruption' (2006) 6 *Public Procurement Law Review* 131; and, for a more recent study, E. Debevoise and C. Yukins, 'Assessing the World Bank's Proposed Revision of Its Procurement Guidelines' (May 2010) 52(21) *The Government Contractor* 1. Also, for a bibliography on this subject, see S. Arrowsmith (ed.), *Bibliography on Public Procurement Law and Regulation* (University of Nottingham, 2011), p. 83 (available at www.nottingham.ac.uk/pprg/documentsarchive/bibliographies/comprehensivepublicprocurementbibliography.pdf (accessed 2 April 2012)).

59 However, when the Bank feels it cannot rely on national systems for the implementation of the funded project, it will resort to the use of project implementation units using resources from outside the recipient's government.

60 The Wold Bank uses two sets of Guidelines: *Guidelines: Procurement of Goods, Works, and Non-Consulting Services under IBRD Loans and IDA Credits and Grants* (January 2011), which cover the procurement of goods, works and work-related services (the Procurement Guidelines); and *Guidelines on the Selection and Employment of Consultants* (January 2011), which cover the procurement of consultancy services (the Consultant Guidelines) by the World Bank. The Guidelines can be found at http://web.worldbank.org/WBSITE/EXTERNAL/PROJECTS/PROCUREMENT/0,,contentMDK:20060840~pagePK:84269~piPK:60001558~theSitePK:84266,00.html (accessed 2 April 2012).

61 The relationship between the Bank and the borrower is governed by the loan agreement which also incorporates the Bank's guidelines.

62 Debevoise and Yukins, 'Assessing the World Bank's Proposed Revision of Its Procurement Guidelines', note 58 above.

are subjected have led some authors to argue that the Bank maintains *de facto* strong control over the procurement process.[63]

As regards the procurement rules applied, for complex and high-value contracts the Bank requires the use of international competitive bidding (ICB), while for the procurement of lower value contracts the Bank often allows the use of the so-called national competitive bidding (NCB) procedure, in which the Bank relies on the national procurement systems of the recipient country and allows the use of national procurement law. However, even when NCB is followed, the recipient will have to respect certain principles set by the Bank – for example, no eligibility restrictions based on the nationality of the bidder and/or the origin of goods can be applied.

The OECD, through various studies conducted in recipient countries, has shown that a number of failings in terms of aid effectiveness and recipients' ownership of aid[64] are caused by the multitude of public procurement procedures specific to each donor. This is especially problematic when recipient countries have newly reformed systems of procurement.[65] Although the donors' and the recipient government's procurement procedures often have common objectives and principles, the donors' procurement procedures are very different to those of the recipient in terms of the devolution of decision-making power to local agencies, procurement thresholds and specific awards and payment methods.[66]

Only rarely do donors let the recipient country use its own procurement rules, as is explained further below in section 4 on the use of country systems. As we will see there, despite the emphasis placed on the use of partners' country systems by the Paris Declaration and the Accra Agenda for Action (AAA), and the recognition that 'bypassing country systems reduces the sustainability of development programs and undermines a partner country's capacity to manage its own development agenda',[67] the use of country systems has not increased to any significant extent in recent years. International institutions such as the World Bank and

63 Arrowsmith, Linarelli and Wallace, *Regulating Public Procurement*, note 58 above, p. 111.

64 See, for example, OECD/DAC, *The Mali Donors' Public Procurement Procedures: Towards Harmonisation with the National Law* (Paris: OECD Publishing, 2000), report summary, p. 2, www.oecd.org/pdf/M00038000/M00038097.pdf (accessed 13 March 2012).

65 *Ibid.* The OECD study suggests that to remedy this situation the easiest choice would be to align with national procedures.

66 *Ibid.*

67 N. Coulson, 'Using Country Systems – Is It All or Nothing?' (1 April 2011), www.unpcdc.org/forum.aspx?g=posts&t=19 (accessed 13 March 2012).

the OECD have been especially vocal in promoting harmonisation of aid procurement practices. However, the latest OECD/DAC survey on implementing the Paris Declaration shows just:

> a moderate increase in the use of partner country's procurement systems by donors over time. For the 32 countries participating in both the 2006 and 2011 Surveys, use of country procurement systems increased from 40% of aid [ODA granted to developing countries] for the government sector in 2005, to 43% in 2007 and 44% in 2010.[68]

As explained above, the multiplicity of aid agencies and of procurement procedures reduces the possibility for bidders to bring actions against breach of procurement rules and undermines the capacity of monitoring entities within the recipient country to verify the correct implementation of the procurement process. This induces the development of practices which do not comply with transparency standards and modern anti-corruption policies. The lack of transparency also risks favouring concealed discriminatory practices which place recipient countries' industries in a disadvantaged position to win aid contracts.

3.4. International initiatives to improve coordination and harmonisation of donors' aid policies

Promoting coherence between development policies and coordination between donors to avoid the problems analysed above are, undoubtedly, major challenges for international donors.[69] Even a small project can have significant effects if it is harmoniously coordinated and followed by the cooperation of all international donors. Lack of coordination between poverty-alleviation initiatives, on the other hand, can lead to inefficiency and to an inability to reach desired goals. For years, donors have supported a large number of unsuccessful individual activities in developing countries; hence, it comes as no surprise that, under the shield of the aid-effectiveness initiatives, one of the major initiatives has been aimed at harmonising and coordinating donors' aid policies.

A landmark event in the aid harmonisation process has been the High Level Forum on Harmonisation (held in Rome in 2003). The overall purpose of this forum was to 'secure broad donor and country support for

68 OECD, *Aid Effectiveness 2005–10: Progress in Implementing the Paris Declaration* (Paris: OECD Publishing, 2011), www.oecd.org (accessed 13 March 2012).

69 See the Aid Harmonization website for more on the harmonisation initiative, www.aidharmonization.org (accessed 13 March 2012).

shifting harmonisation efforts from institutional analysis and diagnosis to voluntary in-country prioritisation, adaptation, implementation and monitoring'.[70]

The Paris Declaration on aid effectiveness also dedicates five paragraphs (paragraphs 32–6) to donors' aid harmonisation. Donors commit to devise common arrangements for planning, funding and monitoring (paragraph 32.2), to reduce the number of duplicative missions and simplify and harmonise procedures (paragraphs 32.3 and 35), to reduce the fragmentation of aid (paragraph 33) while partners commit to provide clear views on donors' comparative advantages (paragraph 34). Both donors and partners commit to reform procedures and provide incentives for staff to work towards 'harmonisation, alignment and results' (paragraph 36). Finally, the commitment to harmonise donors' aid policies has been reiterated by the AAA. Paragraph 17 of the AAA reads:

> [T]he effectiveness of aid is reduced when there are too many duplicating initiatives, especially at country and sector levels. We will reduce the fragmentation of aid by improving the complementarity of donors' efforts and the division of labour among donors, including through improved allocation of resources within sectors, within countries, and across countries.

In some countries, aid harmonisation initiatives have given rise to interesting results in terms of division of labour among donors. Some donors have agreed to designate a lead donor agency to carry out the aid project and administer all other donors' aid money (this has been especially the case at the EU level). Other initiatives to enhance coordination between donors include the launch, in pivotal countries, of a Comprehensive Development Framework (CDF). This initiative aims at bringing together external partners to finance countries' development programmes, rather than conducting numerous individual projects. Assessments of countries where the CDF projects have been experienced are very positive both in terms of deepened coordination and of facilitating recipients' ownership.[71]

Another significant initiative has been undertaken by the Nordic+ Group of donors (Denmark, Finland, Ireland, the Netherlands, Norway, Sweden and the United Kingdom), who have together published a joint

70 See the Documents: Statements from the High Level Forum on Harmonisation, including the Rome Declaration on Harmonisation, www.oecd.org/pdf/M00040000/M00040106.pdf (accessed 13 March 2012). The Rome forum was followed by the Paris Declaration, which is broader than the former and includes harmonisation as one of its objectives.

71 P. Quartey, 'Innovative Ways of Making Aid Effective in Ghana: Tied Aid versus Direct Budgetary Support' (2005) 17 *Journal of International Development* 1077.

action plan aimed at closer harmonisation amongst group members. The plan endorsed by the Nordic+ Group provides for donors to harmonise their aid procurement systems and rules, and to align procurement to partner systems whenever a partner has the appropriate procurement capacity (key policy principle 2.2).

The peculiarity of all the above initiatives is that donors, although coordinating their work, remain responsible for the aid project, and the coordination aspect consists either in the fact that one donor takes the lead in conducting the project or in the fact that the same (donor) rules are applied.

In terms of enhancing cooperation and coordination between donors, the Paris Declaration went a step further than all other initiatives by requiring the use of recipients' country systems for the purchase of aid goods and services and by requiring donors to provide aid as budget support. If aid projects are to be nationally owned, then they should be carried out by the recipient country itself using its own country systems. The Rome and Paris Declarations have given rise to some important initiatives. For example, in Ghana, nine donors agreed to develop the Multi-Donor Budgetary Support Programme (MDBS) which provides budget support to the government of Ghana to implement the second phase of Ghana's Poverty Reduction Strategy (GPRS II). In 2009, a second MDBS was agreed between the government of Ghana and thirteen donors, with the second MDBS donors committing to provide to Ghana US$380 million as budget support.[72]

However, successful stories remain few. The 2011 survey on monitoring the Paris Declaration revealed that in 2010 only 22 per cent of donors' missions were coordinated in the countries participating in the survey, a 2 per cent decrease compared to the level registered in the 2008 survey.[73] The percentage of aid donated as budget support and the use of country systems also remains low, and, as we will see in the next section, the results published in 2008 and 2011 of the pilot projects conducted to assess the implementation of the Paris Declaration are disappointing in this respect.

72 See B. Ellmers (Eurodad), *Tapping the Potential? Procurement, Tied Aid and the Use of Country Systems in Uganda* (April 2010).

73 OECD/DAC, *Aid Effectiveness 2005–10: Progress in Implementing the Paris Declaration*, note 68 above. Thirty-two countries participated in the 2006, 2008 and 2010 Survey on Monitoring the Paris Declaration. Seventy-eight countries participated in the most recent survey. The data reported here refer to the thirty-two countries who participated in all the surveys.

3.5. *Tied aid conditionality*

Another way in which donors influence the aid procurement process is by imposing tied aid conditionality – that is, aid with strings attached. 'Tied aid' refers to aid[74] provided on the condition that goods and services for the aid-financed projects are purchased only from the donor country.[75] When the aid is *formally tied*, the recipient country, in order to receive the grant or the loan, has no other choice but to fulfil the condition imposed by the donor country, even when it would be more convenient to acquire the goods or the services elsewhere. Aid is informally tied when there are no express conditions but the aid is tied in practice because there are no transparent procedures for the relevant procurement. Aid is considered partially tied when eligibility for the procurement process is limited to suppliers and goods originating in specific countries – usually including the donor and all or some developing countries. According to the OECD's definition,[76] aid can be considered partially tied only when suppliers and goods from all developing countries are eligible for the aid tender. However, not all donors agree with the latter definition of partially tied aid and regard aid to be partially tied also when procurement opportunities are open to the donors' industries and goods and to some (but not all) recipient countries' industries, usually including the recipient of the aid and neighbouring developing countries (often limited to a certain region).

Tied aid undermines the effectiveness of aid because it leads to higher costs paid for the goods purchased[77] and to the distortion of the nature of the aid itself, by securing aid for projects that do not meet recipients' real

74 The DAC, *Glossary of Development Terms*, defines 'aid' as flows which qualify as Official Development Assistance (ODA) or Official Aid (OA), www.oecd.org/glossary/0,2586,en_2649_33721_1965693_1_1_1_1,00.html#1965580 (accessed 13 March 2012). See also O. Morrisey and H. White, *How Concessional Is Tied Aid?*, CREDIT Research Paper 93/13 (2003), p. 4.

75 Aid is usually tied when donors grant it bilaterally.

76 OECD/DAC, Statistical Reporting Directives, DC/DAC/(200)10, and in the DAC, *Glossary of Development Terms*, www.oecd.org/glossary/0,2586,en_2649_33721_1965693_1_1_1_1,00.html#1965580 (accessed 13 March 2012).

77 OECD studies demonstrate that tying aid induces a price increase of the goods purchased of between 15 and 30 per cent, to which higher transportation and administrative costs must also be added. See OECD, *Policy Brief: Untying Aid to the Least Developed Countries* (Paris: OECD Publishing, 2001), p. 2, www.oecd.org/pdf/M00006000/M00006938.pdf (13 March 2012). For an extensive account of the effects of tied aid, see C. J. Jepma, *Inter-Nation Policy Co-ordination and Untying of Aid* (Aldershot: Avebury, 1994); and J. Chinnock and S. Collinson, *Purchasing Power: Aid Untying, Targeted Procurement and Poverty Reduction* (ActionAid, 1999).

needs but provide opportunities for the donor's industries.[78] Tied aid also greatly influences developing countries' procurement systems and markets. As Evenett has argued, because a considerable part of developing countries' procurement is financed through aid, loans or grants '[t]o the extent that such aid is tied to purchases from firms in a donor country, then this diminishes the size of the *contestable* national procurement market, and arguably also comes at some cost to the recipient nation'.[79] Tied aid also hampers policy coordination amongst donors. Aid granted from different donors to the same sector often results in incompatible equipment, which requires complex spare parts and training arrangements. For instance, a survey in Kenya found more than sixteen different kinds of water pump in use, each funded by a different donor country.[80]

Economists have concluded that it is very unlikely that aid tying produces benefits for donor economies[81] and it merely serves to undermine the effectiveness of the aid granted. Requiring goods and services to be bought from the donor's industry precludes the recipient country from benefiting from the best value goods and services available in the global and/or local market. When the aid is tied, even the aid-recipient's own competitive industries lose the opportunity to bid for the aid contract. This frustrates the potential of aid to strengthen a recipient country's own domestic market and to foster trade between developing countries – in many of these countries, public bodies and, in particular, aid-financed projects are major potential outlets for trade between neighbouring states. The effects of tied aid on the recipient country might sometimes go beyond the original aid projects; for instance, when the recipient is required to undertake maintenance contracts linked to the original goods or services purchased, these contracts might not always be the cheapest and most convenient option.

Despite its negative effects, tying aid is a well-established practice. Although important initiatives on untying aid have been agreed at the international level (such as the OECD/DAC Recommendation on untying

78 The Caxiguana field station in Brazil is one of these examples. See N. Baird, 'Tied to the Hand That Feeds' (1996) 2051 *New Scientist* 12.

79 Evenett, *Can Developing Countries Benefit from Negotiations on Transparency in Government Procurement in the Doha Round?*, note 19 above, pp. 1–2 (original emphasis).

80 *Ibid.*, p. 13.

81 See L. Tajoli, 'The Impact of Tied Aid on Trade Flows between Donor and Recipient Countries' (1999) 8 *Journal of International Trade and Economic Development* 371, 374. See also Jepma, *Inter-Nation Policy Co-ordination and Untying of Aid*, note 77 above; and Morrissey and White, *How Concessional Is Tied Aid?*, note 74 above.

aid to least developed countries (LDCs) and highly indebted poor countries (HIPCs)[82]), an overwhelming portion of the aid donated continues to be either formally or informally tied.[83]

While donors are always responsible for setting up the tied condition, the actual implementation of the tied condition itself (through the procurement process) can take place in different ways. Specifically, some donors carry out the procurement process themselves while others require the beneficiary country to carry out the procurement.[84] However, even when the recipient carries out the procurement process, given the economic dependence of the beneficiary, the donor maintains strong control over the procurement; although the beneficiary is formally responsible for the procedure and is party to the contract, it is often not free to use its own procurement rules, or to set the conditions of the contract.

The Paris Declaration recognises that untying aid increases aid effectiveness and exhorts donors to continue to make progress on untying aid (paragraph 31). However, little actual progress has been achieved under its auspices. Thus far, the major international effort to untie aid remains the adoption, in 2001, of the OECD/DAC Recommendation on untying aid to LDCs and HIPCs (as modified in 2006 and 2008); no significant further efforts have been undertaken to untie aid since then.[85] However, the OECD Recommendation excludes from its coverage food aid, technical cooperation and all aid granted to developing countries which are

82 The most important initiative in this field is the OECD, *DAC Recommendation on Untying ODA to the Least Developed Countries* (2001). This Recommendation was replaced with the OECD, *DAC Recommendation on Untying ODA to the Least Developed Countries and Heavily Indebted Poor Countries* (July 2008).

83 E. Clay, M. Geddes, L. Natali and D. Willem te Velde, *The Developmental Effectiveness of Untied Aid: Evaluation of the Paris Declaration* (London: Official Development Institute, 2008).

84 See, for instance, Italian commodity aid to Egypt, tender notice NR. PS14TER/03/06: the tender was to be submitted by 10 July 2006, the procurement process was carried out by the government of Egypt and access to procurement opportunities was limited to Italian goods only. See A. La Chimia, 'L'Aiuto Legato Italiano e la Raccomandazione DAC/OECD sullo Slegamento degli Aiuti ai Paesi Meno Avanzati' in M. Zupi (ed.), *La Trasparenza degli Aiuti Internazionali: Il Caso Italiano* (CESPI, 2004), pp. 103–32. More examples of tied aid can be found on the Italian Ministry of Foreign Affairs' website, www.esteri.it/ita/4_28_66_73_23_6.asp (accessed 13 March 2012). France and Spain implement tied aid in a similar way: see K. Outterside, B. Vazquez, A. La Chimia and A. Sneider, *Study on the Further Untying of European Aid* (2004) funded by EC Commission DG Development.

85 On the limits of the DAC Recommendation, see La Chimia, 'L'Aiuto Legato Italiano e la Raccomandazione DAC/OECD sullo Slegamento degli Aiuti ai Paesi Meno Avanzati', note 84 above.

not classified as LDCs or HIPCs (only fifty-two countries are classified as LDCs and another six are HIPCs), covering only 12 per cent of total aid. Hence, the OECD Recommendation, although an important step towards untying aid, is very limited in scope.[86] Besides, the OECD Recommendation is not legally binding; its implementation relies on the goodwill of states, the effectiveness of peer pressure and the OECD/DAC monitoring role.[87] Recent OECD studies show that most OECD countries implement the OECD Recommendation and use the OECD bulletin board, where the untied aid projects and procurement notices are advertised.[88] OECD studies also show that donors have not decreased the level of aid granted as a result of the implementation of the OECD Recommendation.[89] This is certainly good news for the untying debate which suggests that coordination of donors' efforts at the international level has the power to bring about positive results, achieving the target of untying aid while not decreasing the level of aid granted. However, because of its limited coverage, the Recommendation represents only a first step towards untying aid.

As regards food aid, while it has been excluded from the OECD Recommendation, food aid policies are being discussed within the WTO framework for reforming agricultural trade. It is in light of the WTO negotiations on agriculture that the OECD decided not to include food aid within the coverage of the OECD Recommendation. However, the food aid negotiations are suffering from the current impasse faced by the WTO Doha Round of trade negotiations, and the negotiations on untying food aid dealt with under the WTO negotiations for reforming agricultural trade are not advancing.

3.6. Environmental conditionality in the aid procurement process

Some donors, including, surprisingly, some NGOs, have recently advocated the inclusion of environmental and climate-change standards in the aid procurement process, for example by requiring that a certain

86 For an analysis of the 2001 DAC Recommendation, see A. La Chimia, 'International Steps to Untie Aid: The OECD/DAC Recommendation' (2004) 13 *Public Procurement Law Review* 1.

87 *Ibid.*

88 See the OECD website, www.oecd.org (accessed 13 March 2012).

89 OECD, *Implementing the 2001 DAC Recommendation on Untying ODA to the Least Developed Countries: 2005 Progress Report* (2005). This report is available on the OECD website, www.oecd.org (accessed 13 March 2012).

percentage, or the whole of, certain aid contracts are reserved for enterprises that meet environmental/climate-change standards, or giving price preferences to suppliers who meet environmental/climate-change standards. The use of procurement to promote so-called horizontal/secondary policies[90] is common in public procurement generally.[91] While the inclusion of environmental objectives/criteria in the procurement process is now an established phenomenon, the inclusion of environmental/climate-change policies in the aid procurement process is a more recent and unexplored phenomenon, which seems to be expanding.

Thus, NGOs have called for the inclusion of environmental criteria in the aid procurement process,[92] and even for the establishment of a debarment mechanism for enterprises that breach environmental standards.[93]

Although, as far as this author is aware, environmental criteria have not yet been included in the aid procurement process by any specific donor, they have already been considered by international soft law instruments. For example, the OECD Recommendation for untying aid (as updated in 2008) states at paragraph 16:

> [T]hose responsible for procurement should promote respect from suppliers with agreed international standards of corporate social responsibility and environmental behaviour. This could be done through reference to environmental and social considerations in tendering procedures.

If such policies are imposed by the donor country who is directly or indirectly responsible for the procurement process, it is questionable whether developing countries' industries will be ready to implement such policies and to compete on equal grounds with donors' enterprises. Hence, including these requirements could have negative, protectionist, effects which would go against, amongst other things, even the principles and the spirit of the United Nations Framework Convention on Climate Change (see Article 3(5) thereof) which encourages developed countries to take the lead in fighting the environmental problems created by climate change. Further, apart from any consideration linked to the effectiveness

90 Horizontal/secondary policies are policy objectives other than the objective of the acquisition of goods/services on the best possible terms; for example, a national government may pursue social or environmental objectives through its public procurement. See S. Arrowsmith, 'Public Procurement as an Instrument of Policy and the Impact of Market Liberalisation' (1995) 111 *Law Quarterly Review* 235.

91 *Ibid.*

92 See, for example, B. Ellmers (Eurodad), *Tapping the Potential? Procurement, Tied Aid and the Use of Country Systems in Uganda* (April 2010).

93 *Ibid.*, p. 25.

of such policies (which are not limited to the aid procurement process but apply equally when these policies are pursued in any public procurement process),[94] there is a real question of whether recipient countries and donor agencies are really able to monitor the correct implementation of such criteria when they are implemented in an aid project given the multiplicity of rules applied and of agencies involved.

It is submitted that only recipient countries should decide whether to make environmental and climate-change criteria part of the aid procurement process: such policies should be recipient- not donor-driven because only the recipient of the aid is in a position to know whether enterprises in its country can take advantage of these conditions on an equal footing with donors' industries.

4. Donors, aid effectiveness and public procurement reforms in recipient countries

4.1. Introduction

Bilateral and multilateral donors have been and are heavily involved in the processes of reforming national procurement systems in developing countries. Procurement reforms in developing countries have been linked to enhancing trade liberalisation, good governance, capacity building, anti-corruption and, more recently, aid effectiveness and development. The Johannesburg forum on developing a framework on effective procurement systems in developing countries recognised that improvements in the performance of public procurement systems will (among other things) facilitate 'harmonisation and aid effectiveness'.[95] Efficient and effective procurement is an essential element of good governance, which in turn is a 'key driver of economic growth and development'.[96] The emerging message is that 'effective procurement systems are a key part of development'.[97]

94 On this, see Arrowsmith, 'Public Procurement as an Instrument of Policy and the Impact of Market Liberalisation', note 90 above.

95 See 'A Framework for Developing Effective Procurement Systems in Developing Countries: The Johannesburg Declaration' (December 2004), p. 1.

96 The Cusco Declaration of the OECD/DAC Task Force on Procurement, 'Strong Procurement Systems for Effective States' (May 2011), p. 1.

97 United Nations Development Programme, *The Second Meeting of the OECD/DAC Task Force on Procurement, May 4–6 2011 – Cusco, Peru: Summary of the Meeting by the UN Procurement Capacity Development Centre* (2011), p. 2, www.unpcdc.org/media/218131/pcdc_notes_-_2nd_meeting_oecd-dac_task_force_on_procurement_in_cusco_may-2011.pdf (accessed 13 March 2012).

However, albeit that it is widely acknowledged that reforming developing countries' procurement practices is vital for fostering development, it is very difficult to pull off.[98] Leading procurement experts have explored why this is the case and how the obstacles to procurement reforms could be overcome. Hunja, for example, has explained that the reluctance to reform the public procurement systems in developing countries is due to 'deeply vested interests and lack of political will', 'paucity of technical knowledge and capacity, complexity of substantive issues involved' including the types of legal instruments involved, different means of organising procurement functions, and enforcement-related matters.[99]

The solutions proposed by the literature to overcome the obstacles to procurement reforms could be classified into endogenous and exogenous stimuli (or 'commitment mechanisms'[100]) used to kick-start the reforms. Within the category of endogenous stimuli, one could locate Hunja's proposal for implementing such reforms 'within the context of an existing package of reforms aimed at increasing the efficiency of the public sector'.[101] Hunja argues that procurement reforms would fit well into any such programme aimed at reforming governance and are bound to attract 'less direct opposition if it is part of a large reform effort'.[102] A system of good governance applying broadly across the public sector is certainly vital for successful procurement reforms and *vice versa*, i.e. once a country is in the process of implementing a good governance initiative it should deal with its procurement system, or the reforms cannot be deemed completed. One error made in the past by multilateral aid agencies when financing procurement reforms in developing countries was to focus their efforts solely on the procurement system rather than involving the entire system of governance of the country. It is now clear that it is impossible to

98 Evenett, *Can Developing Countries Benefit from Negotiations on Transparency in Government Procurement in the Doha Round?*, note 19 above. See also R. Hunja, 'Obstacles to Public Procurement Reform in Developing Countries' in S. Arrowsmith and M. Trybus (eds.), *Public Procurement: The Continuing Revolution* (London: Kluwer Law International, 2003), Chapter 2.

99 Hunja, 'Obstacles to Public Procurement Reform in Developing Countries', note 98 above.

100 See K. Dawar and S. J. Evenett, 'A Case Study of Regionalism: The EC–CARIFORUM Economic Partnership' in S. Arrowsmith and R. Anderson (eds.), *The WTO Regime on Government Procurement: Challenge and Reforms* (Cambridge University Press, 2011), p. 675. The authors do not explicitly refer to the classification proposed here, but they do refer to international and regional agreements and aid agencies as exogenous commitment mechanism see below in this text.

101 Hunja, 'Obstacles to Public Procurement Reform in Developing Countries', note 99 above.

102 *Ibid.*

expect successful procurement reforms if the entire system of governance is not also involved in the reform process: for example, fighting corruption in the public procurement process is very difficult if the judicial system in charge of reviewing procurement decisions is corrupted. However, good governance initiatives are also difficult to implement especially when the reform process is imposed externally by multilateral institutions and development banks with little or no accountability to local people and communities.[103]

Evenett argues that 'an alternative means for improving procurement practices is in the context of an international trade agreement'.[104] Dawar and Evenett suggest that, 'through effective negotiations, regional and international agreements can serve as a commitment mechanism to incorporate appropriate developmental and social policies while promoting the economic and welfare benefits of transparent and fair procurement systems'.[105] Hence international and regional agreements can act as exogenous stimuli for the reforms. This has proven successful for some countries (for example, for EU member states and EU candidate countries). However, developing countries, and African countries in particular, are notoriously reluctant to join international and regional agreements on procurement.[106]

Within the context of exogenous stimuli for kick-starting procurement reforms one should include development aid, aid agencies and development banks.[107] Development aid is used by donors, directly and indirectly, as an important incentive to reform developing countries' public procurement systems.

A recent survey conducted for the Task Force on Procurement by Pamela Bigart, Kirsten Ejlskov-Jensen and Rita Roos reveals that interviewed countries had indicated as one of the most common factors to kick-start procurement reforms 'donor pressure, or donor assessments

103 Anne Orford offers a brilliant analysis of participatory development and critically assesses World Bank and IMF interventions on governance in developing countries. See A. Orford, 'Globalisation and the Right to Development' in P. Alston (ed.), *People's Rights: The State of the Art* (Oxford University Press, 2001), pp. 127, 150.

104 Evenett, *Can Developing Countries Benefit from Negotiations on Transparency in Government Procurement in the Doha Round?*, note 19 above.

105 Dawar and Evenett, 'A Case Study of Regionalism', note 100 above.

106 The EC–CARIFORUM Economic Partnership agreement is the only EPA which includes procurement provisions. These provisions remain very limited in scope and coverage. For a detailed analysis of the EC–CARIFORUM agreement, see Dawar and Evenett, 'A Case Study of Regionalism', note 100 above.

107 *Ibid.*, p. 673.

that reveal weaknesses in the system'.[108] The survey also makes known that amongst the incentives to initiate procurement reforms, the developing countries interviewed listed 'to satisfy the demands of donors', and 56 per cent of them said 'their reforms had been prioritised jointly with donors'.[109]

As part of the initiatives on enhancing aid effectiveness first launched in Monterrey in 2002,[110] great emphasis has been placed on encouraging donors to support, through aid, countries that have in place good development plans and that have implemented effective country system reforms. Recent examples of donors' activities in this field include the 2003 OECD and the World Bank joint initiative to form a procurement roundtable focused on strengthening procurement capacity in developing countries (the roundtable now includes bilateral and multilateral donors and recipient countries). Other examples include the Joint Venture on Procurement and the task Force on Procurement, operating under the chapeau of the Working Party on Aid Effectiveness (WP-EFF) and the Global Country Systems Cluster.[111]

However, donors do not limit their influence on recipient countries' procurement to participating in international initiatives on procurement reforms. Donors' influence is mostly felt at country level where donors act, directly, as major triggers of the reform process by financing such reforms[112] through the means of development aid, and, indirectly, by promising to developing countries that they will grant aid as budget support or they will procure the aid goods using recipients' procurement systems if the recipient has in place good procurement systems. The prospect of being able to use the aid in the way recipients see fit is used as

108 Bigart, Ejlskov-Jensen and Roos, *Strengthening Country Procurement Systems*, note 48 above, p. 8.

109 *Ibid.*

110 The first call to enhance aid effectiveness was made in Monterrey (2002) at the United Nations Conference on Financing for Development (see United Nations, *Report of the International Conference on Financing for Development* (18–22 March 2002), UN Doc. A/CONF 198/11), followed by the High Level Forums on Aid Harmonisation in Rome (2003) and Paris (2005), which have resulted in a growing consensus on some key principles (embodied in the Paris Declaration on Aid Effectiveness (adopted 2 March 2005), www.oecd.org/dataoecd/11/41/34428351.pdf) – for effective development policies, namely, ownership, partnership, alignment, harmonisation and coordination of donors, management for results and mutual accountability.

111 Bigart, Ejlskov-Jensen and Roos, *Strengthening Country Procurement Systems* note 48 above, p. 2.

112 *Ibid.*

an incentive by donors to encourage the implementation of procurement reform.

The following pages will investigate both the direct and the indirect ways of using development aid as a stimulus for procurement reform in developing countries.

4.2. Donors' direct influence: funding procurement reforms

Donors have committed to assist developing countries to implement procurement reforms and to provide 'sufficient resources to support and sustain medium and long-term procurement reforms and capacity development'.[113]

Since the early 1990s, many initiatives have been undertaken by donors to incentivise developing countries to reform their procurement systems. For example, the World Bank's Country Procurement Assessment Reports (CPARs) have helped set in motion many of the procurement reforms in developing countries. Most of the procurement reforms implemented in Ghana, for example, followed the recommendation given by the World Bank-led CPAR.[114] As a result, 'Ghana's procurement policies and practices have increasingly become a copy of best practices as defined by the [World Bank]'.[115] The World Bank itself (often in association with the IMF) has granted Programmatic and Adjustment loans to many developing countries on condition that structural reforms,[116] including public procurement reforms, were put in place[117] (these reforms being based on the UNCITRAL Model Law on procurement). Both multilateral and

113 The Arusha Statement of the OECD/DAC Joint Venture on Procurement: 'To Support the Implementation of the Paris Declaration Principles by Building Reliable Public Procurement Systems' (May 2008), para. 3, points ii and iii.

114 See Chapter 4 of this volume, on Ghana.

115 B. Ellmers (Eurodad), *Tapping the Potential? Procurement, Tied Aid and the Use of Country Systems in Uganda* (April 2010).

116 On the pros and cons of the World Bank's reforms, see World Bank, *Review of World Bank Conditionality*, issues note (Washington DC: World Bank, 2006), http://siteresources.worldbank.org/PROJECTS/Resources/REVIEWOFBANKCONDITIONALITYJan3105.pdf, pp. 8 and 16. This study shows that a very high number of policy-conditions can be attached to the Bank's loans; for example, it is reported that thirty-five conditions were attached to the Turkey III Programmatic Financial and Public Sector Structural Adjustment Loan, and thirty-one to the Argentina Economic Recovery Support Structural Adjustment Loan (*ibid.*, p. 16 note 39); and S. Devarajan, D. Dollar and T. Holmgren, *Aid and Reform in Africa from Ten Case Studies* (Washington DC: World Bank, 2001).

117 See the World Bank website, www.worldbank.org (accessed 13 March 2012).

bilateral donors continue to finance recipient countries' reforms of their procurement systems.

The study by Bigart, Ejlskov-Jensen and Roos mentioned above reports that 38 per cent of the twenty-three countries analysed had their public procurement reforms financed by donors.[118] The OECD creditor reporting system shows that, since the Paris Declaration, donors' support for public financial management increased more than threefold, for a total of US$644.5 million for all developing countries in 2008.[119] Hence, development aid plays a direct and central role in stimulating the reform process because it is used to finance such reforms.

Unfortunately, however, donors often fail to coordinate their efforts even in this sector. Thus, the study by Bigart, Ejlskov-Jensen and Roos reveals that, in more than one-third of the countries studied, more than one donor is involved in financing the procurement reforms, and donors do not always coordinate their efforts with each other.[120]

4.3. *Indirect ways of influencing procurement reforms*

There are often indirect ways in which donors can influence procurement reforms in developing countries. One such way is to promise to donate aid as budget support when donors deem recipients' systems, including the procurement system, suitable to ensure the aid will be well spent. Aid granted as budget support is not linked to the implementation of a specific project, but is donated directly to the recipient country government and goes to its general budget. Hence when recipient countries receive aid as budget support, they can use the aid as they think best for their country. Authors report that, in countries where aid granted as budget support has increased considerably in recent years, donors have exercised enormous pressure for recipients to implement public financial management and procurement reforms.[121]

Another indirect way of encouraging developing countries to reform their procurement systems is for donors to allow the use of recipient

118 Bigart, Ejlskov-Jensen and Roos, *Strengthening Country Procurement Systems*, note 48 above, p. 8.
119 See the OECD website, www.oecd.org.uk (accessed 13 March 2012).
120 Bigart, Ejlskov-Jensen and Roos, *Strengthening Country Procurement Systems*, note 48 above, p. 8.
121 B. Ellmers (Eurodad), *Tapping the Potential? Procurement, Tied Aid and the Use of Country Systems in Uganda* (April 2010).

countries' systems when aid goods are purchased, provided that recipients' procurement systems are deemed to comply with suitable standards.

The Paris Declaration first, and the Accra Agenda for Action (AAA) later, have placed special emphasis on encouraging donors to let recipient countries use their country systems when implementing aid projects. The use of country systems facilitates the alignment of aid allocation to national priorities and strategies. In the Paris Declaration, developing countries committed to strengthen their systems (including their procurement systems) and donors committed to use those systems to the maximum extent possible.

However, the possibility of using country systems as a means to enhance aid effectiveness is conditional on recipients' procurement systems being able to ensure that the aid will be spent for the 'agreed purposes' (paragraph 17 of the Paris Declaration) and to the systems conforming to 'mutually agreed'[122] standards and processes (i.e. mutually agreed between donor and recipient) (paragraphs 28, 18 and 19). Only when these two conditions are met will recipient countries be able to lead the aid procurement process. The AAA further establishes that '[d]eveloping countries and donors will jointly assess the quality of country systems in a country-led process using mutually agreed diagnostic tools'.[123]

Central to the use of a country system is the requirement that recipient countries have an adequate procurement system, the latter often involving a transparent, competitive, efficient and non-corrupt procurement system. In many developing countries, fulfilment of the above criteria will require the implementation of significant procurement reforms. A detailed methodology for assessing the suitability of a recipient's procurement system has been developed by the OECD (i.e. the Methodology for Assessing Procurement Systems (MAPS), the latest version of which was released in 2010).[124] The methodology is developed around four pillars: 'a) the existing legal framework that regulates procurement in the country; b) the institutional architecture of the system; c) the operation of the system and competitiveness of the national market; and d) the integrity of the procurement system. Each pillar has a number of indicators and sub-indicators to be assessed.'[125]

122 For criticism of these 'mutually agreed standards', see A. La Chimia, *From Monterrey to Bussan, via Paris and Rome* (forthcoming).

123 Para. 15 of the AAA.

124 OECD, Methodology for Assessing Procurement Systems (MAPS) (February 2010), www.oecd.org/dataoecd/50/33/45181522.pdf.

125 *Ibid.*, p. 3.

When recipient countries' systems do not meet the 'mutually' agreed quality standards (and, one could argue, do not satisfy donors' expectation), recipients are encouraged to implement procurement reforms.

Hence, recipient countries have an incentive to reform their procurement system in view of the possibility to use their country systems when purchasing aid goods and services. 'If countries own a set of procurement rules and procedures that would satisfy all donors, the system could then be used to administer donor-financed procurement',[126] with substantial savings in terms of transaction costs but, most importantly, with significant benefits for scaling up development by 'improving all government expenditures not just those funded by donors'.[127]

The World Bank has been one of the major promoters of the use of country systems. In 2008, the Bank launched a Pilot Program for Use of Country Procurement Systems, and this scheme was formally approved by the Bank's Board on 24 April 2008. Twenty countries expressed interest in participating in the pilot programme, fourteen of which made substantial progress, and four countries completed all stages of the selective process and were chosen by the Bank to participate in the pilot, namely, Rwanda, Senegal, Mauritius and Brazil (state of São Paulo).[128] However, after criticism of the effectiveness of the scheme, and of the methodology used to assess the countries,[129] the pilot scheme seems now to have been abandoned by the Bank.[130]

Regrettably, donors do not seem to meet the promises made within the Paris Declaration. The first survey on implementing the Paris Declaration (released in 2008) showed that progress towards the use of country systems was very slow and, 'even when there are good-quality country systems, donors often do not use them, despite the recognition that using country

126 *Summary of the Meeting by the UN Procurement Capacity Development Centre*, note 97 above.

127 *Ibid.*

128 Information available at http://web.worldbank.org/WBSITE/EXTERNAL/PROJECTS/PROCUREMENT/0,,contentMDK:22968216~pagePK:84269~piPK:60001558~theSitePK:84266~isCURL:Y,00.html; see also Wold Bank, *Piloing Program in the Use of Country Procurement Systems Second Progress Report*, http://siteresources.worldbank.org/INTPROCUREMENT/Resources/278019-1311363656902/UCS_Second_Progress_Report_(Final_version)_(22_Dec_2010).pdf.

129 See, for example, C. Pallas and J. Wood, 'The World Bank's Use of Country Systems for Procurement: A Good Idea Gone Bad?' (2009) 27(2) *Development Policy Review* 215.

130 Interviews conducted by this author with World Bank procurement officials in August 2011. The author is grateful to the British Academy for funding the trip to Washington as part of her British Academy-funded project, 'Food Aid on Both Sides of the Atlantic'.

systems promotes their development'. After the disappointing findings in 2008, in Accra donors agreed, in order to strengthen and increase the use of country systems, 'to use country systems as the first option for aid programmes' (AAA, paragraph 15, point a). If donors choose to use another option and 'rely on aid delivery mechanisms outside country systems (including parallel project implementation units), they must transparently state the rationale for this and review their positions at regular intervals' (AAA, paragraph 15, point b).

Unfortunately, despite the further efforts in Accra, the 2011 survey on monitoring the Paris Declaration shows that progress on this front continues to be disappointing.[131] (The 2011 Survey is a useful source of information on the use of country systems, and, together with the Guidance to the Survey,[132] can help in monitoring donors' implementation of their Paris and Accra commitments.)

The report by Bigart, Ejlskov-Jensen and Roos, which includes data on the use of country systems for twenty-three countries also confirms the findings of the 2011 survey, and notes that:

> 60% of countries report that donors do not use the national procurement system in their country. In cases where donors use the national system it is, for the most part, limited to contracts below certain thresholds and/or with additional safeguards such as prior and/or post-reviews.[133]

Many NGO studies also denounce the fact that donors are not fulfilling their promises of using country systems, despite the fact that many of the countries studied had implemented procurement reforms.[134]

131 OECD/DAC, *Aid Effectiveness 2005–10: Progress in Implementing the Paris Declaration* (Paris: OECD, 2011), www.oecd.org/document/1/0,3746,en_2649_3236398_48725569_1_1_1_1,00.html (accessed 25 April 2012).

132 As explained by the survey Guidance (hereafter the guidance), the question asked in the survey in relation to the use of national procurement system was the following: 'Q12: In Calendar year 2010, how much ODA disbursed for the government sector used national procurement systems?' The Guidance also explains that indicator QD12 in the survey 'focuses on the use of national procurement systems when funding is provided for the government sector. It measures the volume of aid that uses national country procurement system as a percent of total aid provided for the government sector' (*Survey on Monitoring the Paris Declaration Fourth High Level Forum on Aid Effectiveness, Survey Guidance* (2011), www.oecd.org/dac/pdsurvey (accessed 11 March 2012)).

133 Bigart, Ejlskov-Jensen and Roos, *Strengthening Country Procurement Systems*, note 48 above, p. 9. The report also notes that this data contrasts with 'the results of the 2008 Paris Declaration Monitoring Survey which reported only 3 countries with no use of country procurement systems (and none of those three are respondents in this survey)'.

134 See, for example, B. Ellmers (Eurodad), *Tapping the Potential? Procurement, Tied Aid and the Use of Country Systems in Uganda* (April 2010).

Eight of the nine African countries studied in the present volume (that is, all except Zimbabwe) have provided data to the OECD on the use of country systems (the data are released by the OECD.StatExtract, Survey on Monitoring the Paris Declaration[135]). OECD.StatExtract reports, in value terms, the amount of ODA granted by donors and disbursed for the government sector, which made use of the recipient's national procurement systems. The data collected reflect those in the 2011 survey, and a legend for the data and guidance on their meaning can be found in the 2011 survey Guidance. As regards the use of country systems, the Guidance specifies that the aim of the survey was to measure the volume of aid that used national country procurement system as a percentage of total aid provided for the government sector.

It appears that OECD.StatExtract contains data for more countries than those released in the 2011 survey. For example, in the 2011 survey, no data are provided for South Africa, while in OECD.StatExtract such data are available – and for this reason the data released by OECD.StatExtract will be used.

In this section, we will mainly look at data related to the use of recipients' country systems. Table 11.3 reproduces the data published on OECD.StatExtract for eight of the countries studied in this collection, relating to the amount of aid procurement granted for the government sector which has been spent using country systems. An analysis of the data will help reveal trends and inconsistencies between donors on the use of country systems in the eight selected countries and gives an indication of the reliance by donors on those country systems.

As already mentioned above, country systems are used when the recipient's national system meets agreed standards and is deemed suitable for undertaking the procurement effectively, and the most popular methodology used to ascertain whether recipients' systems are suitable is the MAPS methodology developed by the OECD. It might be assumed that, once a system is deemed suitable in one country, all donors would use it, and, at the very least, one would expect consistencies of approach between individual donors. Unfortunately, however, the literature and the data available reveal a different picture, and they show that there are inconsistencies of approach between donors.

For example, the World Bank and the United Nations make extensive use of the country system in Nigeria, while the African Development Bank, a donor that seems to use country systems significantly in other countries, does not use the Nigerian country system. Another example

135 See http://stats.oecd.org/Index.aspx?DataSetCode=SURVEYDATA#.

Table 11.3 *Aid procurement granted for the government sector which has been spent using country systems, 2010 (US$ million)*

Partner country	Botswana	Ethiopia	Ghana	Kenya	Namibia	Nigeria	Rwanda	South Africa
African Development Bank	–	64.372022	45.9	38.811256	–	0	18.525779	0
Austria	–	5.403973	–	–	–	–	–	–
Belgium	–	–	–	–	–	–	52.772223	2.87135
Canada	–	18.636698	70.468165	0	–	0	0	7.126726
Denmark	–	–	73.265192	10.96	–	–	–	0
EU institutions	32.34	146.084647	60.658901	0	0	0	80.035594	160.631466
Finland	–	10.568	–	3.293286	0	–	–	–
France	0	1.43965	45.349803	97.905296	–	0	0	0.810214
GAVI Alliance	–	0	0	0	–	–	0	–
GEF	–	–	–	–	–	–	–	0
Germany	–	10.33	27.40634	44.472562	0.88511	–	29.632532	10.564372
Global Fund	2.051655	230.702237	56.974274	0	15.097668	–	137.050722	35.955281
Greece	–	0	–	–	–	–	–	–
Hungary	–	–	–	–	–	–	–	0
IFAD	–	15.542	11.483486	8.842914	–	–	15.082629	–
IOM	–	–	0	–	–	–	–	0
Ireland	–	27.761112	–	–	–	–	–	4.449031
Italy	–	3.296634	0.7	1.818448	–	0	–	0
Japan	0	6.563355	19.781221	34.53	–	0	6.836828	0
Korea	–	0	0	0	–	0	0	–
Netherlands	–	0	69.036171	0	–	–	33.110013	5.017398

New Zealand	–	–	–	–	–	–	–	0
Norway	–	3.536597	–	0.56084	–	–	–	2.919437
OFID	–	–	–	–	–	–	5.855585	–
Spain	–	22.248158	0	–	0	–	–	0
Sweden	–	0	–	14.331757	–	–	7.628893	0
Switzerland	–	–	9.329602	–	–	–	1.080459	0
United Kingdom	–	337.273806	104.898772	6.109067	–	0	95.158436	4.776215
United Nations	1.113984	15.642261	26.324066	36.45	5.332	48.774487	29.863014	0
United States	–	17.500384	3	2.5	0.007423	1.343	0	38.629216
World Bank	0	588.943721	179.460143	35.392344	0	507.52344	164.577984	5.203316
Other donors	–	–	–	–	–	–	–	0
Total	35.505639	1525.845255	804.036136	335.97777	21.322201	557.640927	677.210691	278.954024

Note: data extracted on 5 October 2011 from OECD Stat (http://stats.oecd.org/wbos/index.aspx (last aaccessed 13 March 2012)).

is the fact that the United States make significant use of the country system only in South Africa and (but to a much more limited extent) in Ethiopia; but it does not use country systems significantly in any of the other eight countries studied here despite other donors doing so (for example, in Ghana, the vast majority of donors use the country system, but the United States does not).[136]

Conclusions based on the OECD.StatExtract data need to be treated with caution, and verified from other sources including other data provided by the OECD.StatExtract itself. For example, given that OECD.StatExtract's data on the use of country systems indicate how much aid provided by the government sector uses the country system, to ascertain if use of the country system by one donor is significant it is necessary to know how much aid that donor disbursed for the government sector. For example, Sweden does not use the country system in Ethiopia, but data reveals that Sweden did not actually grant any aid to Ethiopia in the government sector. The same, however, cannot be said for the African Development Bank in Nigeria: the African Development Bank did grant aid to Nigeria for the government sector but simply did not use Nigeria's country system.

It would probably enhance transparency and make the monitoring mechanism more immediate if the OECD.StatExtract released data revealing directly the percentage of government-sector, and total, aid which uses country systems. Although parallel tables published by the OECD itself indicate this, researchers outside the organisation cannot be sure whether the data used for the comparison are the exact same data used by OECD.StatExtract to compile the survey.[137]

5. Concluding remarks

After the criticism raised regarding development aid, new standards and targets have been set to better govern aid policies and projects. Governments, civil society, NGOs and international organisations are all responsible for defining and tackling the problems of aid policies.

136 This is despite the conspicuous amount of money disbursed in those countries by the United States for the government sector. See data on Q3 of the survey at http://stats.oecd.org/Index.aspx?QueryId=34514.

137 Such specific data as this are not easily available to the public and are not (in such detail) published on the OECD website.

Whatever the position endorsed in respect of aid policies, whether constructive or destructive criticism, it remains a fact that aid continues to be donated and, most likely, will be so for a few more years to come. Although the international community is willing to deal with aid effectiveness and to tackle donors' and recipients' practices that have hampered aid success, turning intentions into practice requires more than just debates and high-level forums on aid effectiveness.

Pivotal to the aid-effectiveness debate has been the work on donors' and recipients' procurement practices. Many of the aid-effectiveness goals relate to public procurement. Improving the public procurement sector and development aid procurement can give important results. Small improvements in the aid procurement process can lead to large savings.

The central aim of many aid procurement initiatives is to ensure effective expenditure, fostering ownership of the aid granted through enhanced capacity building, and improving coordination of donors' aid policies to ensure a better partnership between donor and recipient countries.

Donors have many direct and indirect ways of influencing recipient countries' procurement systems. Donors can negatively affect the procurement capacities of developing countries' administrative departments and of local suppliers via complex aid procurement systems and rules. Donors can also act as major triggers of procurement reforms in developing countries, directly, by funding the reforms, and, indirectly, by exercising pressure on developing countries' governments to implement such reforms and by promising to relinquish control of aid funds if the recipient's procurement system is efficient and transparent. While some donor initiatives have produced positive results in developing countries by encouraging reforms of their procurement systems, many problems still remain.

Improvements in the aid procurement systems are needed both in donor and in recipient countries. Donors' practices such as tied aid, which hamper aid success, need to be identified and removed, while recipient countries should reform their procurement systems so as to take full responsibility for, and advantage of, aid funds. The disbursement of aid resources (especially of aid as budget support) has been linked to efficient, transparent and open procurement systems. However, even when recipient countries have implemented procurement reforms, donors remain reluctant to let those recipient countries take full control of the aid procurement process. Recent studies show that donors seldom grant aid as budget support or let the recipient country use their procurement rules and systems when aid funds are at stake.

A consensus has emerged on the need to institute a new partnership for development between developed and developing countries. No battle against poverty can be won without developing countries' active collaboration.[138] Strengthening donor and recipient countries' procurement capacities in the delivery of aid projects would be an important step towards improving the success of aid policies.

138 Maxwell and Riddell suggest that the above would be a sign of strong partnership. See S. Maxwell and R. Riddell, 'Conditionality or Contract: Perspectives on Partnership for Development' (1998) 10 *Journal of International Development* 257.

12

Procurement methods in the public procurement systems of Africa

ELINOR CABORN AND SUE ARROWSMITH

1. Introduction

Public procurement systems generally provide for a variety of different methods – or award procedures, as they are sometimes called – for awarding procurement contracts.[1] These generally range from open tendering, under which all interested and qualified firms may tender, to single-source (or direct) contracting, whereby the procuring entity is permitted to approach a single supplier and award a contract without competition. Procurement methods are at the heart of any public procurement system. Conditions justifying the use of the permitted methods along with the procedural rules for each often form the largest part of any regulatory framework. Thus, for example, over half of the provisions in the UNCITRAL Model Law on Public Procurement[2] (the '2011 Model Law') are concerned with procurement methods and their associated procedures. They are also one of the most visible parts of any public procurement system, governing the key interaction between buyers and suppliers and providing the most visible demonstration of the use, or of course absence, of competition and transparency.

This chapter draws on a number of regulatory frameworks to provide an overview of the procurement methods of certain regulatory systems in Africa and of the influences which have shaped those methods. In the latter respect, we will see that the work of UNCITRAL (the United Nations Commission on International Trade Law), in particular, has had a substantial impact through its 1994 Model Law on Procurement of Goods,

1 See generally S. Arrowsmith, J. Linarelli and D. Wallace, *Regulating Public Procurement: National and International Perspectives* (The Hague: Kluwer Law International, 2000), p. 856.

2 The UNCITRAL Model Law on Public Procurement, adopted 1 July 2011, available at www.uncitral.org/uncitral/uncitral_texts/procurement_infrastructure/2011Model.html. On this, see further section 2 below.

Construction and Services. As we explain below, a revised version of the Model Law was adopted in 2011, and, given the practical importance of UNCITRAL's work for Africa, we will note some of its key revisions that might influence procurement methods in future.

The national frameworks considered are those covered more generally in this book, plus others of which the authors have experience or knowledge. These are mainly (although not exclusively) those of the Anglophone African countries. It is quite possible for reasons related to the differing heritage of the Anglophone countries and of other African countries that the former group are not representative of the continent as a whole. Nevertheless, the analysis provides a starting point for considering this subject in an area in which the current literature is very limited, and it is hoped that it will inspire further research and analysis in both the countries covered and other African countries.

The focus is on the methods that are specifically provided for in the national regulatory frameworks of African countries, for use when those detailed national frameworks apply. However, it is important to mention at the outset that many procurements undertaken by government bodies in Africa or on their behalf do not in fact take place in accordance with those frameworks, but under separate rules imposed by donors who fund the procurement. In view of the importance of this scenario, it is common for African legal regimes to provide specifically for an exception to the usual procurement methods to accommodate donor requirements for use of different procedural rules.[3] The relevant provisions are generally modelled on Article 3 of the 1994 UNCITRAL Model Law;[4] this provides that, to the extent that the provisions of the national rules conflict with, *inter alia*, an agreement entered into between the enacting state and an intergovernmental international financing institution, the requirements of the agreement are to prevail. This phenomenon and the problems to which it gives rise, such as the need for procurement officers to become familiar with various different systems of procurement methods, are discussed in Chapter 11 of this volume.

The present chapter is organised as follows. First, we will consider the various different influences on procurement methods in Africa, including the influence of the UNCITRAL Model Law (section 2). We will then

3 For examples, see Chapter 2, section 2.3; Chapter 3, section 3.2; Chapter 5, section 2.4; and Public Procurement Act 2011 (Swaziland), s. 5.

4 On this, see further section 2.1 below. A parallel provision is found in Art. 3 of the 2011 Model Law.

provide an overview of the tendering methods used for most types of procurement, namely: (i) the default method of open tendering and (ii) the various exceptional methods that sometimes apply, such as two-stage tendering and single-source procurement (section 3). We will then note briefly a distinction sometimes found in the methods above between international and national methods (section 4). We then outline the methods for procurement of consultancy services, which is often treated differently from other procurement (section 5). The next section then considers three related issues that may be relevant for many types of procurement, namely, procurement of common use items, use of supplier lists and use of framework agreements (section 6). Finally, we consider very briefly the subject of electronic procurement (section 7), and make some general concluding remarks (section 8).

2. Influences on procurement methods in Africa

2.1. The UNCITRAL Model Law on procurement

It is useful to begin by considering the key influences that have shaped this area of the law in African countries. Perhaps the most striking feature of the regulatory frameworks in this area is that they often closely follow the 1994 UNCITRAL Model Law.[5] Model laws on procurement have been

5 Available at www.uncitral.org/uncitral/en/uncitral_texts/procurement_infrastructure/1994Model.html. On the role and nature of the Model Law and the 1993 and 1994 Model Law, see further S. Arrowsmith and C. Nicholas, 'The UNCITRAL Model Law on Procurement: Past, Present and Future' in S. Arrowsmith and J. Tillipman (eds.), *Public Procurement Regulation in the 21st Century: Reform of the UNCITRAL Model Law on Procurement* (Eagan, MN: West, 2010), Chapter 1; S. Arrowsmith, 'Public Procurement: An Appraisal of the UNCITRAL Model Law as a Global Standard' (2004) 53 *International and Comparative Law Quarterly* 17; A. Beviglia-Zampetti, 'The UNCITRAL Model Law on Procurement of Goods, Construction and Services' in B. Hoekman and P. Mavroidis (eds.), *Law and Policy in Public Purchasing* (Ann Arbor, MI: University of Michigan Press, 1997), Chapter 15; R. Hunja, 'The UNCITRAL Model Law on Procurement of Goods, Construction and Services and Its Impact on Procurement Reform' in S. Arrowsmith and A. Davies (eds.), *Public Procurement Global Revolution* (London: Kluwer Law International, 1998), Chapter 5; J. Myers, 'UNCITRAL Model Law on Procurement' (1993) 21 *International Business Lawyer* 179; D. Wallace, 'UNCITRAL: Reform of the Model Procurement Law' (2006) 35 *Public Contract Law Journal* 485; D. Wallace, 'The UN Model Law on Procurement' (1992) 1 *Public Procurement Law Review* 406; M. Dischendorfer, 'The UNCITRAL Model Law on Procurement: How Does It Reconcile the Theoretical Goal of Total Objectivity with the Practical Requirement for Some Degree of Subjectivity?' (2003) 12 *Public Procurement Law Review* 100: G. Westring, 'Multilateral and Unilateral Procurement Regimes: To Which Camp Does the Model Law Belong?' (1994) 3 *Public Procurement Law*

developed by UNCITRAL as part of its remit of promoting international trade through the standardisation of commercial laws. They have provided a template for use by states that are developing or reforming their national rules on public procurement, drawing on the wide experiences of procurement regulation around the world, and have two important functions: they avoid the need for states to reinvent the wheel by designing or reforming procurement regimes 'from scratch'; and they also help states to improve the quality of their procurement legislation by drawing on the collective global experience of regulation.[6] The first Model Law on procurement was adopted in 1993,[7] but covered only goods and works, to allow for rapid conclusion of an initial text without the complexity of considering services. A second Model Law was adopted soon afterwards, however, in 1994,[8] that also included rules on procurement of services. It is this 1994 version of the Model Law that is mainly reflected in the current laws in many African countries. As explained further below, a new version of the Model Law was adopted in 2011,[9] but there has not yet been time for this new version of the Model Law to have much impact.

It is important to note that the Model Law is purely a model to assist states and is not a legally binding document. However, as La Chimia explains in Chapter 11 of this volume, there is often pressure to base procurement laws on the Model Law in developing countries, in that many of the legal reforms in the area of procurement are financed, or otherwise influenced, by international development banks such as the World Bank that have required or encouraged use of the Model Law.[10] Whilst the original conception of the Model Law was as an instrument for all countries – and indeed it can be an instrument of trade from a truly global perspective only through such an approach – in practice

Review 142; S. Arrowsmith (ed.), *Public Procurement Regulation: An Introduction*, available at www.nottingham.ac.uk, *passim*; Arrowsmith, Wallace and Linarelli, *Regulating Public Procurement*, note 1 above, *passim*.

6 Arrowsmith (ed.), *Public Procurement Regulation: An Introduction*, note 5 above, section 1.8.

7 Model Law on the Procurement of Goods and Construction (1993), available at www.uncitral.org/uncitral/en/uncitral_texts/procurement_infrastructure/1993Model.html.

8 UNCITRAL Model Law on the Procurement of Goods, Construction and Services (1994), available at www.uncitral.org/uncitral/en/uncitral_texts/procurement_infrastructure/1994Model.html ('1994 Model Law').

9 Model Law on Public Procurement (2011), note 2 above ('2011 Model Law'). For an overview, see C. Nicholas, 'The 2011 UNCITRAL Model Law on Public Procurement' (2012) 21 *Public Procurement Law Review* NA111.

10 See Chapter 11, section 4.2.

it has been used by, and perceived as relevant for, mainly developing countries and transition economies, and this role was emphasised in the Guide to Enactment that was produced to accompany the 1994 Model Law.[11]

Thus, amongst the twenty-nine countries recorded by the UNCITRAL Secretariat as at 10 March 2012 as having legislative texts based on or largely inspired by the 1994 Model Law, there are eleven in Africa – Gambia, Ghana, Kenya, Madagascar, Malawi, Mauritius, Nigeria, Rwanda, Uganda, Tanzania and Zambia.[12] The positions in this regard of Ghana, Kenya, Nigeria and Rwanda are considered respectively in Chapters 4, 5, 7 and 8 of this volume. The influence of the Model Law in Africa is in fact, however, even greater than this. Thus, many countries use the Model Law directly without notifying the UNCITRAL Secretariat, and many regulatory frameworks have also been influenced by those of neighbouring countries, indirectly extending UNCITRAL's influence. Thus, as explained in Chapter 2, for example, Botswana's procurement regulations borrowed heavily from the regulatory framework in Uganda, which is itself listed by the UNCITRAL Secretariat as having legislation inspired by the 1994 Model Law, and, whilst the law of Botswana is not so closely based on the Model Law as that of many other African states, it does have similarities in some areas, including procurement methods.[13] The Model Law has also played an important role under the public procurement project of COMESA (see section 2.3 below). Thus, according to Karangizi and Ndahiro, '[a] key pillar of reform [under the COMESA project] was universal acceptance of the United Nations Commission on International Trade Law (UNCITRAL) Model Law as the basic guiding text for all member states'.[14] As Chapter 3 explains, the methods of procurement provided for in the law of Ethiopia, for example, which is a COMESA member, are based on those of the 1994 Model Law although that country, like Botswana, does not appear in UNCITRAL's list. (In this

11 Guide to Enactment of UNCITRAL Model Law on Procurement of Goods, Construction and Services, available at www.uncitral.org/pdf/english/texts/procurem/ml-procurement/ml-procure.pdf; Introduction, para. 3. On this subject, see generally Arrowsmith, 'Public Procurement: An Appraisal of the UNCITRAL Model Law as a Global Standard', note 5 above.

12 UNCITRAL Secretariat, www.uncitral.org/uncitral/en/uncitral_texts/procurement_infrastructure/1994Model_status.html.

13 See Chapter 2, section 2.4.

14 S. R. Karangizi and I. Ndahiro, 'Public Procurement Reforms and Development in the Eastern and Southern Africa Region' in R. Hérnandez Garcia (ed.), *International Public Procurement: A Guide to Best Practice* (London: Globe Law and Business, 2009), p. 114.

case, as also in Kenya, for example, reforms based to a significant degree on the Model Law actually commenced before the start of COMESA's own project launched in 2002, but the use of the Model Law allowed for consistency with the approach chosen by COMESA). Swaziland, another COMESA member that does not appear in UNCITRAL's list, does not specify all permitted procurement methods in its law, leaving all but the preferred methods of procurement to secondary legislation, but the methods contained in its public procurement regulations are based on those in the 1994 Model Law.[15]

Not all countries in Africa, however, have been influenced in a substantial way in their tendering methods by the Model Law: of the countries covered in this book, this is the case with Namibia and South Africa. These provide (like the Model Law) for open tendering as a general rule but, as is explained further below, in contrast with states using the UNCITRAL approach, regulate in only a very limited way the use of other methods of procurement. The legislation of Zimbabwe – which, as we have seen, is a COMESA member – is interesting, in that the 'open' method of procurement for major contracts and alternative methods that are available for lower value contracts and in certain other cases, which are described in section 4 of Chapter 10, appear in their general design, nomenclature and conditions for use not to have been influenced by the Model Law. However, as is also explained there, the legislation of that country provides for further regulations to be made to regulate procurement of central government under the main Act on this subject – which itself sets out the above methods – specifically on the basis of the provisions of the 1994 Model Law.

In those countries that have been substantially influenced by the Model Law, the methods for the procurement of goods and works for the most part follow the Model Law's approach (although as we will see, without incorporating all of the alternative, more informal, methods contained in the model that are available when it is not feasible to formulate detailed specifications).[16] The focus is thus on formal and open tendering, which is provided by the Model Law as the main method of procurement,

15 S. 42 of the Public Procurement Act 2011; Part 7 of the Regulations on Public Procurement. The Regulations are expected to retain the same procurement methods when updated for issue under the new Public Procurement Act.

16 Two-stage tendering, request for proposals and competitive negotiation: see section 3.6 below.

supplemented by additional methods for low-value and single-source procurement. As explained further below, many African countries also follow the 1994 Model Law's general approach of providing alternative methods for the procurement of consultancy services. On the other hand, we will also see that even those states that are in general influenced by the Model Law often adopt an approach which differs significantly in detail from that of the Model Law in the area of consultancy services, based more on the approach adopted under World Bank guidelines than that adopted under the Model Law.

As mentioned briefly above, in 2011 UNCITRAL adopted a new Model Law in this field, the Model Law on Public Procurement. This resulted from a reform project launched in 2004[17] that aimed both to update the Model Law in light of new developments – notably the growth of electronic commerce – and to improve the existing provisions in light of experience. The main changes affecting procurement methods are explored below, and concern three main issues: adjustment to the structure and details of these methods, in light of experience; introduction of the concept of framework agreements; and introduction of electronic auctions, both as a separate procurement method and as a phase in conducting certain other procurement methods. It is too early to predict how these changes will affect procurement legislation in Africa. Thus, it is not clear whether states – or donors – will find it necessary or appropriate to adjust the details of existing methods to the new Model Law, or whether the new Model Law will provide a catalyst for introducing new approaches through framework agreements or auctions, and how successful these might be in practice. However, it is interesting that a recent review of the procurement regulatory framework in Uganda which was initiated by that country's Public Procurement and Disposal of Public Assets Authority (PPDA), and involved one of the co-authors of this chapter,[18] considered whether to adopt any new provisions from the 2011 Model Law but included only one minor amendment.[19] In particular, the view was taken that Uganda

17 See generally Arrowsmith and Tillipman (eds.), *Public Procurement Regulation in the 21st Century*, note 5 above; S. Arrowsmith, 'Public Procurement: An Appraisal of the UNCITRAL Model Law as a Global Standard', note 5 above.

18 Elinor Caborn, working for Crown Agents under a contract with the government of Uganda to provide consultancy services for amendment of the Public Procurement and Disposal of Public Assets Regulations, Standard Bidding Documents and Guidelines.

19 The addition of a requirement to publish a notice of procurement when using restricted tendering on the ground of availability from only a limited number of sources, in line

was not ready to introduce new approaches, including electronic auctions, before adopting a wider e-procurement strategy; and it was also decided not to add regulatory provisions on framework agreements – which were already permitted in certain forms but addressed in binding guidelines issued by the PPDA rather than primary or secondary law.

2.2. The development banks

We mentioned in the introduction to this chapter that procurements funded by third parties, including the World Bank and other development banks, are often required to be conducted using methods of procurement laid down by the funders themselves rather than those set out in national laws. Of particular importance in this respect, both because of the extent of the funding the World Bank provides and because of its influence on the policy of other institutions, are the World Bank Guidelines.[20]

In addition to this, the content of national procurement laws themselves has sometimes been influenced by the procurement methods in the Guidelines of the World Bank and other institutions.

One reason for this is that, given the number of development-bank-financed projects in developing African economies, their procurement guidelines are familiar to many procurement staff; in a region where procurement capacity is often limited, such expertise as does exist has often developed in Project Implementation Units applying donor guidelines. Both national and international consultants involved in procurement reform programmes may have developed their procurement skills in a project environment and they will tend to favour those methods they know best when developing national regulatory frameworks. Even where alternative methods are considered, in environments of weak

with Art. 34(5) of the 2011 Model Law, although the Model Law applies this requirement to all grounds for restricted tendering and to direct solicitation under other methods, rather than just to these limited circumstances. See further section 3.2. This requirement was not included in legislation, but in draft regulations, which were not finalised at the time of writing.

20 *Guidelines: Procurement of Goods, Works, and Non-Consulting Services under IBRD Loans and IDA Credits and Grants by World Bank Borrowers* (World Bank, January 2011); and *Guidelines: Selection and Employment of Consultants under IBRD Loans and IDA Credits and Grants by World Bank Borrowers* (World Bank, January 2011), available with relevant guidance at http://web.worldbank.org/WBSITE/EXTERNAL/PROJECTS/PROCUREMENT.

capacity it often makes sense to use the most familiar rules as a starting point.

Secondly, as we have already mentioned, the World Bank and other institutions remain significant influencers of any reform process. This applies both when they are funding the reform process and when they are not – even in the latter case they will often comment on draft bills and regulations and may include conditionalities relating to introduction of procurement legislation in other loans or credits, particularly where a country is seeking increased use of direct budgetary support. In exercising their influence, as well as requiring or encouraging use of the Model Law as a basis for reform, the development banks often seek to ensure that borrower countries adopt procurement methods similar to those in their own guidelines in certain areas.

This influence can be seen, for example, in the area of consultancy services where, as described in section 5 below, a number of states that make widespread use of the 1994 UNCITRAL Model Law for most of their law on procurement methods use the approach to selecting consultants that is found in the World Bank's guidelines rather than that provided for in the Model Law. It is also apparent in the distinction made in some states between national and international bidding[21] and also in terminology used in some national procurement systems which, for example, refer to direct contracting rather than (as in the Model Law) to single-source procurement,[22] or to bidding rather than tendering.

2.3. Other influences: applicable trade agreements and the influence of 'foreign' systems

Procurement systems in many countries around the world have been influenced either substantially or to some lesser degree by the need to comply with trade agreements that open up public markets to international trade.[23] In many cases, these are legally binding and require states to use specified procurement procedures. These trade agreements have tended to have a significant focus on procurement methods, as well as (in

21 See section 4 below. 22 See section 3.5 below.

23 On the extent and nature of such trade agreements, see, in particular, R. D. Anderson, A. C. Müller, K. Osei-Lah, J. P. De Leon and P. Pelletier, 'Government Procurement Provisions in Regional Trade Agreements: A Stepping Stone to GPA Accession?' in S. Arrowsmith and R. D. Anderson (eds.), *The WTO Regime on Government Procurement: Challenge and Reform* (Cambridge University Press, 2011), Chapter 20.

some cases) on supplier remedies. In this respect, the WTO's Agreement on Government Procurement (GPA)[24] has either provided the basis for, or influenced to some degree, the procurement rules of many states, either directly, because they are parties to the Agreement (which is optional for WTO member states), or indirectly, because its rules have been used as the basis of other trade agreements.[25] There are also many important regional agreements. In some countries, such as the United Kingdom (where the procurement regime is based almost entirely on EU law), these agreements are the main source of any legal rules on public procurement, including rules on procurement methods.[26]

In this respect, it can be noted that no African country is yet a party to the GPA, or even has 'observer' status, and that particular agreement has had little impact. However, the Common Market for Eastern and Southern Africa (COMESA), an organisation of nineteen countries including four covered in the present study (Ethiopia, Kenya, Rwanda and Zimbabwe), which is focused on trade and regional integration, commenced a reform project on public procurement in 2002.[27] This aimed at the general improvement of public procurement systems and capacity across the whole spectrum of procurement activity, as well as enhancement of competition and awareness of opportunities between the industries of member countries. Whilst, unlike some trade initiatives, it was not focused specifically on regulating methods, this area was covered as one dimension of the programme.[28]

24 As to which, see generally S. Arrowsmith, *Government Procurement in the World Trade Organization* (The Hague: Kluwer Law International, 2003); Arrowsmith and Anderson (eds.), *The WTO Regime on Government Procurement*', note 23 above; A. Gelbrich, *Regulation of Government Procurement within the WTO – Procurement Policies and Multilateral Trade Rules* (Saarbrücken: VDM Verlag Dr Mueller, 2008); A. Reich, *International Public Procurement Law* (The Hague: Kluwer Law International, 1999); and, for the most recent developments, R. Anderson, 'The Conclusion of the Renegotiation of the WTO Agreement on Government Procurement in December 2011: What It Means for the Agreement and for the World Economy' (2012) 21 *Public Procurement Law Review* 83.

25 See Anderson, Müller, Osei-Lah, De Leon and Pelletier, 'Government Procurement Provisions in Regional Trade Agreements', note 23 above.

26 On the UK example, see S. Arrowsmith, *The Law of Public and Utilities Procurement* (2nd edn, London: Sweet & Maxwell, 2005), Chapter 3.

27 See S. Karangizi, 'The COMESA Public Procurement Reform Initiative' (2005) 14 *Public Procurement Law Review* NA51, NA52; Karangizi and Ndahiro, 'Public Procurement Reform and Development in the Eastern and Southern Africa Region', note 14 above; E. Nwogwugwu, 'Towards the Harmonisation of International Procurement Policies and Practices' (2005) 14 *Public Procurement Law Review* 131.

28 Karangizi and Ndahiro, 'Public Procurement Reform and Development in the Eastern and Southern Africa Region', note 14 above.

In this regard, the COMESA directives of 2003 provided for members to adopt national legislation consistent with certain general international standards based mainly on UNCITRAL rules. They require, for example, that states should adopt review mechanisms, and that solicitations should be broadly disseminated through the media and accessible by the general public, including on the COMESA website where possible. The directives themselves did not, however, lay down detailed rules on methods and procedures, nor on other matters such as the content of review mechanisms, in the manner of agreements such as the GPA. The binding COMESA Regulations of 2009, however, now build on the standards in the directives, introducing obligations relating to regional competitive bidding (RCB), and challenge and review procedures. RCB currently applies above thresholds set individually by each member state in its domestic legislation, although the Regulations require member states to work towards a common threshold within five years of adoption of the Regulations.[29] While 'regional competitive bidding' sounds like a specific procurement method, the term is used more to indicate any procurement above the RCB threshold, which requires procurement to be open to regional bidders, rather than restricted to domestic companies only. The Regulations in fact state that the choice of procurement method for RCB is to be determined by domestic legislation, although the procedures and rules in domestic legislation must comply with certain basic obligations contained in the Regulations, such as: prohibiting splitting procurement requirements to avoid a particular method of procurement; use of standard bidding documents; public bid openings; disclosure of evaluation criteria; and application of a standstill period prior to contract award.[30] As many COMESA members adopted procurement laws prior to, or at a similar time to, the adoption of the COMESA directives and Regulations, in practice such regional agreements have in fact been influenced by the content of some members' procurement regimes, as much as they have themselves influenced changes to national regimes.[31]

29 COMESA Public Procurement Regulations 2009, Art. 6.

30 *Ibid.*, Art. 12(1) and (2), 13, 18, 20 and 21.

31 For example, provisions in the COMESA Regulations (Art. 21(1)) requiring a notice of best evaluated bidder and standstill period appear to be directly modelled on similar provisions in Uganda's 2003 procurement law, but COMESA requirements for independent and impartial judicial or administrative challenge and review procedures (Art. 31(1)) may have been an influence on Uganda's establishment of a Public Procurement and Disposal of Public Assets Appeals Tribunal in the 2011 amendments to its law.

As mentioned above, COMESA members have generally accepted use of the UNCITRAL Model Law as the starting point for regulating procurement methods, and COMESA has thus in this area served to promote and reinforce the use of UNCITRAL, rather than to provide a distinct and different influence on the development of national rules on procurement methods. This approach has contributed to, *inter alia*, the greater degree of harmonisation of procurement methods between these countries themselves, and with other countries (including those outside Africa), which use the Model Law. This provides an interesting contrast with the position in some of the former socialist economies in Europe which in the transition to a market economy originally implemented reforms based on the Model Law but have been required to amend their system of procurement methods to conform with those of the EU as a result of trade agreements and/or accession to the EU.[32]

Some other regional agreements in Africa have also addressed public procurement, including the Arab Maghreb Union and the West African Economic and Monetary Union. The latter, an organisation of eight Francophone countries,[33] commenced a regional public procurement reform project in the same year as COMESA, 2002, which similarly has the aim of both modernising regional procurement and achieving a degree of harmonisation, including in methods for awarding contracts.[34]

In other developments, the East African Community (EAC), a regional organisation comprising Burundi, Kenya, Rwanda, Tanzania and Uganda, recently adopted a protocol establishing a common market, with obligations including non-discrimination against suppliers, products or services from other partner states to achieve the benefits of free competition.[35] While no detailed obligations yet apply to public procurement, this field could be the subject of future regulations or directives to implement the protocol. The influence of the EAC Common Market has already been seen in Uganda, where 2011 amendments to procurement legislation amended the definition of 'national provider' to include not only companies owned and controlled by citizens of Uganda, but also those owned and controlled by any EAC citizen. However, no such influence is

32 This is the case, for example, with Poland.

33 Benin, Burkina Faso, Côte d'Ivoire, Guinea-Bissau, Mali, Niger, Senegal and Togo.

34 See further A. Fall and M. Frilet, 'Public Procurement in Francophone Africa' in Hérnandez Garcia (ed.), *International Public Procurement*, note 14 above, p. 75.

35 Protocol on the Establishment of the East African Community Common Market (adopted 20 November 2009, entered into force 1 July 2010), Art. 35.

apparent in, for example, Tanzania, where 2011 procurement legislation retains preferences for national tenderers.[36]

Other regional trade initiatives that are relevant for the countries considered in this volume, such as the Southern African Customs Union (SACU) and the Southern African Development Community (SADC), do not address government procurement at present. However, this could obviously become an issue in future under these agreements, as economic integration becomes increasingly prominent and public procurement more significant as other trade barriers are reduced. Following the COMESA–EAC–SADC agreement in 2011 to start negotiations for a tripartite free trade area, the overlapping membership of some countries and differing levels of procurement regulation in each regional economic community could in future make public procurement a more important issue.

We should also note finally that the clear influence of other specific regimes can sometimes be seen in African procurement laws, which is not surprising given that work on African procurement laws is often undertaken and/or funded by foreign donors (as La Chimia explains in Chapter 11 of this volume). An example of this is the rules on framework agreements adopted in regulations in Malawi, which in certain respects appear to be modelled very closely and directly on those found in EU Public Sector Directive 2004/18.[37]

3. Overview of tendering methods

3.1. The 1994 UNCITRAL Model Law and its use in Africa in the context of tendering methods

Aside from certain methods for complex procurements and those for services, which are discussed further below, the 1994 Model Law sets out four procurement methods:

(1) (Open) tendering, referred to simply as 'tendering' under the 1994 Model Law but by its more common name of 'open tendering' under the 2011 Model Law. This is the default method to be used under the Model Law for all procurements of goods and services except

36 Public Procurement Act 2011, s. 54.

37 On this, see S. R. Karangizi, 'Framework Arrangements in Public Procurement: A Perspective from Africa' in Arrowsmith and Tillipman (eds.), *Public Procurement Regulation in the 21st Century*, note 5 above.

where another method can be justified: all other methods are only available in limited circumstances specified in the Model Law. This method requires a public notice inviting tenders (or applications for pre-qualification, where applicable), a formal solicitation document containing specifications and evaluation criteria, a formal submission and public opening of tenders, and award to the lowest evaluated tender without negotiation.[38] This method of procurement is considered under the Model Law as the appropriate one to use by default to support the key goals of public procurement systems,[39] most notably value for money and integrity, since it provides for the greatest degree of transparency and competition of all procurement procedures; and it also supports the goal of equal treatment which is an additional objective of some systems of procurement. In particular,[40] the possibility for any qualified person to have a tender considered makes for the maximum possible number of participants, which can increase the chances of the procuring entity benefiting from the best supplier available, and also induces suppliers to put forward the best offer they can make because of the level of competition; wide participation reduces the risk of collusion; the absence of any discretion to select which suppliers will be permitted to submit tenders reduces the possibility of abuse of discretion to favour particular suppliers; and the formal nature of open tendering in other respects, including limited possibilities for negotiation, also reduces the possibility for abuse of discretion and facilitates monitoring.

(2) Restricted tendering. This may be used under the 1994 Model Law (and in similar provisions under the 2011 Model Law) where the subject-matter of the contract can be obtained only from a limited number of potential suppliers or the time and cost of evaluating a large number of tenders would be disproportionate to the value of

38 For detail on the 1994 Model Law, see Arrowsmith (ed.), *Public Procurement Regulation*, note 5 above, Chapter 3; and, in the 2011 Model Law, in particular, the provisions of Chapter III of the Model Law. These are very similar to the rules described in Arrowsmith (*ibid.*) relating to the 1994 Model Law, although there are some differences.

39 On these, see Arrowsmith, Linarelli and Wallace, *Regulating Public Procurement*, note 1 above, Chapters 1 and 2; Arrowsmith (ed.), *Public Procurement Regulation*, note 5 above, Chapter 1, section 1.4; S. Schooner, 'Desiderata: Objectives for a System of Government Contract Law' (2002) 11 *Public Procurement Law Review* 103; P. Trepte, *Regulating Procurement: Understanding the Ends and Means of Public Procurement Regulation* (New York: Oxford University Press, 2004), *passim*.

40 This account is based on Arrowsmith (ed.), *Public Procurement Regulation*, note 5 above, Chapter 2, section 2.2.1.1.

the contract.[41] This method follows the same procedures as tendering, with the exception that tenders are solicited directly from all potential suppliers (where only a limited number are available) or (where the method is used on grounds of proportionality) from sufficient suppliers to ensure effective competition, and – very importantly – that there is no public invitation to tender.[42]

(3) Request for quotations.[43] This may be used for readily available goods or services with established markets, provided the estimated value is below a threshold set in regulations. This method requires quotations to be requested from at least three suppliers, where possible,[44] with award to the lowest price quotation that meets the procuring entity's needs without negotiation.

(4) Single-source procurement. The 1994 Model Law provides that this may be used in a variety of situations involving suppliers with exclusive rights, urgent needs, requirements for standardisation, research and development, or defence and security contracts. A price quotation is solicited from a single supplier, but no further procedures are provided in the 1994 Model Law for this method.

We will see that these methods are closely mirrored by many regulatory frameworks in Africa, albeit with alternative terminology in some cases – for example, the term 'direct procurement' is used for single-source procurement in several countries and 'bidding' in place of 'tendering',[45] and there are often some minor differences in conditions justifying such use.

As in the 1994 Model Law, procurement methods are selected in Africa, as we will see, on the basis of the dual factors of estimated value linked to prescribed thresholds and circumstances surrounding the nature of the procurement and the market.

41 1994 Model Law, Art. 20; 2011 Model Law, Art. 29(1).

42 Under the 2011 Model Law, a public notice of the procedure is required before the procedure commences (Art. 34(5)), but this is not a public solicitation.

43 1994 Model Law, Arts. 21(1) and 50; 2011 Model Law, Arts. 29 and 46.

44 The 2011 version of the Model law does not include this qualification and thus requires quotations from three suppliers in all cases.

45 For example, Botswana and Uganda use open and restricted bidding and direct procurement (see Chapter 2, section 4.2, of this volume; and Uganda's Public Procurement and Disposal of Public Assets Act 2004, Fourth Schedule), Nigeria and Kenya use direct procurement (see respectively Chapter 5, section 4, and Chapter 7, section 4, of this volume), while Liberia and Sierra Leone use open and restricted bidding (see Liberia's Public Procurement and Concessions Act 2005, Part V; and Sierra Leone's Public Procurement Act 2004, Part V).

3.2. Open tendering as the preferred method and the approach to exceptions to the preferred method

As under the UNCITRAL Model Law in all its versions, open tendering is generally the preferred procurement method in the case of goods and works procurement in African countries. Thus, this is stated as the method of procurement to be used as a general rule in all the countries studied for this book,[46] and the authors are not aware of any African countries that adopt a different approach. Some countries formally differentiate further certain species of open tendering, with separate formal methods for national and international tendering, as discussed in section 4 below.

It is interesting that many African countries in fact provide for the same formal open tendering method as the general method for procurement not only for goods and works but also for non-consultancy services. This is even the general method in some countries for consultancy services, although alternative methods are more commonly provided for consultancy, as discussed further in section 5 below. Thus, for example, Botswana provides for open bidding as the preferred method for all procurement, including both consultancy and non-consultancy services,[47] while Ethiopia, Rwanda, Kenya and Ghana provide for open tendering as the default method for non-consultancy services.[48] This is not formally the position under the 1994 Model Law. That formally provides a different method, the principal method for procurement of services, which is in reality suitable mainly for purchasing complex services, as the general method for all services – but then provides for open tendering to be used for services as an 'exception' to this general method where it is feasible to formulate detailed specifications and tendering proceedings would be more appropriate taking into account the nature of the services to be procured.[49] Since most services procurement is relatively standardised, this 'exception' is frequently relevant – the inclusion of a separate 'general' method of services in the Model Law was a reflection more of the historical development of the Model Law, in which services were added

46 See section 4 of each of the country study chapters. 47 See Chapter 2, section 4.2.

48 See Chapter 3, section 4; ss. 23 and 1 of Rwanda's Procurement Act 2007, which requires open competitive bidding for goods, works and 'other services' and defines 'services' as 'any services other than consultant services'; ss. 29 and 76 of Kenya's Public Procurement and Disposal Act 2005, which make open tendering the default method for all procurement, but with the request for proposals method always available for services which are 'advisory or otherwise of a predominantly intellectual nature'; and Chapter 4, section 4.1, on Ghana.

49 1994 Model Law, Art. 18(3)(a).

later and the focus was on adding new rules for complex services, than of a rational approach to regulation. Hence, when enacting the Model Law, the 'exception' was made the rule for services in some African procurement systems as described above, with other methods being provided as an exception to that rule for the more complex services. This is now also the approach under the 2011 UNCITRAL Model Law, which provides for open tendering as the default method for *all* procurement, whether goods, works or services, and leaves the more complex services to be addressed through the other 'exceptional' methods in the Model Law.[50] This is one way in which the Model Law has been adapted to match the reality of procurement practice during the 2011 reforms.

Regulatory systems that make open tendering the default method because of the perceived value of open tendering in achieving procurement goals usually provide for various controls over derogations from this method. At some risk of simplification,[51] controls can be divided into two broad types: legal, in which the circumstances in which the methods can be used are specified in detail in the procurement laws; and institutional, in which some form of higher approval is required for the use of other methods.

In this respect, all versions of the UNCITRAL Model Law have specified in some detail the conditions under which methods other than open tendering may be used, as well as requiring the justification for use of these methods to be specified in the record of the procurement as a means of enhancing monitoring and enforcement of the legal rules. There was, however, a very important gap in the system of legal control under the 1994 Model Law in that, although there was provision for a system of supplier review, the choice of procurement method was excluded from the scope of review,[52] thus leaving even abusive choices at this point outside one important part of the enforcement system. The position of the Model Law in this respect was widely criticised[53] and the 2011 Model Law no longer provides for such an exclusion.[54] At the same time, the 2011

50 2011 Model Law, Art. 28(1).

51 For example, institutional control can be exercised according to formal guidelines or policies setting out conditions for use which could mirror those found in some states' procurement laws.

52 1994 Model Law, Art. 52(2)(a).

53 See, for example, Arrowsmith, 'Public Procurement: An Appraisal of the UNCITRAL Model Law as a Global Standard', note 5 above; J. Myers, 'UNCITRAL Model Law on Procurement' (1993) 21 *International Business Lawyer* 179.

54 It does not in fact contain any explicit exclusions from review.

reforms also greatly strengthened the system of supplier remedies that can be used to secure compliance with these and other legal controls, both by providing stronger remedies and – of particular importance in the context of control of procurement methods – including a new requirement for an advance notice of the procurement whenever the procuring entity uses a method of procurement that does not involve an open solicitation with a public advertisement.[55]

As regards institutional control, the 1994 Model Law provided for this also, including a provision for approval by a higher authority (as designated by the enacting state) of the use of any of the methods for goods and construction other than open tendering.[56] It was envisaged that this approval could be given by an organ independent of the procuring entity (for example, a national Public Procurement Office or Ministry of Finance), or at a supervisory level within the procuring entity. Such approval can help prevent abuse (at a stage at which correction without disruption is still possible); ensure sound decision-making; help to ensure consistency in decision-making; and assist in capacity-building at the procuring entity level through the process of justifying the decision and receiving feedback. However, the 2011 Model Law takes a diametrically opposite approach to the issue of institutional control, and no longer provides for approval for most methods – even as a possible option for enacting states, let alone as a requirement. This is included (as a requirement) only for the method of request for proposals with dialogue,[57] which is envisaged as a highly exceptional method which most developing countries will not want to include at all. Apparently, the UNCITRAL Working Group considered approval requirements in general to be detrimental to capacity building in procuring entities themselves in that they limit opportunities for real decision-making by entities. Approval requirements can also cause delay, which may be disproportionate if approving bodies are not properly resourced. The argument regarding capacity building is, however, somewhat debateable: as just noted, it can be argued that such a process can in fact be operated to help *build* capacity.

As regards legal control in Africa, African countries that provide for open tendering as the default method provide, in all cases within the authors' experience, for some legal control over the use of other methods by specifying the circumstances for the use of other methods in legal

55 See, in particular, 2011 Model Law, Art. 34(5).

56 See 1994 Model Law, Arts. 19(1), 20(1), 21(1) and 22(1).

57 2011 Model Law, Art. 30(2).

rules. However, this general statement masks some important differences between states.

Thus, on the one hand, in many countries, including, for example, Rwanda, Ghana, Kenya, Botswana, Ethiopia and Nigeria, the circumstances in which methods other than open procurement can be used are set out with precision in the law,[58] providing for close legal control such as is found under the UNCITRAL Model Law. These countries in fact base their law in this respect quite closely on the UNCITRAL Model Law and the specified circumstances (as is discussed below) are modelled to a significant degree on those set out in the Model Law itself. In Zimbabwe, this is the case for alternative methods other than direct contracting, the position of which is discussed later below.

On the other hand, however, a rather different approach to derogation from open tendering is found in both Namibia and South Africa, which, as we have seen, show little, if any, influence, of the Model Law in their regulatory systems. In both these countries, the conditions for using methods other than open tendering are open-ended, rather than closely defined. Thus, in Namibia, apart from defined exceptions relating mainly to agreements with other public bodies, different methods may be used whenever the Tender Board of Namibia has 'good cause' to deem open tender impractical or inappropriate – a very broad and discretionary 'ground' for derogation. In this case, legal control is effectively *substituted* by institutional control with hierarchical approval serving actually to define the circumstances in which other methods can be used, rather than this being done in the legal rules themselves. In South Africa, the law also contains much less well-defined exceptions than are found under the UNCITRAL-type model, including the possibility for using other methods when open tendering is impractical.[59]

It is also worth noting that, whilst Ethiopia has a system predominantly based on the Model Law in which exceptional methods and grounds for use are similar in many respects to those of the Model Law, as noted above, there is also provision for authorisation of different procurement methods altogether from those specified in the law, as well as the

58 See, respectively, Chapters 2, 3, 4, 5, 7 and 8.

59 See Chapter 9, and for critique P. Bolton, 'Grounds for Dispensing with Public Tender Procedures in Government Contracting' (2006) 9(2) *Potchefstroom Electronic Law Journal* 1; J. Laing, 'Deviations from Procurement Processes: Do Public Entities Enjoy Too Much Discretion?', paper presented at conference on Public Procurement in Africa, University of Stellenbosch, 24–25 October 2011.

established and defined ones.[60] In Zimbabwe (see section 4 of Chapter 10), the conditions for use of alternatives to open tendering are prescribed for central government in most cases by value or by reference to specified circumstances – but it is possible also to dispense with tenders altogether on the broad ground of 'public interest'. In addition, in Botswana there is a rather open-ended possibility for using direct contracting – this may be done, alongside precisely specified grounds, where its use is 'justified in the circumstances' (see section 4 of Chapter 2). Whilst such general provisions can provide a welcome degree of flexibility to deal with particular unforeseen situations in what are essentially systems that emphasise transparency, this benefit needs to be balanced against the potential for abuse of such provisions.

As regards the possibility of supplier review to help enforce the rules of legal control, in line with the approach of the 1994 Model Law, review of the choice of procurement method is expressly excluded in a number of African countries. For example, this is the case in Ethiopia, Ghana and Botswana,[61] whilst in Kenya legal review of the choice of method is excluded, although aggrieved persons may petition the Kenyan Public Procurement Oversight Authority to examine the choice of method made.[62] On the other hand, several African countries have chosen *not* to exclude review in this situation. This is the case, for example, in Nigeria, South Africa, Rwanda, Zimbabwe, Namibia[63] and Uganda. Of these, South Africa, Zimbabwe and Namibia are countries that can be said not to use the 1994 Model Law as the main basis for their procurement systems. However, Nigeria does so yet nevertheless chose to provide for review of choice of procurement methods;[64] and Uganda, whilst basing many of its review provisions on the 1994 Model Law, also chose not to exclude review of the choice of procurement method but to allow bidders to seek review of any omission or breach of the law.[65] It will be interesting to see if the unfortunate exclusion from review of choice of methods that still applies in many African countries is removed in those countries in which it does currently apply, in line with the revised position under the 2011 version of the Model Law. In Tanzania, the revised Public Procurement Act published in December 2011 retains the existing exclusion from review of the choice of procurement method,

60 See Chapter 3. 61 See Chapter 13. 62 See Chapter 5, section 4.
63 See Chapter 13. 64 See Chapter 7, section 4.
65 Public Procurement and Disposal of Public Assets Act 2003, s. 89 (Uganda).

although the Bill may have been prepared before the 2011 Model Law was finalised.[66]

It will also be interesting to see if African countries that have based their systems on the 1994 Model Law introduce the prior notice requirement of the 2011 Model Law as described above in order to enhance supplier scrutiny and other control over use of procurement methods. In Uganda, a requirement to publish a notice of procurement when using restricted tendering was added to draft regulations[67] during the recent ongoing revision of the regulatory framework, but this draft envisages including such a requirement only when the method is used on grounds of availability from only a limited number of sources and does not extend it to other circumstances or methods of procurement as in the Model Law.

As regards institutional approval requirements, these are common in African laws, in line with the approach of the 1994 Model Law. Thus, in Ghana,[68] for example, prior approval is required from the Public Procurement Authority for use of either restricted tendering or single-source procurement (neither of which requires a notice to be published and which thus can be particularly open to abuse); in Ethiopia, permission to use methods other than open tendering must generally be obtained from the Public Procurement and Property Administration Agency; and in Zimbabwe permission to dispense with the usual tendering procedure must be obtained from the State Tender Board or its chairperson. In Botswana, approval is required from the Public Procurement and Asset Disposal Board for use of either restricted bidding or direct procurement, and the Board can also authorise use of procedures other than open bidding in circumstances not provided in regulations. In Uganda, approval of the choice of procurement procedure is a function of the Contracts Committee within each procuring entity.[69] In Malawi, use of a method other than tendering or request for proposals for consultancy services is subject to approval by the Director of Public Procurement,[70] and in Nigeria the use of methods other than open competitive bidding must be approved by the Bureau of Public Procurement.[71] In South

66 Public Procurement Act 2011, s. 95(2)(a). 67 Not published. 68 See Chapter 4.
69 Public Procurement and Asset Disposal Regulations 2006 (Botswana), Part V; Public Procurement and Disposal of Public Assets Act 2003 (Uganda), ss. 28–29.
70 Public Procurement Act 2003 (Malawi), s. 30(11). 71 See Chapter 7, section 4.

Africa, approval is also necessary to dispense with competitive award procedures.[72]

It will be interesting to see whether any changes are made in this respect in line with the changed approach adopted in the 2011 Model Law as outlined above. The establishment of new systems of institutional control, including both procurement regulatory bodies and authorising boards or committees within procuring entities, has been a central part of procurement reforms in many African countries during the past decade and requirements to seek authorisations from a central tender board often existed prior to the adoption of UNCITRAL-based laws. Thus, reducing or removing such authorisation requirements would in many cases constitute a significant change to the traditional approach to control and require alternative solutions to the challenges of weak capacity and corruption. The approach of the World Bank, which as we have seen is a significant influence in many African countries, is consistent with that commonly adopted in Africa; it not only specifies conditions for use of methods other than its default procurement and selection methods in its guidelines, but also requires review and no objection by the Bank of a detailed justification prior to the use of direct contracting for goods, works and non-consultancy services or single-source selection for consultancy services.[73]

3.3. Restricted tendering

As regards alternative methods to open tendering, we can first note that, in those African states that specify the nature and conditions of alternative methods in detail using the UNCITRAL Model Law, some form of restricted tendering is usually available. This is the case, for example, in Rwanda, Ethiopia, Kenya, Botswana and Ghana.[74] Justifications generally include, as under the Model Law, the availability of only limited sources and the time and cost of open tendering being disproportionate to the contract value. In the latter case, this consideration is sometimes linked to a threshold provided for in regulations rather than a

72 See Bolton, 'Grounds for Dispensing with Public Tender Procedures in Government Contracting', note 59 above.

73 *Guidelines: Procurement of Goods, Works, and Non-Consulting Services under IBRD Loans and IDA Credits and Grants by World Bank Borrowers*, note 20 above, para. 3.7; *Guidelines: Selection and Employment of Consultants under IBRD Loans and IDA Credits and Grants by World Bank Borrowers*, note 20 above, para. 3.9.

74 See respectively Chapters 2, 3, 4, 5 and 8.

case-by-case consideration of the nature of the specific procurement. This is the case in, for example, Ethiopia and Botswana (although in Botswana no threshold has yet been set in the regulations and this ground is not used in practice).[75] Additional conditions for use may apply; thus, in Ethiopia, restricted tendering is permitted where open advertisements have failed to attract bidders,[76] while, in Uganda and Botswana, emergency situations can justify restricted tendering.[77] We can note that, in Kenya, where restricted tendering is used on grounds of value, at least ten suppliers must be invited,[78] arguably negating the purpose of reducing the time and cost of evaluating a large number of tenders.

3.4. Request for quotations and other methods for low-value procurement

The request for quotations method is also widely available in Africa, being used for purchases below prescribed thresholds. While some countries, such as Ghana, use the 1994 Model Law's wording relating to 'readily available goods or services', others, such as Uganda, focus only on value as a condition and clearly make the method available for works, in addition to goods and services.[79] In Botswana, UNCITRAL's requirement to request quotations from at least three suppliers is increased to five.[80]

In addition to the basic UNCITRAL methods, many African countries also include an additional method to cater for very low-value procurement for situations in which even the request for quotations method would involve disproportionate effort for the value involved. This is referred to as 'petty cash purchases' in South Africa[81] and micro procurement in Botswana and Uganda.[82] In the latter two countries, documentation requirements are limited to a copy of a receipt or invoice, without any need for written solicitation, quotation or contract. The method thus largely satisfies requirements for a financial audit trail, without requiring application of the usual procurement principles.

75 See Chapter 2. 76 See Chapter 3.

77 See Chapter 2, section 4.2; Public Procurement and Disposal of Public Assets Act 2003 (Uganda), Fourth Schedule.

78 See Chapter 5, section 4.

79 Public Procurement and Disposal of Public Assets Act 2003 (Uganda), Fourth Schedule.

80 See Chapter 2, section 4.2. 81 See Chapter 9.

82 See Chapter 2, section 4.2; Public Procurement and Disposal of Public Assets Act 2003 (Uganda), Fourth Schedule.

3.5. Single-source procurement

Single-source procurement, as it is called in the Model Law, and which is also sometimes referred to as direct procurement or contracting – for example, in Botswana, Rwanda and Kenya – is also widely available. In general, such procurement is subject to minimal control by way of legal requirements for the conduct of the procedure and involves merely negotiating with one or more directly selected suppliers. However, this is not always the case – it is interesting to note that in Botswana, for example, this procedure must be conducted in accordance with the rules of bidding so far as possible in the circumstances.[83]

The precise list of justifying conditions differs in each country. The existence of only a single supplier and emergency situations appear to be almost universal criteria in those systems in which detailed criteria are set out in law,[84] with the need for standardisation often also included.

Grounds of these kinds are all provided for under the 1994 Model Law.[85] The first and third are found in similar form also in the 2011 Model Law.[86] However, it is interesting that the 2011 Model Law has narrowed the grounds for use of single sourcing in cases of urgency from that applicable under the 1994 version of the Model Law: whereas the 1994 Model Law provided for its use for all cases of urgent need in which other procurement methods were impractical and the urgency was neither foreseeable by the procuring entity nor the result of dilatory conduct,[87] as well as for catastrophic events, the 2011 Model Law now provides for this method only in the latter case (where, '[o]wing to a catastrophic event, there is an extremely urgent need for the subject-matter of the procurement, and engaging in any other method of procurement would be impractical because of the time involved in using those methods'[88]). It will be interesting to see whether this narrower approach is introduced into national systems in the future. It can perhaps be argued that a better solution is the kind of approach provided in Botswana or Uganda. In Botswana,[89] single-source procurement is made available more widely than in cases of catastrophe but the rules of ordinary bidding can be dispensed with only to the extent that compliance is not possible in

83 See Chapter 2, section 4.2.

84 See, for example, Chapter 3, section 4; Chapter 4, section 4.1; and Chapter 2, section 4.2.

85 1994 Model Law, Art. 22(1)(b), (c) and (d).

86 2011 Model Law, Art. 30(5)(a) and (c).

87 1994 Model Law, Art. 22(1)(b).

88 2011 Model Law, Art. 30(5)(b).

89 See Chapter 2, section 4.2.

the particular case. In Uganda, a regulation on 'emergency situations' provides that competition shall not be automatically excluded in emergency situations and that procuring entities are to obtain competition to the extent practicable; it further allows for modifications to the usual rules – such as reduced timescales or simplified documents – and specifies a hierarchy of methods, with open bidding preferred over restricted bidding or quotations procurement (equivalent to request for quotations) and any competitive method with modifications to be considered before recourse to direct procurement.[90] While neither country has adopted the wording of the 2011 Model Law, both Uganda and Tanzania have included greater definition of and guidance on emergency procurement in 2011 revisions to their procurement legislation.[91] In Uganda, the definition of 'emergency situation' was moved from regulations to primary law and various provisions on arrangements for institutional control of such procurement added. In Tanzania, a new section on emergency procurement provides strict defining criteria (including where there is a threat to life, health, welfare or safety by reason of natural disaster, epidemic, riot, war, fire or similar, where continued functioning of government would suffer irreparable loss or for preservation or protection of irreplaceable public property), requires additional approvals, allows modified procedures and provides for further regulations on emergency procurement (not yet issued).

Additional justifications for use of single-source procurement vary, and include both grounds found in the 1994 Model Law and further grounds which are not found there, but which are found in some cases in other international instruments. Thus, to give some examples,[92] in Ethiopia single-source procurement is available where exceptionally advantageous conditions present themselves; in Ghana for research and development; and in Rwanda for procurement related to items available from a monopolist.

3.6. *Two-stage tendering and other methods for complex procurement*

In addition to the common procurement methods outlined above, the UNCITRAL Model Law also provides for flexible methods for use for,

90 Public Procurement and Disposal of Public Assets Regulations 2003 (Uganda), reg. 110.

91 Public Procurement and Disposal of Public Assets (Amendment) Act 2011 (Uganda), ss. 3 and 26–27; Public Procurement Act 2011 (Tanzania), s. 65.

92 See respectively Chapters 3, 4 and 9.

inter alia, more complex procurement. In this respect, Article 19 of the 1994 Model Law provided for two-stage tendering, request for proposals and competitive negotiations:

(1) in cases of difficulty in drafting the specification ('when it is not feasible for the procuring entity to formulate detailed specifications, and either i) to obtain the most satisfactory solution to its needs it seeks offers to various possible means of meeting those needs or ii) because of the technical character of the requirement, it is necessary to negotiate with suppliers');
(2) for contracts for research, experiment, study or development;
(3) for defence and security procurement, where this is covered by the procurement law; and
(4) where open tendering procedures have failed.

Two-stage tendering[93] is similar to open tendering and involves a similar degree of competition and transparency. The difference is that it involves, in addition, a first tendering stage in which firms submit tenders on any relevant aspects of the contract (which may include the contract terms as well as technical features), followed by negotiations on any aspects of the tenders – a process which is used by the procuring entity to set a common specification. Tenderers then submit further, complete tenders in a second tendering stage against this specification, following the rules of open tendering. The request for proposals procedure in the 1994 Model Law was a more flexible method whereby suppliers submit their own proposals for addressing an issue, followed by discussion on those proposals and submission of final offers covering all aspects of their proposal. Request for proposals[94] is less transparent and potentially less competitive than open tendering in that it provides for the possibility of dispensing with a public advertisement in certain cases and of inviting only a limited number of suppliers to participate, and also in that there is no common specification, but each supplier tenders on the basis of its own solution, making comparison of offers more difficult. It is a useful method to allow procuring entities to take advantage of different possible solutions to a requirement, including to benefit from, and encourage, innovative

93 See further Arrowsmith (ed.), *Public Procurement Regulation*, note 5 above, Chapter 2, section 2.2.2.

94 See further Arrowsmith (ed.), *Public Procurement Regulation*, note 5 above, Chapter 2, section 2.3.1.

approaches by suppliers. Competitive negotiation[95] is less structured – and less transparent and competitive – than either two-stage tendering or request for proposals, involving simply selecting a limited number of suppliers without any advertisement, and negotiating the terms of the contract with them, although it does conclude with a formal offer process.

Advice in the Guide to Enactment to the 1994 Model Law is that an enacting state should incorporate at least one of the three situations when detailed specifications cannot be formulated prior to inviting tenders,[96] but it is not envisaged that states will include all of them.

The approach in Africa has generally been to prefer the transparent two-stage tendering for complex procurement of goods and construction. Thus, a number of African countries permit the use of two-stage tendering for situations in which detailed specifications cannot be formulated prior to soliciting tenders. This method is found, for example, in the regulatory framework in Ethiopia, Rwanda and Ghana and at local government level in South Africa.[97] In Uganda, two-stage tendering is permitted, but treated as an alternative method of bid submission, rather than a separate procurement method, while, in Kenya, regulations merely stipulate that tender documents must contain the procedures and criteria where a procuring entity decides to invite tenders in two separate phases.[98] In many of the African regulatory frameworks, two-stage tendering is *only* available on the ground of the need for discussions to draft specifications. However, in some, it is also made available on other grounds found under the Model Law: for example, in Rwanda, it is available where single-stage tendering procedures have failed, and, in Ghana, for research and development contracts.[99]

Most African countries do not include the other more flexible of the alternative procurement methods contained in Article 19 of the 1994 Model Law, namely, request for proposals or competitive negotiation.[100] (Further, whilst as we have seen some include two-stage tendering, there

95 1994 Model Law, Art. 49. See further Arrowsmith (ed.), *Public Procurement Regulation*, note 5 above, Chapter 2, section 2.3.2.

96 Guide to Enactment, Introduction, para. 19.

97 See respectively Chapters 3, 4, 8 and 9.

98 Public Procurement and Disposal of Public Assets Regulations 2003 (Uganda), reg. 155; Public Procurement and Disposal Regulations 2006 (Kenya), reg. 38.

99 See respectively Chapters 4 and 8.

100 Although the term 'request for proposals' is typically used to describe the method for procurement of consultancy services described in section 5 below, this should not be confused with use of the request for proposals method in the 1994 Model Law.

are countries, Tanzania being one example, which do not include any of the three alternative methods, despite the exhortation to do so in the Guide to Enactment.) Indeed, it seems that the use of the less structured methods with greater dialogue or negotiations is uncommon, at best – and the authors are unaware of any countries that actually include such methods for goods and works. There are a number of reasons for this.

First, due to high levels of corruption in many African countries, opportunities for malpractice when using such flexible methods are often seen as unacceptably high and to outweigh the potential benefits from negotiated procurement. Secondly, weak procurement capacity means that most procurement officers lack the skills to manage such procurement effectively; in such environments, more structured tendering methods may deliver better value for money. The influence of the World Bank and other development banks provides a third reason; due to concerns over corruption and weak capacity, the World Bank discourages the use of negotiated methods in its borrower countries. Its own procurement guidelines allow only two-stage bidding, the least flexible of the alternative Model Law methods.[101] A policy of preferring the most transparent method of procurement where there is a choice in the Model Law is also stated in a World Bank 'Note for Drafting Public Procurement Regulations' dated March 2002 and issued to consultants working on some World-Bank-funded projects. Fourthly, in many developing countries, fewer complex contracts are generally awarded than in developed countries, thus reducing the need for such flexible methods. While consultancy services are frequently purchased, these can use a structured selection process without negotiations, as described below. Privately financed infrastructure projects which have driven the need for flexible methods elsewhere are less commonly used. In addition, larger, more complex contracts tend to be donor-financed, often requiring use of the donor's own procurement rules rather than national regulations.

Some African countries provide for privately financed infrastructure contracts and any other specialised or unusual procurement by allowing that alternative or special methods may be used where justified, often subject to authorisation by a procurement regulatory authority. For example, in Kenya, the Public Procurement Oversight Authority may permit special procurement procedures, such as concessions and design

101 *Guidelines: Procurement of Goods, Works, and Non-Consulting Services under IBRD Loans and IDA Credits and Grants by World Bank Borrowers*, note 20 above.

competitions.[102] In Ethiopia, grounds are less specific, but use of the 'specially permitted procurement' procedure may be authorised by the Public Procurement and Property Administration Agency whenever its use is justified on sound grounds.[103]

We can note that the 2011 Model Law provides for two-stage tendering in a similar form to the 1994 Model Law for cases of difficulty in drafting specifications and where open tendering has failed.[104] The 2011 Model Law also provides for a request for proposals with dialogue method[105] which is available in similar circumstances to the 1994 request for proposals method, and also involves a similar procedure in many respects, although some aspects are regulated in more detail[106] – in part, a reflection of the greater attention that the 2011 Model Law gives in general to methods other than open tendering. However, as the current draft of the Guide to Enactment indicates,[107] the multilateral development banks may remain cautious over use of this method and over its use for bank-funded projects; thus, it might not be considered suitable at all for inclusion in some countries (particularly those first developing a procurement regime), and other approaches (two-stage tendering or other tendering methods preceded by a design study) may be preferred by some countries for cases in which there is difficulty in setting a specification. As already mentioned above, the 2011 Model Law also treats request for proposals with dialogue as a special and exceptional method in that it provides for hierarchical approval of its use, something which is no longer provided for with other procurement methods. It is also relevant to mention that the 2011 Model Law now provides a single set of methods for use for procurement of goods, construction and services, and that the request for proposals methods that it provides may be more relevant for

102 See Chapter 5. 103 See Chapter 4.

104 2011 Model Law, Art. 30(1) (grounds for use) and Art. 48. Defence and security procurement is now subject to the general rules of the Model Law, rather than being treated as an exceptional case.

105 There is also a method called request for proposals without negotiation directed at procurements – including for services – of a relatively standard nature which are not complex enough to require discussions of what is offered, but in which quality issues are very important so that it is appropriate to evaluate the financial aspects of proposals separately from other aspects. It provides for a single submission of proposals without discussions of those proposals, but with an evaluation procedure at the end under which first non-financial aspects are evaluated and then financial aspects are considered: see 2011 Model Law, Arts. 29 and 49.

106 See 2011 Model Law, Art. 49. 107 A/CN.9/WG.I/WP.79/Add.7, para. 11.

procurement of services than for goods and construction. The method of competitive negotiations also remains under the 2011 Model Law, but its role is much reduced. It is no longer provided as a method for cases where it is not possible to formulate specifications (or for where open tendering has failed), but only for cases of urgent procurement[108] and where needed for protection of the essential security interests of the state.[109] Thus, the approach of the 2011 Model Law now perhaps reflects more than the 1994 Model Law the approach that is actually adopted in practice to complex procurement in those African countries that base their systems on the Model Law.

3.7. Community participation

We can finally note that an approach to procurement referred to as community participation is available in a few countries. Such a 'method' is found, for example, in Rwanda's procurement legislation, in local government procurement regulations in Uganda,[110] and in legislation in Tanzania, as discussed below. This is used to refer to an approach in which special preference is given to the participation in implementing the project of users of the subject-matter of the contract. It is considered that this may be the most efficient way to implement some projects, since users have an incentive to ensure good quality in the performance of work affecting them directly. Participation of users can in fact be obtained through inclusion of various provisions relating to the 'standard' procurement methods – for example, through award criteria, through single sourcing to user groups in specified cases, or for requirements to use community resources in certain project components – and an approach that takes into account community participation is perhaps not to be regarded as a distinct method of procurement in the usual sense. The World Bank guidelines relating to procurement of goods, works and non-consulting services in fact provide for community participation in components of Bank-funded projects both for reasons of sustainability of the project and to achieve social objectives, this being possible on a case-by-case basis and in a flexible manner subject to Bank approval of the

108 In circumstances set out in 2011 Model Law, Art. 30(4)(a) and (b).

109 2011 Model Law, Art. 30(4)(c).

110 Local Governments (Public Procurement and Disposal of Public Assets) Regulations 2006 (Uganda), reg. 42.

relevant proposals.[111] Tanzania's regulatory framework contains similar provisions, allowing community participation for project sustainability or to achieve the social objectives of the project; procurement procedures, specifications and contract packaging may be suitably adapted, and the beneficiary community be made responsible for procurement, subject to guidance from the project authorities.[112]

4. National and international methods

A number of African countries distinguish between national and international methods of procurement. A distinction of broadly this kind is found in the UNCITRAL Model Law.[113] It is also found in development bank guidelines, which often distinguish between 'international competitive bidding' and 'national competitive bidding' to denote a distinction between procurements in which borrowers must follow the Bank's own guidelines and those in which borrowers are permitted use of tendering methods found in their national systems.[114] The difference between national and international tendering in most national regulatory frameworks is, however, minimal. Thus, procedural differences are generally limited to the location for publication of notices and perhaps a lengthening of any mandatory timescales, such as minimum bidding periods. In some countries, such as Ghana,[115] requirements for international tendering are linked to a value threshold, while in others, such as Uganda and Botswana,[116] the need for international tendering is based on considerations regarding the location of potential sources and the need for foreign participation to obtain sufficient competition.

111 *Guidelines: Procurement of Goods, Works, and Non-Consulting Services under IBRD Loans and IDA Credits and Grants*, note 20 above, para. 3.19.

112 Public Procurement Act 2011, s. 64(2)(c); Public Procurement (Goods, Works, Non-Consultant Services and Disposal of Public Assets by Tender) Regulations 2005, reg. 75.

113 Thus, in the 1994 Model Law, for example, the requirement to publish a notice in an international language and publication did not apply in Art. 23 where (i) participation was limited to domestic suppliers or (ii) when the procuring entity considered that only domestic suppliers are likely to be interested because of the low value.

114 See, for example, World Bank, *Guidelines: Procurement of Goods, Works, and Non-Consulting Services under IBRD Loans and IDA Credits and Grants*, note 20 above.

115 See Chapter 4, section 4.1.

116 See respectively Public Procurement and Disposal of Public Assets Act 2003 (Uganda), Fourth Schedule, and Chapter 2, section 4.2.

Greater differences between national and international tendering are seen in countries where the official language is not one customarily used in international trade. Thus, both international competitive bidding and national competitive bidding are included in the regulatory framework of Ethiopia, where the official language is Amharic. In this country,[117] the international method is linked to both a value threshold and considerations of availability of the subject-matter of the contract in the local market. Differences extend beyond the location for publication, with requirements for international competitive bidding notices and documents to be in English (while national competitive bidding notices may be in Amharic) and international procurement contracts to be based on international commercial terms and conditions.

Other countries, such as Zimbabwe,[118] include rules on advertising which require international publications to be used where foreign participation is sought, without defining international tendering as a separate method.

The 2009 COMESA Regulations, discussed in section 2.3 above, define national competitive bidding, regional competitive bidding and international competitive bidding, and require the domestic legislation of member states to include the latter two methods. National competitive bidding means procurement limited to suppliers registered in a member state; regional competitive bidding is procurement within thresholds set by member states under which participation must be open to regional suppliers; and international competitive bidding means procurement open to bidders of all nationalities, but in which preferences for regional suppliers must be applied. The authors are not aware of any member states which have yet included these methods within their domestic procurement laws, and it remains to be seen what influence they have on future revisions to national procurement laws. However, as discussed above, these COMESA requirements are not specific new methods as such, but rather rules governing eligibility to participate and evaluation criteria, which can be applied within the context of existing national procurement methods.

5. Methods for consultancy services

As we have seen in section 3.2, the 1994 Model Law dealt separately with goods/construction and services for historical reasons, and included a

117 See Chapter 3, section 4. 118 See Chapter 10.

separate chapter containing the principal method for procurement of services.[119] We saw above that this was stated to be the default method for all services procurement, but was actually aimed mainly at consultancy services and other intellectual services. Similarly, the development banks issue separate guidelines governing the selection of consultants (an important area of procurement in this context).[120] Following this approach of using a different method for this type of procurement, many African countries also regulate the procurement of consultancy services through alternative procurement methods to those described in section 3 above. Examples include Ethiopia, Rwanda, Ghana, Kenya and Swaziland.[121] In Tanzania, not just alternative methods, but separate regulations, are provided to regulate consultancy services.[122] Few take the approach now adopted in the 2011 Model Law, which is to make the same range of methods available for goods, works and services, recognising that any type of procurement can be either simple or complex and that methods should be selected according to complexity and other relevant factors. Uganda previously provided a rare example of a country that did adopt this latter approach, with its 2003 Act and Regulations providing a single set of methods for all procurement; however, in the 2011 revisions to its regulatory framework, it introduced alternative methods for consultancy services,[123] thus moving in the opposite direction to the recent changes in the UNCITRAL Model Law.

While the approach of providing alternative procurement methods for consultancy services is consistent with the 1994 Model Law, the procedural rules of such methods in many African states are much closer to the guidelines of the development banks in substance than they are to the provisions of the 1994 Model Law. The 1994 Model Law provided a choice of selection procedures within the single principal method for procurement of services: selection without negotiation, selection with simultaneous negotiations and selection with consecutive negotiations, the first based on either lowest price or best combined evaluation in terms

119 1994 Model Law, Chapter IV.

120 For example, *Guidelines: Selection and Employment of Consultants under IBRD Loans and IDA Credits and Grants by World Bank Borrowers*, note 20 above.

121 See respectively Chapters 3, 4, 5 and 8. For Swaziland, see the Public Procurement Regulations 2008, Part 7, with the approach now confirmed in the Public Procurement Act 2001, s. 42.

122 Public Procurement (Selection and Employment of Consultants) Regulations 2005.

123 Public Procurement and Disposal of Public Assets (Amendment) Act 2011, ss. 79 and 88A.

of price and other criteria.[124] By contrast, development bank guidelines are primarily focused on selection without negotiation, with a preference for selection based on a combination of quality and cost.[125] While development bank guidelines do permit negotiations with the successful consultant, such 'negotiations' are strictly limited in scope under any competitive procedure and might be better described as technical discussions.[126] A range of alternative selection methods is provided, for use in specified circumstances,[127] but simultaneous negotiations are never permitted.

Many regulatory frameworks in Africa have adopted the World Bank's selection methods for consultancy services, or a selection of them, often adopting both the rules to be applied and the conditions for use of each, based verbatim on the World Bank provisions. Thus, quality and cost based selection, quality based selection, fixed budget selection and least cost selection are widely used. Ghana, Uganda, Botswana and Tanzania provide examples of this approach.[128] Even where not all development bank selection methods are included, quality and cost based selection is often provided as the default method, as is the case in Swaziland, where only least cost selection is provided as an alternative.[129] Some countries, for example Ethiopia and Tanzania,[130] also include the World Bank's selection method for small assignments – selection based on the consultants' qualifications – where a single company is invited to submit a proposal following publication of a request for expressions of interest and evaluation and ranking of the responses.

The strong influence of development bank guidelines can also be seen in rules on the selection of consultants to be invited to submit proposals. Thus, many countries require a pre-selection process for all but small or urgent requirements, with a notice seeking expressions

124 1994 Model Law, Arts. 42–44. For detail, see further Arrowsmith (ed.), *Public Procurement Regulation: An Introduction*, note 5 above, section 4.3.

125 For example, *Guidelines: Selection and Employment of Consultants under IBRD Loans and IDA Credits and Grants by World Bank Borrowers*, note 20 above, para. 1.5.

126 For example, *ibid.*, paras. 2.27–2.29.

127 For example, *ibid.*, section III.

128 See respectively Chapter 4 at section 4.1, Public Procurement and Disposal of Public Assets Regulations 2003 (Uganda), regs. 198–213 and 288, Chapter 2 at section 4.3 and Public Procurement (Selection and Employment of Consultants) Regulations 2005 (Tanzania), Part IV.

129 Public Procurement Regulations 2008, reg. 72.

130 See Chapter 3, section 4; and Public Procurement (Selection and Employment of Consultants) Regulations 2005 (Tanzania), reg. 41.

of interest used to help draw up a limited shortlist. This approach is included, for example, in the regulatory frameworks of Tanzania, Ghana and Swaziland.[131] This contrasts with the 1994 Model Law, which provides for greater transparency and competition than is found in the rules of the development banks, focusing on either open participation in the sense that any interested firm may submit a proposal, or merely applying a pre-qualification process with all qualified suppliers invited to submit a proposal.[132]

6. Procurement of common use items, supplier lists and framework agreements

At one time, procurement in many African countries was highly centralised, with government ministries and departments typically obtaining goods from one or more central stores or supply organisations and all but the smallest procurement activities controlled by a central body. This central body was often a central tender board, sometimes supported by regional tender boards or others for specialised requirements. These centralised bodies were often part of, or reported to, the finance ministry, which was usually responsible for regulation of procurement through finance or administration rules or other circulars. For example, in Uganda, all contracts over US$1,000 were awarded by the Central Tender Board in the Ministry of Finance, with further tender boards for the police and military, and district tender boards for local governments; and procurement of many items was undertaken centrally by the government Central Purchasing Corporation.[133] Similarly, Rwanda operated a National Tender Board until 2007, and Ghana conducted its procurement through a number of centralised bodies, including the Ghana Supply Commission and the Ghana National Procurement Agency,[134] whilst in Malawi public procurement for central government was the responsibility of the

131 See respectively Public Procurement (Selection and Employment of Consultants) Regulations 2005 (Tanzania), reg. 49; Chapter 4, section 4.2; and Public Procurement Regulations 2008 (Swaziland), regs. 67–69.

132 1994 Model Law, Chapter IV; see Arrowsmith (ed.), *Public Procurement Regulation*, note 5 above, Chapter 4, section 4.1.

133 E. Agaba and N. Shipman, 'Public Procurement Reform in Developing Countries: The Uganda Experience' in K. V. Thai and G. Piga (eds.), *Advancing Public Procurement: Practices, Innovation and Knowledge-Sharing* (Boca Raton, FL: PrAcademics Press, 2007).

134 See Chapter 8, section 2.2; and Chapter 4, section 2.4.

Central Government Stores and Central Tender Board until the latter was dissolved in 2001.[135]

However, from the late 1990s, reforms have resulted in significant changes to institutional frameworks for public procurement. Although the trend is not universal (as Chapter 10 explains, central government tendering in Zimbabwe is still largely done centrally), many African countries have decentralised procurement responsibilities, often setting up tender boards or equivalent bodies within individual ministries and departments, as well as creating regulatory bodies with responsibility for procurement policy and supervision. Decentralisation has been driven by a number of factors, including inefficiencies and poor value for money due to the inability of centralised arrangements to cope with the expansion of government procurement (which was increasingly including more complex purchases, such as consultancy services as well as construction, which were previously performed in-house) and the need to separate operational functions from policy and oversight roles. The difficulty of balancing operational and other roles was an important driver in Rwanda,[136] while inefficiencies, delays and poor value for money in procurement were noted in Ghana, Uganda and Malawi.[137]

Given the decentralisation that now exists in many African countries, the question of how to obtain best value for items commonly purchased across government and how to maintain and share information on suppliers has become a key challenge. As part of the decentralisation process explained above, many countries have disbanded any central purchasing body or government stores, or at least made its use optional. Often a procurement regulatory body is instead given functions relating to maintaining databases of suppliers and the coordination of common use items (that is, items purchased by more than one procuring entity). Thus, for example, in Uganda, the regulatory authority is required to maintain a register of suppliers; the functions of Tanzania's regulatory body includes agreeing a list of goods and services in common use which may be subject to common procurement;[138] while in Sierra Leone the National Public

135 Office of the Director of Public Procurement, Introduction, available at www.odpp.gov.mw/home/index.php?option=com˙content&view=article&id=158&Itemid=147.

136 See Chapter 8, section 2.2.

137 Chapter 4, section 2.4; Agaba and Shipman, 'Public Procurement Reform in Developing Countries', note 133 above; and Office of the Director of Public Procurement, note 135 above.

138 See respectively the Public Procurement and Disposal of Public Assets Act 2003 (Uganda), s. 7; and the Public Procurement Act 2011 (Tanzania), s. 9.

Procurement Authority is required to publish a database of suppliers and records of prices and may designate a body to conduct procurement of common use items.[139] In practice, such functions have not always been high priorities for newly established procurement regulatory bodies and can result in a blurring of the newly created distinction between operational and regulatory functions.

One tool that is common outside Africa for the procurement of common use items and services – as well as for items and services required repeatedly by individual procuring entities, or urgent procurement – is the framework agreement.[140] A framework agreement is simply a list of suppliers able to perform specific contracts which also establishes some or all of the terms on which the contracts in question will be made,[141] allowing for orders to be placed swiftly and without repeating all the stages of a competition every time the need for a specific item arises. Such an agreement (which may or may not take the form of a binding contract) may be concluded with a single supplier, with purchasers simply 'calling off' goods, works or services under the agreement as and when a need for the covered item arises. It may also take the form of multi-supplier arrangements, involving an initial competition to select several potential suppliers for the framework, followed by a second phase of the procedure when a requirement arises, when the procuring entity chooses one of these several 'framework suppliers' to fulfil the order. Such framework agreements are often placed by central purchasing bodies or others for use by more than one procuring entity, allowing for benefits such as economies of scale, savings on procedural costs, central monitoring and

139 Public Procurement Act 2004, s. 14; Public Procurement Regulations 2006, reg. 19.

140 See generally S. Arrowsmith, 'Methods for Purchasing Ongoing Requirements: The System of Framework Agreements and Dynamic Purchasing Systems under the EC Directives and UK Procurement Regulations' in Arrowsmith and Tillipman (eds.), *Public Procurement Regulation in the 21st Century*, note 5 above, Chapter 3; L. Folliot Lalliot, 'The French Approach to Regulating Frameworks under the New EC Directives' in Arrowsmith and Tillipman (eds.), *Public Procurement Regulation in the 21st Century*, note 5 above, Chapter 4; D. Gordon and J. Kang, 'Task-Order Contracting in the US Federal System: The Current System and Its Historical Context' in Arrowsmith and Tillipman (eds.), *Public Procurement Regulation in the 21st Century*, note 5 above, Chapter 5; S. Arrowsmith, 'Framework Purchasing and Qualification Lists under the European Procurement Directives' (1999) 8 *Public Procurement Law Review* 115, 115–26; S. Arrowsmith and C. Nicholas, 'Regulating Framework Agreements under the UNCITRAL Model Law on Procurement' in Arrowsmith and Tillipman (eds.), *Public Procurement Regulation in the 21st Century*, note 5 above, Chapter 2; Arrowsmith (ed.), *Public Procurement Regulation*, note 5 above, Chapter 5, section 5.3.

141 Arrowsmith (ed.), *Public Procurement Regulation*, note 5 above, Chapter 5, section 5.3.

use of centralised purchasing expertise, whilst at the same time retaining user flexibility. At the call-off stage in an arrangement involving more than one supplier, there may be no need for further competition (the best supplier can be selected by considering the initial tenders); there may be competition to supplement the original tenders (for example, to seek discounts for specific bulk purchases); or work might be allocated by rotation between framework suppliers.

Such framework agreements, if used appropriately, can provide a better means for obtaining value for money and also provide for lower procedural costs than repeat micro purchasing – benefits which, as we mentioned, can sometimes be enhanced where such agreements are placed on behalf of more than one entity or otherwise to cover the spend of more than one entity on common use items. The 1994 Model Law[142] contained no explicit provisions on framework agreements but its general procedures did not preclude use of frameworks with one supplier – contracts of this kind can simply be placed with the supplier using the ordinary procurement methods, usually open tendering. On the other hand, the Model Law methods and procedures under the 1994 version did not appear to accommodate the possibility of single framework arrangements concluded with more than one supplier, which may involve certain advantages, including security of supply, and enhanced competition for individual requirements.[143] One of the main revisions in the 2011 Model Law has been the introduction of explicit new measures to provide for, and regulate, various kinds of framework agreements.[144]

In this respect, the Model Law now provides for three different types of framework agreements, two 'closed' (that is, in which suppliers may not join the framework after initial tenders have been held to choose the framework suppliers) and one 'open' (where new suppliers can join the framework agreement throughout its lifetime).[145] The three types are:

(1) A closed framework agreement with a full set of terms and conditions set at the initial tendering stage, which are then used to place call-offs.

142 On framework agreements under the 1994 Model Law, see further Arrowsmith and Nicholas, 'Regulating Framework Agreements under the UNCITRAL Model Law on Procurement', note 140 above.

143 On possible reasons for such multi-supplier arrangements, see Arrowsmith, 'Framework Purchasing and Qualification Lists under the European Procurement Directives', note 140 above.

144 See C. Nicholas, 'A Critical Evaluation of the Revised UNCITRAL Model Law Provisions on Regulating Framework Agreements' (2012) 21 *Public Procurement Law Review* 19.

145 See the definitions in 2011 Model Law, Art. 2(e)(i)–(v).

This kind of arrangement may be with one supplier or more than one supplier.

(2) A closed framework agreement made with more than one supplier which contains the main terms and conditions but which involves an element of further tendering between the framework suppliers when call-offs are made, to place the orders.

(3) An 'open' framework agreement with more than one supplier and involving a competition between the framework suppliers for orders. This is to be operated exclusively online and is directed at commonly used, off-the-shelf purchases.

It is not proposed to address this complex area in any detail in this short chapter, but it can be observed that an analysis of provisions on framework agreements in African legislation undertaken by Karangizi in 2008[146] found that a number of systems surveyed provided specifically for these in legislation (for example, Uganda, Tanzania, Malawi, Ethiopia, Rwanda, Burkina Faso, Mali, Niger and Senegal),[147] whilst others did not include any explicit provisions (Cameroon, Egypt, Nigeria, Sierra Leone, Kenya, Ghana and Zambia).[148] Of those countries mentioned above that did address them, explicit provisions appeared to be concerned only with frameworks with one supplier, which are generally awarded using ordinary tendering methods. Further, the degree of regulation of their use (regarding requirements to use them, limits on use, maximum duration etc.) was variable. Only in the laws of two of these states, Malawi and Ethiopia, did Karangizi find explicit provision for the possibility of using the more complex types of framework agreements that involve selection of more than one supplier for the same requirement, such as are found in the 2011 Model Law. Further, only the provisions in Malawi made explicit provision for the type of framework that involves a second-stage competition between suppliers on the framework (modelled, as we have mentioned in section 2.3, on provisions of EU legislation).[149] This appears to indicate that such arrangements are not available in other countries since they do not fit within traditional tendering rules.

When considering legal rules on frameworks, an important area to consider alongside the explicit provisions on this subject is the issue of aggregation as there is often an important relationship between rules on aggregation and framework agreements. Rules on aggregation are rules

146 Karangizi, 'The COMESA Public Procurement Reform Initiative', note 27 above.
147 *Ibid.* 148 *Ibid.* 149 *Ibid.*

that prohibit entities from splitting contracts in order to fall below the thresholds for using formal tendering or – more rarely – that require the positive aggregation of certain requirements for the purpose of calculating whether relevant thresholds are met. Requirements of the latter kind are found under the EU procurement regime, where entities must aggregate repeat purchases of similar supplies and services over a year, as well as all procurement relating to the same single work, to determine whether formal tendering is required.[150] Where such rules apply, they tend to increase the importance, or potential importance, of framework agreements as these are, as we have seen, a useful method of tendering larger requirements for repeat needs. In Africa, rules prohibiting the division of requirements to keep contracts below thresholds and avoid use of tendering methods are common,[151] but such rules are hard to monitor and enforce and strict aggregation rules such as are found in EU law are not generally applied. This can tend to limit recourse to the framework approach in practice. Further, practical skills in planning, aggregating procurement (including between different entities purchasing the same requirements), and actually using frameworks are often weak; and these problems are compounded by a lack of coordination between procurement and financial systems and other financial challenges, such as uncertain budgetary releases.[152] The overall result is that there can often be seen in African countries frequent low-value tenders or requests for quotations for common use and regularly purchased items, with many procuring entities repeatedly buying the same items without any centralised coordination or use of available types of frameworks.

There are, however, exceptions to the general fragmented approach to purchasing common items. Exceptions are often seen, in particular, in the health sector. In this sector, a central medical store or ministry of health often leads the procurement of pharmaceuticals and other medical items and the priority given to the sector results in greater funding and greater

150 See e.g. Directive 2004/18/EC of the European Parliament and of the Council of 31 March 2004 on the coordination of procedures for the award of public works contracts, public supply contracts and public service contracts [2004] OJ L134/114, Art. 9. All the purchases do not need to be tendered in one contract, but the natural tendency of such positive aggregation rules is to encourage this because of the cost of using formal tendering for many different small contracts.

151 For example, see Public Procurement Act 2004 (Sierra Leone), s. 37; Public Procurement and Disposal of Public Assets Act 2003 (Uganda), s. 58(2)(c); Public Procurement Act 2011 (Tanzania), s. 49(1)(c); Public Procurement Act 2003 (Ghana), s. 21(5); Chapter 2, section 4.2; Public Procurement and Disposal Act 2005 (Kenya), s. 30(1); and the position of Nigeria, mentioned in Chapter 7, section 4.

152 See also Karangizi, 'The COMESA Public Procurement Reform Initiative', note 27 above.

investment in areas such as forecasting, modern procurement techniques and stock management systems. The Kenya Medical Supplies Agency and Tanzania's Medical Stores Department are examples of agencies operating in this area.[153] Another exception can be seen in South Africa, where the National Treasury facilitates 'transversal term contracts' for goods and services required by more than one government department, where such arrangements would be cost-effective.[154] Other recent reforms have also sought to address the problem. Thus, in Uganda, where framework contracts have long been expressly permitted in legislation,[155] growing recognition of the need to ensure value for money in the procurement of common use items resulted in the issue of a guideline on framework contracts in 2011[156] and a prohibition being introduced in revisions to its procurement legislation on using micro procurement for works, services or supplies required continuously or repeatedly over a set period of time, or for which a framework contract is required.[157] In Tanzania, revisions to the Public Procurement Act in 2011 included a new Government Procurement Services Agency (to assist the regulatory authority in setting procedures for procurement of common items and services by procuring entities through framework agreements that these entities may use) and definitions of closed and open frameworks, although detailed rules for use of frameworks and the agency's role are yet to be established by regulations.[158]

However, for the most part, providing for a suitable regulatory system for purchasing common use items and ensuring its effective use in practice remains a major and difficult challenge for the procurement systems of Africa. It will be interesting to see whether this is addressed in future reforms and what use, if any, is made in any such process of the new provisions on framework agreements – and the accompanying practical

153 The Kenya Medical Supplies Agency is a state corporation established in 2000 to provide a secure source of drugs and other medical supplies for public health institutions in Kenya: see www.kemsa.co.ke/index.php?option=com_content&view=article&id=19&Itemid=20; Tanzania's Medical Stores Department is an autonomous department of the Ministry of Health, created by statute to furnish good quality drugs and medical equipment at accessible prices: see www.msd.or.tz/about-us.

154 See Chapter 8, section 4.

155 See the account of Karangizi, 'The COMESA Public Procurement Reform Initiative', note 27 above, pp. 247–8.

156 Guideline 1/2011, Guidance on Use of Framework Contracts for procurement of supplies and services.

157 Public Procurement and Disposal of Public Assets (Amendment) Act 2011, Fourth Schedule.

158 Public Procurement Act 2011, ss. 50, 56 and 105.

guidance in the Guide to Enactment – that are contained in the 2011 Model Law.

A related topic is the use of supplier lists, sometimes also referred to as approved lists or qualification systems.[159] These are simply lists of suppliers that are interested in, or qualified for, certain types of procurements. They can be classified into mandatory lists, which can be defined as lists on which suppliers are required to register as a condition of being considered for a contract, and 'optional' lists – that is, lists that entities use to identify potential suppliers, and registration on which may evidence some of the supplier's qualifications, but on which registration is not compulsory for suppliers to be considered for contracts.

Many African countries permit procuring entities, a regulatory authority, or both, to maintain supplier lists. For example, in Sierra Leone, both procuring entities and any special agency designated to conduct the procurement of common use items may establish a register of suppliers; this is intended to provide information on potential suppliers, and to facilitate development of shortlists and the identification of sole sources.[160] In Ethiopia and Botswana, registration with the central procurement body is mandatory under procurement legislation for domestic suppliers as a condition of participation in procurement.[161] It is not legally required in most states to be registered on a supplier list as a condition of access to any procurement contract, and when open tendering is used any interested and qualified firm must be admitted to the procedure regardless of prior registration on a list. However, in some countries, registration *is* required in order for suppliers to be eligible to receive an invitation to tender in certain types of procurement: this is the case, for example, in some sectors in Zimbabwe for participation in most procedures other than open formal tendering, as Chapter 10 explains (section 4.7). Further, even where there is no legal requirement for registration, *in practice* registration on such lists may be the only way of being included on

159 Framework agreements as defined above and supplier lists can in fact be regarded as shades on a spectrum rather than as distinct concepts. On supplier lists, see further Arrowsmith (ed.), *Public Procurement Regulations*, note 5 above, Chapter 5, section 5.2; S. Arrowsmith, *Government Procurement in the WTO* (The Hague: Kluwer Law International, 2003), pp. 232–6; S. Arrowsmith, 'Public Procurement: An Appraisal of the UNCITRAL Model Law as a Global Standard', note 5 above, section C; Arrowsmith, Linarelli and Wallace, *Regulating Public Procurement*, note 1 above, pp. 639–45; C. Maund, 'The Development of Vendor Registration Systems for European Utilities' (1996) 5 *Public Procurement Law Review* CS51.

160 Regulations on Public Procurement, reg. 26.

161 See further Chapter 3, section 4; and Chapter 2, section 4.1.

shortlists for non-advertised procurement, since the legislation – following the pattern of the 1994 Model Law – often does not provide for any method for identifying firms to participate in such procurement, and there is a practice of using lists in order to do this. For example, in both Kenya and Ghana, registration is, in effect, essential in practice for participation in restricted tendering or request for quotations procedures, although Ghana's legislation is silent on the maintenance of closed supplier lists by procuring entities.[162] In South Africa, contractors can apply to be listed as prospective suppliers for contracts below the open tendering threshold.[163]

With the exception of contractors for works, registration on lists in those African countries that use them is often a process limited to verifying key legal documents, such as trading licences. More rigorous assessment of qualifications is generally found only for the construction sector, where contractors are often classified according to capability to manage contracts of differing sizes, thereafter being qualified to tender for contracts in their designated grade only. In Sierra Leone, only the Ministry of Works, Housing and Technical Maintenance is permitted to maintain a register for contractors and supervising engineers,[164] while in Botswana, where registration is mandatory for domestic companies, registration for construction contracts has been the Public Procurement and Asset Disposal Board's first priority, with works contractors being registered under six different grades, before registration requirements for services or supplies were enforced.

While supplier lists are used in Africa in the ways set out above, rules controlling their use and the conditions for registration are often limited, although some exist either under procurement legislation or (for example, in South Africa)[165] under general principles of administrative law. This perhaps reflects the absence of similar provisions in either the Model Law or donor guidelines on which to model such provisions. Such provisions are found in some other systems, however. It can be noted, in particular, that the WTO's GPA expressly allows use of mandatory lists, but applies to supplier lists certain controls included to secure transparency and to prevent the lists being used – intentionally or otherwise – as obstacles to participation in procurement. These rules[166] require entities to publicise

162 See Chapter 5, section 4; and Chapter 4, section 4.3. 163 See Chapter 8, section 4.
164 Regulations on Public Procurement, reg. 50. 165 See Chapter 9, section 4.
166 Which are also found in a similar form in the revised text of 2006, available at www.wto.org/english/thewto_e/minist_e/min11_e/brief_gpa_e.htm (as to which, see generally

a list when it is set up and periodically thereafter;[167] require that suppliers must be able to apply for qualification at any time and must be included within a reasonably short period;[168] and state that the process of registration and the time taken to complete it must not be used to keep suppliers off the list.[169] Controls over payments by suppliers may also be useful to ensure these do not operate as a barrier to participation and are not used simply for generating revenue (as appears to happen in Nigeria[170]) – for example, requirements that (as is often provided with tender documents) any payments must be limited to the costs of operating the list, or even prohibitions on payment, requiring the cost to be borne by government. The 1994 Model Law and the 2011 Model Law neither permit mandatory lists,[171] nor provide any transparency rules for lists that are used in practice (i.e. mandatory lists (which the Model Law assumes are not used), purely optional lists, or *de facto* mandatory lists in the sense of lists that are used in practice to select participants for non-advertised procurements). As Arrowsmith has argued elsewhere, it might be useful to include explicit provisions in the Model Law both to facilitate entities taking advantage of mandatory lists, and – through provisions modelled on those of the GPA – to improve transparency and competition in the use of lists of all kinds.[172] Even if the concept of formally mandatory lists is rejected, such provisions would be useful to regulate the operation of *de facto* mandatory lists and optional lists. However, the idea of including provisions on supplier lists was rejected when the Model Law was revised.[173]

Anderson, 'The Conclusion of the Renegotiation of the WTO Agreement on Government Procurement in December 2011', note 24 above).

167 GPA 1994, Art. IX.9. 168 *Ibid.*, Art. VIII(d). 169 *Ibid.*, Art. VIII(c).

170 See Chapter 7, section 4. See also Chapter 10, section 4.7, where it is explained that greatly differing fees are charged to register in Zimbabwe for foreign and domestic firms; the reasons are not clear but this could be done, *inter alia*, in order to raise revenue, or to provide more favourable participation conditions for local suppliers.

171 2011 Model Law, Art. 9(4) (similarly to Art. 6(3) of the 1994 Model Law) prohibits entities from imposing any 'criterion, requirement or procedure' with respect to qualifications other than those in Art. 6, and Art. 6 does not refer to registration on a list. That mandatory lists are intended to be precluded is confirmed by the Working Group of the 2011 revisions: see UNCITRAL, Report of Working Group I (Procurement) on the work of its thirteenth session (New York, 7–11 April 2008), A/CN.9/648, para. 136. The exception is the open framework agreement described above, which functions mainly as a list of suppliers interested in certain types of contract.

172 Arrowsmith, 'Public Procurement: An Appraisal of the UNCITRAL Model Law as a Global Standard', note 5 above.

173 See, most recently, Doc. A/CN.9/648, para. 136, cited in note 171 above.

7. E-procurement

At present, it appears that few African countries use electronic tools for procurement, beyond the use of websites to publish procurement notices. Even in South Africa, where infrastructure is relatively developed, electronic procurement is not widely used in the public sector: as in most other countries, opportunities may be advertised by electronic means, but hard copy tenders are generally still required, and no provision is made in legislation for electronic procurement.[174] In Nigeria, provision is made in legislation both for advertising electronically and to require procurement records to be maintained in electronic form, but reality differs from aspirations in this respect – a culture of advertising and searching electronically has not developed, and actual maintenance of electronic records has not proved practical.[175] Infrastructure challenges and private sector connectivity remain a concern in many African countries. However, e-procurement methods may also potentially be seen as partial solutions to challenges of weak capacity and corruption in Africa. Recent revisions to regulatory frameworks for public procurement in Uganda, Tanzania and Ethiopia suggest that these countries are considering the future introduction of e-procurement. Thus, in Tanzania, a definition of e-procurement was added, along with a provision enabling the future issue of regulations with procedures for conducting e-procurement; in Uganda, definitions of information and records were updated to include electronic formats;[176] and the recent legislation in Ethiopia envisages authorising use of electronic means for procurements once the necessary capacity is in place.[177]

In this respect, it is relevant to mention that one of the main objectives of the revisions to the UNCITRAL Model Law in 2011 was to update the Model Law to take account of the growth of electronic procurement.[178] Thus, the 2011 Model Law now includes explicit provisions to ensure that electronic and paper-based communications are treated on an equivalent basis (so that documents etc. are equally valid in

174 See Chapter 9, section 4. 175 See Chapter 7, section 4.

176 Public Procurement Act 2011 (Tanzania), ss. 3 and 105; Public Procurement and Disposal of Public Assets (Amendment) Act 2011 (Uganda), s. 3.

177 See Chapter 3, section 4.

178 On the issues and the rules of the Model Law, see further Nicholas, 'The 2011 UNCITRAL Model Law on Public Procurement', note 9 above; Arrowsmith (ed.), *Public Procurement Regulation*, note 5 above, Chapter 7.

electronic as in paper form);[179] and that the procuring entity may choose any form of communication in award procedures.[180] However, it also includes provisions requiring entities to ensure appropriate standards of authenticity, integrity and confidentiality[181] regardless of the means of communication, as well as provisions to safeguard the accessibility of the procedure to suppliers, so that use of electronic means does not operate as an obstacle to participation.[182] Thus, the Model Law now offers a ready-made legal framework for African states that may wish to make greater use of electronic technologies in their procurement, whilst the Guide to Enactment that will accompany the 2011 Model Law (which at the time of writing was yet to be formally adopted) will provide some detailed guidance on how to implement the provisions.

The development of electronic procurement has resulted not only in the application of electronic communications and other technologies to enhance traditional tendering and other procurement methods, but also in the development of different approaches to procurement altogether. Of particular note is the emergence of the auction as a significant procurement technique, since auctions are much easier to conduct and more effective when operated online than through other methods.[183] The 2011 Model Law thus also includes explicit provisions to permit use of electronic auctions, either as a separate procurement method or as a phase in other procurement methods, and to regulate in detail the conduct of such auctions.[184] As we have already mentioned above, it also provides for an open framework agreement for off-the-shelf products which operates entirely online. In view of the limited use of electronic procurement in general, it is not surprising that such approaches are not yet generally found in the procurement laws of African states. However, it is again important that a template for regulation and guidance on further implementation now exists to assist in the expected future development of this area of procurement practice on the African continent.

179 2011 Model Law, Art. 7(1). 180 *Ibid.*, Art. 7(3). 181 *Ibid.*, Art. 7(5).

182 *Ibid.*, Art. 7(4) requiring, in particular, that means of communication must be 'in common use by suppliers or contractors in the context of the particular procurement'.

183 On electronic auctions in public procurement and the regulatory issues, see generally S. Arrowsmith, 'Regulating Electronic Reverse Auctions under the UNCITRAL Model Law on Procurement' in Arrowsmith and Tillipman (eds.), *Public Procurement Regulation in the 21st Century*, note 5 above, Chapter 11, and the works cited there, and the other chapters in Part IV of that book.

184 2011 Model Law, Chapter VI.

8. Concluding remarks

We have seen that, despite differences in terminology and detail, there is a striking degree of similarity in procurement methods used in many African countries, largely as a result of the common influences of the UNCITRAL Model Law and the procurement guidelines of the development banks. However, there are still, on the other hand, a number of states whose procurement law follows a different pattern – even though similar in some important respects, such as in the general priority given to open tendering. As regional integration continues and increasingly addresses public procurement issues, further harmonisation is likely, with regional agreements both influencing national regulatory frameworks and building on existing commonalities.

It remains to be seen whether the adoption of the 2011 Model Law will lead countries to update their regulatory frameworks on procurement methods. It seems unlikely that states will want to revise their alternative methods to tendering merely for the sake of bringing them into line with those under the new Model Law: in this respect, we can note that the differences between the old and new approaches are quite limited; that some differences lie in areas, notably the purchase of consultancy services, where the Model Law has had less influence in the first place; and that some of the features of the new Model Law, such as use of ordinary open tendering for simple services, are already found in national laws, the changes to the Model law being a reflection of that existing practice. However, it will be interesting to see if important improvements of detail introduced in 2011, such as the new provision made for suppliers to seek review of the choice of procurement method, and the requirement for an advance public notice of procurement that is not the subject of a public solicitation, will be widely adopted in states that do not currently apply them. It will also be interesting to see the extent to which the Model Law's provisions in the wholly new areas of framework agreements and electronic procurement (including electronic auctions) will be used to assist states in addressing these issues in future, or even serve as an early driver to the change that – in the area of electronic procurement, at least – seems ultimately inevitable.

13

A comparative perspective on supplier remedies in African public procurement systems

GEO QUINOT

1. Introduction

Some of the biggest concerns in public procurement in Africa are a perceived lack of transparency, accountability and fairness in procurement, or what can collectively be termed integrity in the procurement process. There are many studies and reports that have pointed to this overarching concern with integrity as of primary importance in reforming African public procurement systems.[1] From a legal perspective, one of the key ways to address concerns regarding integrity is to develop an effective regime of supplier remedies,[2] that is, legal mechanisms that allow suppliers to challenge public procurement decisions and to obtain relief where it can be shown that procurement rules were not adhered to.

Designing an effective supplier remedies regime is obviously only part of the solution. Success depends largely on the effective implementation of the regime, which is a much more complex issue depending not only on the design of the particular mechanisms, but also on much

1 See the World Bank Institute's Contract Monitoring Initiative at http://wbi.worldbank.org/wbi/content/transparent-contracting-and-procurement (accessed 5 March 2012); W. Odhiambo and P. Kamau, 'Public Procurement: Lessons from Kenya, Tanzania and Uganda', OECD Development Centre: Working Paper No. 208 (2003); OECD, *Enhancing Integrity in Public Procurement: OECD Joint Learning Study on Morocco* (Paris: OECD, 2008) and most of the Country Procurement Assessment Reviews on African countries conducted by the World Bank; T. Asare, A. Kane, F. Leautier and S. Majoni, 'Trends in Public Procurement in Africa: Opportunities and Challenges of Capacity Building Interventions', presentation at the III Global Conference on Electronic Government Procurement (2009); R. Hunja, 'Obstacles to Public Procurement Reform in Developing Countries' in S. Arrowsmith and M. Trybus (eds.), *Public Procurement: The Continuing Revolution* (The Hague: Kluwer Law International, 2003), pp. 13–22.

2 D. I. Gordon, 'Constructing a Bid Protest Process: The Choices That Every Procurement Challenge System Must Make' (2006) 35 *Public Contract Law Journal* 427, 428, 430–1, 445.

broader institutional factors.[3] Nevertheless, putting in place a supplier remedies regime is a critical first step towards enhanced integrity in public procurement. Furthermore, in designing that regime one can already enhance its potential effectiveness by calibrating particular aspects of the regime within the broader procurement system in such a way that effective implementation is facilitated. Coherence within the remedies regime between different challenge forums and the relationships between different remedies that may be granted are also of key importance in designing an effective supplier remedies system. In this respect, the significant developments in remedies regimes in more mature procurement systems, national, regional and international, can serve the development of supplier remedies in more fledgling African systems well. At the same time, there is real value to be had by comparing African systems *inter se*.[4] The benefit lies particularly in the shared social context within which African supplier remedies systems must operate, which is quite often far removed from the context of more mature non-African and international systems.

In this chapter, I compare supplier remedies regimes in a number of African systems. First, I compare them *inter se* in order to assess the state of supplier remedies in a sample of African systems and to discern trends in remedies regimes. These trends not only help us to develop an understanding of the nature of procurement remedies on the continent, but can also help us to develop an understanding of the underlying objectives and priorities that drive public procurement regulation in Africa. As Gordon effectively argues:

> The relative importance a nation, state, or other procuring entity gives to . . . competing demands will drive the trade-offs made in defining the structure of its protest system.[5]

The purpose of the comparison is, however, not to provide a detailed account or analysis of the remedies regimes in all these systems or on the continent. It is necessarily a broad overview, and my aim is thus to highlight patterns and paint an African remedies picture in broad brush strokes. Secondly, although not in a separate section, I assess those trends

3 See S. Arrowsmith, J. Linarelli and D. Wallace, *Regulating Public Procurement: National and International Perspectives* (The Hague, London: Kluwer Law International, 2000), p. 749.

4 See G. Quinot, 'Enforcement of Procurement Law from a South African Perspective' (2011) 20 *Public Procurement Law Review* 193, 206.

5 Gordon, 'Constructing a Bid Protest Process', note 2 above, p. 432.

against experiences and developments elsewhere, particularly in leading international and regional procurement systems. This second purpose is a tentative attempt to benchmark the African systems scrutinised against international standards.

The systems included in this comparative overview are those covered in the first part of the book, namely, Botswana, Ethiopia, Ghana, Kenya, Namibia, Nigeria, Rwanda, South Africa and Zimbabwe. The chapter will start by providing an overview of the basic structure of supplier remedies in these systems. It will consequently consider the operation of multiple remedies regimes in a single system and standstill periods before moving on to an analysis of the relief available in supplier challenges. The rules governing interim relief, invalidation of procurement decisions and compensation awards will be considered in turn. In the final section, I will draw out a number of conclusions from the broad comparative overview, pointing out the tensions inherent in these remedies systems.

2. Basic structure of challenge proceedings

All but two[6] of the systems under review provide for administrative review mechanisms, that is, mechanisms to challenge procurement decisions at an administrative level. In four of these systems, the types of procurement decisions subject to review are limited in that a number of decisions are expressly excluded from review.[7] The decisions exempt from review closely follow the review exemptions under the 1994 UNCITRAL Model Law on Procurement of Goods, Construction and Services ('1994 UNCITRAL Model Law').[8] In all these systems, the choice of procurement method[9] and a decision to reject all bids are exempt from review. The choice of an evaluation procedure is also exempt in Botswana[10] and Ghana,[11] again mirroring the 1994 Model Law. In Ghana, a decision to limit procurement proceedings on the basis of nationality is also exempt,[12] making it the only system of which all the exemptions are also found in

6 The exceptions are Namibia and Zimbabwe.

7 These are Botswana (Public Procurement and Asset Disposal Regulations, reg. 77(2)); Ethiopia (Federal Government Procurement and Property Administration Proclamation No. 649/2009, Art. 73(2)); Ghana (Public Procurement Act 2003 (Act 663), s. 77(2)); and Kenya (Public Procurement and Disposal Act 2005, s. 93(2)).

8 Art. 52(2).

9 The rules governing the choice of procurement method are discussed in detail in Chapter 12 of this volume.

10 Public Procurement and Asset Disposal Regulations (Botswana), reg. 77(2)(b).

11 Public Procurement Act 2003 (Act 663) (Ghana), s. 77(2)(b).

12 *Ibid.*, s. 77(2)(c).

the 1994 Model Law, although not adopting all the exemptions of the Model Law. In Botswana, 'a refusal by the procuring entity to respond to an unsolicited offer of an interest to bid' is also exempt from review,[13] and in Kenya the conclusion of the contract is expressly excluded from review.[14]

In the majority of systems, administrative challenge involves in the first place a review or appeal to a superior official, usually the head, of the relevant procuring entity. In most of these systems, a subsequent appeal or review is available to a central administrative oversight body. In some systems, there are even multiple administrative appeal opportunities subsequent to the original challenge of the procurement decision at issue. For example, in Rwanda, this oversight structure, the Independent Review Panels (IRP), exist at district and national levels with consecutive appeals available against challenge decisions of procurement entities. An adverse decision of a procurement entity on a challenge may first be appealed to the district-level IRP and subsequently to the national-level IRP, thus providing multiple administrative appeal opportunities.[15] Another example is Botswana, where challenge decisions at the procuring entity level may be appealed to the Public Procurement and Asset Disposal Board, whose decisions may in turn be appealed to the Independent Complaints Review Committee.[16]

A variation on this common structure of challenge proceedings is where the administrative review lies directly to the central oversight body, in other words where provision is not made for challenge within the procurement entity. Kenya is an example of such structure where the review lies in the first place to the Public Procurement Administrative Review Board, a centralised review body specifically created for this purpose.[17]

The South African system is an exception to the common structure set out above. While there are also administrative challenge mechanisms available in South Africa, these are not as systemised as in the other systems. Instead, one finds a number of diverse administrative mechanisms at different levels of government with no overarching or

13 Public Procurement and Asset Disposal Regulations (Botswana), reg. 77(2)(d).

14 Public Procurement and Disposal Act 2005 (Kenya), s. 93(2)(c). See also section 6.1 below on the remedy of invalidation of concluded contracts.

15 Law No. 12/2007 of 27 March 2007, Law on Public Procurement (Rwanda) Arts. 69–70. See Chapter 8, section 2.3.3, of this volume.

16 Public Procurement and Asset Disposal Act 2001 (Botswana), s. 104. See Chapter 2, section 2.3, of this volume.

17 Public Procurement and Disposal Act 2005 (Kenya), ss. 25 and 93. See Chapter 5, section 2.3, of this volume.

coherent structure.[18] Thus, at national and provincial level, the relevant treasury is obliged in terms of the Treasury Regulations 2005 under the Public Finance Management Act[19] to 'establish a mechanism . . . to receive and consider complaints regarding alleged non-compliance with the prescribed minimum norms and standards' in the supply chain management system.[20] No further guidance is given in the regulations on how these mechanisms should operate or what they can do. At local government level, there are multiple internal review mechanisms allowing challenges against procurement decisions mostly within the procuring entity.[21]

As noted above, two of the systems under review here, namely, Namibia and Zimbabwe, do not provide for administrative review. Instead, supplier remedies are purely judicial in these two systems. In Namibia, there is no specific provision for supplier remedies in the public procurement regulatory regime. The only recourse open to suppliers is in the ordinary courts based on general principles of especially administrative law, but also law of contract and delict (tort).[22] The Zimbabwean Public Procurement Act provides for challenges against procurement decisions directly to the Administrative Court.[23] South Africa, Namibia and Zimbabwe thus differ markedly from the other systems under review in that there are no central administrative bodies to which challenges against procurement decisions may be made in these systems.

All of the systems with administrative review mechanisms, in addition, also provide for recourse to courts if a bidder is dissatisfied with the relief at administrative level or as an alternative to administrative review. Such judicial recourse takes different forms. In a number of systems, such as Nigeria and Kenya, the aggrieved bidder may take the complaint on appeal to the courts.[24] In other systems, such as Ghana and South Africa, judicial recourse is in the form of review only.[25] In this latter category, the judicial review powers are generally not created in the public procurement rules themselves, but rather are based on general

18 See Quinot, 'Enforcement of Procurement Law from a South African Perspective', note 4 above, pp. 195–7.

19 Act 1 of 1999 (South Africa).

20 Reg. 6A9.3 (South Africa).

21 Quinot, 'Enforcement of Procurement Law from a South African Perspective', note 4 above, pp. 195–7.

22 See Chapter 6, section 2.3, of this volume.

23 Procurement Act (Zimbabwe), s. 43. See Chapter 10, section 2.3, of this volume.

24 Chapter 7, section 2.3, of this volume; Chapter 5, section 2.3, of this volume.

25 Quinot, 'Enforcement of Procurement Law from a South African Perspective', note 4 above, pp. 200–3; Chapter 4, section 2.3, of this volume.

administrative justice provisions in either the constitution[26] or general administrative law enactments.[27] Another distinction in judicial supplier remedies lies in the focus of judicial scrutiny. In some systems, it is the original procurement decision that may be challenged in court (either on appeal or review) while in others it is the administrative review of the original procurement decision that may be brought to court, and in yet another category both these decisions may be challenged. In most systems, judicial redress is available in the ordinary civil courts, with the exception of Zimbabwe where procurement decisions fall within the jurisdiction of the specialised Administrative Court.[28] While courts in some systems, for example Kenya and South Africa, seem to be very active in fulfilling this supreme supervisory function,[29] the trend seems to be for courts rarely to use their supervisory function over procurement, despite the notional existence of their review/appeal powers.

One can only speculate on the reasons for this trend in the absence of any empirical study on supplier use of remedies. One reason may be long delays in obtaining an outcome in judicial proceedings, which is fairly common in many African systems.[30] Delays are particularly problematic in the context of public procurement where any significant delay in litigation may render the outcome ineffective against the background of a procurement contract that had already been completed by the time the litigation renders an outcome.[31] Another potential reason is the fact that many of the regulatory systems under review are of fairly recent origin. Most of these systems have adopted their core public procurement rules only in the last decade with the result that one would expect low levels of experience and familiarity among suppliers in respect of available remedies.[32] Finally, one can ask whether the extensive administrative

26 For example, Art. 23 of the Constitution of the Republic of Ghana 1992 and s. 33 of the Constitution of the Republic of South Africa, 1996.

27 For example, the Promotion of Administrative Justice Act 3 of 2000 in South Africa.

28 Procurement Act (Zimbabwe), s. 43.

29 See Chapter 5, section 2.3, of this volume; Quinot, 'Enforcement of Procurement Law from a South African Perspective', note 4 above, pp. 198–201.

30 See Penal Reform International, *Access to Justice in Sub-Saharan Africa: The Role of Traditional and Informal Justice Systems* (2000), p. 17, which argues, albeit in the criminal justice context, that one reason 'why the majority of people in Africa continue to settle their disputes using traditional and informal systems' is because '[m]ost [formal judicial] proceedings are subject to considerable delays at all stages'.

31 See Gordon, 'Constructing a Bid Protest Process', note 2 above, p. 437.

32 In her study of the effectiveness of bidder remedies in the UK and Greece, Pachnou found that 'ignorance of the substantive and procedural law' and 'unpredictable outcome at trial' were factors that discouraged firms from litigating public procurement disputes in the UK and Greece: D. Pachnou, 'The Effectiveness of Bidder Remedies for Enforcing the

review mechanisms available to bidders in most of these systems contribute to low levels of recourse to judicial remedies. Comparing the high levels of procurement litigation in South Africa, where there is limited effective administrative review opportunities, with low levels of procurement litigation in most other systems where there are extensive administrative review opportunities, it is certainly arguable that this is a factor inhibiting procurement litigation.

An interesting institutional difference between the systems is that, in some of them, judicial intervention follows as a particular step within the overall remedies scheme, in particular in the form of an appeal or review against the final administrative review decision, whereas, in other systems, judicial intervention stands further apart from the administrative review. In some of these latter instances, there may be no link with the administrative review, in other words, the procurement decision is simply challenged in court quite independently of any administrative challenge. In other instances, there may be a link to the administrative review, although the judicial review still stands on its own and distinct from the administrative proceedings. In these latter cases, exhausting an administrative review may be a prerequisite for approaching a court, but, without any further links between the two reviews, the link between administrative and judicial review is thus only a formal one, not one of substance.[33]

From this overview of the basic structure of challenge proceedings in the systems under review, it should already be evident that the 1994 UNCITRAL Model Law's review provisions are closely followed in most of the systems,[34] which is not surprising given the significant influence that the Model Law has had on most of these systems as highlighted in Part I of this volume. However, the choices made (or the apparent absence of a choice) in these systems between the different remedy mechanisms put forward in the 1994 Model Law are interesting. By and large, the

EC Public Procurement Rules: A Case Study of the Public Works Sector in the United Kingdom and Greece' (unpublished PhD thesis, University of Nottingham, 2003). It is thus to be expected that, in systems with fairly new procurement rules and thus few judgments in this area, these two factors will play an even more significant role in inhibiting procurement litigation.

33 In South Africa, s. 7(2) of the Promotion of Administrative Justice Act 3 of 2000 provides that judicial review can only proceed after administrative remedies have been exhausted, and in Nigeria the Federal High Court confirmed the same principle in *A. C Egbe Nig Ltd* v. *DG BPP and 4 Others*, Suit No. FHC/B/CS/116/2010 (see Chapter 7, section 2.3, of this volume).

34 Chapter VI of the 1994 Model Law.

systems that have been influenced by the 1994 Model Law have adopted all of the remedy mechanisms proposed in the Model Law and have created supplier remedies at all three potential levels or places where a bid protest forum can be located, namely, at the level of the procuring entity, with an administrative oversight body, and within courts.[35] In a number of instances, systems have even gone further than the 1994 Model Law in providing for multiple remedies at one particular level, while also providing for remedies at the two other levels; examples outlined above are Rwanda and Botswana. These choices are interesting since one would have expected to find more limited and streamlined challenge mechanisms in order to 'limit disruption of the procurement process'[36] in light of the extreme resource constraints faced by most African systems and the dire need for cost-effective administration, including public procurement. However, the quite extensive supplier remedies regimes found in these systems, enacting the full ambit of, and at times going beyond, the 1994 Model Law's remedies provisions and mostly exceeding what is required as a minimum of remedies under the WTO's Agreement on Government Procurement,[37] probably again emphasise the determinative role that the objective of integrity in procurement plays in designing remedies in Africa.

3. Single or multiple remedies regimes

An interesting issue is whether there is only one (domestic) remedies regime applicable to public procurement within a system[38] or whether potentially multiple remedies regimes may be at play. Of particular interest is whether suppliers have access to an alternative remedies regime to the domestic one in procurement funded by external donors, such as the World Bank.[39] The 2011 OECD/DAC survey on implementing the

35 See Gordon, 'Constructing a Bid Protest Process', note 2 above, p. 433.

36 See UNCITRAL, 'Main Features of the Model Law' in *Guide to Enactment of UNCITRAL Model Law on Procurement of Goods, Construction and Services*, para. 33.

37 On the remedies requirements of the WTO Agreement on Government Procurement, see S. Arrowsmith and R. D. Anderson (eds.), *The WTO Regime on Government Procurement: Challenge and Reform* (Cambridge University Press, 2011), Part VI.

38 This domestic remedies system may consist of different sub-systems applicable at different levels of government in a particular country or between different categories of contracting authorities within the same country. However, for present purposes, these different sub-systems are treated as a single national, domestic system of remedies.

39 On the influence of donors on African procurement regulation generally, see Chapter 11 of this volume.

Paris Declaration indicates that 'the use of donor systems continues to be prevalent amongst donors, and less than half of all aid reported in the Survey uses countries' procurement systems'.[40] That means that, for more than half of the aid reported in the countries included in the survey, which include eight of the systems under review here,[41] procurement systems other than the domestic one were used.[42] In many instances, that would include remedies regimes other than the domestic one.[43]

From a remedies perspective, the question of interest is whether this practice may result in parallel challenge mechanisms or actual parallel proceedings. While information on actual practices in this regard is scarce, it seems as if in some systems, for example Ethiopia,[44] remedies may be pursued in terms of more than one mechanism simultaneously. However, it also seems that a finding in terms of the 'external' remedies regime may have a determinative influence on any ongoing challenge in the domestic system.[45]

In those systems where judicial procurement remedies are obtained in terms of normal judicial systems, in other words based on general review or appeal jurisdiction, mostly in terms of general administrative law, like Ghana, Namibia and South Africa, the use of external procurement rules, including remedies, may cause particular problems. Such external rules will generally not be able to displace the review jurisdiction of the national courts.[46] This can quite easily result in duplicate and divergent remedies systems. Since the distinct challenge procedures

40 OECD/DAC, *Aid Effectiveness 2005–10: Progress in Implementing the Paris Declaration* (Paris: OECD, 2011), p. 49.

41 The only system not included is Zimbabwe.

42 The figures for the eight countries individually range from 14 per cent of aid for the government sector using country procurement systems in Namibia to 64 per cent in Rwanda: OECD/DAC, *Aid Effectiveness 2005–10*, note 40 above, pp. 124–5.

43 It does not follow necessarily that use of the donor's procurement rules will result in the use of an 'external' remedies regime, i.e. a regime other than that of the relevant country, since the donor's rules may simply rely on the local remedies system, e.g. judicial review in the national courts.

44 Chapter 3, section 2.2, of this volume.

45 *Ibid.*

46 For example, while the 'Bid Challenge System' of the Millennium Challenge Account (the organisational unit established within the National Planning Commission by the Namibian government to manage the aid granted under the Millennium Challenge Compact entered into between the United States and Namibia) expressly provides that the decision of the final administrative review body under that system (the Independent Appeals Panel) will be 'final, binding and enforceable', it is highly unlikely that this system can oust the ordinary judicial review jurisdiction of the Namibian High Court over public procurement decisions taken under this programme.

in such an instance, that is the external system's administrative review and the domestic judicial review, originate from different systems, it is to be expected that problems of alignment may emerge. These problems may be as basic as conflicting time frames for pursuing the different remedies or more complicated such as the distinct remedial powers granted to various levels within the different remedies regimes and the relationships created within a single system between the various levels, which may now be lost because of the intersecting application of distinct remedies systems. This may result in significant disruption to the coherence within any one of these remedies systems. Another difficult issue may be the fairly general requirement found in most systems that administrative remedies be exhausted before judicial intervention is pursued.[47] In an instance of multiple applicable remedies regimes, one wonders whether a domestic review court will include the external procurement rules' administrative remedies as falling within the scope of this rule, in other words whether domestic courts will also require bidders to first exhaust the administrative remedies under the external procurement rules before approaching the court as it would *vis-à-vis* domestic administrative remedies.

While the procurement laws of some systems contain conflict clauses to resolve potential conflicts between domestic procurement rules and rules of donors,[48] such clauses will not be of particular use in resolving the remedial issues raised above. First, such conflict clauses are mostly only aimed at resolving conflicts between the domestic procurement statute and the external set of rules. The problems outlined above do not emerge from the domestic *procurement* laws, but rather from more general laws pertaining to judicial remedies on which a conflict clause in the procurement act can have little impact. Secondly, in most of the questions raised above, there is no true conflict between the domestic laws and external procurement rules. The issues rather emerge from the combined application of domestic and external rules.

47 See note 33 above.

48 E.g. s. 6(1) of the Kenyan Public Procurement and Disposal Act 2005 states that '[w]here any provision of this Act conflicts with any obligations of the Republic of Kenya arising from a treaty or other agreement to which Kenya is a party, this Act shall prevail except in instances of negotiated grants or loans'; and s. 7(1) states that '[i]f there is a conflict between this Act, the regulations or any directions of the Authority and a condition imposed by the donor of funds, the condition shall prevail with respect to a procurement that uses those funds and no others'.

4. Standstill period

Some of the systems provide for a mandatory standstill period between the award decision and the conclusion of the contract to allow for challenges to the award before signing of the contract. In Ethiopia and Rwanda, the standstill period is seven days,[49] while in Kenya it is fourteen days.[50] In this regard, these systems are aligned to international standards in terms of which standstill periods have become a common feature of remedies regimes.[51]

Most systems under review, however, have no standstill periods. The absence of a standstill period is inevitably linked to the availability of interim relief when a challenge is brought, either in the form of an automatic suspension of the procurement or upon application as well as to the eventual substantive relief that may be granted in response to the challenge and in particular whether a concluded contract may be invalidated. Both of these issues will be considered below. In systems with generous interim relief arrangements, particularly where suspension is automatic, there seems little point in having a standstill period in addition to prompt notification of the award decision to all bidders. Likewise, where a concluded contract may be invalidated in challenge proceedings, the argument in favour of a standstill period is considerably weaker, which is often to avoid a 'race to sign the contract' that will undermine the possibility of any effective remedy in subsequent challenge proceedings.[52] The generous suspension rules in most systems under review, outlined below, thus explain the absence of standstill periods. Whether this is the most appropriate design for remedies regimes in African systems is a different question to which I shall return in the conclusion below.

South Africa provides an interesting African example of a 'judicially engineered' standstill period, albeit not in the strict sense of the term used above. There is no mandatory standstill period in South African public procurement regulations. However, the judgment of the South African Constitutional Court, the highest court in the country, in *Steenkamp*

49 *Ibid.*; Law No. 12/2007 of 27 March 2007, Law on Public Procurement (Rwanda), Art. 43.

50 Chapter 5, section 2.3, of this volume.

51 Both the 2011 UNCITRAL Model Law (Art. 22) and EU Remedies Directive 2007/66 [2007] OJ L134/114 (Art. 2a) provide for mandatory standstill periods.

52 See H.-J. Prieß and P. Friton, 'Designing Effective Challenge Procedures: The EU's Experience with Remedies' in Arrowsmith and Anderson (eds.), *The WTO Regime on Government Procurement*, note 37 above, pp. 526–8, on the rationale for introducing a mandatory standstill period in EU procurement law.

NO v. *Provincial Tender Board, Eastern Cape*[53] may be said effectively to amount to a type of standstill period between award of the tender and effective implementation, if not conclusion, of the tender contract. In this matter, a tender contract was set aside on judicial review just over a year after award of the tender.[54] However, while the initially successful bidder had not performed under the contract yet, it had already incurred expenses in preparation for performance. The initially successful bidder thus instituted a claim for damages against the contracting authority for the losses it incurred as a result of the contract being set aside. The matter eventually ended up in the Constitutional Court, which refused to recognise a claim for damages under these circumstances. The Court held, *inter alia*, that the successful bidder acted too quickly following the award of the tender and should have waited before it acted on the tender award to see if the award was not challenged on review.[55] As I have argued elsewhere,[56] this approach of the Court effectively results, or at least judicially sanctions, a standstill period between award of the tender and the expiry of the time frame for challenging the award upon judicial review.[57]

5. Temporary or interim relief

A common feature in many of the systems is the suspension of procurement procedures when a challenge is lodged. Again, the strong influence of the 1994 UNCITRAL Model Law is evident in this regard.[58] However, it is of interest to see the different ways that suspension is dealt with in the various systems. In some systems, such as Nigeria, Ghana and Kenya, the suspension is discretionary. The reviewing body, either the procuring entity or a centralised review body, must decide in every case whether

53 2007 (3) SA 121 (CC).

54 The review judgment was reported as *Cash Paymaster Services (Pty) Ltd* v. *Eastern Cape Province* 1999 (1) SA 324 (CkH).

55 *Steenkamp*, 2007 (3) SA 121 (CC) at [51]–[52].

56 G. Quinot, 'Worse Than Losing a Government Tender: Winning It' (2008) 19 *Stellenbosch Law Review* 101, 113–14.

57 That period is generally a maximum of 180 days after notification of the decision under the Promotion of Administrative Justice Act 3 of 2000 (South Africa), s. 7(1), but may be extended either by agreement between the parties or by the court in terms of s. 9 of the Act.

58 Art. 56 of the 1994 Model Law provides for suspension of the procurement proceedings for seven days when a complaint is lodged.

suspension is warranted.[59] In Nigeria, suspension is to be ordered if the relevant accounting officer seized with the review 'deems it necessary',[60] and in Kenya the Review Board must communicate to the procuring entity 'suspension of the procurement proceedings in such manner as may be prescribed'.[61] In Ghana, the discretion is clearly circumscribed by means of the conditions to be met for a suspension.[62] These mirror the 1994 UNCITRAL Model Law's conditions for suspension,[63] namely, that the complaint is not frivolous; that the bidder will suffer irreparable damage if the procurement is not suspended; that the challenge is likely to succeed and that the suspension will not cause disproportionate harm to others. Suspension will also not be possible in the face of certification by the procuring entity that the procurement should continue on urgent public interest grounds.

In most of the systems, however, the suspension will be automatic, that is, suspension will not depend on the discretion of the reviewing body, thereby following the approach of the 1994 UNCITRAL Model Law. Interestingly, in Nigeria, appeals against challenge decisions of procuring entities to the Bureau for Public Procurement automatically suspend procurement proceedings.[64] This is in contrast, as we have noted above, to suspension at the first level of administrative review in Nigeria, which is discretionary. The 1994 Model Law's conditions for suspension are also clearly influential in systems with automatic suspensions. In many of these systems, such as Botswana and Zimbabwe, the suspension will not lie if the complaint does not comply with these conditions, for example if the complaint is found frivolous or only aimed at delay etc.[65] The net result may thus be the same as with discretionary suspensions based on these conditions. In yet another use of the conditions to virtually the same effect, of which Kenya provides an example,[66] the reviewing body may simply immediately reject a complaint that does not meet these conditions, hence rendering suspension moot. This is arguably the most effective mechanism, taking into account these conditions. It brings immediate certainty on the complaint and the procurement can proceed

59 This is also the approach adopted in the 2011 UNCITRAL Model Law in Arts. 66 and 67.
60 Public Procurement Act 2007 (Nigeria), s. 54(2).
61 Public Procurement and Disposal Act 2005 (Kenya), s. 94.
62 Public Procurement Act 2003 (Act 663) (Ghana), s. 81(1).
63 1994 UNCITRAL Model Law, Art. 56.
64 Public Procurement Act 2007 (Nigeria), s. 54(4).
65 Public Procurement and Asset Disposal Regulations (Botswana), reg. 79; Procurement Act (Zimbabwe), s. 44.
66 Public Procurement and Disposal Act 2005 (Kenya), s. 95.

without delay and without the fear of later disruption. It is difficult to see why a complaint should be allowed to proceed, even without suspension, if it has no *prima facie* merit or is frivolous or will cause disproportionate harm to others.

In South Africa, no provision is made in any of the administrative review mechanisms for suspension of the procedure. However, at judicial level an applicant may ask the court for an interim order to suspend the procurement pending the finalisation of the review application in terms of normal interim relief rules in civil suits,[67] as is the case under judicial remedies of many other systems.[68] The conditions for granting an interim order of this nature, which is the same as in any judicial review application, closely resemble the 1994 UNCITRAL Model Law's conditions. The applicant must show a clear right, which, 'though *prima facie* established, is open to some doubt', the apprehension of irreparable harm if the relief is not granted and the absence of an alternative remedy.[69] It is a discretionary remedy and the court weighs the interests of the respective parties in granting or withholding the relief, referred to as the balance of convenience.[70]

In this type of case, the first requirement, that of a *prima facie* right, is established by indicating that the procurement decision stands to be reviewed in terms of general administrative law principles, in other words that the applicant can make out a *prima facie* case for the judicial review of the decision.[71] This leg of the inquiry does not present particular

67 Quinot, 'Enforcement of Procurement Law from a South African Perspective', note 4 above, pp. 198–200.

68 See e.g. *RBH Construction and Another* v. *Windhoek Municipal Council and Another* 2002 NR 443 (HC) (Namibia); *AFS Group Namibia (Pty) Ltd* v. *Chairperson of the Tender Board of Namibia* (A55/2011) 2011 NAHC 184 (1 July 2011) (Namibia); S. Gbadegbe, 'Overview of the High Court (Civil Procedure) Rules', paper presented at the induction course for newly appointed circuit judges at the Judicial Training Institute (Ghana); *Medical Rescue International Botswana Ltd* v. *Attorney General and Others* (Civil Appeal No. 55 of 205) [2006] BWCA 6 (10 March 2006) (Botswana); *Airfield Investments (Pvt) Ltd* v. *Minister of Lands, Agriculture and Rural Resettlement and Others* (64/03) [2004] ZWSC 36; SC36/04 (3 June 2004) (Zimbabwe).

69 See *Eriksen Motors (Welkom) Ltd* v. *Protea Motors* 1973 (3) SA 685 (A); *Hix Networking Technologies* v. *System Publishers (Pty) Ltd* 1997 (1) SA 391 (A).

70 *Ibid.* These requirements closely resemble that of the European Court of Justice in similar cases: see S. Treumer, 'Enforcement of the EU Public Procurement Rules: The State of the Law and Current Issues' in S. Treumer and F. Lichère (eds.), *Enforcement of the EU Public Procurement Rules* (Copenhagen: DJØF Publishing, 2011), pp. 20–1; S. Arrowsmith, *The Law of Public and Utilities Procurement* (2nd edn, London: Sweet & Maxwell, 2005), paras. 21.57–21.64.

71 See *TBP Building and Civils (Pty) Ltd* v. *East London Industrial Development Zone (Pty) Ltd* [2009] JDR 0203 (ECG) at [14]; *Actaris South Africa (Pty) Ltd* v. *Sol Plaatje Municipality*

problems. It is rather the second and third requirements, which also inform the balance-of-convenience analysis, that tend to be problematic in procurement cases.[72] It may be quite difficult for a disappointed bidder to prove the harm that she attempts to avoid in applying for interim relief in such a case. The same considerations will also make it difficult to show the absence of an alternative remedy, particularly in the contemplated review application.[73] While the motivation behind these cases is obviously to get the contract,[74] the unsuccessful bidder will mostly not be able to show that such a result will follow even pursuant to a successful review application, that is, if the *prima facie* right is vindicated. First, the outcome of the review will mostly only be the invalidation of the tender decision and only in the most exceptional cases will the review court actually order the tender to be awarded to the applicant. The disappointed bidder-applicant's legal entitlements under the judicial review are thus extremely limited. Her entitlement to the contract is highly speculative and will mostly not swing the balance of convenience in her favour. Secondly, the applicant will find it difficult to prove that the contract will be awarded to her following the set-aside upon review. Thus, as a matter of both law and fact, the harm that the applicant for interim relief seeks to avoid mostly cannot be the failure to secure the contract.[75] The harm is located in a more generalised interest in administrative justice and fair public contracting, and, at best for the applicant, the opportunity to participate in such a fair tender process. It seems that in South Africa this interest, despite its constitutional pedigree, quite easily bends the knee to the more immediate and concrete competing commercial interests of the contracting authority and often the public that is served by the procurement in the background at the interim relief stage.[76]

[2008] 4 All SA 168 (NC) at [17] and [26]; *Indo Contractors CC* v. *TFMC (Pty) Ltd* [2009] JOL 23768 (KZD) at [5]; *Lohan Civil-Tebogo Joint Venture* v. *Mangaung Plaaslike Munisipaliteit* (Case 508/2009 (O)) 27 February 2009 at [37]–[39]; *Matlafalang Training CC* v. *MEC: Free State, Department of Public Works* (5412/2008) [2008] ZAFSHC 136 (11 December 2008) at [8] and [11]–[13].

72 See e.g. *Actaris South Africa*, note 71 above, at [27]; and *Eskom Holdings Ltd and Another* v. *New Reclamation Group (Pty) Ltd* 2009 (4) SA 628 (SCA) at [11].

73 See *Matlafalang Training*, note 71 above, at [21].

74 See G. Quinot, 'Towards Effective Judicial Review of State Commercial Activity' (2009) *Journal of South African Law* 436, 442–3.

75 See *Matlafalang Training*, note 71 above, at [21].

76 See *Digital Horizons (Pty) Ltd* v. *South African Broadcasting Corporation* (2008/19224) [2008] ZAGPHC 272 (8 September 2008) at [24]–[28]; *Indo Contractors*, note 71 above, at [11]–[13].

In most of the African systems under review, there is clearly a close adherence to the 1994 UNCITRAL Model Law's approach to interim relief in the form of suspension. In this regard, it is thus worth noting that the 2011 UNCITRAL Model Law on Procurement of Goods, Construction and Services ('2011 UNCITRAL Model Law') moves away from the automatic suspension approach of the earlier Model Law in favour of discretionary suspensions to be ordered by the relevant review body.[77]

Interim relief, either at administrative or judicial level, is a key aspect of any supplier remedies regime. It needs to balance the trade-off between preserving an effective remedy in a challenge to a procurement decision thereby promoting integrity, on the one hand, and the need to minimise disruption to the procurement process thereby enhancing efficient procurement, on the other. This is what Gordon has called the 'overarching tension' in all remedies systems as a whole.[78] The question is thus not whether to allow interim relief as part of a remedies regime – clearly an effective remedies regime cannot do without it – but rather how interim relief should be crafted. A generous interim relief regime will favour the objective of integrity, while a strict or narrow approach to interim relief will favour efficiency. In this regard, the desirability of the high prevalence of automatic suspension in the African systems under review is questionable. In the first place, this approach may favour the incumbent supplier who will often continue to supply the goods or services during the suspension of the new tender, thus creating skewed incentives for such incumbent to challenge when losing a new tender round.[79] This may eventually undermine the goal of integrity in the procurement process, which is one of the main drivers of the generous automatic suspension approach. In adopting this approach, African systems are certainly also wanting to improve their systems' reputation in order to attract more competition in their procurement markets, especially from foreign suppliers.[80] However, a system that inherently favours the incumbent supplier will clearly undermine this purpose. Secondly, even the conditions commonly set for automatic suspension or to override such suspension, as noted above, may not prove to be effective. Where the suspension is automatic, the burden will be largely placed on the

77 2011 UNCITRAL Model Law, Arts. 66 and 67.

78 Gordon, 'Constructing a Bid Protest Process', note 2 above, p. 430.

79 *Ibid.*, p. 442.

80 See Gordon, 'Constructing a Bid Protest Process', note 2 above, pp. 430–1, on this 'reputational' objective.

contracting authority, or the reviewing authority, to ascertain whether these conditions are met in order to override the automatic suspension. In systems with limited public procurement capacity, which certainly include all of the systems under review here, such an approach may not achieve the necessary balance that is crucial to an effective interim relief regime. In such systems, it is to be expected that suspensions will follow as a matter of course since officials will not be equipped to take up compliance with the conditions. A far better approach would be to allow for suspension upon application, as is commonly the approach to interim relief at judicial level. Under such an approach, the burden is largely placed on the challenging supplier to show compliance with the conditions for suspension. This will counter any advantages that an incumbent supplier may see in bringing a challenge for the sole reason of suspension and would also help address the problem of lack of capacity on the part of contracting authorities.

6. Final relief

6.1. Invalidation

The general relief available in most systems is for the review/appeal body to review the relevant decision and set it aside if found irregular. The matter may then be referred back to the relevant procuring entity with instructions or may in most cases be replaced by the review body. This is the essential hallmark of an effective remedies system: the ability to have the impugned decision invalidated. In Ethiopia and South Africa, it is not clear that the administrative review body may indeed replace the procuring entity's decision. In Ethiopia, this power is not expressly granted to the Complaints Review Board,[81] and the Board is expressly prohibited from 'making decisions in regard to selection of the successful bidder or entering into a contract'.[82] It thus seems that the Board can at least not replace the procuring entity's award decision upon review. In South Africa, much depends on the particular mechanism put in place by the relevant treasury or procuring entity since the applicable regulations do not set out the remedial powers of the complaints mechanisms to

81 See Federal Government Procurement and Property Administration Proclamation No. 649/2009 (Ethiopia), Arts. 72(3), 75(2).

82 Federal Government Procurement Directive 2010 (Ethiopia), Art. 41.

be created by these bodies.[83] Only at local government level within the limited scope of the appeal mechanism under the Municipal Systems Act[84] is the power expressly given to vary the decision under scrutiny. However, as I have argued elsewhere,[85] this power is circumscribed in a way that may undermine its effectiveness in procurement disputes by the strange provision of that Act stating that 'no such variation or revocation of a decision may detract from any rights that may have accrued as a result of the decision'.[86]

Judicial remedies follow broadly the same pattern as above. Most procurement enactments are fairly vague on the nature of the proceedings before a court, with terms such as 'review' and 'appeal' being used interchangeably.[87] The Ethiopian Procurement Direction, for example, simply states that a bidder 'may take the matter to a competent court' without indicating what court that may be and what the powers of the court in such applications are.[88] Zimbabwe is a rare exception in the systems under review here, in that its Procurement Act explicitly sets out in what court judicial remedies may be pursued and what the nature of such proceedings and remedies are.[89] Given the strong influence of the 1994 UNCITRAL Model Law on most of these systems and the Model Law's explicit 'minimal approach in Article 57' to judicial review,[90] setting out judicial intervention only in the broadest terms, it is not surprising to find very little detail and thus a fair amount of uncertainty on judicial remedies in most of the present systems' procurement laws. It is submitted that, in most systems with a common law tradition, which includes the bulk of the systems under review, judicial intervention will be in the form of ordinary administrative law judicial review. The default remedy in such

83 Quinot, 'Enforcement of Procurement Law from a South African Perspective', note 4 above, pp. 195–7.
84 Act 32 of 2000 (South Africa), s. 62.
85 Quinot, 'Enforcement of Procurement Law from a South African Perspective', note 4 above, pp. 195–6.
86 Local Government: Municipal Systems Act 32 of 2000 (South Africa), s. 62(3).
87 See e.g. Public Procurement and Disposal Act 2005 (Kenya), s. 100, which states, in subsection (2): 'Any party to the review aggrieved by the decision of the Review Board may *appeal* to the High Court', and in subsection (4): 'If *judicial review* is not declared by the High Court . . . ' (emphasis added).
88 Federal Government Procurement Directive 2010 (Ethiopia), Art. 50; see Chapter 3, section 2.2, of this volume.
89 Procurement Act (Zimbabwe), s. 43.
90 See UNCITRAL, note 36 above, comment on Art. 57. The provisions dealing with judicial review in the new 2011 UNCITRAL Model Law are even more skeletal.

applications will be invalidation of the challenged decision. Under exceptional circumstances, review courts may in some systems, such as Namibia[91] and South Africa,[92] be able to replace the procurement decision with its own decision.[93]

One of the biggest issues in final relief in procurement disputes is whether a concluded contract can be overturned. Internationally there was traditionally strong support for the approach that concluded contracts cannot be upset.[94] This is also the approach adopted by the 1994 UNCITRAL Model Law and as a result is reflected in most of the systems under review here. In Nigeria and South Africa, however, concluded contracts may be administratively cancelled. In Nigeria, the Bureau of Public Procurement enjoys wide powers of investigation whether there was a challenge by a bidder or not and may as a consequence of its investigations cancel a contract.[95] In South Africa, the power to administratively cancel a contract is more circumscribed. In terms of procurement regulations applicable to all three levels of government, contracting authorities *must* cancel a contract if the supplier or any official 'committed any corrupt or fraudulent act during the bidding process or the execution of that contract' to the benefit of the supplier.[96] Judicial invalidation of contracts

91 *Waterberg Big Game Hunting Lodge Otjahewita (Pty) Ltd* v. *Minister of Environment and Tourism* 2010 (1) NR 1 (SC).

92 Promotion of Administrative Justice Act 3 of 2000 (South Africa), s. 8(1)(c)(ii)(aa).

93 Factors that will move a court to grant such a substitution order include bias or gross incompetence on the part of the decision-maker, where the end result is a foregone conclusion and referring it back will simply be a waste of time and where the court is in as good a position as the original administrator to make the decision. See *Premier, Mpumalanga, and Another* v. *Executive Committee, Association of State-Aided Schools, Eastern Transvaal* 1999 (2) SA 91 (CC) (South Africa); *Waterberg Big Game Hunting Lodge Otjahewita*, note 91 above (Namibia).

94 See Arrowsmith, Linarelli and Wallace, *Regulating Public Procurement*, note 3 above, pp. 786–7, indicating that this was the approach favoured in the 1994 UNCITRAL Model Law, the 1994 WTO Agreement on Government Procurement and in EU procurement law under the Remedies Directive and the Utilities Remedies Directive (Directive 89/665 [1989] OJ L395/33 and Directive 92/13 [1992] OJ L2/76).

95 Public Procurement Act 2007 (Nigeria), ss. 53(4) and 54(4). While the language of private law is used here to refer to 'cancellation' rather than 'invalidation' or 'setting aside', it is clear that 'cancel' should be understood in this context as meaning 'invalidate', i.e. the act of bringing the contract to an end not on the basis of the contract (i.e. as a contractual remedy) but based on legislative powers and due to reasons outside the contractual relationship.

96 Treasury Regulations 2005 (South Africa), reg. 16A9.1(f), applying to national and provincial government procurement; Municipal Supply Chain Management Regulations 2005 (South Africa), reg. 38(1)(f), applying to local government procurement.

is also possible in a number of systems such as in the Administrative Court in Zimbabwe[97] and the High Courts in South Africa[98] and probably also Namibia.[99] Botswana presents an interesting variation on this theme. While contracts are expressly declared to be 'irrevocable' and their 'execution shall proceed without interruption' despite a challenge to the procurement process, the Public Procurement and Asset Disposal Act empowers the Independent Complaints Review Committee to 'suspend' execution where 'the execution of such a contract may cause substantial loss to the public revenue or that it will prejudicially affect the public interest'.[100] It is not altogether clear whether this power to 'suspend' would in effect amount to the setting aside of the contract. While 'suspend' is patently not equivalent to 'invalidate', it is difficult to see how this power to suspend under these circumstances will be of any effect if the intention is that execution of the contract can only be temporarily halted.

There has recently been a growing trend internationally to move away from the once strict notion of the irrevocability of concluded contracts or what some authors have called the notion of concluded public contracts as 'sacred cows'.[101] In EU procurement law, the new Remedies Directive 2007/66,[102] following judgments of the European Court of Justice, now requires national remedies regimes in the EU to provide for invalidation of concluded contracts under certain circumstances.[103] Importantly, the new 2011 UNCITRAL Model Law also now provides, as an option, that independent administrative review bodies may overturn concluded contracts.[104] This is a significant move away from the approach under the 1994 Model Law, as noted above, and which has influenced many African

97 Procurement Act (Zimbabwe), s. 43(3), read with Administrative Court Act (Zimbabwe), s. 4.

98 *Eskom Holdings* v. *New Reclamation Group* 2009 (4) SA 628 (SCA) (South Africa).

99 While there is no case law on point, Namibia shares the same administrative law and common law as South Africa, and it thus follows that, since contracts may be set aside upon review in South Africa, the same would be true in Namibia.

100 Public Procurement and Asset Disposal Act 2001 (Botswana), s. 104.

101 Cf. S. Treumer, 'Towards an Obligation to Terminate Contracts Concluded in Breach of the EC Procurement Rules: The End of the Status of Concluded Public Contracts as Sacred Cows' (2007) 16 *Public Procurement Law Review* 371; Treumer, 'Enforcement of the EU Public Procurement Rules', note 70 above, p. 32; see Chapter 3, section 2.2, of this volume.

102 Directive 2007/66 [2007] OJ L134/114.

103 Treumer, 'Enforcement of the EU Public Procurement Rules', note 70 above, pp. 32–7, also see the various country studies in the same book setting out how each system has implemented this requirement.

104 2011 UNCITRAL Model Law, Art. 67(9)(f).

systems. The question emerges whether African systems that currently do not provide for invalidation of concluded contracts should follow suit. The answer to that question links on to the next section and the availability of compensation as an alternative remedy, and I shall return to it in the conclusion.

6.2. Compensation

The award of compensation as relief is less uniformly regulated in African systems. A number of systems unequivocally provide for compensation, such as Ghana[105] and Botswana.[106] However, in both these systems, the ambit of the compensation is circumscribed. In Ghana, only 'compensation for reasonable costs' may be ordered,[107] and in Botswana the compensation that may be awarded by the Independent Complaints Review Committee is capped at the maximum of the commercial outlay for the preparation of a bidding package.[108] Strangely, there is no equivalent cap on compensation awards by the Public Procurement and Asset Disposal Board, although aggrieved bidders must submit 'documentary evidence of loss' when claiming compensation, which suggests that only out-of-pocket expenses may be contemplated.[109]

In a number of other systems, the relevant regulations are rather less clear on compensation awards. In Kenya, for example, provision is made for 'payment of costs as between parties to the review'.[110] It is not clear if this is meant to include substantive compensation claims or simply the costs of the review itself. One finds a similar position in Zimbabwe, where the Administrative Court 'may make such order as to costs as it thinks fit'.[111] However, in Zimbabwe there seems to be some indication that this is meant only to cover litigation costs as opposed to compensation claims in light of the exact same wording found in the Administrative Court Act where it clearly only refers to litigation costs.[112]

In Ethiopia, Namibia, Nigeria and South Africa, no provision is made for compensation whatsoever. However, the power given to accounting

105 Public Procurement Act 2003 (Act 663) (Ghana), s. 79(3)(f).
106 Public Procurement and Asset Disposal Act 2001 (Botswana), s. 108.
107 Public Procurement Act 2003 (Act 663) (Ghana), s. 79(3)(f).
108 Public Procurement and Asset Disposal Act 2001 (Botswana), s. 108(2).
109 Public Procurement and Asset Disposal Regulations (Botswana), reg. 78(2).
110 Public Procurement and Disposal Act 2005 (Kenya), s. 98(d).
111 Procurement Act (Zimbabwe), s. 43(3).
112 Administrative Court Act (Zimbabwe), s. 18.

officers in Nigeria to take any 'corrective measures'[113] and the general tenure of the mandate to establish complaint mechanisms in South Africa[114] may be interpreted to include the power to order compensation. Additionally, in these systems, aggrieved bidders may be able to claim compensation in judicial proceedings, either through a civil claim or as part of an application for judicial review. In South Africa, the latter possibility is expressly recognised in the Promotion of Administrative Justice Act under exceptional circumstances.[115] In addition, while civil claims for damages in procurement disputes have been granted for some time in South Africa, the judgment in *Steenkamp NO* v. *Provincial Tender Board, Eastern Cape*[116] has now restricted such claims to instances where *mala fides* can be shown on the part of the contracting authority. It is of interest to contrast this ruling with those of the European Court of Justice in recent years holding that culpability or fault may not be stated as a condition for damages claims in EU member states' remedies regimes under the EU procurement directives.[117] In the *Steenkamp* judgment, the South African court also seems to suggest that out-of-pocket expenses, such as bid preparation costs, will never be recoverable, because in the court's view such 'class of expenses is always irrecoverable whatever the fate of the tender is. On any outcome, expenses for preparing a tender have to be incurred.'[118]

The very narrow approach to compensation as a supplier remedy in African systems stands in contrast to the trend in European law towards a wider ambit for damages claims.[119] In terms of the 1994 UNCITRAL Model Law, those few African systems that do provide for compensation

113 Public Procurement Act 2007 (Nigeria), s. 54(2)(b).

114 Reg. 50(1)(b) of the Municipal Supply Chain Management Regulations (South Africa) states that an independent person must be appointed 'to deal with objections, complaints and queries', and the Treasury Regulations (South Africa) state that an accounting officer must 'take steps' against an official that fails to comply with procurement rules (reg. 16A9.1(b)(ii)).

115 Act 3 of 2000, s. 8(1)(c)(ii)(bb).

116 *Steenkamp*, 2007 (3) SA 121 (CC). See Quinot, 'Enforcement of Procurement Law from a South African Perspective', note 4 above; and Quinot, 'Worse Than Losing a Government Tender', note 56 above.

117 D. Fairgrieve and F. Lichère, 'Introduction' in D. Fairgrieve and F. Lichère (eds.), *Public Procurement Law: Damages as an Effective Remedy* (Oxford: Hart Publishing, 2011), pp. 2–4; and S. Treumer, 'Basis and Conditions for a Damages Claim for Breach of the EU Public Procurement Rules' in the same volume at pp. 155–61.

118 *Steenkamp*, 2007 (3) SA 121 (CC) at [53].

119 See generally D. Fairgrieve and F. Lichère (eds.), *Public Procurement Law: Damages as an Effective Remedy* (Oxford: Hart Publishing, 2011).

have clearly followed or are aligned to the first, more limited option to compensation provided for in Article 54(3)(f). The 2011 Model Law also seems to suggest a broader approach to compensation claims, even though the wording in Article 67(9)(i) of the new law closely reflects that of the 1994 Model Law. Signals of a broader approach can be found in the replacement of the two distinct options to compensation set out in the 1994 Model Law with a single approach that includes both 'reasonable costs' and 'any loss or damages suffered'. The new Model Law also only provides as an option the restriction of the latter type of compensation claims to 'the costs of the preparation of the submission or the costs relating to the application, or both', in other words excluding lost profits.

7. Concluding remarks

From the broad overview of the remedies regimes in nine African systems in this chapter, one can draw a number of conclusions.

The first observation is the close adherence to the 1994 UNCITRAL Model Law regarding challenge proceedings in most of these systems. The structures of challenge proceedings as well as the basic remedies available are mostly those set out in the 1994 Model Law. Interesting though is the divergence in respect of compensation remedies. In this respect, the systems under review show less adherence to the options regarding compensation awards set out in the 1994 Model Law and seem to be more restrained in allowing compensation claims. One possible explanation for this position may be the severe shortage of resources in most African systems. This factor clearly plays an important role in the South African system where the courts have in recent years significantly narrowed down the scope of damages claims in the procurement context, even in the absence of strict limitations on compensation claims in procurement law itself like those found in many other African systems. In *Steenkamp NO* v. *Provincial Tender Board, Eastern Cape*,[120] the South African Constitutional Court noted:

> The resources of our state treasury, seen against the backdrop of vast public needs, are indeed meagre. The fiscus will ill-afford to recompense by way of damages disappointed or initially successful tenderers and still remain with the need to procure the same goods or service.

120 *Steenkamp*, 2007 (3) SA 121 (CC) at [55].

Against this background context, it is not to be expected that these African systems will follow the lead of other procurement regimes towards a broader approach to compensation claims. However, compensation remedies cannot be viewed in isolation. As I have indicated above, the availability of compensation as a remedy is one important factor in deciding whether to allow concluded contracts to be invalidated upon challenge. Both of these remedies are in turn linked to the availability of interim relief and the existence of standstill periods. The discussion above indicated that concluded contracts cannot be invalidated in most of the systems under review. In light of the limited availability of compensation remedies, the effectiveness of supplier remedies in the post-award stage of procurement in these African countries must consequently be questioned. One counter-argument may be to point to the fairly generous interim relief measures, especially suspension when challenges are lodged, found in most of these systems as a means of addressing the potential ineffectiveness of the remedies regime once a contract is concluded. As I have argued above, however, automatic suspension is also not ideal in these African systems. Furthermore, in all the systems with automatic suspension rules there is considerable scope to avoid suspension altogether. Providing for standstill periods may be a more sensible way of dealing with this difficulty since standstill periods may increase the likelihood of a challenge being brought before conclusion of the contract and thus preserving an effective remedy, while at the same time avoiding the potential dangers of suspensions in creating skewed incentives for incumbent suppliers. In this respect, African systems may thus want to seriously consider adopting the new standstill rules of the 2011 UNCITRAL Model Law. Another solution may be to take a more nuanced view of the invalidation remedy that does not approach invalidation on an all-or-nothing basis. In other words, it may be useful to consider designing an invalidation remedy that does not only amount to either complete invalidation of the concluded contract or no invalidation, but also provides for some middle ground. An example of such an approach can be found in the South African judgment in *Millennium Waste Management (Pty) Ltd* v. *Chairperson, Tender Board: Limpopo Province*,[121] in which what can be called a conditional invalidation order was granted. In this case, the court found the award of a tender for the removal of medical waste from public hospitals reviewable at a time when the contract was already concluded and performance under it ongoing. Rather than simply invalidating the contract,

121 2008 (2) SA 481 (SCA).

as is often the automatic remedial response to a finding of reviewable irregularity in South Africa,[122] the court fashioned a creative remedy tailored to the specific challenge and the interests affected. It invalidated the tender award only if, on a proper re-evaluation of the affected tenders by the contracting authority within a stated time frame, it emerged that the applicant's tender should have won. In other words, the court invalidated the contract only if, on the contracting authority's own assessment, the irregularity impacted on the outcome of the decision. While this re-evaluation was ongoing, the current contract would thus remain in place. The court also preserved any monetary claims that the initially successful tenderer may have under the current tender up to the date of setting aside, if that is the eventual outcome. The invalidity in this sense did not act retrospectively.[123] This conditional, *ex nunc* invalidation provides an effective remedy to the challenger, but does not cause disproportionate disruption to the procurement at issue or the government function dependent on the procurement. It thus shows that a more nuanced approach to invalidation than the common all-or-nothing approach may be able to balance integrity and efficiency concerns in supplier remedies.

A second, somewhat surprising observation that one can draw from the overview of African supplier remedies in this chapter is the generous scope of the challenge proceedings in most of these systems. As noted above, they mostly provide for administrative review challenges at multiple levels, up to three consecutive levels of scrutiny. Less than half of the systems reviewed exempt certain procurement decisions from review. In addition, judicial review or appeal is uniformly available. The remedies provided for in these administrative challenges are also generally extensive, allowing in most cases for substitution of the decision under scrutiny at least prior to conclusion of the contract. This trend seems counter-intuitive when viewed against the observation regarding limited compensation claims noted above. One would expect that, in systems with significantly limited resources, the remedies regimes would not be as extensive. One would expect to find perhaps one level of administrative review and a narrow scope for judicial intervention, with narrowly circumscribed relief. One would furthermore expect reliance on existing, general oversight or

122 See Quinot, 'Worse Than Losing a Government Tender', note 56 above, pp. 117–20; Quinot, 'Enforcement of Procurement Law from a South African Perspective', note 4 above, p. 203.

123 See Quinot, 'Towards Effective Judicial Review of State Commercial Activity', note 74 above, p. 445.

review mechanisms rather than the creation of dedicated, expert public procurement review bodies.

I believe that these two seemingly contradictory observations demonstrate the tension inherent in the creation of a public procurement remedies regime in most African systems. On the one hand, given the perceived lack of accountability and transparency in African procurement systems, maximum control is of high importance, thus leading to extensive, generous and formal remedies regimes, typically in dedicated oversight bodies and/or courts. Undoubtedly, Gordon's argument that an important objective of a national remedies regime may be 'an effort to improve a system's reputation' in order to attract foreign investment[124] is at play in these systems. On the other hand, given the extreme lack of resources in most African systems, both financial and human resources, and thus the need to optimise procurement in terms of best value for money, one expects remedies regimes that are informal, less generous, speedy and as effective as possible: aimed at minimum disruption of the procurement process and cost to government.

The close adherence to the 1994 UNCITRAL Model Law that we saw in most of these African systems, at least on paper, does not seem to provide the answer to the negotiation of this tension. This is compounded by the strong indications, judging from commentary emanating from some of these systems, that the rather ambitious remedies regimes created in the legal frameworks are not and/or cannot be effectively implemented in these countries.[125] Perhaps one of the reasons for this seeming failure of the Model Law to enhance procurement regulation in African systems in this respect lies in the tentative and skeletal nature of the review provisions in the Model Law.[126] It may indeed be a failure to take the Model Law's remedies provisions as optional and providing guidance rather than a strict set of rules to be adopted wholesale that has led many African systems down the problematic path of over-ambitious remedies regimes. But, in

124 Gordon, 'Constructing a Bid Protest Process', note 2 above, pp. 430–1.

125 See U. Awom, 'FRSC, Public Procurement Act: As Senate Wields the Big Axe', *Leadership* (4 March 2012); 'PS Warned on Procurement Scams', *PSNews* (13 March 2012); B. Agande, 'Reps Accuse FEC of Illegal Approval of Contracts', *Vanguard* (7 March 2012); Editorial, 'Contracting Sovereignty', *The Nation* (1 March 2012); F. Links and C. Daniels, 'The Tender Board: Need for Root and Branch Reform', Anti-Corruption Research Programme Paper 3 (2011).

126 See S. Arrowsmith and C. Nicholas, 'The UNCITRAL Model Law on Procurement: Past, Present, and Future' in S. Arrowsmith (ed.), *Reform of the UNCITRAL Model Law on Procurement: Procurement Regulation for the 21st Century* (Eagan, MN: West, 2009), pp. 1, 44–6.

the two African systems under scrutiny where the Model Law has not had any significant influence, namely, Namibia and South Africa, the locally developed remedies regimes do not present any better solution to these tensions either. The South African system, as we have noted, is haphazard, unclear and fragmented, especially with regard to administrative review. The result has been excessive reliance on judicial intervention, which is slow, costly and not geared towards the improvement of procurement decisions at the administrative level. It is therefore also not an ideal model or one worth following. The Namibian system is equally unclear and provides only minimal protection to suppliers. It is thus not surprising to find very low levels of use of Namibia's own procurement rules for procurement in externally funded aid programmes.

The provisions on challenge proceedings in the new 2011 UNCITRAL Model Law are in some ways an improvement on those of the old law in the context of the tensions discussed above, and may provide some answers to these problems. However, I am not sure that these new rules will completely resolve the tensions on the assumption that the Model Law will continue to play a significant role in public procurement reform in Africa. The new review rules are not presented as optional and are not as tentative as the old ones, and the choices that a system has to make are much more clearly set out in the new rules. This may bring the realisation home that African systems need not have all of the review mechanisms mentioned in the Model Law. For example, the new rules present application for review to an independent administrative review body and judicial review as alternatives and also move away from reconsideration by the procuring entity as a mandatory element of a remedies regime.[127] However, the much broader possibility of overturning concluded contracts in administrative review under the new rules[128] may extend the scope of the already wide ambit of relief in challenge proceedings even further, which may not be the best route for African systems to take, at least not in an all-or-nothing approach to invalidation. Given that many of the African systems under scrutiny here have also only recently adopted their procurement laws, it may not be realistic to think that many of them will be willing to entertain reforms in this regard under the guise of the new Model Law at this time.

The quest thus remains for models of appropriate supplier review mechanisms in the African procurement systems under review.

127 2011 UNCITRAL Model Law, Art. 64(2). 128 *Ibid.*, Art. 67(9)(f).

However, whether it will ever be possible to reconcile the twin problems of a perceived lack of accountability and transparency in public procurement and extreme resource constraints by means of a system of supplier remedies in African systems is highly doubtful. Perhaps the reality is that an uncomfortable choice will have to be made between these problems and a remedies regime designed in light of that choice, which would result in a less-than-ideal regime, but at least one that is more realistically suited to the African context.

14

A perspective on corruption and public procurement in Africa

SOPE WILLIAMS-ELEGBE

1. Introduction

Corruption, like most crime, is a problem of antiquated origin. In the ancient Greek and Roman Empires, corruption was reportedly widespread and deplored by the thinkers of that time as much as it is today.[1] In the fourteenth century, Abdul Rahman Ibn Khaldun located the root cause of corruption in the desire by the ruling class to live in luxury.[2] Writing about seventeenth-century England, Linda Peck gives a detailed account of monarchical and bureaucratic corruption.[3] In the early twentieth century, Lord Bryce recorded the prevalence of corruption in America and its transfer to post-First World War Europe.[4] The literature on corruption is extensive, and there is no shortage of material on the history, nature, effects and consequences of corruption.

Like most social issues, corruption can be defined in any number of ways, to cover a range of behaviours from 'venality to ideological erosion'.[5] A wide definition of corruption will take account of its operation in both public and private sectors, and may extend to cover activities that strictly speaking consist of fraud, extortion, embezzlement and abuse of office. However, this chapter will focus on bureaucratic corruption, which

1 See Plato, *The Laws* (E. Hamilton and H. Cairns, eds., New York: Pantheon, 1961), Book 12, section d. See also R. MacMullen, *Corruption and the Decline of Rome* (New Haven, CT: Yale University Press, 1988); N. Jacoby, P. Nehemkis and R. Eells, *Bribery and Extortion in World Business: A Study of Corporate Political Payments Abroad* (London: Macmillan Publishing, 1977), pp. 7–43.

2 See S. H. Atlas, *The Sociology of Corruption: The Nature, Function, Causes and Prevention of Corruption* (Singapore: Times Books, 1980), pp. 9, 77.

3 See L. L. Peck, *Court Patronage and Corruption in Early Stuart England* (London: Routledge, 1990).

4 See J. Bryce, *Modern Democracies* (New York: Macmillan Publishing, 1921), vol. II, p. 509.

5 See J. S. Nye, 'Corruption and Political Development: A Cost–Benefit Analysis' (1967) 61 *American Political Science Review* 417, 419.

includes bribery, kickbacks, 'gifts' and illicit payments to government officials in their capacity as public servants, in order for the giving party to achieve a stated purpose.

One area in which bureaucratic corruption manifests is public procurement. As is discussed further below, procurement corruption can take different forms and is one of the main avenues through which corruption manifests in public life. This chapter will examine the issue of corruption and public procurement and is divided into five parts. The first part attempts to define corruption, and analyses the concept, nature and effects of corruption, analysing whether corruption is an economic, social or political phenomenon. The second part will examine the relationship between corruption and public procurement, explaining why public procurement appears to be susceptible to corruption. The third part examines some of the measures that may be implemented through public procurement regulation to combat corruption. The fourth part discusses some of the techniques that may be used to discover whether corruption has occurred in public procurement, and the fifth part examines the main international instruments against corruption to give a general overview of the drivers behind anti-corruption measures.

2. The concept, nature and consequences of corruption

2.1. Defining corruption

Corruption as an economic, social, legal or political concept can be hard to define. First of all, corruption is an issue that is steeped in morality[6] and ethics[7] and even in secular societies it is imbued with elements of moral approbation, shame and wrongdoing, making it a sensitive subject to address.[8] Secondly, although corruption might offend inherent (and possibly universal) values of morality and ethics, it is also to some extent culturally specific, with a dichotomy between Western and non-Western conceptualisations of corruption.[9]

6 J. Wilson, 'Corruption Is Not Always Scandalous' in J. A. Gardiner and D. J. Olson (eds.), *Theft of the City: Readings on Corruption in America* (Bloomington, IN: Indiana University Press, 1968), p. 29.

7 J. Noonan, *Bribes* (Berkeley, CA: University of California Press, 1987), pp. 702–3.

8 R. Klitgaard, *Controlling Corruption* (Berkeley, CA: University of California Press, 1988), p. ix.

9 See, for instance, J. Kim and J. Kim, 'Cultural Differences in the Crusade against International Bribery: Rice Cake Expenses in Korea and the Foreign Corrupt Practices Act' (1997) 6 *Pacific Rim Law and Policy Journal* 589; J. Hooker, *Working Across Cultures* (Palo

In spite of the definitional difficulties recognised by most writers on the subject, definitions of corruption are not lacking. One widely used definition states that corruption is 'behaviour which deviates from the formal duties of a public role because of private-regarding (personal, close family, private clique) pecuniary or status gains; or violates rules against the exercise of certain types of private-regarding influence'.[10]

For the purposes of delimiting the scope of this chapter, the focus will be on public sector corruption, or the corruption that occurs between private individuals and public sector agents. Thus, the chapter will not include a consideration of pure private sector corruption, or, in the procurement context, the corruption that occurs between two private contractors such as collusion. This is not to deny the corruption which takes place in the private sector, but it appears that private sector corruption poses less of a problem to governments and the international community, since market forces invariably dictate the price that people pay for a good or service. In addition, private sector corruption is less likely to become systemic and cannot be sustainable in the long run, as the increased costs of doing business will decrease a firm's competitiveness over time as long as that firm is not a monopoly. Furthermore, some private sector corruption (such as insider trading, overvaluations for credit/mortgage purposes, or insurance collusion) does not produce the social costs of public sector corruption such as the 'contagion of corruption'[11] or the waste and inefficient allocation of public resources.[12]

2.2. The nature of corruption

2.2.1. Introduction

There is a diversity of opinions as to whether corruption is an economic, social or political issue, with each perspective providing models for analysing and understanding corruption.

Alto, CA: Stanford University Press, 2003), pp. 88, 204, 317. Note that non-Western cultures generally have accepted practices of 'gift-giving' which may amount to bribery in a Western context. For this reason, the United Nations, in its *Anti-Corruption Tool Kit* (3rd edn, Vienna: United Nations, 2004), which is aimed at providing assistance to countries and institutions wishing to prevent corruption, refrains from defining corruption, and, instead, defines the various types or levels of corruption such as 'grand' and 'petty' corruption, 'active' and 'passive' corruption, bribery, embezzlement, theft, fraud, extortion, abuses of discretion, etc.

10 Nye, 'Corruption and Political Development', note 5 above, p. 417.

11 G. Caiden and O. Dwivedi, 'Official Ethics and Corruption' in G. Caiden (ed.), *Where Corruption Lives* (West Hartford, CT: Kumarian Press, 2001), p. 245.

12 S. Rose-Ackerman, *Corruption and Government: Causes, Consequences, Cures* (Cambridge University Press, 1999), pp. 3, 30.

2.2.2. Economic theories of corruption

Within the economic framework,[13] the agency model of corruption appears to be the most dominant.[14] At its most basic form, this model assumes that the public servant is the agent of a specific government agency and is employed to further that agency's (the principal's) interests in whatever the objectives of the agency might be. In addition to this public interest that the agent is supposed to be furthering, the agent also has his own private interests, which may conflict with that of his principal. Corruption occurs when the agent decides to pursue his private ends at the expense of the public interest, or subordinates the public interest to his private goals. The economic model assumes that the agent is a rational (if amoral) being and will weigh up the benefits of being corrupt against the costs. Where the net benefits of corruption exceed the net costs of the corrupt activity, the agent will act corruptly.[15]

The problem with economic models of corruption, is that they are sterile to the point that they do not take into account any inclinations towards morality or ethics which may dissuade a public agent from acting corruptly and ignore the normative undertones of corruption which can impact the agent's decision. In assuming that all officials are morally neutral and will act corruptly if it benefits them, the models are subsequently unable to explain why some agents are not corrupt, and how the non-economic motivations of non-corrupt officials may be harnessed as an anti-corruption tool. The assumption that, once it is beneficial and the opportunity presents itself, all public officials will act corruptly is also not based on the evidence in cases where there are few detriments to an agent for acting corruptly, in countries where corruption is systemic, tolerated and rarely penalised, and some officials still do not engage in corrupt activities. Whilst economic models of corruption are helpful in understanding the economic drivers behind corruption, they are limited in the nature of solutions that can be proffered as the solutions are also economically driven, often ignoring the complexity of the subject-matter.[16]

13 See other economic propositions in Rose-Ackerman, *Corruption and Government*, note 12 above, Chapter 2.

14 N. Groenendijk, 'A Principal–Agent Model of Corruption' (1997) 27 *Crime, Law and Social Change* 207–29; O. H. Fjeldstad, J. C. Andvig, I. Amundsen, T. Sissener and T. Soreide, *Corruption: A Review of Contemporary Research* (Bergen: CMI, 2001).

15 Klitgaard, *Controlling Corruption*, note 8 above, pp. 69–74.

16 See G. Becker, 'Crime and Punishment: An Economic Approach' (1968) 76 *Journal of Political Economy* 169–217.

2.2.3. Political theories on corruption

The political and social conceptualisations of corruption have similar shortcomings. In relation to the political, here corruption might be perceived either as a consequence of a particular system of government (democratic or non-democratic),[17] or a failure of leadership.[18] Here, the arguments usually are that the non-democratic and therefore non-accountable nature of the political machinery contributes to corruption[19] or that the existing personalities in government are the cause of the problem.[20] Where corruption is thought to be a result of the system of government, the theories afford little explanation for the corruption that takes place in developed democracies, and, in any event, there is conflicting evidence on whether non-democratic societies are more corrupt than democratic ones.[21] In fact, it is claimed that democratic societies may create an atmosphere more conducive to corrupt activity, as:

> democratic society encourages wheeling and dealing and give and take. They support negotiation and persuasion. This can mean some persons back into committing technical violations without the intention to commit a crime... For elected officials, the line between political contributions and buying favours and extortion can be thin.[22]

17 See generally A. Doig and R. Theobald, *Corruption and Democratisation* (London: Frank Cass, 2000).

18 K. R. Hope, 'Corruption and Development in Africa' in K. R. Hope and B. C. Chikulu (eds.), *Corruption and Development in Africa: Lessons from Country Case Studies* (New York: St Martin's Press, 2000), Chapter 1, p. 19.

19 J. Friedrich, 'Corruption Concepts in Historical Perspective' in A. Heidenheimer, M. Johnston and V. LeVine (eds.), *Political Corruption: A Handbook* (New Brunswick, NJ: Transaction Publishers, 1989).

20 See J. Coolidge and S. Rose-Ackerman, 'Kleptocracy and Reform in African Regimes: Theory and Examples' in Hope and Chikulu (eds.), *Corruption and Development in Africa*, note 18 above, Chapter 3.

21 See A. Doig and R. Theobald, *Corruption and Democratisation* (London: Frank Cass, 2000), who trace the absence of grand corruption in developed countries to the existence of a private sector that offers better opportunities for self-enrichment, and because the state occupies a less strategic role and also because of better functioning control bodies and greater transparency. See also Fjeldstad, Andvig, Amundsen, Sissener and Soreide, *Corruption: A Review of Contemporary Research*, note 14 above, Chapters 4.2 and 6.2, illustrating that competitive politics may lead to questionable political influence. See also D. Treisman, 'The Causes of Corruption: A Cross National Study' (2000) 76 *Journal of Public Economics* 399–457.

22 G. T. Marx, 'When the Guards Guard Themselves: Undercover Tactics Turned Inwards' (1992) 2 *Policing and Society* 166.

Where corruption is blamed on the personalities in government, this removes the responsibility for individual actions from public officials and agents and places it with the leadership. Whilst it may be true that a corrupt leadership will invariably reproduce itself,[23] even in the most corrupt of regimes, public servants retain the responsibility for their actions in deciding to be corrupt.

2.2.4. Social explanations for corruption

Finally, corruption might be considered to be an anthropological problem[24] or a consequence of the failings inherent in the organisation of society, such as a failure of capitalism.[25] In this respect, the argument is that corruption comes into play where market forces are unable to efficiently allocate resources, and, in fact, corruption ensures that opportunities are allocated to the highest bidder.[26] Whilst there may be merit in this argument to the extent that, in an inefficient society, corruption might ensure that opportunities are given to those who desire them the most (or who are willing to pay an increased premium for them), the argument fails to realise that political participation, state resources and opportunities are not private property and should not be for sale. Furthermore, if corruption is used as the means to distribute resources that are intended for the greater good, the re-distribution of those resources will reflect the increased costs of obtaining them, which will adversely affect society as a whole.[27]

From the above, it can be seen that none of the above conceptualisations is sufficient in itself to explain the complex nature of corruption. Rather, corruption can only be explained by taking all factors into account, the political, the economic and the social.

23 D. Windsor and K. Getz, 'Multilateral Cooperation to Combat Corruption: Normative Regimes Despite Mixed Motives and Diverse Values' (2000) 33 *Cornell International Law Journal* 731, 757.

24 For an excellent review of anthropological theories on corruption, see T. Sissener, *Anthropological Perspectives on Corruption* (Bergen: CMI, 2001); Fjeldstad, Andvig, Amundsen, Sissener and Soreide, *Corruption: A Review of Contemporary Research*, note 14 above, Chapter 5.4.

25 See generally M. Blomstrom and B. Hettne, *Development Theory in Transition* (London: Zed Books, 1984); W. Pfaff, 'A Pathological Mutation in Capitalism', *International Herald Tribune*, 9 September 2002, for an alternative explanation on how the failure of capitalism leads to corruption in corporate America.

26 See Rose-Ackerman, *Corruption and Government*, note 12 above, Chapter 2.

27 See W. Witting, 'A Framework for Balancing Business and Accountability within Public Procurement' (2001) 10 *Public Procurement Law Review* 139–64.

2.3. *The consequences of corruption*

It is surprising to find that scholars are not in universal agreement on the consequences of corruption. One school of thought opines that corruption is intrinsically bad because it undermines the legitimacy of governments and increases public spending without a corresponding increase in public welfare.[28] Most modern writers agree that the perceived end result of corruption where it is systemic is an adverse effect on development as the state becomes incapable of meeting basic needs or sustaining economic development.[29] The effect of corruption on development has been illustrated by studies showing that corruption or the opportunity to obtain bribes can affect the allocation of public spending and lead to large unnecessary (construction) projects being given priority over health and education.[30]

Apart from its impact on development, corruption can have direct effects on public welfare. For instance, if one considers the allocation of a hypothetical water distribution contract to a supplier who bribed the public sector decision-makers to obtain the contract, it is clear that the provision of water to the end consumer will either reflect the increased costs to obtain the contract, or will be provided at a sub-standard quality, in order to recoup the increased costs of obtaining the contract. Even if the quality of the water is unaffected by the corrupt activity, the contractor may not be the most efficient or cost-effective, thereby leading to a waste

28 See P. Mauro, 'Corruption and Growth' (1995) 110 *Quarterly Journal of Economics* 681, who provides empirical evidence of the link between increased corruption and reduced gross domestic product. See also P. Ward, *Corruption, Development and Inequality: Soft Touch or Hard Graft* (London: Routledge, 1989), p. 170; Rose-Ackerman, *Corruption and Government*, note 12 above, Chapter 1.

29 See F. Khan, 'Top Down or Bottom Up? The Spread of Systemic Corruption in the Third World' (December 2001), www.colbud.hu/honesty-trust/khan/pub01.rtf (accessed 26 March 2012). See also N. Kofele-Kale, *International Law of Responsibility for Economic Crimes: Holding Heads of State and Other High Ranking Officials Individually Liable for Acts of Fraudulent Enrichment* (The Hague: Kluwer Law International, 1995), pp. 105–7; D. Frisch, 'The Effects of Corruption on Development' (1996) 158 *The Courier ACP–EU* 68–70; C. Gray and D. Kaufman, 'Corruption and Development' (1998) *Finance and Development* 7–10.

30 See P. Mauro, 'The Effects of Corruption on Growth, Investment and Government Expenditure: A Cross Country Analysis' in K. A. Elliot (ed.). *Corruption and the Global Economy* (Washington DC: Institute for International Economics, 1997), who found that government expenditure on education and health is negatively correlated with higher levels of corruption. See V. Tanzi, 'Corruption around the World: Causes, Consequences, Scope and Cures' (1998) 45 *IMF Staff Papers* 559. See also T. Soreide, *Corruption in Public Procurement: Causes, Consequences, Cures* (Bergen: CMI, 2002), Chapter 2.

of public funds. In any event, society at large bears the brunt of the corrupt activity.

Other studies into the effects of corruption have revealed that it reduces private investment, foreign direct investment and consequently, the rate of economic growth,[31] as it effectively acts as a tax on foreign direct investment thereby reducing real capital flows.[32] Other effects of corruption include the fact that it disrupts democracy and the citizenry's right to political participation;[33] if one considers that, where a public agent alters his decision-making because of the receipt of a bribe or other inducement, he is thereby denying the right of other people to participate in that process, and subverting democracy by flouting formal processes.

In addition to its effect on economic development, political infrastructure and democracy, corruption can also have fatal and disastrous consequences, especially where the construction of infrastructure is concerned. For instance, in Egypt in 2007, a building collapsed killing several people.[34] Similarly, in India in 2010, sixty-five people were killed when a building collapsed.[35] These tragedies were blamed on corruption and lax enforcement of building regulations.

On the other hand are the scholars who believe that a limited amount of corruption can often be beneficial to society if it succeeds in making markets more efficient and aiding in the allocation of scarce resources.[36] The problem with this reasoning, however, is in defining and imposing the

31 Mauro, 'Corruption and Growth', note 28 above, pp. 700–4.

32 N. Rubin, 'Note and Comment, a Convergence of 1996 and 1997 Global Efforts to Curb Corruption and Bribery in International Business Transactions: The Legal Implications of the OECD Recommendations and Convention for the United States, Germany and Switzerland' (1988) 14 *American University International Law Review* 257, 315. In addition, increased levels of corruption may decrease investor interest in a country, further reducing the rate of growth. See Shing-Jin Wei, 'How Taxing Is Corruption on International Investors?', NBER Working Paper 6030 (1997).

33 See T. Donaldson, *The Ethics of International Business* (Oxford University Press, 1989), pp. 89–94.

34 See www.msnbc.msn.com/id/22432355/ns/world_news-mideast_n_africa/t/corrupt-work-blamed-egypt-building-collapse/ (accessed 26 March 2012).

35 See www.allvoices.com/contributed-news/7345623-the-worst-disaster-of-building-collapse-in-delhi-killing-60-people (accessed 26 March 2012).

36 See Nye, 'Corruption and Political Development', note 5 above, pp. 417, 419–22; P. Huntington, 'Modernization and Development' in M. U. Ekpo (ed.), *Bureaucratic Corruption in Sub-Saharan Africa: Towards a Search for Causes and Consequences* (Washington DC: University Press of America, 1979); N. Leff, 'Economic Development through Bureaucratic Corruption' in M. U. Ekpo (eds.), *Bureaucratic Corruption in Sub-Saharan Africa*; T. Olsen and G. Torsvik, 'Collusion and Renegotiation in Hierarchies: A Case of Beneficial Corruption' (1998) 39 *International Economic Review* 413–38.

'limits' of this corruption. In a study into the telecommunications sector in India, Rashid argued that bribes to obtain a telephone line began as price discrimination among customers in an egalitarian system, but quickly degenerated into extortion against customers that impeded service so that the officials in charge could obtain even larger bribes.[37] Whether or not there is evidence to suggest that corruption can be beneficial for economic development,[38] the majority of economists and other social scientists affirm the undesirable effects and consequences of corruption.

3. Public procurement and corruption

3.1. Introduction

This section will define public procurement and discuss the reasons behind corruption in public procurement and the kinds of corrupt activity that occur in public procurement.

3.2. Defining public procurement

As is explained in Chapter 1, public procurement is the purchasing by a government or other public body of the goods and services it requires to function and to ensure and maximise public welfare. In doing so, a government tries to ensure that it obtains these goods, services or 'works' (in the case of construction contracts) at the most economically advantageous price. Ideally, procurement regulation is designed to ensure that the process or procedures in place for obtaining these goods and services are transparent and competitive. As was discussed in Chapter 1 of this volume, it is believed that transparency in procurement regulation[39] will help in the fulfilment of the other goals of procurement regulation, such as obtaining value for money.[40]

In addition to the 'primary' goals of procurement regulation, public procurement may also – as was again highlighted in Chapter 1 – be a tool of horizontal (or 'secondary') objectives, in the sense that a government

37 S. Rashid, 'Public Utilities in Egalitarian LDCs: The Role of Bribery in Achieving Pareto Efficiency' (1981) 34 *Kyklos International Review for Social Sciences* 448, 448–55.

38 Nye, 'Corruption and Political Development', note 5 above, pp. 417, 419–22.

39 S. Arrowsmith, *The Law of Public and Utilities Procurement* (2nd edn, London: Sweet & Maxwell, 2005), Chapter 3; S. Schooner, 'Desiderata: Objectives for a System of Government Contract Law' (2002) 11 *Public Procurement Law Review* 103.

40 See the discussion in Chapter 1 of this volume and the literature cited there.

may decide to use public procurement to achieve non-procurement-related goals such as the development of a particular industrial sector or segment of society (such as 'disadvantaged' groups), or encouraging environmentally friendly manufacturing, by favouring these groups or industries in public contract awards.[41] The use of procurement for social policy purposes is discussed further in Chapter 15 of this volume.

3.3. *The incidence and types of corruption in public procurement*

As will be seen below, the major international instruments on corruption require the maintenance of transparent, competitive and efficient procurement systems as part of the measures to address corruption. This is because, as stated earlier, public procurement as a sphere of government activity is one of the areas in which bureaucratic corruption manifests. There are several reasons why public procurement is susceptible to corruption,[42] and these include the large sums involved in public procurement, the (usually) non-commercial nature of contracting entities, the nature of the relationship between the decision-maker and the public body,[43] the measures of unsupervised discretion, bureaucratic rules, and budgets that may not be tied to specified goals as well as non-performance-related pay and low pay.

Apart from the above, public procurement also presents the opportunity for corruption because of the asymmetry of information between the public official and his principal, i.e. the government. As the public official

41 P. Bolton, 'The Use of Government Procurement as an Instrument of Policy' (2004) 121 *South African Law Journal* 619; P. Bolton, 'Government Procurement as a Policy Tool in South Africa' (2006) 6 *Journal of Public Procurement* 193; P. Bolton, 'An Analysis of the Preferential Procurement Legislation in South Africa' (2007) 16 *Public Procurement Law Review* 36; S. Arrowsmith and P. Kunzlik (eds.), *Social and Environmental Policies in EC Procurement Law: New Directives and New Directions* (Cambridge University Press, 2009); C. McCrudden, *Buying Social Justice* (Oxford University Press, 2007).

42 See generally Soreide, *Corruption in Public Procurement*, note 30 above; S. Kelman, *Procurement and Public Management: The Fear of Discretion and the Quality of Government Performance* (Washington DC: AEI Press, 1990); F. Anechiarico and J. Jacobs, *The Pursuit of Absolute Integrity: How Corruption Control Makes Government Ineffective* (University of Chicago Press, 1996), Chapter 8.

43 See 'Measures to Prevent Corruption in EU Member States', European Parliament Directorate General for Research Working Paper, Legal Affairs Series JURI 101 EN 03-1998, Annex, 'Combating Corruption in Public Procurement Contracts'. In a firm, it is less likely that the decision-maker's interests will diverge from those of the firm, as his financial situation depends on the continued success of the firm, this being enough to prevent him from taking decisions that might jeopardise the firm.

holds more information about the procurement process and the procurement market, i.e. the nature and availability of the goods and services the government requires, the official is able to use this knowledge to his advantage by manipulating the procurement process, should he choose to do so. The incidence of corruption within government procurement is well documented in developing and transition economies, where there is little regulation and non-transparency.[44]

There are three ways in which procurement corruption manifests, and it can take the form of public, private or auto-corruption.[45] Public corruption is that which moves from a private individual (the supplier) to the public official responsible for taking procurement decisions. This corruption will frequently take the form of bribes or other non-monetary advantages or inducements granted to the public official in order to influence the exercise of his discretion. In the procurement context, the public official may improperly exercise his discretion in, for example, deciding which firms to invite for tender, or by emphasising or designing evaluation criteria that favour a preferred company.[46] Improper exercises of discretion may also occur where a procurement official decides to split a large contract into several small contracts that fall below legislative thresholds for complying with certain procedural requirements, in order to circumvent the requirement for publication of the tender in the required medium,[47] again in order to favour a preferred supplier. Other benefits that a supplier may seek include the avoidance of a government-imposed cost or requirement such as fees, taxes or production of various

44 I. Hors, 'Shedding Light on Corrupt Practices in Public Procurement' (2003) 14 *Public Procurement Law Review* NA101–NA108; P. Nichols, G Siedel and M Kasdin, 'Corruption as a Pan-Cultural Phenomenon: An Empirical Study in Countries at Opposite Ends of the Former Soviet Empire' (2004) 39 *Texas International Law Journal* 215–50; B. Earle, 'Bribery and Corruption in Eastern Europe, the Baltic States and the Commonwealth of Independent States: What Is To Be Done?' (2000) 33 *Cornell International Law Journal* 483–512; T. Jingbin, 'Public Procurement in China: The Way Forward' (2001) 10 *Public Procurement Law Review* 207–28; O. Oko, 'Subverting the Scourge of Corruption in Nigeria: A Reform Prospectus' (2002) 34 *New York University Journal of Law and Politics* 397.

45 V. Key, 'Techniques of Political Graft' in A. Heidenheimer, M. Johnston and V. LeVine (eds.), *Political Corruption: A Handbook* (New Brunswick, NJ: Transaction Publishers, 1989), pp. 46–8.

46 Rose-Ackerman, *Corruption and Government*, note 12 above, p. 64; Soreide, *Corruption in Public Procurement*, note 30 above, Chapter 3.

47 See J. P. Bueb, 'Identifying Risks to Prevent and Sanction Corruption in Public Procurement', OECD Global Forum on Governance: Fighting Corruption and Promoting Integrity in Public Procurement (December 2004).

documents.[48] Public corruption is arguably the most pervasive type of corruption that occurs in public procurement,[49] and is one reason behind the criminalisation of the bribery of foreign public officials in domestic and international anti-corruption instruments.

The second type of corruption that occurs in public procurement is private corruption, which manifests as collusion, price-fixing, maintenance of cartels or other uncompetitive practices committed by suppliers which prevent the government from obtaining value for money.[50] While this kind of corruption falls outside the scope of this chapter, it is important to mention that it forms a part of the activities that could be targeted under national or international procurement regulation.

Thirdly, auto-corruption occurs in public procurement when a public official wrongly secures for himself or an associate (such as a close friend or family member) the privileges which rightly belong to the public,[51] by by-passing or manipulating the formal procedures necessary for the award of these privileges. This type of corruption might manifest where conflicts of interest[52] cause an official to corruptly favour the company in which he is interested,[53] or where an official uses a dummy corporation to hide awards involving personal interest.

48 See Tanzi, 'Corruption around the World', note 30 above, p. 559.

49 If the increasing focus of organisations such as the EU, the OECD, Transparency International and the World Bank on corruption in public procurement is anything to go by. See 'Measures to Prevent Corruption in EU Member States', European Parliament Directorate General for Research Working Paper, Legal Affairs Series JURI 101 EN 03-1998. See also OECD Reports on OECD Global Forum on Governance, Fighting Corruption and Promoting Integrity in Public Procurement, available at www.oecd.org (accessed 26 March 2012); Soreide, *Corruption in Public Procurement*, note 30 above, Chapter 2.

50 See Klitgaard, *Controlling Corruption*, note 8 above, Chapter 6.

51 See Key, 'Techniques of Political Graft' note 45 above, pp. 46–8. An example given by Tanzi, 'Corruption around the World', note 30 above, p. 559, is where a public official has a facility such as an airport built in his small hometown.

52 See OECD, *Managing Conflicts of Interest in the Public Sector: A Toolkit* (Paris: OECD, 2001), p. 2, where conflict of interests are said to be financial, economic and personal interests or other undertakings and relationships which may compromise directly or indirectly the performance of duties of public office holders. See also S. Arrowsmith, J. Linarelli and D. Wallace, *Regulating Public Procurement: National and International Perspectives* (The Hague: Kluwer Law International, 2000), pp. 39–40.

53 See H.-J. Prieß, 'Distortions of Competition in Tender Proceedings: How to Deal with Conflicts of Interest (Family Ties, Business Links and Cross-representation of Contracting Authority Officials and Bidders) and the Involvement of Project Consultants' (2002) 11 *Public Procurement Law Review* 153, 154–5, who identifies the types of conflicts of interest as family ties and business links, where the public official owns or has a stake in a bidder for a public contract, as well as cross-representation, where a member of the board of a company competing for a public contract is also an official of the contracting authority.

4. Measures used in procurement regulation to fight corruption

4.1. Introduction

There are various tools available to a government which can be used against corruption, which can be classified into three broad categories: administrative, regulatory and social tools. Administrative measures refer to the various measures which may not be specifically required by legislation, but which are permitted under the exercise of executive discretion. Regulatory tools on the other hand are the range of binding and obligatory measures which must be imposed where corrupt activity is found to have occurred, including requirements to impose penal and civil sanctions. Social tools encompass the societal pressures, ridicule, shame and infamy that attend corrupt activity where it is exposed.

These categories are not necessarily exclusive, and administrative and regulatory measures will frequently overlap in cases where government regulations or legislation authorise the use of a particular administrative measure against corruption. In addition, social tools may accompany the use of certain types of regulatory and administrative measures.

Apart from measures in the general law against corruption, most procurement laws have measures within them directed at reducing or preventing corruption in public procurement. The measures used in procurement regulation against corruption might not be explicitly directed at corruption such as requirements for transparency,[54] open competition and increased accountability in government contracts,[55] but others might be directly concerned with ensuring that an environment exists where corruption cannot thrive and that neither public officials nor contractors may engage in corrupt practices.

4.2. Administrative measures

Administrative tools against corruption include the range of measures that are implemented under the exercise of official discretion on the part of a public official. These may include executive restrictions on obtaining government patronage, licences, approvals, permits, etc. placed upon persons who are adjudged corrupt. An example is a denial of registration

54 See, for example, Arrowsmith, *The Law of Public and Utilities Procurement*, note 39 above, at [7.12].

55 J. Hansen, 'Limits of Competition: Accountability in Government Contracting' (2003) 112 *Yale Law Journal* 2465.

as a company or other legal person,[56] where the proposer has bankruptcies or criminal or fraudulent convictions against him/her.

Administrative tools also include measures that deny corrupt firms or persons access to government contracts. Such denials may either be temporary or permanent. Such measures are utilised by procurement systems in developing and developed countries, and may be used to deny corrupt persons access to contracts for procurement or non-procurement-related violations.[57] Similar measures which have the effect of denying access to government contracts are those which deny corrupt persons registration on qualifying lists for government contracts.[58]

Other administrative measures which can be utilised to curb corruption are increased levels of public sector financial management, such as accounting and audit requirements. Public sector financial management is on the rise, as financial controls become an increasingly important part of public sector reform and, consequently, an important part of corruption control.[59] As a method of corruption control, public sector financial management seeks accountability in terms of results, and not just in terms of the process.[60] Specifically, the purpose of such audits is to ensure that any imbalances or areas of leakage in public finances are identified and properly addressed.[61]

56 See TMC Asser Institute, *Prevention of and Administrative Action against Organised Crime: A Comparative Study of the Registration of Legal Persons and Criminal Audits in Eight EU Member States* (The Hague: TMC Asser Press, 1997).

57 E. Piselli, 'The Scope for Excluding Providers Who Have Committed Criminal Offences under the EU Procurement Directives' (2000) 9 *Public Procurement Law Review* 267; S. Williams, 'The Mandatory Exclusions for Corruption in the New EC Procurement Directives' (2006) 31 *European Law Review* 711; T. Medina, 'EU Directives as an Anti-Corruption Measure: Excluding Corruption-Convicted Tenderers from Public Procurement Contracts' in K. V. Thai (ed.), *International Handbook of Public Procurement* (Boca Raton, FL: CRC Press, 2008); S. Williams, 'The Debarment of Corrupt Contractors from World Bank-Financed Contracts' (2007) 36 *Public Contract Law Journal* 277; S. Williams, 'The Use of Exclusions for Corruption in Developing Country Procurement: The Case of South Africa' (2007) 51 *Journal of African Law* 1; S. Williams and G. Quinot, 'Public Procurement and Corruption: The South African Response' (2007) 124 *South African Law Journal* 339; S. Williams, 'The Mandatory Contractor Exclusions for Serious Criminal Offences in UK Public Procurement' (2009) 15 *European Public Law* 429.

58 H. Xanthaki, 'First Pillar Analysis' in S. White (ed.), *Procurement and Organised Crime* (London: Institute of Advanced Legal Studies, 2000).

59 Anechiarico and Jacobs, 'The Pursuit of Absolute Integrity', note 42 above, Chapter 9.

60 Hood, 'The New Public Management in the 1980s: Variations on a Theme' (1995) 20 *Accounting, Organisations and Society* 93–100.

61 C. Walsh, 'Creating a Competitive Culture in the Public Service: The Role of Audits and Other Reviews' (1995) 54 *Australian Journal of Public Administration* 325; M. Power,

In addition to public sector financial controls, increased supervision of public officials is another tool that can be used to control corruption. This can be implemented through a series of approvals necessary before major decisions can be taken and implemented. The supervision of public officials is closely tied to restricting the levels of discretion available to public agents, which some jurisdictions consider a necessary component of corruption control.[62] In addition, in relation to public officials, measures which may protect the government against conflicts of interest are the procedures which provide for the rotation of officials to prevent the formation of relationships which may lead to corruption. Other administrative/regulatory measures could include those which require officials to declare their assets at the inception and termination of public office, and those which require the disclosure of public officials' business interests in order to ensure impartiality.[63]

Another measure used against procurement corruption is to require various levels of approval before a public contract is awarded. Another administrative measure is the creation of a division that ensures that prices paid for procured goods (or services) are fair and reflect market rates.

Other administrative/regulatory measures directed towards contractors include the use of 'integrity pacts' or the extraction of a (binding or non-binding) commitment from a supplier not to engage in corrupt activities, which is obtained at some point during the procurement process. These might extend beyond a commitment not to bribe, and include commitments not to collude with competitors to obtain the contract. Similar undertakings which might be extracted from a contractor include those which are currently utilised by the World Bank under which a bidder for a Bank-financed contract undertakes to comply with the borrowing country's anti-corruption legislation.[64]

'Evaluating the Audit Explosion' (2003) 25 *Law and Policy* 185. Note that, in relation to procurement, post-contract audits can be used to ascertain whether any corrupt acts were committed during the execution of a public contract.

62 See Kelman, *Procurement and Public Management*, note 42 above, Chapter 1; C. Gray, *Anti-Corruption in Transition 2: Corruption in Enterprise–State Interactions in Europe and Central Asia 1999–2002* (Washington DC: World Bank Publications, 2004), p. 11.

63 See Prieß, 'Distortions of Competition in Tender Proceedings', note 53 above, pp. 153, 156.

64 See World Bank Procurement Guidelines, para. 1.16.

4.3. *Regulatory measures*

Regulatory measures include the legislation, regulations and other binding measures that a government may adopt against corruption. This will include legal prohibitions against corruption as well as criminal and civil penalties and forfeitures that are directed at both the public and private sector.

Many jurisdictions outside Africa have followed the example set by the United States[65] and criminalised overseas bribery. This means that, where a private individual is found to have bribed a foreign public official, such a person will be liable to conviction in his home state. Although the increasing criminalisation of overseas bribery can be traced directly to the efforts of the United States government, many countries which have criminalised overseas bribery have done so in order to meet their obligations under the OECD Convention on Combating Bribery of Foreign Public Officials.[66]

South Africa is the only African country to have criminalised foreign bribery,[67] and did so in order to accede to the OECD Convention.[68] It is also the only African state to have ratified this Convention. Although other African nations such as Nigeria have anti-corruption laws that pre-date that of South Africa, these anti-corruption laws focus on the criminalisation of domestic corruption and do not have extra-territorial reach.[69]

In public procurement, the most obvious regulatory measures against corruption are criminal sanctions for bribes. Although the prohibitions against bribery may not be found within procurement legislation itself, it is usually a criminal offence for any public official to accept bribes or other inducements in the exercise of his public function. The prohibition

65 Foreign Corrupt Practices Act 1977, Pub. L. No. 95–213, 91 Stat. 1494. See N. Colton, 'Foreign Corrupt Practices Act' (2001) 3 *American Criminal Law Review* 891; S. Salbu, 'The Foreign Corrupt Practices Act as a Threat to Global Harmony' (1999) 20 *Michigan Journal of International Law* 419; B. C. George, J. Birmele and K. Lacey, 'On the Threshold of the Adoption of Global Anti-Bribery Legislation: A Critical Analysis of Current Domestic and International Efforts towards the Reduction of Business Corruption' (1999) 32 *Vanderbilt Journal of Transnational Law* 1.

66 37 ILM 1 (1997).

67 Prevention and Combating of Corrupt Practices Act 12 of 2004, s. 5.

68 O. Sibanda, 'The South African Corruption Law and Bribery of Foreign Public Officials in International Business Transactions: A Comparative Analysis' (2005) 18 *South African Journal of Criminal Justice* 1.

69 Corrupt Practices and Other Related Offences Act 2000.

against bribery is frequently accompanied by custodial sentences[70] and other punishments. For instance, a corrupt public official, in addition to a fine or custodial sentence that may be imposed during a criminal trial, will invariably also lose his employment and in some jurisdictions may forfeit his pension and related benefits.[71]

As mentioned above, conflicts of interest may frequently be targeted through administrative procedures, but it is not uncommon for legislative intervention to exist to prevent such conflicts.[72] Such legislation may require the official with an interest in the contract to disclose such an interest as soon as possible and take no part in the contract award procedure.[73]

As mentioned in the context of administrative measures, in relation to contractors, mandatory legislative provisions which blacklist, exclude or disqualify from public contracts, contractors who are seen as unethical or corrupt and, conversely, provisions which 'white list' or grant access to public contracts to firms who can certify that they meet minimum ethical requirements and have sound internal management practices are some of the regulatory measures which could be integrated into procurement legislation. Thus, for instance, in South Africa, the Public Finance Management Act Treasury Regulations provide that a procuring authority must exclude a bidder who commits a fraudulent act in competing for a contract.[74]

It was stated above that there are other regulatory measures which are not solely directed towards corruption in public procurement, but serve to create an environment where corruption cannot thrive. These include the requirements for transparency, open competition and best value. Transparency in public procurement is often touted as one of the goals of a procurement system[75] and is usually a mandatory

70 S. 26 of the South African Prevention and Combating of Corrupt Activities Act 12 of 2004 punishes a person convicted of corruption in the High Court to a fine or imprisonment for up to life. Under ss. 8–10 of the Nigerian Corrupt Practices and Other Related Offences Act 2000, a person convicted of bribery is liable to imprisonment for seven years.

71 See G. Becker and G. Stigler, 'Law Enforcement, Malfeasance and Compensation of Enforcers' (1974) 3 *Journal of Legal Studies* 1–19.

72 See Prieß, 'Distortions of Competition in Tender Proceedings', note 53 above. See also Arrowsmith, Linarelli and Wallace, *Regulating Public Procurement*, note 52 above, Chapter 2.

73 See Anechiarico and Jacobs, 'The Pursuit of Absolute Integrity', note 42 above, pp. 50–3.

74 Reg. 16A9.1.

75 See Schooner, 'Desiderata: Objectives for a System of Government Contract Law', note 39 above, pp. 103, 105.

requirement in regulated procurement systems. Transparency suggests that the procurement procedure is conducted in an open and impartial manner and that the parties to the process are aware of information on specific procurements,[76] and, further, that all participants to the procurement process are subject to the rules applicable to the process. A transparent procurement system can ensure the absence of corruption where the rules that define the procurement process and the opportunities for contracting are publicly available, making it more difficult to conceal improper practices.[77]

The requirement for open competition is also one of the pillars of a developed procurement system.[78] The requirement for open competition supports anti-corruption efforts by ensuring that all qualified suppliers have access to available contracts and limits the scope for corruption-induced favouritism and cronyism. Open competition also removes the restrictions to participation created against non-corrupt suppliers and is supported by a transparent regime where contracting opportunities and the rules of the process are publicly available and applicable to all participants of the process.

The third regulatory obligation which may support anti-corruption measures is that requiring that contracting entities obtain the best value for money in their procurements. Best value, also termed 'value for money', may be defined as a policy goal that desires to obtain the best bargain with the public's money.[79] Best value is not synonymous with lowest price, as quality or total life-cycle considerations may mean that the cheapest products do not necessarily provide the best value.

Best value can be achieved through the other regulatory provisions discussed above. For instance, the requirement for competition supports best value, as a competitive environment ensures that the government has a 'pool' of suppliers to choose from and will pay a competitive price and avoid monopolistic prices.[80] The requirements for transparency also support best value by promoting a competitive environment, and making

76 See S. Arrowsmith, 'Towards a Multilateral Agreement on Transparency in Government Procurement' (1998) *International and Comparative Law Quarterly* 793, 796.

77 Note that transparency supports other objectives of the procurement process such as competition. See Arrowsmith, *The Law of Public and Utilities Procurement*, note 39 above, Chapters 3 and 7.12, and Chapter 1 of this volume.

78 Schooner, 'Desiderata: Objectives for a System of Government Contract Law', note 39 above, pp. 103, 105.

79 *Ibid.*, p. 108.

80 See A. Beviglia-Zampetti, 'The UNCITRAL Model Law on Procurement of Goods, Construction, Services' in B. Hoekman and P. Mavroidis (eds.), *Law and Policy in Public*

it clear when the government has not obtained value for money. The relationship between best value and anti-corruption provisions is found in the fact that, where contracts are awarded as a result of corrupt activity, this will have adverse implications for best value, if one considers that corruption stifles competition and the costs of corruption may be passed on to the government. However, it should be noted that, in some cases, there could be conflict between the requirements for best value and anti-corruption measures. This may occur where anti-corruption mechanisms are expensive to implement and cause transactional inefficiencies in the procurement process.[81]

4.4. Social measures

Social measures against corruption are those elements of disapprobation which a society attaches to corrupt activity. These include the shame, ridicule and disgrace that should normally follow the exposure of bribe taking or other corrupt activity. Social tools against corruption are hardly used as primary instruments against corruption, since they are largely informal and unorganised mechanisms. Nevertheless, social tools might follow the use of regulatory tools, where, for instance, the press sensationalises corruption scandals and publishes the names of the parties involved, possibly at the conclusion of criminal trials. Social tools may also accompany the use of administrative measures where, for instance, it becomes publicly known that a firm has been excluded from government contracts as a result of corruption.

In public procurement, although social tools may not be expressed as an anti-corruption tool, they will frequently attend the use of administrative and regulatory measures. For instance, where a supplier has been convicted of, or otherwise involved in corruption, the infamy that results from such a conviction where it is published in the media will frequently lead to a loss of business and may in some cases signal the end for that company. Likewise, where a firm is excluded or disqualified from public contracts as a result of corruption, such a firm may find that its tarnished reputation makes it difficult for it to obtain business elsewhere.

Purchasing: The WTO Agreement on Government Procurement (Ann Arbor, MI: University of Michigan Press, 1997), Chapter 15.

81 F. Anechiarico and J. Jacobs, 'Purging Corruption from Public Contracting: The "Solutions" Are Now Part of the Problem' (1995) *New York Law School Law Review* 143; Arrowsmith, Linarelli and Wallace, *Regulating Public Procurement*, note 52 above, Chapter 2.

Although social tools might act as a restraint on corruption in societies where strong notions of ethics prevail, in countries where the illicit acquisition of wealth is celebrated and not denounced, social tools against corruption will have a limited impact as an anti-corruption tool.

5. Discovering corruption in public procurement: investigations, audits and reporting

5.1. Introduction

The clandestine nature of procurement corruption makes discovery extremely difficult. Although transparency in public procurement may make it more difficult to conceal improper practices, transparency alone is insufficient to uncover procurement corruption, especially where the perpetrators have gone to great lengths to ensure that corrupt activity cannot be discovered.

The other means by which corruption in public procurement may be discovered is through audits, investigations and reporting mechanisms. Audits may be *ex ante* or *ex post* the conclusion of the procurement process, in most systems occurring at various specified points during the process. Investigations are *ex post* and may be triggered by the revelation of improprieties during the procurement process. Reporting mechanisms usually take the form of processes (sometimes anonymous) by which persons who allege impropriety in the procurement process may report this without fear of retaliation. Reporting mechanisms are often supported by whistleblower protections.

5.2. Audits

Most countries mandate the auditing of the procurement function through internal or external audits. Internal audits are of course those conducted internally within the agency carrying out the procurement function, and external audits are those conducted by individuals or bodies such as an audit institution unrelated to the agency which is being audited. Audit institutions are usually state audit institutions like the Auditor-General in South Africa, the National Audit Office in the United Kingdom and the Government Accountability Office in the United States. The United States also makes use of Inspectors-General within some federal agencies which are also authorised to conduct audits.

Most procurement audits are designed with a limited objective, such as ensuring that procurement was done in accordance with the rules or that the bulk of purchasing was done competitively or that purchasing was done through centrally managed contracts.

However, audits may have a broader mandate as is the case in South Africa where the audits conducted by the Auditor-General are to consider issues such as 'public interest; accountability; probity; effective legislative oversight, the compliance with law, regulation or other authority; performance against pre-determined objectives; and economic efficient, and effective procurement of resources. The ultimate goal of the audits concerned is to strengthen the South African democracy.'[82]

The main function of audits can be described as ensuring that 'value for money is achieved, appropriate controls are in place so that expenditure is reliably recorded; that it complies with all relevant accounting requirements, authorities and regulations . . . and that the risks of waste, impropriety and fraud are minimised'.[83] Public procurement audits examine the procurement function (compliance auditing), as well as the management of expenditures related to the procurement function (financial auditing), as well as the performance of the procurement system more generally or within an agency (performance audits). For auditors to be able to properly perform their functions, they need to have a clear mandate, some level of independence and adequate funding and staff, irrespective of whether the audit is internal or external.[84]

5.3. *Investigations*

As mentioned above, investigations in public procurement are usually *ex post* and may be triggered by the suspicion that there has been impropriety or criminality in the procurement process. Depending on the country and the context, such investigations may be carried out by police/judicial or prosecutorial authorities or in countries in which an oversight authority exists within a government agency; investigations may be conducted by that oversight official. In many contexts, the audit and the investigatory function may be located within the same office.

82 Auditor-General South Africa, Reporting Guide 2009.
83 National Audit Office, Getting Value for Money: How Auditors Can Help.
84 K. Dye and R. Stapenhurst, 'Pillars of Integrity: The Importance of Supreme Audit Institutions in Curbing Corruption' (Washington DC: World Bank Institute, 1998).

Thus, for instance, in South Africa, the Public Finance Management Act provides that the head of every public department must act as the accounting officer and is responsible for maintaining a system of internal audit and uncovering and taking action where there is 'unauthorised, irregular or fruitless expenditure'.[85]

Another example from the United States is the office of the Inspector General. This is a statutory office established in some federal agencies by the Inspector General Act of 1978 in order to detect and prevent fraud, waste, abuse and violations of law and to promote economy, efficiency and effectiveness in the operations of the federal government. Essentially, Inspectors General are required to conduct independent and objective audits, investigations and inspections. Because the Inspectors General are fully independent from the agencies they oversee, they can be totally objective in their work. Where there is an allegation of impropriety in public procurement, the Inspector General investigates this and produces an investigative report, which may be passed on to the police authorities or Congressional oversight committees where relevant.

5.4. *Reporting mechanisms*

As stated above, reporting mechanisms are designed to provide an avenue for people (often referred to as whistleblowers) to report suspicious or criminal activity within a government agency. Encouraging this kind of reporting as well as ensuring the safety of whistleblowers and the absence of retaliatory measures where this reporting occurs is often seen as central to the success of discovering procurement corruption. In fact, many countries establish anonymous reporting lines within government agencies or externally through reporting to an anti-corruption or similar body.

For example, in South Africa, the Public Finance Management Act Treasury Regulations provide that the National Treasury and each provincial treasury must establish a mechanism to consider complaints regarding alleged non-compliance with the prescribed minimum norms and standards and make recommendations for remedial action if non-compliance is established.[86] In addition, the South African Office of the Public Protector (OPP), established under the South African Constitution,[87] is empowered to investigate conduct in the public administration that is suspected

85 Public Finance Management Act 1 of 1999, Part 5. 86 Ibid., reg. 16A9.3.
87 Constitution of the Republic of South Africa, 1996, s. 182.

to be improper or that will result in impropriety or prejudice and to take appropriate remedial action.[88] These mechanisms may be used to report improper activity in the procurement context.

Apart from avenues for reporting wrongdoing, the protection of whistleblowers is essential to ensuring that such reporting mechanisms are utilised. Such protection takes the form of ensuring that government employees who report their superiors for improper activity cannot face retaliatory measures such as loss of employment, loss of promotion or other opportunities, demotion or out-of-town transfers.

Many countries have legislation which protects whistleblowers in the event that misconduct in the workplace is reported. In the United Kingdom, for instance, an employee is protected by law from dismissal where a disclosure is made and can make a claim for unfair dismissal against the employer where his appointment is terminated. Similar protections exist in the United States, where the Inspector General is responsible for whistleblower protection within a federal agency.

6. International measures against corruption

6.1. Introduction

Corruption is a problem that is regarded as so pervasive that it has necessitated concerted efforts to fight it.[89] It is currently being addressed by various multilateral and intergovernmental bodies such as the United Nations, the World Bank, the Organization for Economic Co-operation and Development and the African Union, as well as non-governmental organisations such as Transparency International. It is widely accepted that corruption undermines democratisation, the rule of law and the consolidation of market economies,[90] and is a threat to the international economy. To counter this threat, anti-corruption measures have become increasingly global in outlook. The OECD was

88 *Ibid.*, s. 182(1).

89 For instance, the creation of a Global Programme against Corruption by the United Nations in 1999 designed to assist mainly developing countries wishing to strengthen legal and institutional anti-corruption frameworks.

90 Rose-Ackerman, *Corruption and Government*, note 12 above; Soreide, *Corruption in Public Procurement*, note 30 above; P. Nichols, 'Outlawing Transnational Bribery through the World Trade Organization' (1997) 28 *Law and Policy in International Business* 305, 337; P. Nichols, 'Regulating Transnational Bribery in Times of Globalization and Fragmentation' (1999) 24 *Yale Journal of International Law* 257; J. Noonan, *Bribes* (New York: Macmillan, 1984).

the first intergovernmental institution to seek a coherent international framework for combating corruption in 1994.[91] This was accomplished by the enactment of instruments directly addressing corruption in government procurement[92] as well as more generally.

Anti-corruption measures on the international or multilateral plane can be divided into binding international instruments such as treaties and conventions, soft law instruments such as OECD recommendations,[93] United Nations and General Assembly resolutions and declarations,[94] and non-binding instruments from the EU.[95] Technical assistance programmes[96] (mainly directed at developing and transition economies) and 'naming and shaming' corrupt nations[97] are also included in the range of international and multilateral initiatives that may be used against corruption. For depth of analysis, this chapter is not limited to African instruments but will include all the international/multilateral binding instruments against corruption which are regarded as the most important in terms of their geographical significance and/or number of ratifications/accessions. In addition to the strategic importance of the instruments which have been selected for

91 Recommendations on Bribery in International Business Transactions adopted by the Council on 27 May 1994.

92 See Recommendations for Anti-Corruption Proposals for Aid-Funded Procurements, 1997.

93 See, for instance, OECD Recommendation of the Council on Bribery in International Business Transactions (27 May 1994) C94 (75)/FINAL; OECD Recommendation of the Council on the Tax Deductibility of Bribes to Foreign Public Officials, 35 ILM 1311; OECD Revised Recommendation of the Council on Combating Bribery in International Business Transactions, 36 ILM 1016 (1997); OECD Recommendation of the Council on Guidelines for Managing Conflict of Interest in the Public Service.

94 United Nations General Assembly Resolution 51/59 on Action against Corruption and the International Code of Conduct for Public Officials, A/RES/51/59; United Nations Declaration against Corruption and Bribery in International Commercial Transactions, A/Res/51/191; General Assembly Resolution 55/61 on an Effective International Legal Instrument against Corruption, A/RES/55/61.

95 Communication from the Commission to the Council and European Parliament on a Union Policy against Corruption, COM (97) 0192; Communication from the Commission to the Council and European Parliament on a Comprehensive EU Policy against Corruption, COM (2003) 0317; Action Plan to Combat Organised Crime [1997] OJ C251/1; Resolution on the Communication from the Commission to the Council and the European Parliament on a Union Policy against Corruption [1998] OJ C328/46.

96 Technical assistance is provided by the EU (through SIGMA, PHARE), the OECD and the United Nations through its anti-corruption toolkit.

97 Such as in the Corruption Perceptions Index, the Bribe Payers Index and the Global Corruption Barometer which are compiled and provided by Transparency International. See www.transparency.org (accessed 26 March 2012).

consideration, all the instruments (excepting the OECD Convention) are of particular importance in the context of public procurement as they all refer to the maintenance of transparent procurement systems as one of the ways to combat corruption.

6.2. The OECD Anti-Bribery Convention

The OECD Convention on Combating Bribery of Foreign Public Officials[98] had an interesting legislative history.[99] After the enactment of the US Foreign Corrupt Practices Act in 1977 (FCPA) and its subsequent amendment in 1988,[100] it became apparent to the US government that it could not single-handedly and in the absence of international cooperation, solve the problem of international corruption. Instead, the FCPA was largely criticised for harming US interests by making it more difficult for US firms to obtain foreign business as non-US firms who were still willing to pay bribes now had a significant advantage over their US competitors.[101] To ensure that US firms were not prejudiced by the

98 37 ILM 1 (1997).

99 See generally A. Posadas, 'Combating Corruption under International Law' (2000) 10 *Duke Journal of Comparative and International Law* 345; D. Tarullo, 'The Limits of Institutional Design: Implementing the OECD Anti-Bribery Convention' (2004) 44 *Virginia Journal of International Law* 665; D. Windsor and K. Getz, 'Multilateral Cooperation to Combat Corruption: Normative Regimes Despite Mixed Motives and Diverse Values' (2000) 33 *Cornell International Law Journal* 731; B. George, K. Lacey and J. Birmele, 'The 1998 OECD Convention: An Impetus for Worldwide Changes in Attitudes toward Corruption in Business Transactions' (2000) 37 *American Business Law Journal* 485; N. Rubin, 'A Convergence of 1996 and 1997 Global Efforts to Curb Corruption and Bribery in International Business Transactions: The Legal Implications of the OECD Recommendations and Convention for the United States, Germany and Switzerland' (1998) 14 *American University International Law Review* 257; J. Nesbitt, 'Transnational Bribery of Foreign Officials: A New Threat to the Future of Democracy' (1998) 31 *Vanderbilt Journal of Transnational Lawaw* 1273; P. Nicholls, 'The Myth of Anti-Bribery Law as Transnational Intrusion' (2000) 33 *Cornell Journal of International Law* 627; C. Hudson and P. Pieros, 'The Hard Graft of Tackling Corruption in International Business Transactions: Progress in International Cooperation and the OECD Convention' (1998) 32 *Journal of World Trade* 77–102; S. Salbu, 'A Delicate Balance: Legislation, Institutional Change and Transnational Bribery' (2000) 33 *Cornell International Law Journal* 657; P. Jennings, 'Public Corruption: A Comparative Analysis of International Corruption Conventions and United States Law' (2001) 18 *Arizona Journal of International and Comparative Law* 793.

100 Pub. L. No. 95-213, 91 Stat. 1494.

101 See Tarullo, 'The Limits of Institutional Design', note 99 above, p. 665; Windsor and Getz, 'Multilateral Cooperation to Combat Corruption', note 99 above, pp. 731, 748.

government's desire to eradicate bribery, the US government put increasing pressure on its peers at the OECD[102] and was able to convince them that bribery hindered international trade, leading to the adoption of a similar approach to criminalising overseas bribery by means of a Recommendation in 1994.[103]

This Recommendation was followed by the Convention three years later, which entered into force in 1999. The Convention addresses only supply-side bribery. In other words, the obligation is on states to prevent their citizens from bribing foreign officials, but does not address the taking of bribes by those foreign officials. The major obligations imposed by the Convention can be broken into three parts.

The main obligation is provided in Article 1, which obliges signatories to:

> take such measures as may be necessary to establish that it is a criminal offence under its law for any person intentionally to offer, promise or give any undue pecuniary or other advantage . . . to a foreign public official for that official or for a third party, in order that the official act or refrain from acting in relation to the performance of official duties, in order to obtain or retain business or other improper advantage in the conduct of international business.

This obligation is supported by subsequent Articles providing for appropriate criminal and civil sanctions against firms that are guilty of foreign bribery.[104]

The second major obligation imposed by the Convention is one to discourage accounting and financial recording mechanisms that disguise or hide foreign bribes. In addition, member states are obliged to punish such accounting malpractices by effective, proportionate and dissuasive penalties.[105] The third major obligation imposed on member states is an obligation under which the parties to the Convention must provide mutual legal assistance to each other, for the purposes of investigating relevant cases,[106] including the possibility of extradition where necessary.[107]

The OECD monitors compliance with the Convention through a process of peer reviews of the anti-corruption legislation adopted by member states. In doing this, the OECD works through the medium of self- and mutual examination, whereby OECD member states may review each

102 Posadas, 'Combating Corruption under International Law', note 99 above, pp. 345, 377–9.

103 33 ILM 1389 (1994). 104 OECD Anti-bribery Convention, Art. 3(1).

105 *Ibid.*, Art. 8. 106 *Ibid.*, Art. 9(1). 107 *Ibid.*, Art. 10.

other's anti-corruption regimes. The process also includes a formal evaluation procedure by the OECD itself. The OECD also conducts an examination into the enforcement mechanism of member states[108] to assess how effective the anti-corruption legislation is in practice.[109]

As an organisation, the OECD has focused on ensuring that the administrative and legislative mechanisms necessary to implement the Convention are in place in signatory states. It is not yet clear whether the Convention has had much success in reducing foreign bribery among its signatories, and, while many commentators view the Convention as a positive step towards eradicating corruption, most are of the view that the Convention has not been as successful in combating international bribery as had been hoped.[110] This is due in part to what is regarded as the major loopholes in the Convention which are that it excludes passive bribery and 'small facilitation payments' from its ambit[111] as well as similar lacunae in the implementing legislation of states parties.[112] In addition, because the Convention is not a model for legislation, but a set of guidelines mandating a broad outcome, it does not 'require uniformity or changes in the fundamental principles of a Party's legal system'.[113] As a result, states parties are not required to do much more than criminalise foreign bribery in order to have complied with the Convention.[114] Coupled with a weak

108 See www.oecd.org (accessed 26 March 2012).

109 See C. Corr and J. Lawler, 'Damned If You Do, Damned If You Don't? The OECD Convention and the Globalisation of Anti-Bribery Measures' (1999) 32 *Vanderbilt Journal of Transnational Law* 1249, 1319–24.

110 For a review of the various reasons why it appears that the Convention has not succeeded, see L. Miller, '"No More This for That?" The Effect of the OECD Convention on Combating Bribery of Foreign Public Officials in International Business Transactions' (2000) 8 *Cardozo Journal of International and Comparative Law* 139; C. Calberg, 'A Truly Level Playing Field for International Business: Improving the OECD Convention on Combating Bribery using Clear Standards' (2003) 26 *Boston College International and Comparative Law Review* 95; Tarullo, 'The Limits of Institutional Design', note 99 above, p. 665.

111 See Commentaries on the Convention on Combating Bribery of Officials in International Business Transactions, OECD Negotiating Conference, para. 1, available at www.oecd.org (accessed 26 March 2012).

112 Miller, '"No More This for That?"', note 110 above, pp. 150–8; D. Heifetz, 'Japan's Implementation of the OECD Anti-Bribery Convention: Weaker and Less Effective Than the US Foreign Corrupt Practices Act' (2002) 11 *Pacific Rim Law and Policy Journal* 209.

113 Commentaries on the Convention on Combating Bribery of Officials in International Business Transactions, OECD Negotiating Conference, para. 2, available at www.oecd.org (accessed 26 March 2012).

114 P. Ala'I, 'The Legacy of Geographical Morality and Colonialism: A Historical Assessment of the Current Crusade against Corruption' (2000) 33 *Vanderbilt Journal of Transnational Law* 877, 923–4.

implementation mechanism, the Convention's success may be found in the harmonisation of a set of norms on foreign bribery and not much more.[115] The shortcomings of the Convention led to the adoption in 2009 of a Recommendation for Further Combating Bribery of Foreign Public Officials in International Business Transactions, which suggests further measures to combat international bribery.[116]

6.3. The Organization of American States Corruption Convention

The Organization of American States (OAS) is a regional organisation of western hemisphere states. The OAS path to a multilateral convention against corruption began in 1994 at the Miami Summit, where the adopted Declaration of Principles and Plan of Action[117] made the link between effective democracy and the eradication of corruption.[118] As a result of the commitments outlined in the Plan of Action, the member states of the OAS adopted the Inter-American Convention against Corruption,[119] which took effect in March 1997.

The Inter-American Convention follows the same pattern of criminalisation of overseas bribery that is present in the OECD Convention. The Inter-American Convention is, however, broader in scope than the OECD Convention in that it addresses both the demand and the supply-side of corruption and applies not only where a corrupt act was committed in a state party, but also where the act has *effects* in a state party.[120] Presumably, an effect would include where a firm from a state party was denied a contract because the firm refused to give a bribe. It is not clear, however, how this might be addressed by the Convention.

The Inter-American Convention also contains measures necessary to prevent corruption,[121] thus adopting a more holistic approach to corruption control. It provides for the implementation in national systems of measures to prevent corruption in government activities, including, but not limited to, the tax system, the procurement system[122] and the civil service. It also provides for the creation of mechanisms that will support

115 *Ibid.*, p. 928.
116 See also OECD Recommendation on Tax Measures for Further Combating Bribery of Foreign Public Officials in International Business Transactions, 2009.
117 Summit of the Americas: Declaration of Principles and Plan of Action, 34 ILM 808 (1995).
118 *Ibid.* 119 35 ILM 724 (1996).
120 Inter-American Corruption Convention, Art. IV.
121 See *ibid.*, Art. III. 122 *Ibid.*, Art. III(5) and (6).

good accounting practices within firms as a means of detecting corrupt acts where they occur.[123]

The Inter-American Convention contains a series of mandatory multilateral obligations. These include a commitment to extradite persons found to have committed acts of corruption which have either been defined as such in the Convention, or have been established as offences by the state party.[124] State parties are also enjoined to afford each other wide measures of mutual assistance in preventive, investigative and enforcement efforts,[125] including assistance in the seizure and forfeiture of assets connected with 'acts of corruption'.[126] In addition, states parties may not use bank secrecy laws or the political nature of the act of corruption as a basis for refusing to cooperate with other states parties.[127]

Unlike the OECD Convention, however, there is no monitoring or compliance mechanism, leaving implementation to the discretion of states parties. Another feature of the Inter-American Convention, which does not have parallels in the OECD Convention, is that some of the offences listed therein are declared to be subject to the constitution and fundamental principles of the state party.[128] Thus, a state party may refrain from adopting the offences in question if it feels they are incompatible with its legal system.

6.4. The African Union Convention on Preventing and Combating Corruption

The African Union Convention on Preventing and Combating Corruption[129] is the most recent of the regional instruments against corruption, having been adopted by the member states of the African Union in July 2003. The object of the Convention is to promote and strengthen measures to prevent and combat corruption in Africa. This includes the facilitation of cooperation in respect of anti-corruption measures and the

123 *Ibid.*, Art. III(8). 124 *Ibid.*, Art. XIII.

125 *Ibid.*, Art. XIV. 126 *Ibid.*, Art. XV.

127 *Ibid.*, Arts. XVI and XVII. See L. Low and J. de Gramont, 'The Inter-American Convention against Corruption: Overview and Status at Three Years since its Inception' (2000) 15 *American University International Law Review* 768.

128 Such as the illicit enrichment of public officials under Art. IX.

129 43 ILM 5 (2004). For an analysis of the Convention, see N. J. Udombana, 'Fighting Corruption Seriously? Africa's Anti-Corruption Convention' (2003) 7 *Singapore Journal of International and Comparative Law* 447.

harmonisation of anti-corruption policies and legislation among states parties.[130]

The Convention is similar to the Inter-American Convention in its thrust, as the states parties consider in the preamble to the Convention that corruption is undermining political stability and socio-economic development in Africa.[131] The body of the Convention reiterates this theme in Article 2, where the stated objectives of the Convention include promoting socio-economic development by removing obstacles to the enjoyment of economic, social, cultural, civil and political rights.

The African Convention deals with corrupt acts that might be particular to Africa. The Convention thus defines the acts to which it applies as including the offences of giving or receiving a bribe (or other benefit) and the diversion of public funds or state property.[132] The Convention also applies to private sector corruption.[133] States parties are also enjoined to criminalise conspiracy and the concealment of fraudulently obtained proceeds.[134] The Convention also criminalises the laundering of corruptly obtained property[135] and illicit enrichment,[136] while seeking to protect whistleblowers.[137]

The Convention does not follow the general pattern of existing multilateral anti-corruption instruments, as it is designed to combat the specific issues that African nations face in relation to corruption. The Convention thus includes a commitment that states parties will require public officials to declare their assets at the inception and conclusion of their period in public service and further requires states parties to create a body devoted to the training of civil servants and the establishment of public codes of conduct.[138] It also requires states parties to ensure transparency in public procurement.

Like most multilateral corruption conventions, there are provisions relating to international cooperation, mutual assistance and extradition.[139] The Convention also provides for the establishment of

130 African Union Convention on Corruption, Art. 2.

131 See also Y. Osinbajo, 'Human Rights, Economic Development and the Corruption Factor' in P. Zeleza and P. McConnaughay (eds.), *Human Rights, the Rule of Law and Development in Africa* (University of Philadelphia Press, 2004), who argues that human rights repression was a façade for grand corruption during past military regimes in Nigeria.

132 African Union Convention on Corruption, Art. 4.

133 *Ibid.*, Arts. 4(e) and (f) and 11.

134 *Ibid.*, Art. 4(1)(h).

135 *Ibid.*, Art. 6.

136 *Ibid.*, Art. 8.

137 *Ibid.*, Art. 5.

138 *Ibid.*, Art. 7.

139 *Ibid.*, Arts. 15–19.

a monitoring mechanism, through the Advisory Board on Corruption within the African Union. This body is to promote the adoption and implementation of anti-corruption legislation in states parties, and submit regular reports to the Executive Council of the African Union on the progress made by states parties in complying with the Convention.[140]

6.5. The United Nations Convention against Corruption

The United Nations Convention is the only truly international instrument against corruption, being open to all members of the United Nations. Its origins date back to General Assembly Resolution 55/61 of December 2000, where it was recognised that an effective international legal instrument against corruption was necessary. This led to the establishment of an *ad hoc* committee for the negotiation of the Convention. Three years later, the Convention approved by the *ad hoc* committee was adopted by the General Assembly by Resolution 58/4 of October 2003. The Convention came into force on 14 December 2005.

The Convention is very ambitious in its scope[141] and can be divided into four parts: the prevention of corruption,[142] the criminalisation of corruption,[143] international cooperation[144] and asset recovery.[145] The Convention's methods for preventing corruption include the development of anti-corruption policies, and the establishment of an anti-corruption agency or body which will implement those policies. In addition, the Convention imposes a commitment on states parties to maintain an educated and well-trained civil service, which is adequately remunerated to reduce their vulnerability to corruption. It also touches on measures necessary to establish transparent and competitive procurement systems, as well as measures necessary to secure the integrity of the judiciary. The Convention also enjoins states parties to prevent corruption in the private sector. In providing for the criminalisation of corruption, the Convention casts its net wide to include public sector corruption, the bribery of foreign public officials and officials of international organisations, private sector corruption, diversion of public funds, or *anything of value* entrusted to a public official. The Convention goes

140 *Ibid.*, Art. 22.

141 See generally I. Carr, 'Fighting Corruption through the United Nations Convention on Corruption 2003: A Global Solution to a Global Problem' (2005) 11 *International Trade Law and Regulation* 24.

142 See United Nations Corruption Convention, Chapter II.

143 *Ibid.*, Chapter III. 144 *Ibid.*, Chapter IV. 145 *Ibid.*, Chapter V.

further than most international anti-corruption instruments by criminalising trading in influence and private sector embezzlement.

In relation to international cooperation on corruption matters, the Convention is again quite ambitious in calling for the mutual extradition of offenders, whether or not the offences for which extradition is sought are punishable under the law of the extraditing state, and whether or not an extradition treaty exists between the concerned states. The Convention extends the requirement of cooperation to include the transfer of sentenced persons, or criminal proceedings from the territory of one member state to another, as well as the 'widest measure' of mutual legal assistance. Mutual legal assistance includes the taking of evidence, the service of judicial documents, executing searches, freezing assets, and the provision of required information. International cooperation also extends to cooperation between the law enforcement agencies of states parties and the establishment of channels of communication between the same. Under the asset recovery provisions of the Convention, states parties are enjoined to afford each other the widest measure of cooperation and assistance in detecting the existence of corruptly obtained proceeds and permitting each other directly to recover assets by means of civil action.

Although the Convention goes into great detail on the abovementioned areas, its monitoring and compliance provisions are sadly lacking.[146] The Convention merely provides for a Conference of the States Parties to the Convention,[147] which is aimed at improving 'the capacity of and cooperation between States Parties' to achieve the objectives of the Convention and review its implementation.

6.6. The Southern Africa Development Community Protocol Against Corruption

The Southern Africa Development Community (SADC) was initially established in 1980 by the democratic states in Southern Africa with the aim of liberating South Africa from minority rule. Its mandate was enlarged in 1992 to include economic growth and economic integration among member states. There are currently fifteen members of SADC. The

146 See P. Webb, 'The United Nations Convention against Corruption: Global Achievement or Missed Opportunity?' (2005) 8 *Journal of International Economic Law* 191, 218–23.

147 United Nations Corruption Convention, Art. 63.

SADC Protocol Against Corruption was adopted by the SADC Council of Ministers in August 2001 and signed by fourteen of the SADC members.

The Protocol is quite broad in its scope and contains provisions to detect, prevent and punish acts of corruption. Specifically, and similarly to the African Union Convention, the Protocol criminalises the solicitation, giving or receiving of a bribe or other inducement in the course of a public official's duties, trading in influence, the diversion of state property, the fraudulent concealment of corruptly obtained property and conspiracy to commit any of the offences under the Protocol.[148]

In relation to its preventive provisions, the Protocol is not prescriptive, but merely lists the sectors in which states parties should take action, including but not limited to the public procurement system, government recruitment, taxation administration, whistleblower protection and the public education system.[149] The Protocol also criminalises overseas bribery and requires states parties to afford each other assistance in relation to overseas corruption.[150] Similarly to the other international instruments discussed above, the Protocol also calls for cooperation amongst states parties in relation to the confiscation and seizure of the proceeds of corruption, extradition and mutual legal assistance.[151]

6.7. Economic Community of West African States Protocol on the Fight against Corruption

The Economic Community of West African States (ECOWAS) is a regional organisation of fifteen West African states formed in 1975. The main objective of ECOWAS at its formation was to achieve economic integration in West Africa. This scope was subsequently expanded to include socio-political interactions and mutual development in related spheres.

The Protocol on the Fight against Corruption of the Economic Community of West African States was adopted with the objective of strengthening effective mechanisms to prevent, suppress and eradicate corruption in each of the states parties through cooperation between the states parties. It was signed on 21 December 2001, but has not yet entered into force as it has not obtained a sufficient number of ratifications.

Similarly to the SADC Protocol and the African Union Convention, the ECOWAS Protocol obliges states parties to adopt the necessary legislative measures to criminalise active and passive bribery in the public and

148 SADC Protocol, Art. 3. 149 *Ibid.*, Art. 4.
150 *Ibid.*, Art. 6. 151 *Ibid.*, Arts. 8–10.

private sectors; illicit enrichment, false accounting, as well as acts of aiding and abetting corrupt practices, and the laundering of the proceeds of corruption; to ensure the protection of victims; and to provide each other with judicial and law enforcement cooperation. The Protocol further calls upon states parties to harmonise their national anti-corruption laws, to adopt effective preventive measures against corruption and to introduce proportionate and dissuasive sanctions.

15

Promotion of social policy through public procurement in Africa

GEO QUINOT*

1. Introduction

While obtaining value for money is often considered to be the primary objective of public procurement regimes,[1] many countries also use procurement as a tool to implement other policies. These are sometimes referred to as 'horizontal policies' in that they are not necessarily directly connected with the functional purposes of the goods, works or services acquired in the procurement.[2] The aims pursued in horizontal policies in public procurement vary from environmental concerns to labour and equality, industrial development and economic growth, crime prevention and social concerns such as poverty alleviation and wealth distribution.[3]

From a legal perspective these parallel objectives in a public procurement system raise a number of concerns. On the one hand, there is the matter of incorporating the achievement of these horizontal policy objectives in the public procurement rules. In other words, there is a need to develop rules within the public procurement regulatory regime that can

* My thanks to Jan-Hugo Fyfer for excellent research assistance in writing this chapter.

1 S. Arrowsmith, J. Linarelli and D. Wallace, *Regulating Public Procurement: National and International Perspectives* (The Hague; London: Kluwer Law International, 2000), pp. 28–31.

2 These are sometimes also referred to as secondary or collateral policies. The label 'horizontal policies' was adopted by Arrowsmith and Kunzlik in preference to these other terms, in part because the label 'horizontal policies' does not imply that these policies are in any way of lesser importance than other objectives of procurement: see S. Arrowsmith and P. Kunzlik (eds.), *Social and Environmental Policies in EC Procurement Law: New Directives and New Directions* (Cambridge University Press, 2009), Chapter 1.

3 See generally C. McCrudden, *Buying Social Justice* (Oxford University Press, 2007); Arrowsmith and Kunzlik (eds.), *Social and Environmental Policies in EC Procurement Law*, note 2 above; Arrowsmith, Linarelli and Wallace, *Regulating Public Procurement*, note 1 above, Chapter 5; R. Caranta and M. Trybus (eds.), *The Law of Green and Social Procurement in Europe* (Copenhagen: DJØF Publishing, 2010).

facilitate the realisation of horizontal policy objectives. On the other hand, parallel objectives create tension within the regulatory regime in that different rules aimed at achieving different objectives may be in conflict with each other.

In this chapter, I consider the rules aimed at the promotion of social policy in public procurement in a number of African systems. The chapter provides a broad overview of horizontal policy in public procurement and the way that it generally impacts on the law of public procurement, that is the mechanisms found in public procurement regulation to implement such policies. I then consider the use of procurement for social policy objectives as reflected in the public procurement rules of African countries, with a particular focus on Southern Africa where public procurement has been seen as a major tool to address the wealth inequalities brought about by colonisation and apartheid, in other words as a tool to pursue distributive justice. The chapter subsequently focuses in detail on the legal mechanisms used in Kenya and South Africa to promote social policy objectives through public procurement. These two systems have both recently adopted new detailed legal rules on preferential procurement and thus provide an interesting set for comparison in this regard.

2. Horizontal policies and the regulation of public procurement

The use of public procurement to further horizontal policies is a widely accepted tool of public administration. It is also certainly not a new phenomenon. In the United States, for example, public procurement has been used to support local industries under the Buy American Act[4] for almost a century,[5] and the massive US small business programmes, which include the use of public procurement to support small and medium-sized enterprises (SMEs), have been in operation since 1953.[6] While a number of more recent international and regional trade regimes, such as those of the WTO, UNCITRAL and the EU, have ostensibly problematised the use of procurement to pursue horizontal policies, the practice remains

4 41 USC §§ 10a–10d.

5 The Buy American Act was first enacted in 1933: see M. J. Golub and S. L. Fenske, 'US Government Procurement: Opportunities and Obstacles for Foreign Contractors' (1987) 20 *George Washington Journal of International Law and Economics* 567, 573.

6 J. Linarelli, 'The Limited Case for Permitting SME Procurement Preferences in the Agreement on Government Procurement' in S. Arrowsmith and R. D. Anderson (eds.), *The WTO Regime on Government Procurement: Challenge and Reform* (Cambridge University Press, 2011), p. 444.

common in both developed and especially developing countries.[7] But, even the so-called free trade regimes that have included rules on public procurement, such as the WTO Agreement on Government Procurement, the UNCITRAL Model Law on Procurement of Goods, Construction and Services ('UNCITRAL Model Law') and the various EU Directives on public procurement, cannot be viewed as opposed to the use of procurement for horizontal policy purposes despite seeming opposition to such use in some of the mechanisms.[8] In a sense, these instruments can all be viewed as endorsing the use of procurement for horizontal policy purposes in that free trade, global market integration or open competition may in itself be viewed as a horizontal policy, that is a policy objective external to the purpose of the procurement of goods, services or construction in a given instance. At least to the extent that these regimes attempt to implement a particular economic policy, that of free trade and open competition, by means of public procurement they endorse horizontal policy objectives in public procurement as much as protectionist economic policies, as evidenced by preferences to local suppliers, do. In addition, a number of horizontal policy objectives currently enjoy particular prominence in regional and international policy debates. These include environmental concerns, human rights abuses and the fight against corruption.[9] The increased importance and urgency that these issues have garnered in recent years have also led to more emphasis on and awareness of the use of public procurement as a tool to implement these policies. EU public procurement law is a good example of this development with the EU Public Sector

7 See generally McCrudden, *Buying Social Justice*, note 3 above; F. Ssennoga, 'Examining Discriminatory Procurement Practices in Developing Countries' (2006) 6 *Journal of Public Procurement* 218.

8 See A. Davies, 'The National Treatment and Exceptions Provisions of the Agreement on Government Procurement and the Pursuit of Horizontal Policies' in Arrowsmith and Anderson (eds.), *The WTO Regime on Government Procurement*, note 6 above, pp. 429 *et seq.*; and, in the same volume, P. Bolton and G. Quinot, 'Social Policies in Procurement and the Agreement on Government Procurement: A Perspective from South Africa', pp. 459 *et seq.*; Linarelli, 'The Limited Case for Permitting SME Procurement Preferences', note 6 above, pp. 453–8; 459 *et seq.*; R. Caranta, 'Sustainable Public Procurement in the EU' in Caranta and Trybus (eds.), *The Law of Green and Social Procurement*, note 3 above, pp. 15 *et seq.*; S. Arrowsmith, 'Application of the EC Treaty and Directives to Horizontal Policies: A Critical Review' in Arrowsmith and Kunzlik (eds.), *Social and Environmental Policies in EC Procurement Law*, note 2 above, pp. 147 *et seq.*; McCrudden, *Buying Social Justice*, note 3 above, pp. 225–30 and Chapters 11, 12 and 15–17. See also Ssennoga, 'Examining Discriminatory Procurement Practices in Developing Countries', note 7 above, p. 221, on other regional trade agreements.

9 This last issue and its influence on procurement law are discussed in detail in Chapter 14.

Directive[10] and the Utilities Directive[11] both now imposing obligations on contracting authorities to exclude bidders on corruption grounds[12] and a host of legal provisions requiring attention to what is called 'sustainable public procurement'[13] taking into account environmental and particular social policy issues.[14] A final factor that has brought horizontal policies in public procurement to the fore is governments' responses to the global recession. Public procurement, and state commercial activity more broadly, has played a major role in governments' efforts to counter the effects of the crisis in financial markets and its aftermath since 2007. The United States is again a good example. Under the American Recovery and Reinvestment Act of 2009, significant federal funding was earmarked for government contracts to be awarded to domestic suppliers in an attempt to stimulate US economic activity.[15]

For the most part, the law does not play a significant role in decisions to use public procurement for horizontal policy purposes. Those policy decisions are mostly based on economic and political rationales, not legal ones. The law may play some role in limiting the options available to policy-makers, although even then it may only really impact on the way that policy decisions are implemented rather than the decisions themselves. There are some exceptions where higher order legal rules, such as constitutional provisions, dictate particular usage of public procurement. A number of constitutions in Southern Africa provide examples of such exceptions where the constitution commits the administration to programmes of wealth distribution, poverty alleviation and the general transformation of the economy. These legal rules may thus implicitly or explicitly determine the use of public procurement for horizontal policy purposes even in the absence of an actual decision on the part of the administration to use procurement as such. For example, the Namibian Constitution mandates the creation of 'policies and programmes' through legislation to redress social and economic inequalities brought about by

10 Directive 2004/18 [2004] OJ L134/114.

11 Directive 2004/17 [2004] OJ L134/1.

12 S. Williams, 'Coordinating Public Procurement to Support EU Objectives – A First Step? The Case of Exclusions for Serious Criminal Offences' in Arrowsmith and Kunzlik (eds.), *Social and Environmental Policies in EC Procurement Law*, note 2 above, pp. 479–80.

13 Caranta, 'Sustainable Public Procurement in the EU', note 8 above, p. 17.

14 *Ibid.*, pp. 15 *et seq.*; Arrowsmith and Kunzlik (eds.), *Social and Environmental Policies in EC Procurement Law*, note 2 above, Chapters 7 and 9.

15 From February 2009 (when the Act came into operation) to March 2012, US$227.4 billion had been spent under the Act on federal contracts, grants and loans. See www.recovery.gov for more details on the programmes under the Act.

past discriminatory laws or practices.[16] This provision is seen as implicitly mandating (or even dictating) the use of public procurement for social policy purposes.[17] The South African Constitution provides an example of an explicit mandate for the use of public procurement for social policy purposes.[18]

The law does play a significant role in the context of horizontal policies in public procurement in the *way* that these policies are implemented, in other words in designing the mechanisms used to implement these policies. Arrowsmith's useful taxonomy of horizontal policies in public procurement sets out these mechanisms as the third element of the taxonomy and lists nine distinct mechanisms.[19] The taxonomy is helpful in this regard in that it allows for closer analysis of the advantages and disadvantages of various legal mechanisms aimed at implementing horizontal policies through procurement. It thus shifts the focus away from the policies themselves, which as I have argued above are mostly functions of extra-legal considerations, to an appropriate focus in legal analysis of this phenomenon. The nine mechanisms identified by Arrowsmith are:

(1) The decision to purchase, or not to purchase.
(2) The decision on what to purchase.
(3) Contractual requirements laid down by the purchaser.
(4) Packaging and timing of orders.
(5) Set-asides.
(6) Exclusion from contracts for non-compliance with government policies.
(7) Preferences in inviting firms to tender.
(8) Award criteria.
(9) Measures for improving access to government contracts.[20]

Based on this taxonomy, Watermeyer has put forward a useful table, which is reproduced here as Table 15.1. The table effectively captures the range of legal mechanisms available to implement horizontal policies through public procurement, and clearly shows how the choice of mechanism

16 Constitution of the Republic of Namibia 1990, Art. 23(2).

17 See Chapter 6, section 2.1, of this volume.

18 Constitution of the Republic of South Africa, 1996, s. 217(2). See Chapter 9, section 2.1, of this volume; and section 4.2 below.

19 S. Arrowsmith, 'A Taxonomy of Horizontal Policies in Public Procurement' in Arrowsmith and Kunzlik (eds.), *Social and Environmental Policies in EC Procurement Law*, note 2 above, pp. 127–46.

20 *Ibid.*

Table 15.1 *Legal mechanisms aimed at implementing horizontal policies through procurement*

Scheme type	Methods	Actions associated with the method
Reservations	#1 Set asides	Allow only enterprises that have prescribed characteristics to compete for the contracts or portions thereof, which have been reserved for their exclusive execution.
	#2 Qualification criteria	Exclude firms that cannot meet a specified requirement, or norm, relating to the policy objective from participation in contracts other than those provided for in the law.
	#3 Contractual conditions	Make policy objectives a contractual condition, e.g. a fixed percentage of work must be subcontracted out to enterprises that have prescribed characteristics or a joint venture must be entered into.
	#4 Offering back	Offer tenderers that satisfy criteria relating to policy objectives an opportunity to undertake the whole or part of the contract if that tenderer is prepared to match the price and quality of the best tender received.
Preferencing	#5 Preferences at the short listing stage	Limit the number of suppliers/service providers who are invited to tender on the basis of qualifications and give a weighting to policy objectives along with the usual commercial criteria, such as quality, at the short listing stage.
	#6 Award criteria (tender evaluation criteria)	Give a weighting to policy objectives along with the usual commercial criteria, such as price and quality, at the award stage.

(cont.)

Table 15.1 (*cont.*)

Scheme type	Methods	Actions associated with the method
Indirect	#7 Product/service specification	State requirements in product or service specifications, e.g. by specifying labour-based construction methods.
	#8 Design of specifications, contract conditions and procurement processes to benefit particular contractors	Design specifications and/or set contract terms to facilitate participation by targeted groups of suppliers.
Supply side	#9 General assistance	Provide support for targeted groups to compete for business, without giving these parties any favourable treatment in the actual procurement.

Source: R. B. Watermeyer, 'Facilitating Sustainable Development through Public and Donor Procurement Regimes: Tools and Techniques' (2004) 13 *Public Procurement Law Review* 30, 43, Table 3.

impacts on the effect of horizontal policy considerations on public procurement decisions. The degree of impact of horizontal policies on public procurement decisions is thus greatly dependent on the legal mechanism adopted. Such impact ranges from determinative in the case of reservation schemes where for example only goods or suppliers complying with the horizontal policy objective at issue are eligible to bid, to simply supportive in the case where suppliers complying with the horizontal policy objective are given support in preparing bids, but with no further advantage in the actual procurement decision. The realisations that the particular legal mechanism adopted determines the scope of impact of horizontal policies in procurement and that there is a range of different mechanisms available providing vastly different degrees of impact play an important role in any analysis of the desirability of horizontal policy objectives in public procurement as well as on the internal tensions that may emerge between various objectives of a public procurement system and how those tensions can be managed in the regulatory regime. In other words, it is not sensible simply to debate the use of public procurement for horizontal policy purposes without close attention to the various legal mechanisms used (or available) to implement such policy objectives in the procurement system.

Regarding the tensions created within a procurement system when horizontal policy objectives are included, it is often argued that the use of procurement for horizontal policy purposes adversely affects the more general aim of value for money.[21] McCrudden shows how mechanisms to implement horizontal policies in procurement may result in three different types of discrimination, namely, 'entry discrimination', 'price discrimination' and 'cost discrimination', each of which may result in higher procurement costs to contracting authorities utilising these mechanisms.[22] Under most of these schemes, the pool of competing bidders will be reduced, which may lead to higher prices. Bidders may also increase prices to counter additional contractual burdens placed on them in pursuit of horizontal policies. Of course, goods may also simply cost more because of particular horizontal policy requirements attached to them. However, as Arrowsmith indicates, such cost increases are not always inevitable and

21 Arrowsmith, 'A Taxonomy of Horizontal Policies in Public Procurement', note 19 above, p. 128; McCrudden, *Buying Social Justice*, note 3 above, pp. 115–18, 595–617, discussing various empirical studies on the effect of horizontal policies on procurement systems; Linarelli, 'The Limited Case for Permitting SME Procurement Preferences', note 6 above, pp. 448–50.

22 McCrudden, *Buying Social Justice*, note 3 above, p. 117.

some mechanisms may in fact lead to cost reduction.[23] For example, in the long run, support to new entrants to a market may lead to more competition and lower prices, or goods that may cost more at the outset may be more cost-effective over the full life-cycle of the product, good examples being many environmentally friendly products such as low-energy light bulbs or water-saving plumbing equipment that may not only last longer than conventional products, but also result in savings in running costs. However, the important point here is that different mechanisms used to implement horizontal policies in procurement may have vastly different implications for the objective of value for money. It is thus not the use of procurement to pursue horizontal policies *per se* that results in tension with the value-for-money objective, but rather the particular mechanism used to implement such policies. As Linarelli cogently notes in this regard: 'The emphasis should be on careful design.'[24]

The same point emerges when one considers the relationship between horizontal policy objectives and another key aim in procurement, namely, that of efficient procurement. Pursuing horizontal policies through procurement may result in considerable additional administration in the procurement process. Again, the focus is on the mechanisms used to implement policy objectives and what the administrative implications are of the particular mechanism for both contracting authorities and suppliers. Additional qualification or award criteria may, for example, be difficult, time-consuming and costly to adjudicate adding to the burden of contracting authorities. Conversely, compliance (or simply proof of compliance) with such additional criteria may impose significant burdens on suppliers, again resulting in adverse efficiency and cost implications. Supervision of compliance with such additional elements of the procurement system and the increased possibility of challenges on these additional grounds add yet another layer to the process with potential efficiency (and cost) implications. A good example of this danger is anti-corruption mechanisms such as the exclusion of certain suppliers from government contracts because of past corrupt practices. As is pointed out in Chapter 14 where corruption in public procurement is discussed, such mechanisms may be very difficult and thus costly to implement given

23 Arrowsmith, 'A Taxonomy of Horizontal Policies in Public Procurement', note 19 above, p. 128. See also Linarelli, 'The Limited Case for Permitting SME Procurement Preferences', note 6 above, pp. 448–50, where he notes a number of recent empirical studies that indicate decreased procurement costs as an outcome of preferential schemes.

24 Linarelli, 'The Limited Case for Permitting SME Procurement Preferences', note 6 above, p. 450.

the challenges in tracing bidders' backgrounds and effectively screening all potential suppliers.[25] Again, as with value for money, it is the particular mechanism that may lead to adverse efficiency implications rather than the pursuit of policy objectives *per se*. A legal perspective on the use of procurement for horizontal policy purposes should thus focus closely on these implications of different legal mechanisms implementing such use.

A final consideration in a legal perspective on horizontal policies in procurement is the need for clear procurement rules. Efficiency, value for money and integrity can only be achieved in public procurement systems if procurement is conducted in terms of a set of clear rules.[26] In fact, the notion of transparency in procurement, as an important means of achieving these core objectives of most procurement systems as was explained in Chapter 1, is mostly understood as meaning a system that is characterised by a set of clear rules.[27] As Arrowsmith, Linarelli and Wallace point out, '[a] first and fundamental requirement of transparency is that the "rules of the game" are known to participants.'[28] This also implies that procurement officials should not enjoy wide discretionary powers, but that decisions should rather be closely rule-based.[29] This is also true for the use of procurement for horizontal policy purposes. If public procurement is thus to be used to achieve horizontal policy objectives as a political, public policy and/or economic choice, it is imperative that such policy objectives in procurement be properly translated into public procurement rules. It is particularly in relation to horizontal policy influences on procurement decisions that wide discretionary powers should not be granted to procurement officials. In the absence of clear rules, it is extremely difficult to assess whether a particular procurement decision was properly made in terms of the range of objectives pursued in the procurement system. Thus, where horizontal policy objectives form part of the procurement system, the absence of clear rules would make it virtually impossible to assess whether a given decision rests solely, largely, somewhat or not at all on such policy objectives and conversely what role other objectives such as value for money played, if any, in the decision. The pursuit of horizontal policy objectives in public procurement thus necessitates clear rules that

25 See Chapter 14, section 4.2, of this volume.

26 R. J. Hunja, 'Obstacles to Public Procurement Reform in Developing Countries' in S. Arrowsmith and M. Trybus (eds.), *Public Procurement: The Continuing Revolution* (The Hague: Kluwer Law International, 2003), p. 15.

27 Arrowsmith, Linarelli and Wallace, *Regulating Public Procurement*, note 1 above, p. 73.

28 *Ibid.*, p. 74. 29 *Ibid.*, pp. 22–3 and 74–5.

define the balance between the different objectives of the system, especially where those objectives may be in tension in particular procurement decisions.

3. Social policy in African public procurement

3.1. The objectives pursued

An overview of the objectives of the public procurement regulatory systems of the African countries investigated in this book (Botswana, Ethiopia, Ghana, Kenya, Namibia, Nigeria, Rwanda, South Africa and Zimbabwe) shows that all the systems provide for some measure of social policy to be pursued in public procurement.[30] The most common policy objectives relate to support of local goods and/or suppliers, thus promoting local economic development, and support for (local) SMEs. A significant number of these systems also include anti-corruption measures in public procurement laws as is discussed in more detail in Chapter 14, indicating that the fight against corruption is also a common policy objective pursued in public procurement. Other policy objectives are, however, largely absent from these regulatory regimes. For example, one does not find any significant indications that environmental policies feature in these systems.[31]

While there is commonality between these African systems in support of local goods and/or suppliers, the exact policies underlying such local

30 See section 2.1 of the respective chapters in Part I of this volume.

31 There are indications that environmental concerns are beginning to receive some attention in public procurement in a number of these African systems. In South Africa, for example, one of the nine provinces, the Western Cape, recently published a draft policy on green procurement: Western Cape Department of Environmental Affairs and Development Planning, 'Draft White Paper on Greening the Procurement of Goods and Services in the Provincial Government of the Western Cape', *Province of the Western Cape: Provincial Government Gazette Extraordinary*, No. 6880, 21 June 2011. See also S. De la Harpe, 'Green Public Procurement – An Option for South Africa?' (2008) 22 *Speculum Juris* 53; P. Bolton, 'Incorporating Environmental Considerations into Government Procurement in South Africa' (2008) *Journal of South African Law* 31; International Institute for Sustainable Development, *Sustainable Public Procurement in South Africa* (Winnipeg: International Institute for Sustainable Development, 2008). In Ghana, the International Institute for Sustainable Development (IISD) is also working with the Ghanaian Public Procurement Authority under the IISD's Country Projects on Sustainable Public Procurement to develop a framework for sustainable public procurement. In Kenya, the *Public Procurement and Disposal General Manual* (2009) of the Public Procurement Oversight Authority notes in section 2.13 that environmental considerations should be taken into account in the design of procurement requirements and during the evaluation process.

support mechanisms seem to differ judging from the relevant public procurement rules. In some systems, such as Ghana, Nigeria, Ethiopia and Rwanda, the policy pursued by these mechanisms seems purely economic, that is, an attempt to generate domestic economic growth and foster local industrial development. In a number of other systems, such as Botswana and Namibia, the mechanisms seem to be premised on a more mixed policy basis. In these systems, while economic considerations such as economic growth clearly play a role in providing support to local suppliers, there are important additional social policy objectives, namely, support of marginalised groups in society. In Namibia, for example, price preferences may be given at the award stage based on a number of criteria, some of which focus on local content, while others, in the same preferential scheme, focus on social objectives such as employment of women and disabled persons.[32] In Botswana, one finds a similar mix of local preference based on 'economic . . . objectives'[33] and preference to targeted groups such as 'disadvantaged women's communities and regions and areas subject to occasional calamities'[34] based on 'social objectives'.[35] In a third group of systems, such as Kenya, South Africa and Zimbabwe, both these types of policy objectives, economic and social, are present, but are pursued in distinct mechanisms in the procurement regime. In other words, unlike in the previous group of systems, the policy objectives are not combined behind a single set of mechanisms. The Kenyan Public Procurement and Disposal Act 2005 clearly contemplates both economic policy objectives and social objectives. While the Act provides for reservations and preferences in the same section,[36] the recent Public Procurement and Disposal (Preference and Reservations) Regulations 2011 provide for distinct forms of preference to various categories of bidders, differentiating between the different objectives as is discussed below.[37] In Zimbabwe, distinct preferences are given for local content on the one hand and bids by previously disadvantaged groups on the other.[38] In South Africa, as is

32 See Chapter 6, section 4, of this volume.

33 Public Procurement and Asset Disposal Act 2001 (Botswana), s. 66(1).

34 *Ibid.*, s. 66(3)(ii).

35 *Ibid.*, s. 66(1). See Chapter 2, section 2.1, of this volume.

36 S. 2(f) of the Act lists as an objective of the procurement regime 'to facilitate the promotion of local industry and economic development', while the section that actually provides for reservation and preference schemes, s. 39, explicitly also provides for preferences to be given to 'candidates such as disadvantaged groups, micro, small and medium enterprises', indicating that social policy objectives beyond that listed in s. 2 of the Act are at issue here. See Chapter 5, section 2.1, of this volume.

37 On these regulations, see section 4.1 below.

38 See Chapter 10, section 2.1, of this volume.

discussed in more detail below, preference is given to bidders based on their status under that country's comprehensive economic empowerment regime representing a major social policy dimension to public procurement, whereas, most recently, a system of reservations for local products has been introduced quite separate from the economic empowerment scheme in furtherance of economic objectives.[39]

Of particular interest are the clear indications in the procurement laws of the three Southern African systems of Namibia, Zimbabwe and South Africa, and to a lesser extent also that of Kenya, regarding the use of public procurement to redress past discriminatory practices and actively pursue wealth redistribution. These systems thus employ public procurement for particular, expressed social-political purposes, which go beyond simple domestic preference. I will return to this aspect of the Kenyan and South African systems in more detail below.[40]

3.2. Mechanisms used to implement social policy objectives

If one turns to the legal mechanisms utilised in these African systems to promote social policy objectives, one finds a broad range of scheme types and mechanisms from Table 15.1 above. At one end of the scale, one finds relatively innocuous supply-side schemes that mandate assistance to domestic suppliers in bidding for public contracts, but without any actual preference in a particular bid. For example, the Ghanaian Public Procurement Act obliges the Public Procurement Authority to 'assist the local business community to become competitive and efficient suppliers to the public sector'.[41] However, the most common mechanisms found in these systems are on the other end of the scale involving reservations in the form of set-asides and preferential schemes. Reservations or set-asides are mostly mandated only under very limited circumstances. For example, in Botswana and Kenya, contracts may only be reserved for local bidders in cases of low-value and low-complexity procurement.[42] In South Africa, only contracts in particular sectors may be reserved for locally produced

39 Preferential Procurement Regulations 2011 (South Africa) in *Government Gazette*, No. 34350, 8 June 2011 ('2011 Procurement Regulations'), reg. 9.

40 See section 4 below.

41 Public Procurement Act 2003 (Ghana), s. 3(t); Chapter 4, section 2.1, of this volume.

42 Public Procurement and Asset Disposal Act 2001 (Botswana), s. 71; Public Procurement and Disposal Act 2005 (Kenya), s. 39(8).

goods.[43] The most common mechanism is preferencing, and in particular price preference at the award stage, which is found in all of the systems under review.

In comparing these preference mechanisms, a number of interesting differences emerge. There are differences in the way that preferences to local suppliers and preferences to local goods are dealt with.[44] In most systems, one finds preference schemes of both types, that is, preferences for local bidders and content. In some systems, the preferences for domestic goods and suppliers are provided for in a single mechanism, suggesting that the same policy objective informs both types, mostly economic objectives of local industrial development.[45] In other systems, while preferences to domestic goods and suppliers respectively are dealt with in distinct provisions, it seems that the distinction is only driven by the need to differentiate in the *mechanism* used to implement the same policy objectives, again mostly, but not exclusively, economic in nature.[46] One such difference lies, for example, in the discretionary-versus-mandatory nature of the preference (to which I shall return below). In a third category, the two types of preferences are distinct and clearly pursue different policy objectives.[47] Another distinction relates to the identity of local suppliers entitled to preferences. In some systems, the preference is simply to all local suppliers, suggesting in most cases an economic policy

43 2011 Procurement Regulations, reg. 9. At present, these sectors are buses (bus bodies), textiles, clothing, leather and footwear, power pylons, canned/processed vegetables, rolling stock: National Treasury, *Circular: Supply Chain Management: Local Production and Content as Announced by the Minister of Trade and Industry* (20 January 2012).

44 This distinction only relates to procurement for goods, rather than procurement for services or construction. In these latter two categories, such a distinction is mostly not possible and preference schemes will for the most part apply simultaneously in both these ways, i.e. a preference in a service procurement for local bidders will also mostly amount to a preference for local services.

45 E.g. in the Nigerian Public Procurement Act 2007, s. 34(1); Ethiopia: Federal Government Procurement and Property Administration Proclamation No. 649/2009, Art. 25 read with Federal Government Procurement Directive 2010, Art. 16.20; and Ghana: Public Procurement Act 2003, s. 59(1). However, the draft Guidelines for Margins of Preference published by the Ghanaian Public Procurement Board expressly state that preference should only be granted to local goods and not to local bidders.

46 E.g. Kenya: Public Procurement and Disposal Act 2005, s. 39(8)(a) and (b) read with the Public Procurement and Disposal (Preference and Reservations) Regulations 2011; and Botswana: Public Procurement and Asset Disposal Act 2001, ss. 66 and 75.

47 Ethiopia is an example where preferences for local goods are granted in all instances, but preferences to local small and micro enterprises are only granted in certain procurement methods. Federal Government Procurement Directive 2010 (Ethiopia), Art. 16.20.5(b). On procurement methods, see Chapter 12 of this volume.

objective.[48] In other systems, a distinction is drawn between different types of local suppliers with preferences either given to only one type[49] or in a differentiated manner to different types.[50] These distinctions suggest that different policy objectives are at play, for example economic growth policies informing preferences to all domestic suppliers, and social policies of wealth distribution or poverty alleviation informing preferences to circumscribed categories of local suppliers such as women or historically disadvantaged bidders. Where different categories of domestic suppliers are accorded different preferences, it may also indicate different social policy objectives being pursued, for example policies of rural development, gender equality and/or redress of past discriminatory practices. A third distinction between preference mechanisms relates to the mandatory or discretionary nature of the scheme. In some systems, preferences are mandatory in the sense that contracting authorities must accord preferences to bidders in terms of the relevant scheme set out in the legal rules.[51] In other systems, the decision to award preferences is discretionary, and the contracting authority has to decide whether preferences will be allowed in a given case.[52] Another variation is where the procurement rules make granting preferences mandatory where a preferential scheme has been adopted by another administrative body, such as a procurement board or responsible member of the executive, without compelling such body to implement a preference scheme. In such instances, there is thus no discretion in the hands of the particular

48 E.g. in Rwanda: Law on Public Procurement No. 12/2007 of 29 March 2007, Art. 41; and Nigeria: Public Procurement Act 2007, s. 34(1).

49 Ethiopia is an example of preferences granted only to small and micro local suppliers and not all local suppliers, Federal Government Procurement Directive 2010 (Ethiopia), Art. 16.20.

50 Zimbabwe, Namibia, Kenya and South Africa are examples of differentiated preferences granted to different categories of local suppliers. In Zimbabwe, all locally based suppliers are granted a 10 per cent price preference and 'previously economically disadvantaged contractors' are ostensibly granted an additional 10 per cent preference: Procurement Regulations, Statutory Instrument 171 of 2002 (Zimbabwe), reg. 20(1) and (2). In Namibia, different preferences are given to 'small scale industries' and 'tenderers located in communal areas or notified underdeveloped areas': Tender Board Regulations 1996 (Namibia), Annexure A. On the Kenyan and South African models, see section 4 below.

51 E.g. in Zimbabwe: Procurement Regulations, Statutory Instrument 171 of 2002 (Zimbabwe), reg. 20; and Ethiopia: Federal Government Procurement and Property Administration Proclamation No. 649/2009, Art. 25, and Federal Government Procurement Directive 2010, Art. 16.20.

52 E.g. in Nigeria: Public Procurement Act 2007, s. 34(1); and Ghana: Public Procurement Act 2003, s. 59(1). In Ghana, the discretion is, however, subject to the approval of the Public Procurement Board (s. 59(3)).

contracting authority, but preferences are still an administrative discretion in terms of the procurement rules, that is, the rules themselves do not compel preferences.[53] This comparative perspective indicates that, while there is significant convergence on the particular mechanisms used to promote social policies in these African countries' procurement systems, there is considerable divergence in the exact form of those mechanisms.

As I have noted above, social policies are mostly implemented in these African procurement systems by way of domestic reservations and/or preferences. However, international trade agreements have had some impact on such mechanisms. In some instances, trade agreements have resulted in domestic preference schemes being extended beyond national borders to also provide preferences to bidders from a particular region. Rwanda provides an example of such an instance where section 41 of the Rwandan Law on Public Procurement provides for a maximum 10 per cent price preference not only to domestic bidders, but also to 'bidders in regional economic integration bodies' member states'. This provision caters, *inter alia*, for Rwanda's obligations as a member of the East African Community Common Market, which prohibits discrimination against bidders from other member states in public procurement.[54] International trade agreements will, however, more likely restrain African states from implementing domestic preferences. In this regard, many of the systems under review provide in their procurement rules that preferential schemes must be implemented in a manner that is consistent with the country's international trade obligations.[55]

Of particular relevance in the legal analysis of preferential procurement schemes is the level of detail found in the actual procurement rules as opposed to discretion left to contracting authorities in granting

53 See e.g. Botswana: Public Procurement and Asset Disposal Act 2001, s. 66, where 'the government' is empowered to introduce preference schemes, and s. 68, where contracting authorities are obliged to apply preference schemes where they are implemented.

54 Chapter 8, section 2.1, of this volume.

55 E.g. Botswana, where the Public Procurement and Asset Disposal Act 2001, s. 66, states that preferential procurement must be 'consistent with [Botswana's] external obligations and its stable, market oriented, macro-economic framework'. In most other systems, trade-agreement limitations on preferential procurement schemes are contained in a more general statutory provision following that found in the UNCITRAL Model Law (Art. 3) stating that in case of conflict between the relevant procurement Act and a trade agreement the latter shall prevail. Since trade agreements are generally aimed at opening up trade between the parties to the agreement, it is to be expected that schemes granting preference to domestic bidders will fall foul of non-discrimination clauses typical of such agreements, at least to the extent that the agreement applies to public procurement markets.

preferences. As noted above, this aspect of the use of procurement for social policy purposes is crucial in the design of a transparent procurement regulatory system. In this regard, there are again marked differences among the African systems under review. At the one end of the spectrum, one finds systems such as that in Botswana, where the procurement rules only set out the basic framework within which preferences may be granted, but leave the detail of the actual preferences to be worked out administratively within a given preference scheme. At the other end of the spectrum – and this seems to be the more common approach – the procurement rules set out in significant detail what the preferences are, how they must be calculated and when they will apply, leaving very little to administrative discretion. In this respect, the recent regulatory changes in Kenya and South Africa on preferential procurement provide interesting examples of how social policy objectives can be translated into law.

4. Detail preferential procurement rules in Kenya and South Africa

4.1. Introduction

Both Kenya and South Africa adopted new preferential procurement regulations in 2011[56] providing in significant detail for legal mechanisms to implement social policy objectives in public procurement. A close look at these two systems thus provides interesting examples of recent African developments in crafting legal rules to use public procurement for policy purposes.

4.2. Kenya

While the Kenyan Public Procurement and Disposal (Preference and Reservations) Regulations 2011 (the 'Kenyan Preference Regulations 2011' or 'the Regulations') state as their underlying objective 'to promote local, national and regional industry and support socio-economic development',[57] their purpose is more directly stated in what follows this statement in regulation 4, namely, to set out the legal rules to achieve these

56 Coincidentally on the very same day: 8 June 2011.

57 It is of interest to note the slightly different formulation of these policy objectives in the recent Kenyan Public Procurement Oversight Authority's Circular No. 10/2011 of 29 November 2011 where the purpose of the new Regulations are stated as 'promoting the growth of local, national and regional industry and *thereby* supporting socio-economic development' (emphasis added). This slight reformulation suggests a different view of the objectives of the Regulations in which support for local industry and socio-economic development are not co-objectives, but rather stand in a means–end relationship.

objectives. As such, the Regulations build on section 39 of the Kenyan Public Procurement and Disposal Act 2005, which mandates reservations and preferences to be given under certain conditions. The Act only sets out the most basic framework for these schemes and mandates the Minister of Finance to create further detailed rules.[58]

The Regulations create at least six different preferential procurement schemes, set out in Table 15.2. As can be gleaned from the table, the mechanisms employed in the Regulations provide for a range of different preferential targets including both defined domestic suppliers and goods in an interesting number of variations.

The key target groups are all defined in the Act or Regulations. These include 'citizen contractors', which is defined as 'a natural person or an incorporated company wholly owned and controlled by persons who are citizens of Kenya';[59] 'local contractors', which is defined as 'a contractor who is registered in Kenya under the Companies Act and whose operation is based in Kenya';[60] 'small enterprises', which is defined as 'a business undertaking with an initial (a) staff establishment of not less than eleven and not more than fifty employees, and (b) annual turnover or investment not exceeding five million Kenya Shillings';[61] and 'micro enterprises', which is defined as 'a business undertaking with an initial (a) staff establishment of not more than ten employees, and (b) annual turnover or investment not exceeding Kenya Shillings five hundred thousand'.[62] These first four targeted groups as well as the shareholding preferences in item 5 in Table 15.2 follow the fairly familiar African approach to social policy objectives in public procurement by focusing on preferences to local suppliers and/or goods and SME support. As argued above, these mechanisms are mostly aimed at advancing policies of domestic economic growth and industrial development. A number of noteworthy points already emerge from the Kenyan regulatory approach to these familiar mechanisms. It is interesting to note the variation in preferences based on citizenship and locality, being the main difference between the defined target groups of 'citizen contractors' and 'local contractors', the latter not necessarily having to be citizens or controlled by citizens. One thus sees in these variations domestic preferences in two distinct forms, and an interesting question, to which the answer is not apparent, at least from the regulatory regime, is whether these distinctions in the mechanisms reflect different policy objectives or perhaps different degrees of implementation of local economic support policies. For example, preferences to 'local contractors'

58 Public Procurement and Disposal Act 2005 (Kenya), s. 39(2). 59 *Ibid.*, s. 3(1).
60 *Ibid.* 61 Kenyan Preference Regulations 2011, reg. 2. 62 *Ibid.*

Table 15.2 *Kenyan preferential procurement schemes*

	Authority	Mechanism	Target	Procurement
1	Regulation 11	Reservation	'Citizen contractors' in the relevant region	Any procurement in defined regions using the Constituency Development Fund or the Local Authority Transfer Fund
2	Regulation 12 read with section 39(4)(b) of the Act	Reservation	'Local contractors'	Contracts for defined Kenyan goods[a]
3	Regulation 13 read with section 39(8)(a) of the Act	Reservation	'Citizen contractors'	Procurements that are 100% funded by the Kenyan government or 'Kenyan bodies' and are under the following thresholds: (a) five hundred million shillings for procurements in respect of road works; (b) two hundred million shillings for procurements in respect of other works; and (c) fifty million shillings for procurements in respect of goods or services.

4	Regulation 14 read with section 39(8)(b)(i) of the Act	15% price preference	All bidders	Offers of Kenyan goods
5	Regulation 15 read with section 39(8)(b)(ii) of the Act	6% price preference	Less than 20% Kenyan shareholding in bidder	All procurements
		8% price preference	Greater than 20% and less than 51% Kenyan shareholding in bidder	
		10% price preference	Greater than 50% Kenyan shareholding in bidder	
6	Regulation 20	Reservation	'Disadvantaged groups', 'small enterprises' and 'micro enterprises'	Unbundled contracts

[a] These goods are described as '(a) motor vehicles, plant and equipment which are assembled in Kenya; (b) furniture, textile, foodstuffs and other goods made in Kenya; (c) goods manufactured, mined, extracted or grown in Kenya'.

may suggest a policy of support for local industries, but also in support of attracting foreign investors to establish operations in Kenya. In contrast, preferences to 'citizen contractors' only support domestic industries, but do not attract foreign investment, since Kenyan-based but foreign-owned bidders will not be entitled to such preference. The choice between these two different mechanisms thus plays a significant role in the impact of the adopted preferential procurement mechanism on attracting foreign investment. Of course, each of these distinct categories also impact differently on the competition within a given procurement subject to these schemes. In the first scheme in Table 15.2, where citizenship and locality both define the target group, competition will be limited to the greatest extent, whereas with the second and third schemes competition will be limited to a lesser extent, but in varying ways when compare *inter se*. In order to assess whether the horizontal policy objectives that are being pursued by these mechanisms justify the impact on competition, or, put differently, can be justifiably balanced against other objectives such as value for money, one would of course need a clear understanding of what exactly is being pursued by these different mechanisms.[63] The graded manner in which mechanism 5 in Table 15.2 awards preference is also of interest in that it creates strong incentives for increasing local ownership, but not in an all-or-nothing manner. This seems an effective mechanism to support local industries and foreign investment without excluding any potential bidders and thereby managing the trade-off between the horizontal policy objectives and other objectives such as value for money.

The most interesting target-group definition from a social-policy perspective is that of 'disadvantaged groups', which is defined as 'persons perceived to be denied, by mainstream society, access to resources and tools which are useful for their survival in a way that disadvantages them, or individuals who have been subjected to prejudice or cultural bias because of their identities as members of groups without regard to their individual qualities, and includes enterprises owned by women, the youth and persons with disabilities'.[64] 'Youth', in turn, is defined as a person between the ages of eighteen and thirty-five; and 'disability' is defined as 'a physical, sensory, mental or other impairment, including any visual, hearing, learning or physical incapability, which impacts adversely on social, economic or environmental participation'.[65] The sixth mechanism

63 See McCrudden, *Buying Social Justice*, note 3 above, p. 13.
64 Kenyan Preference Regulations 2011, reg. 2.
65 Persons with Disabilities Act 2003 (Kenya), s. 2.

in Table 15.2 clearly indicates horizontal social-policy objectives beyond simple domestic industrial or economic growth policies being pursued in Kenyan public procurement. It is a clear example of what McCrudden calls 'equality linkages' in procurement,[66] that is, a mechanism which attempts to use procurement to advance status equality between different groups or individuals within a system. In the definition of 'disadvantaged groups', one finds the express inclusion of women, youth and persons with disabilities, which is not surprising since one would expect these groups to be typically subjected to status inequality and thus to qualify for equality-based protection or advancement. Of interest are the additional persons included in the definition. These two additional groups are defined more generally as subjected to discrimination. For the first category, the test is a perception of denied access to resources.[67] This is clearly an individual standard of equality status, in other words membership of a particular group is not required to fall within this part of the definition. Particularly interesting is the perception test. The definition does not provide any guidance on whose perception is at issue here. The syntax suggests that it is not the perception of 'mainstream society' that is at issue here, but that the phrase 'by mainstream society' rather qualifies 'denied'. The qualifying phrase 'which are useful for their survival' to the terms 'resources and tools' is also interesting. It is again not clear what exactly is meant by this qualification. It seems that luxuries or non-essential goods would be excluded from this description, but since the qualifier refers to 'useful' rather than 'necessary' the meaning of the relevant deprivation may at best be established in terms of degree rather than concept. For example, education is certainly a resource or tool 'useful for . . . survival', but can this view be applied equally to primary and higher education? It seems that there are thus significant interpretative difficulties in applying this part of the definition of 'disadvantaged groups', leaving considerable scope for discretionary decisions. The second of the general categories in the definition of 'disadvantaged groups' brings in a group perspective. Here, it is group membership that qualifies a person as falling within the definition. The interesting question on this second category is whether actual prejudice or bias towards the individual concerned is required or

66 McCrudden, *Buying Social Justice*, note 3 above.

67 The approach here seems to resonate with the capability approach of Sen and Nussbaum. See I. Robeyns, 'The Capability Approach: A Theoretical Survey' (2005) 6 *Journal of Human Development* 93, for an overview of the literature on the capability approach. This approach may provide a useful theoretical framework for more in-depth analyses of preferential procurement regimes aimed at development.

whether membership of the group that suffers from such prejudice or bias would be adequate. While the text seems to suggest the former, it will be extremely difficult to assess such status in every case, which may hold adverse efficiency implications for the procurement system.

Many of these difficulties in identifying the target group may be ameliorated by the registration requirement in the Regulations. Before any bidder belonging to one of the target groups under scheme 6 in Table 15.2 can obtain a preference in procurement, that bidder must be registered as such.[68] The Regulations thus contemplate that the Ministry of Finance will maintain a system of registration of bidders within the categories of 'disadvantaged groups', 'small enterprises' and 'micro enterprises'. In addition to such registration, the Ministry of Finance will also certify membership of the category 'disadvantaged groups', and such certificate will be the basis for registration.[69] Proof of registration will in turn be the basis for preference in a given procurement so that it is not up to individual contracting authorities to establish whether a particular bidder falls within one of the target groups. In this approach, there is thus no additional burden placed on each contracting authority when procuring under these preference schemes, but there is an additional administrative cost in the form of the additional functions allocated to the Ministry of Finance.

Two further rules regarding preferences are noteworthy. First, the Regulations provide that a bidder may only benefit from one preference scheme in any given procurement. When a bidder thus qualifies for more than one scheme, the one with the greatest advantage will be applied to the exclusion of others.[70] Secondly, the Regulations place a time limit of five years on preferences to any given bidder, which period may be renewed once.[71] Any particular bidder may thus only enjoy preferences under any of the target group schemes for a maximum of ten years and only under one in any procurement. These are important rules to ensure that the policy objectives underlying these preferences remain the focus of

68 Kenyan Preference Regulations 2011, regs. 5(2) and 6.

69 According to information obtained from the Kenyan Ministry of Finance Directorate of Public Procurement, the Ministry has to date not itself certified membership of 'disadvantaged groups' despite calls for applications, but contemplates relying on certification from other relevant government departments such as the Ministry of Youth Affairs and Sport and the Ministry of Gender, Children and Social Development for relevant certification by those departments that may also indicate membership of the category 'disadvantaged groups'.

70 Kenyan Preference Regulations 2011, regs. 17 and 18.

71 *Ibid.*, reg. 22.

preferential procurement and are thus good examples of alignment between the mechanisms and the policies by means of the legal rules. They ensure that a particular bidder cannot be continuously enriched by preferences and create incentives for bidders to leverage preferential procurement towards eventual integration in the mainstream competitive market. The bar on multiple preferences within a given procurement also keeps the balance between the pursuit of horizontal policies, through preferences, and other objectives such as value for money and efficiency pursued through open competition in check.

While the Kenyan system thus now contains detailed rules on how social policies will be implemented in the procurement scheme, which raises the level of certainty and transparency, there remains some questions about the alignment of the Regulations and the Act. First, it is curious to note that, while the Act provides in mandatory terms for preferences and reservations to apply to 'micro, small and medium enterprises',[72] the Regulations only provide for micro and small enterprises as outlined above. It seems that there is thus still a category of bidders entitled to preferences under the Act that is left out in the cold under the Regulations. Secondly, it is not altogether clear what the statutory basis for the reservations under scheme 6 in Table 15.2 is. Section 39(2) of the Act mandates the Minister to prescribe preferences and reservations, but crucially this is 'subject to subsection (8)'. Subsection (8) in turn seems to provide for reservations only under very limited circumstances, essentially what is captured in scheme 3 in Table 15.2. It is thus not clear whether other forms of reservations may also be implemented without further statutory authority. Much will depend on the interpretation of section 39(2) read with section 39(8), and in particular whether the latter section is interpreted to limit the powers granted in the former or whether the latter is only understood as providing the minimum reservations and preferences that must be provided for without limiting the general powers given to the Minister under the former section to implement preferential mechanisms.

4.3. *South Africa*

As noted above, a new set of regulations, the 2011 Procurement Regulations, was published in South Africa on the same day as the Kenyan Preference Regulations 2011. However, unlike the position in Kenya, the South African Regulations did not introduce a new preference scheme.

72 Public Procurement and Disposal Act 2005 (Kenya), s. 39(4)(a).

Preferential procurement has been an integral part of South African public procurement since the adoption of the Preferential Procurement Policy Framework Act (PPPFA) in 2000.[73] The PPPFA aims to implement the constitutional mandate of using public procurement towards distributive justice, in particular redressing past discriminatory practices in terms of the government's Black Economic Empowerment (BEE) policy.[74] This is premised on section 217(2) of the South African Constitution[75] that mandates 'categories of preference' in awarding contracts through mechanisms providing for 'the protection or advancement of persons, or categories of persons, disadvantaged by unfair discrimination'. However, the PPPFA only provides for the framework in terms of which this social policy objective is to be implemented, leaving the details to be worked out in regulations.

Immediately following the enactment of the PPPFA, a set of regulations, the Preferential Procurement Regulations 2001, was promulgated and provided in detail for mechanisms implementing BEE in public procurement.[76] However, subsequent to these Regulations, the Broad-Based Black Economic Empowerment Act[77] (the 'B-BBEE Act') was enacted providing for the implementation of BEE in a comprehensive manner across the entire public administration as well as in private enterprises, called 'broad-based black economic empowerment' (B-BBEE). Since the B-BBEE Act adopted a different approach to BEE targets than the Preferential Procurement Regulations 2001 under the PPPFA, it was realised that the existing approach to preferential public procurement, as an important aspect of the government's BEE strategy, had to be realigned to the general approach to B-BBEE under the B-BBEE Act. This realignment took seven years and culminated in the 2011 Procurement Regulations, published on 8 June 2011 and which came into operation on 7 December 2011.[78]

Prior to the adoption of the 2011 Procurement Regulations, not all public procurement was subject to the same approach to preferencing. While section 217(3) of the Constitution makes it clear that the

73 Act 5 of 2000.

74 Constitution of the Republic of South Africa, 1996, s. 217(2) and (3).

75 *Ibid.*

76 For a discussion of these regulations, see Bolton and Quinot, 'Social Policies in Procurement and the Government Procurement Agreement', note 8 above, pp. 460–5.

77 Act 53 of 2003.

78 The implementation of the Regulations by state-owned enterprises was, however, extended to 7 December 2012. GN R1027, *Government Gazette*, No. 34832, 7 December 2011.

advancement of the BEE policy through public procurement *must* be done in terms of the framework provided for in the PPPFA, that section only covers government departments and other institutions identified in national legislation as subject to it. Since not all public entities and in particular state-owned enterprises had been so identified as subject to section 217 and the PPPFA, South African courts have held that, subject to general fairness, contracting authorities may depart from the preferential procurement system created in the PPPFA where such bodies are not strictly subject to the PPPFA.[79] Contracting authorities that were not strictly subject to the PPPFA indeed adopted approaches to preferential procurement that differed markedly from that adopted by the PPPFA, by for example making use of reservations schemes and preferences in invitations to tender whereas the PPPFA approach is one of price preferences only.[80] This situation created significant uncertainty as to how the social policy of wealth distribution was to be achieved in public procurement as well as confusion and frustration among bidders who had to comply with different preferential approaches for tenders issued by different public bodies. In particular, this lack of certainty and coherence, and thus failure on the part of the legal rules, undermined the realisation of the policy objective since they did not create a clear set of incentives for bidders towards wealth distribution. The 2011 Procurement Regulations drastically changed this position by subjecting all public entities to the same approach to preferential procurement set out in the Regulations.[81] This is the first noteworthy characteristic of the new Regulations that shows a better design in preferential procurement towards the achievement of the horizontal social policy at issue.

The 2011 Procurement Regulations, however, in principle retain the existing model for preferential procurement under the 2001 Regulations using a preference points system in terms of which preference is granted

79 See G. Quinot, 'Public Procurement' (2009) *Juta's Quarterly Review of South African Law*, No. 1, para. 2.1.

80 See *Digital Horizons (Pty) Ltd* v. *South African Broadcasting Corporation* (unreported, Case No. 2008/19224 (W), 8 September 2008), para. 6, in which it emerged that the South African Broadcasting Corporation adopted a set-aside approach in its preferential procurement policy; *Manong and Associates (Pty) Ltd* v. *City Manager, City of Cape Town, and Others* 2009 (1) SA 644 (EqC); *Manong and Associates (Pty) Ltd* v. *Department of Roads and Transport, Eastern Cape, and Others (No. 2)* 2008 (6) SA 434 (EqC); G. Quinot, 'Public Procurement' (2008) *Juta's Quarterly Review of South African Law*, No. 4, para. 2.1; G. Quinot, 'Public Procurement' (2008) *Juta's Quarterly Review of South African Law*, No. 2, para. 2.2.

81 2011 Procurement Regulations, reg. 2.

to qualifying bidders at the award stage. For all contracts between the value of R30,000 and R1 million, an 80/20 preference points system is used, and, for all contracts of a value above R1 million, a 90/10 preference points system is used. This basic framework is set out in the PPPFA,[82] with the values determined in the Regulations.[83] Under these preference points systems, 80 or 90 points, depending on the value of the contract, will be awarded for price in the evaluation of the bids. The remaining 20 or 10 points are preference points representing the realisation of the social policy objectives and calculated as set out below. These two sets of points are then combined to a total score for each bidder out of 100 points, and the bidder with the most points should generally be awarded the contract.[84] Already from this basic structure, it is clear that the margin of preference is relatively small and that price plays the most important role in the award decision. This clearly indicates that the balance which the South African public procurement system strives for between social policy objectives and value for money is heavily in favour of the latter.

Another major development under the new 2011 Procurement Regulations when compared to the 2001 Regulations lies in the manner in which the preference points are calculated. Under the 2001 Regulations, each tender had to specify how the preference points would be awarded, with only minimal requirements set out in the Regulations, namely, that points may be awarded 'for being an HDI [historically disadvantaged individual] and/or contracting with an HDI' and/or achieving any of a number of stated goals.[85] An HDI was defined as 'a South African

82 Preferential Procurement Policy Framework Act, s. 2(1)(b).

83 2011 Procurement Regulations, regs. 5 and 6.

84 Preferential Procurement Policy Framework Act, s. 2(1)(f). The only exception to an award to the highest scoring bidder is when 'objective criteria' other than price and BEE preference justify such award to the non-highest scoring bidder.

85 Preferential Procurement Regulations 2001, regs. 3(2) and 4(2). These goals were listed in reg. 17: '(a) The promotion of South African owned enterprises; (b) The promotion of export orientated production to create jobs; (c) The promotion of SMMEs [small, medium and micro enterprises]; (d) The creation of new jobs or the intensification of labour absorption; (e) The promotion of enterprises located in a specific province for work to be done or services to be rendered in that province; (f) The promotion of enterprises located in a specific region for work to be done or services to be rendered in that region; (g) The promotion of enterprises located in a specific municipal area for work to be done or services to be rendered in that municipal area; (h) The promotion of enterprises located in rural areas; (i) The empowerment of the work force by standardising the level of skill and knowledge of workers; (j) The development of human resources, including by assisting in tertiary and other advanced training programmes, in line with key indicators such as percentage of wage bill spent on education and training and improvement of

citizen (1) who, due to the apartheid policy that had been in place, had no franchise in national elections prior to the introduction of the Constitution of the Republic of South Africa, 1983 (Act No. 110 of 1983) or the Constitution of the Republic of South Africa, 1993 (Act No. 200 of 1993) ("the Interim Constitution"); and/or (2) who is a female; and/or (3) who has a disability: Provided that a person who obtained South African citizenship on or after the coming to effect of the Interim Constitution, is deemed not to be an HDI.'[86] The strong resemblance to the Kenyan category of 'disadvantaged groups' is evident, although the South African HDI concept was more specific in the criteria that qualified a person as marginalised. It is also evident that this definition of HDI allowed considerable discretion to contracting authorities to decide who would qualify for HDI points under a given contract. Furthermore, since the definition focused on individuals, it did not give a clear indication of how firms should be treated. In this regard, the 2001 Regulations stated that 'equity ownership by HDIs' must be taken into account as part of the preference points calculation.[87] It set out a formula essentially amounting to a grading of the percentage HDI ownership of a bidder against that of other bidders.[88] Apart from the discretion created in the determination of what amounts to an HDI, the choice between awarding preference points to 'being an HDI', 'contracting with an HDI', the long list of other objectives listed in regulation 17, which included preference to domestic bidders, and the further mandate to award preference points to locally manufactured goods,[89] increased the significant discretion granted to contracting authorities under this scheme. This had a severe impact on the efficiency of the procurement system since contracting authorities not only had to design a preference scheme, either in general or per procurement, but also had to adjudicate each bidder's qualification in terms of these preferences in every procurement. Furthermore, given the generous judicial remedies available in South Africa for bidders to challenge procurement decisions, which is discussed in detail in Chapter 13 of this volume, the award of preference points became a rich source of litigation. In light of the small weight given to the social policy objective in procurement compared to value for money represented by the overwhelming weight given to price, this approach was certainly not efficient nor justifiable.

management skills; and (k) The upliftment of communities through, but not limited to, housing, transport, schools, infrastructure donations, and charity organisations.'

86 *Ibid.*, reg. 1. 87 *Ibid.*, reg. 13(1). 88 *Ibid.*, reg. 13(5). 89 *Ibid.*, reg. 12(1).

Table 15.3 *Preference points per B-BBEE status level*

B-BBEE status level of contributor	Number of preference points
For contracts between the value of R30,000 and R1 million	
1	20
2	18
3	16
4	12
5	8
6	6
7	4
8	2
Non-compliant contributor	0
For contracts of a value above R1 million	
1	10
2	9
3	8
4	5
5	4
6	3
7	2
8	1
Non-compliant contributor	0

The 2011 Regulations radically changed the way in which preference points are determined. Instead of the wide discretion found in the 2001 Regulations and the complicated decisions and adjudication that followed, the new Regulations simply set out the amount of preference points to be awarded to a bidder based on a bidder's certified B-BBEE status in terms of the B-BBEE Act. The 2011 Regulations thus grant no discretion to contracting authorities in calculating preference points and greatly reduce the obligation to determine compliance with the preference criteria to a simple exercise of checking the B-BBEE status certificate submitted by the relevant bidder against the categorisation shown in Table 15.3 and identifying the relevant number of preference points stated against that bidder's 'B-BBEE status level' as certified.[90]

90 2011 Procurement Regulations, regs. 5(2) and 6(2).

The relevant points from Table 15.3 (depending on the size of the contract) will thus simply be added to the points calculated for the price offered to make up the final number of points scored by each tenderer. Subcontracting may, however, have an impact on the preference points awarded to a tenderer. A tenderer may not be awarded preference points if it intends to subcontract more than 25 per cent of the value of the contract to an entity that does not qualify for at least the same amount of preference points on the above scale.[91] Likewise, once the tender has been awarded, a contractor may not subcontract more than 25 per cent of the value of the contract to an entity that does not have an equal or higher B-BBEE status level than the main contractor.[92] It is beyond the scope of this chapter to provide a detailed account of how a bidder's B-BBEE status level will be calculated in terms of the B-BBEE Act. Such status is determined by accredited verification agencies upon (paid) application by the relevant entity seeking certification. The B-BBEE Act defines B-BBEE status with reference to a 'scorecard' consisting of various elements against each of which a firm can be assessed to eventually arrive at a score that translates into a B-BBEE status.[93] While there are a number of sector-specific scorecards, there is a generic scorecard that consists of seven core elements, namely: ownership; management control; employment equity; skills development; preferential procurement; enterprise development; and socio-economic development and sector-specific contributions.[94] An entity's initiatives under each of these contribute to its eventual score and status. It is thus evident that 'being an HDI' is no longer the sole requirement and it is possible for a completely non-HDI entity (for example, a previously advantaged South African bidder or a foreign bidder) to have a higher B-BBEE status (and thus obtain more preference points in procurements) than an HDI, based on the former's initiatives under elements other than 'ownership' and 'management control'. What is of particular interest in the current context is that 'preferential procurement' is one of the seven core elements. This element refers to procurement by the evaluated private entity, thus *private* procurement. In essence, it means that private entities can earn preference points in public procurement for themselves by procuring preferentially in the private market. If a private entity itself procures from a private

91 *Ibid.*, reg. 11(8). 92 *Ibid.*, reg. 11(9).

93 Codes of Good Practice on Black Economic Empowerment issued under the B-BBEE Act (GN No. 112, *Government Gazette*, No. 29617, 9 February 2007).

94 *Ibid.*, code series 000 statement 000, para. 7.

supplier with a high B-BBEE status level, the status level of the buying entity will be increased resulting in higher preference points when it submits a bid in a public procurement. In this manner, the mechanism created in the 2011 Procurement Regulations manages to 'export' horizontal policy objectives in public procurement to the private market.

The 2011 Procurement Regulations are a vast improvement on the 2001 Regulations in the way that the new rules provide for preferences. The burden on contracting authorities in a given procurement is greatly reduced and efficiency in procurement thus promoted. By removing the bulk of the discretion from contracting authorities and replacing it with an external verification tool (in the form of the B-BBEE status level certificates), the rules bring about a high level of certainty and transparency in preferential procurement and it is submitted that challenges based on preference will be significantly reduced under the new regime. This is a clear indication of how a different design of the mechanism used to implement a social policy can make a significant difference in the trade-off between the social policy objectives and other objectives such as value for money, efficiency and integrity and the eventual achievement of a transparent procurement system. Since the new approach to preferences also places less emphasis on domestic bidders and goods, the tension between the preference scheme and international trade is greatly reduced.[95]

In clear distinction to the social policy objectives pursued through the price preference mechanism discussed above, the 2011 Procurement Regulations also introduce a reservation scheme for the procurement of defined local goods.[96] In terms of this approach certain tenders may be set aside for local production and content within sectors designated by the Department of Trade and Industry. For tenders falling outside the designated sectors, contracting authorities retain a discretion to call for minimum local content in bids. In contrast to the 2001 Regulations, which provided for support to local suppliers and goods in the same preference scheme as the social objective of BEE, the new Regulations thus create a different mechanism altogether, thereby separating in terms of mechanisms the economic and social policy objectives in public procurement. The 2011 Regulations also state that it may be necessary to adopt a two-stage tendering process to keep these different mechanisms apart in

95 See Bolton and Quinot, 'Social Policies in Procurement and the Government Procurement Agreement', note 8 above, pp. 467, 472, 478–9.

96 2011 Procurement Regulations, reg. 9.

terms of which the economic objectives pursued through the reservation mechanism will be implemented in the first stage of tendering and the preference scheme promoting the social policy objective of BEE in the subsequent second stage.[97] The differentiation between the mechanisms aimed at different policy objectives seems a sensible approach since it allows for a much clearer assessment of the trade-off between different objectives in the procurement system.

5. Concluding remarks

The comparative overview of the use of public procurement for horizontal policy purposes in the African systems under review in this book indicates that such use is a common phenomenon. The analysis also shows that there is a large measure of commonality between these systems in terms of the type of policies pursued, which are mostly economic in nature, pursuing domestic economic growth and industrial development, and are only to a limited extent social in nature. In this latter sense, one finds policy objectives in public procurement relating to support for marginalised regions and groups, typically women and persons with disabilities. In the Southern African systems under review, there is clearly also a common objective of redressing past discriminatory practices.

There is also a significant level of conformity in the legal mechanisms employed to implement horizontal policies through procurement. Reservation schemes and especially price preferences at the award stage are the most common mechanisms. However, if one looks closer at the detail of the particular mechanisms, divergences between the systems emerge. The analysis above shows up a number of interesting differences between the systems in relation to price preference schemes for example. These differences relate to the mandatory or discretionary nature of the scheme, the level of detail set out in the regulatory instruments, and the different ways in which the targets of the preferences are defined.

The closer look at the Kenyan and South African preferential procurement rules as two systems with very recent developments in this area, takes this comparative analysis further. Through the closer analysis of these two regimes one can identify a number of characteristics of mechanisms aimed at promoting social policies through procurement that seem either sensible or problematic. In both systems the definition of the target

97 *Ibid.*, reg. 9(5).

group in especially the social policy dimension of the preference scheme is clearly an area of difficulty. In Kenya, the definition of 'disadvantaged groups' raises a number of questions and generally lacks clarity in a way that would allow easy application. It is therefore not surprising that this part of the preference scheme has not been effectively implemented. In South Africa, the shift in approach to preferences from the 2001 Regulations to the 2011 Regulations has this very issue at its core. As the discussion above indicates, the open-ended nature of the description of the target groups that may qualify for preference in the 2001 Regulations has been completely replaced by the simply mechanical approach to preferences under the 2011 Regulations doing completely away with any need to grapple with problematic definitions of target groups. Both systems have also opted for an external verification tool to measure compliance with the criteria for preference, which seems another sensible approach to the difficulty of identifying qualifying bidders. Another problem that emerges from the Kenyan example and that underlies the changes in South Africa is the fusion of various distinct policy objectives in a single mechanism or set of mechanisms. As I have noted, it is very difficult to properly assess the various competing objectives in procurement systems if the mechanisms put in place to pursue such objectives are not clearly designed to facilitate particular objectives.

These examples drawn from the discussion in this chapter underscore Linarelli's insight that much depends on careful design in a procurement system when it comes to successful implementation of horizontal policy objectives. The question is thus not whether horizontal policies should be pursued through public procurement, but rather how such pursuit should be designed. In this regard, there is significant potential benefit in comparing the mechanisms adopted in various African systems with each other in order to see how different systems have responded to very similar social concerns within their procurement systems. The more detailed analysis of the Kenyan and South African systems in this chapter illustrates this potential. That analysis holds important lessons for both systems. For example, Kenya can learn from the recent South African refinement of a preference system that has been in place for a decade and consider a clearer distinction between mechanisms aimed at economic policy objectives and those aimed at social objectives. South Africa, on the other hand, can learn from the Kenyan model in the way that the latter has placed a time limitation on entitlement to preferences.

In the final analysis, these comparative perspectives can help African countries develop more refined legal rules on horizontal policy objectives in procurement systems, in particular social policy objectives, which is an obvious high priority in Africa given the high developmental needs. The broad overview in this chapter indeed suggests that there is still a need for more development in this area of procurement law towards clearer, specific legal rules instead of fairly broad discretionary powers.

MATERIALS ON PUBLIC PROCUREMENT REGULATION IN AFRICA

General and comparative works

B. Basheka, 'Public Procurement Reforms in Africa: A Tool for Effective Governance and the Public Sector and Poverty Reduction' in K. V. Thai (ed.), *International Handbook of Public Procurement* (Boca Raton, FL: Taylor & Francis, 2009), p. 131

E. Caborn and S. Arrowsmith, 'Procurement Methods in the Public Procurement Systems of Africa' in G. Quinot and S. Arrowsmith (eds.), *Public Procurement Regulation in Africa* (Cambridge University Press, 2012), Chapter 12

A. Fall and M. Frilet, 'Public Procurement in Francophone Africa' in R. Hérnandez Garcia (ed.), *International Public Procurement: A Guide to Best Practice* (London: Globe Law and Business, 2009), p. 75

K. Jacobs, 'Naval Programmes – Procurement Programmes of Middle-East and North-African Navies' (2007) 27 *Naval Forces* 83

S. R. Karangizi, 'Framework Arrangements in Public Procurement: A Perspective from Africa' in S. Arrowsmith (ed.), *Reform of the UNCITRAL Model Law on Procurement: Procurement Regulation for the 21st Century* (Eagan, MN: West, 2009), p. 243

J. O. Kuye and U. Kakumba, 'The Ombudsman Institutions in the Procurement of Legal Responsibilities in the Commonwealth: An Overview of Canada, South Africa and Uganda' (2008) 43(3) *Journal of Public Administration* 156

A. La Chimia, 'Donors' Influence on Developing Countries' Procurement Systems, Rules and Markets: A Critical Analysis' in G. Quinot and S. Arrowsmith (eds.), *Public Procurement Regulation in Africa* (Cambridge University Press, 2012), Chapter 11

F. Lichere and B. Martor, 'On the Development of Public–Private Partnerships in Africa: Current Reforms and Future Prospects' (2007) 3 *International Business Law Journal* 297

W. Odhiambo and P. Kamau, 'Public Procurement: Lessons from Kenya, Tanzania and Uganda' (OECD Development Centre, 2006), www.oecd-ilibrary.org/docserver/download/fulltext/5lgsjhvj7843.pdf?expires=1289653149&id=0000&accname=guest&checksum=21011C9633AD1509062E3309A11D170B

G. Quinot, 'A Comparative Perspective on Supplier Remedies in African Public Procurement Systems' in G. Quinot and S. Arrowsmith (eds.), *Public Procurement Regulation in Africa* (Cambridge University Press, 2012), Chapter 13

'Promotion of Social Policy through Public Procurement in Africa' in G. Quinot and S. Arrowsmith (eds.), *Public Procurement Regulation in Africa* (Cambridge University Press, 2012), Chapter 15

G. Quinot and S. Arrowsmith, 'Introduction' in G. Quinot and S. Arrowsmith (eds.), *Public Procurement Regulation in Africa* (Cambridge University Press, 2012), Chapter 1

Report on the Proceedings of the Conference of the Public Procurement Reform in Africa, Abijan, 1998 (World Bank, African Development Bank, United Nations Development Programme, International Trade Centre UNCTAD/WTO, 1998)

S. Willet, 'Defence Expenditures, Arms Procurement and Corruption in Sub-Saharan Africa' (2009) 36 *Review of African Political Economy* 335

S. Williams-Elegbe, 'A Perspective on Corruption and Public Procurement in Africa' in G. Quinot and S. Arrowsmith (eds.), *Public Procurement Regulation in Africa* (Cambridge University Press, 2012), Chapter 14

Common Market for Eastern and Southern Africa (COMESA)

S. R. Karangizi, 'The COMESA Public Procurement Reform Initiative' (2005) 14 *Public Procurement Law Review* NA51

S. R. Karangizi and I. Ndahiro, 'Public Procurement Reform and Development in the Eastern and Southern Africa Region' in R. Hérnandez Garcia (ed.), *International Public Procurement: A Guide to Best Practice* (London: Globe Law and Business, 2009), p. 113

E. Nwogwugwu, 'Towards the Harmonisation of International Procurement Policies and Practices' (2005) 14 *Public Procurement Law Review* 131

Organization for the Harmonisation of Business Law in Africa (OHBLA)

P. K. Agboyibor, 'OHBLA – Business Law in Africa' (2000) *International Business Law Journal* 490

O. Fille-Lambie, 'Legal Aspects of Project Financing as Applied to Public Utilities in the OHBLA Zone' (2001) *International Business Law Journal* 925

Individual country materials

Botswana

R. Kumar and E. Caborn, 'The Regulatory Framework for Public Procurement in Botswana' in G. Quinot and S. Arrowsmith (eds.), *Public Procurement Regulation in Africa* (Cambridge University Press, 2012), Chapter 2

Egypt

M. A. M. Ismail, 'Legal Globalization and PPPs in Egypt: An Analytical and Comparative Perspective on the Current Legislative and Judicial Modifications to and Enhancements of the Administrative Contractual Regime on PPP Transactions' (2010) 5 *European Public Private Partnership Law* 54

A. Y. Zohny, 'Egypt's Procurement Regime and Building an Export Oriented Economy' (2003) 18 *Arab Law Quarterly* 169

Ethiopia

T. H. Bahta, 'The Regulatory Framework for Public Procurement in Ethiopia' in G. Quinot and S. Arrowsmith (eds.), *Public Procurement Regulation in Africa* (Cambridge University Press, 2012), Chapter 3

'Adjudication and Arbitrability of Government Construction Contract Disputes in Ethiopia' (2009) 3 *Mizan Law Review* 1

D. Rene, 'Administrative Contracts in the Ethiopian Civil Code' 4(1) *Journal of Ethiopian Law* 143 (translated into English by Michael Kindred)

Gambia

W. A. Wittig and H. Jeng, 'Challenges in Public Procurement: Comparative Views of Public Procurement Reform in Gambia' in K. V. Thai, A. Araujo, R. Y. Carter *et al.* (eds.), *Challenges in Public Procurement: An International Perspective* (Boca Raton, FL: PrAcademics Press, 2005), vol. 3, p. 21

Ghana

D. N. Dagbanja, 'The Regulatory Framework for Public Procurement in Ghana' in G. Quinot and S. Arrowsmith (eds.), *Public Procurement Regulation in Africa* (Cambridge University Press, 2012), Chapter 4

The Law of Public Procurement in Ghana (Saarbrücken: Lambert Academic Publishing, 2011)

D. Ofosu-Dorte, I. Boaten and F. Adadzi, 'Ghana' in H.-J. Prieß (ed.), *Getting the Deal Through: Public Procurement 2010* (London: Law Business Research Ltd, 2010), p. 115

R. Verhage, J. van der Gronden, K. Awanyo and S. Boateng, 'Procurement Reform in the Ghana Health Sector' (2002) 2 *Journal of Public Procurement* 261

Kenya

J. M. M. Akech, 'Development Partners and Governance of Public Procurement in Kenya: Enhancing Democracy in the Administration of Aid' (2006) 3 *International Law and Justice Working Paper* (Global Administrative Law Series), www.iilj.org

A. J. M. Migai, 'Development Partners and Governance of Public Procurement in Kenya: Enhancing Democracy in the Administration of Aid' (2005) 37 *New York University Journal of International Law and Politics* 829

V. Mosoti, 'Reforming the Laws on Public Procurement in the Developing World: The Example of Kenya' (2005) 54 *International Commercial Law Quarterly* 621

M. Nyaoga and C. Odhiambo, 'Kenya' in H.-J. Prieß (ed.), *Getting the Deal Through: Public Procurement 2010* (London: Law Business Research Ltd, 2010), p. 152

'Kenya' in H.-J. Prieß (ed.), *Getting the Deal Through: Public Procurement 2009: Public Procurement: An Overview of Regulation in 43 Jurisdictions Worldwide* (London: Law Business Research Ltd, 2009), p. 136

M. Ogot, M. Mulinge and R. Muriuki, 'Impact of Public Procurement Law in Profit-Oriented State-Owned Corporations in Kenya' in K. V. Thai (ed.), *Towards New Horizons in Public Procurement* (Boca Raton, FL: PrAcademics Press, 2010), p. 372

K. T. Udeh, 'The Regulatory Framework for Public Procurement in Kenya' in G. Quinot and S. Arrowsmith (eds.), *Public Procurement Regulation in Africa* (Cambridge University Press, 2012), Chapter 5

Lesotho

F. Darroch, 'The Lesotho Corruption Trials – A Case Study' (2003) 29 *Commonwealth Law Bulletin* 901

Liberia

D. Ofosu-Dorte, I. Boaten and F. Adadzi, 'Liberia' in H.-J. Prieß (ed.), *Getting the Deal Through: Public Procurement 2010* (London: Law Business Research Ltd, 2010), p. 163

Mali

J. Ruche and E. Garandeau, 'The Mali Donors' Public Procurement Procedures: Towards Harmonisation with the National Law 6 (2000)', available at http://webdomino1.oecd.org/COMNET/DCD/ProcurementCWS.nsf/viewHtml/index/$FILE/1_MaliProcurement-website.pdf.

Namibia

S. K. Amoo and S. Dicken, 'The Regulatory Framework for Public Procurement in Namibia' in G. Quinot and S. Arrowsmith (eds.), *Public Procurement Regulation in Africa* (Cambridge University Press, 2012), Chapter 6

F. Links and C. Daniels, 'The Tender Board: Need for Root and Branch Reform', Anti-Corruption Research Programme Paper 3 (2011)

E. Tjirera, 'Public Procurement in Namibia: The Role of Codes of Conduct in Reducing Corruption', Anti-Corruption Research Programme Paper 3 (2011)

Nigeria

S. Ekpenkhio, 'Public Sector Procurement Reforms: The Nigerian Experience', paper presented to Regional Workshop on Procurement Reforms and Transparency in Government Procurement for Anglophone Countries, Tanzania, 16 January 2003

A. J. Osuntogun, 'Procurement Law in Nigeria: Challenges in Attaining Its Objectives' (2012) 21 *Public Procurement Law Review* (forthcoming)

G. Oyebode and O. Fayokun, 'Nigeria' in H.-J. Prieß (ed.), *Getting the Deal Through: Public Procurement 2010* (London: Law Business Research Ltd, 2010), p. 185

K. T. Udeh and L. Ahmadu, 'The Regulatory Framework for Public Procurement in Nigeria' in G. Quinot and S. Arrowsmith (eds.), *Public Procurement Regulation in Africa* (Cambridge University Press, 2012), Chapter 7

S. Williams, 'The Development of Defence Procurement Policy in Nigeria and the Case for Reform' (2005) 14 *Public Procurement Law Review* 153

S. Williams-Elegbe, 'The Reform and Regulation of Nigerian Public Procurement' (2011) 41 *Public Contract Law Journal* 339

Rwanda

I. Rugema, 'The Regulatory Framework for Public Procurement in Rwanda' in G. Quinot and S. Arrowsmith (eds.), *Public Procurement Regulation in Africa* (Cambridge University Press, 2012), Chapter 8

F. Zigirinshuti, 'Rwanda' in R. Noguellou and U. Stelkens (eds.), *Droit Comparé des Contrats Publics/Comparative Law on Public Contracts* (Brussels: Bruylant, 2010), p. 858

Sierra Leone

F. J. Elliott, 'Procurement Reform in Sierra Leone: A Public Choice Model of Analysis' (2004) 3 *International Public Procurement Conference Proceedings* 189

South Africa

Books

P. Bolton, *The Law of Government Procurement in South Africa* (Durban: LexisNexis Butterworths, 2007)

T. E. Manchidi and I. Hammond, *Targeted Procurement in the Republic of South Africa: An Independent Assessment* (International Labour Organization, 2002)

G. Quinot, *State Commercial Activity: A Legal Framework* (Cape Town: Juta & Co., 2009)

Articles and essays in edited collections

P. Bolton, 'The Regulatory Framework for Public Procurement in South Africa' in G. Quinot and S. Arrowsmith (eds.), *Public Procurement Regulation in Africa* (Cambridge University Press, 2012), Chapter 9

'Afrique du Sud/South Africa' in R. Noguellou and U. Stelkens (eds.), *Droit Comparé des Contrats Publics/Comparative Law on Public Contracts* (Brussels: Bruylant, 2010), p. 281

'Municipal Tender Awards and Internal Appeals by Unsuccessful Bidders' (2010) 13:3 *Potchefstroom Electronic Law Journal* 1

'South Africa' in H.-J. Prieß (ed.), *Getting the Deal Through: Public Procurement 2010* (London: Law Business Research Ltd, 2010), p. 227

'The Regulation of Preferential Procurement in State-Owned Enterprises' (2010) *Journal of South African Law* 101

'Overview of the Government Procurement System in South Africa' in K. V. Thai (ed.), *International Handbook of Public Procurement* (Boca Raton, FL: Taylor & Francis, 2009), p. 357

'The Committee System for Competitive Bids in Local Government' (2009) 12(2) *Potchefstroom Electronic Law Journal* 56

'The Status of Contracts Exceeding a Municipal Tender Call' (2009) *Journal of South African Law* 382

'Incorporating Environmental Considerations into Government Procurement in South Africa' (2008) *Journal of South African Law* 31

'Protecting the Environment through Public Procurement: The Case of South Africa' (2008) 32(1) *Natural Resources Forum* 1

'The Public Procurement System in South Africa: Main Characteristics' (2008) 37 *Public Contract Law Journal* 781

'An Analysis of the Preferential Procurement Legislation in South Africa' (2007) 16 *Public Procurement Law Review* 36

'Government Procurement as a Policy Tool in South Africa' (2006) 6 *Journal of Public Procurement* 193

'Grounds for Dispensing with Public Tender Procedures in Government Contracting' (2006) 9(2) *Potchefstroom Electronic Law Journal* 1

'The Exclusion of Contractors from Government Contract Awards' (2006) 10 *Law, Democracy and Development* 25

'Scope for Negotiating and/or Varying the Terms of Government Contracts Awarded by Way of a Tender Process' (2006) 17 *Stellenbosch Law Review* 266

'Government Contracts and the Fettering of Discretion – A Question of Validity' (2004) 19 *South African Public Law* 90

'Government Dealings and the Intention to Create Legal Relations' (2004) 16 *South African Mercantile Law Journal* 196

'The Use of Government Procurement as an Instrument of Policy' (2004) 121 *South African Law Journal* 619

P. Bolton and G. Quinot, 'Social Policies in Procurement and the Government Procurement Agreement: A Perspective from South Africa' in S. Arrowsmith and R. D. Anderson (eds.), *The WTO Regime on Government Procurement: Recent Developments and Challenges Ahead* (Cambridge University Press, 2011), p. 459

D. C. Campbell, 'US Firms and Black Labour in South Africa: Creating a Structure of Change' (1986) 7 *Journal of Labour Research* 1

D. D. Caron, 'The Structure and Pathologies of Local Selective Procurement Ordinances: A Study of Apartheid-Era South Africa Ordinances' (2003) 21 *Berkeley Journal of International Law* 159

S. De la Harpe, 'Green Public Procurement – An Option for South Africa?' (2008) 22 *Speculum Juris* 53

G. Devenish, 'The Legal and Constitutional Position of the Tender Board in KwaZulu-Natal and Related Matters' (1998) *Journal of South African Law* 398

J. Dohrman and J. Aiello, 'Public–Private Partnerships for Waste Management: Challenges for Policies and Procedures' (1999) 16 *Development South Africa* 691

C. Ferreira, 'The Quest for Clarity: An Examination of the Law Governing Public Contracts' (2011) 128 *South African Law Journal* 172

R. Ferreira and I. Liebenberg, 'Civil–Military Relations and Arms Procurement in South Africa: 1994–2002' (2004) 35 *Society in Transition* 61

B. M. Jackson and M. Hlahla, 'South Africa's Infrastructure Delivery Needs: The Role and Challenge for Public–Private Partnerships' (1999) 16 *Development South Africa* 551

J.-P. Labuschagne, 'Public–Private Partnerships in the Health Industry' (1998) 15 *Development South Africa* 133

D. Letchmiah, 'The Process of Public Sector Procurement Reform in South Africa' (1999) 8 *Public Procurement Law Review* 15

C. McCrudden, 'Social Policy Choices and the International and National Law of Government Procurement: South Africa as a Case Study' in H. Corder (ed.), *Global Administrative Law* (Cape Town: Juta & Co., 2009), p. 123

J. C. Pauw and J. S. Wolvaardt, 'Multi-Criteria Decision Analysis in Public Procurement – A Plan from the South' (2009) 28 *Politeia* 66

G. Penfold and P. Reyburn, 'Public Procurement' in S. Woolman, T. Roux, J. Klaaren, A. Stein, M. Chaskalson and M. Bishop (eds.), *Constitutional Law of South Africa* (2nd edn, Cape Town: Juta & Co., 2008), pp. 25–1

C. Plasket, 'Tendering for Government Contracts: Public Procurement and Judicial Review' in G. Glover (ed.), *Essays in Honour of A. J. Kerr* (Durban: LexisNexis Butterworths, 2006), p. 159

G. Quinot, 'Enforcement of Procurement Law from a South African Perspective' (2011) 20 *Public Procurement Law Review* 193

'Towards Effective Judicial Review of State Commercial Activity' (2009) *Journal of South African Law* 436

'Worse Than Losing a Government Tender: Winning It' (2008) 19 *Stellenbosch Law Review* 101

R. Roos and S. De La Harpe, 'Good Governance in Public Procurement: A South African Case Study' (2008) 11(2) *Potchefstroom Electronic Law Journal* 1

C. Scott and P. Macklem, 'Constitutional Ropes of Sand or Justiciable Guarantees? Social Rights in a New South African Constitution' (1992) 141 *University of Pennsylvania Law Review* 1

M. Sinclair, 'Regulation and Facilitation of Public–Private Partnerships: The MSP Policy' (1999) 16 *Development Southern Africa* 585

N. Steytler and J. De Visser, *Local Government Law of South Africa* (Durban: Lexis-Nexis Butterworths, 2007), Chapter 14

H. Van As, 'The Right to Information and the Tender Process' (1999) 34 *Journal of Public Administration* 257

K. Van Vuuren and J. A. Badenhorst-Weiss, 'South African Provincial Government Reform: Using a Shared Services Model to Transform "Back-Office" Support in Gauteng Province' in L. Knight, C. Harland, J. Telgen, K. V. Thai, G. Callender and K. McKen (eds.), *Public Procurement: International Cases and Commentary* (London: Routledge, 2007), p. 278

R. Watermeyer, 'Facilitating Sustainable Development through Public and Donor Procurement Regimes: Tools and Techniques' (2004) 13 *Public Procurement Law Review* 30

'The Use of Targeted Procurement as an Instrument of Poverty Alleviation and Job Creation in Infrastructure Projects' (2000) 9 *Public Procurement Law Review* 226

S. Williams, 'The Use of Exclusions for Corruption in Developing Country Procurement: The Case of South Africa' (2007) 51 *Journal of African Law* 1

S. Williams and G. Quinot, 'To Debar or Not to Debar: When to Endorse a Contractor on the Register for Tender Defaulters' (2008) 125 *South African Law Journal* 248

'Public Procurement and Corruption: The South African Response' (2007) 124 *South African Law Journal* 339

Notes

P. Bolton, 'Checks and Balances: Service Delivery by External Providers' (2010) 12(1) *Local Government Bulletin* 15

'Tender Awards in the Spotlight: Limitations of Internal Appeal Procedures' (2010) 12(3) *Local Government Bulletin* 18

'The Different Hats Worn by the Municipal Manager in the Tender / Bid Process' (2010) 12(2) *Local Government Bulletin* 10

'Notifying the Correct Bidder of Its Success' (2009) 11(5) *Local Government Bulletin* 25

'The Municipal Manager's Supervisory Role over Bid Committees' (2009) 11(2) *Local Government Bulletin* 26

'The Roles and Functions of Bid Committees' (2009) 11(4) *Local Government Bulletin* 19

'When Can Bidders with Bad Track Records Be Rejected?' (2009) 11(1) *Local Government Bulletin* 22

'Who Excludes Bidders from Future Contracts?' (2008) 10(5) *Local Government Bulletin* 22

'Supply Chain Management and Public–Private Partnership Provisions' (2004) 6(4) *Local Government Bulletin* 4

B. M. Jackson and M. Hlahla, 'South Africa's Infrastructure Service Delivery Needs: The Role and Challenge for Public–Private Partnerships' (1999) 16 *Development Southern Africa* 1

V. Johnson, 'Service Delivery Agreements: Who Reads Them?' (2005) 7(2) *Local Government Bulletin* 7

G. Mawoneke, 'The PPP Procurement Process' (2005) 7(3) *Local Government Bulletin* 11

D. McMeekin, 'State Procurement: The Public/Private Divide' (2009) *Responsa Meridiana* 35

N. Muvangua, 'Tokenism and the Constitutional Court Finding on Viking Pony Africa Pumps Africa and Hidro-Tech Systems (Pty) Ltd and City of Cape Town' (Center for Constitutional Rights, 2009), www.polity.org.za/article/okenism-and-the-constitutional-court-finding-on-viking-pony-africa-pumps-pty-ltd-ta-tricom-africa-and-hidro-tech-systems-pty-ltd-and-city-of-cape-town-2010-11-29

G. Quinot, 'Public Procurement' (2012) *Juta's Quarterly Review of South African Law*

'Public Procurement' (2011) *Juta's Quarterly Review of South African Law*

'Public Procurement' (2010) *Juta's Quarterly Review of South African Law*

'Public Procurement' (2009) *Juta's Quarterly Review of South African Law*

'Public Procurement' (2008) *Juta's Quarterly Review of South African Law*

F. Venter, 'Competitive Tendering: A Perspective on PPP/PFI from the Mangaung Maximum Security Prison, South Africa' (2003) *Prison Service Journal* 149

P. J. Visser, 'Damages Recoverable for Prospective Loss of Profit Caused by Non-Awarding of a Tender – Transnet Ltd v. Sechaba Photoscan (Pty) Ltd 2005 1 SA 299 (SCA)' (2005) 68 *Journal of Contemporary Roman Dutch Law* 510

Uganda

E. Agaba and N. Shipman, 'Procurement Systems in Uganda' in K. V. Thai (ed.), *International Handbook of Public Procurement* (Boca Raton, FL: Taylor & Francis, 2009), p. 393

B. C. Basheka, M. Tumutegyereize and E. Agaba, 'Public Procurement Capacity Building Reform Initiatives in Uganda: A Performance Measurement Approach' in K. V. Thai (ed.), *Towards New Horizons in Public Procurement* (Boca Raton, FL: PrAcademics Press, 2010), p. 60

J. M. Ntayi, I. Namugenyi and S Eyeaa, 'Supplier Delivery Performance in Ugandan Public Procurement Contracts' (2010) 4 *Journal of Public Procurement* 479

N. Shipman and E. Agaba, 'Public Procurement Reform in Developing Countries: The Uganda Experience' in G. Piga and K. V. Thai (eds.), *Advancing Public Procurement: Practices, Innovation and Knowledge-Sharing* (Boca Raton, FL: PrAcademics Press, 2007), p. 373

F. Ssennoga, 'Discriminatory Public Procurement Policies' (PhD thesis, University of Twente, 2010)

Zimbabwe

J. Zowa, N. Machingauta and P. Bolton, 'The Regulatory Framework for Public Procurement in Zimbabwe' in G. Quinot and S. Arrowsmith (eds.), *Public Procurement Regulation in Africa* (Cambridge University Press, 2012), Chapter 10

INDEX

1994 Model Law *see* UNCITRAL Model Law on Procurement (1994 Model Law)
2011 Model Law *see* UNCITRAL Model Law on Procurement (2011 Model Law)

academic studies on public procurement
  overview, 5–6
Accra Agenda for Action (AAA)
  as to aid harmonisation, 239
  as to procurement reform, 252
  as to use of country systems, 237–8
Africa
  aid generally, 225–31
  DAC donors' aid to (table), 227
  Millennium Development Goals (MDGs), 225–6
  public procurement reform initiatives, 1–6
  total aid in selected years (table), 229
African Development Bank
  use of country systems, 255–8
African Union Convention on Preventing and Combating Corruption
  overview, 364–6
aggregation rules
  framework agreements and, 299–300
aid
  bilateral, 230
  coordination/harmonisation initiatives, 238–40
  by DAC donors (table), 227
  donors' influence *see* donors' influence on procurement
  environmental conditionality, 244–6
  fluctuating levels of, 226–30
  generally, 225–31
  importance of, 226
  as incentive for procurement reform, 248, 251
  international initiatives on aid policies, 222, 226–30, 237–40
  multilateral, 230
  Paris Declaration *see* Paris Declaration on aid effectiveness
  as percentage of GDP, 226
  as percentage of government expenditure, 222–3
  predictability, 231
  selected years (table), 229
  theories on, 219–22
  tied aid conditionality, 219, 241–4
anti-corruption measures *see* corruption
Arab Maghreb Union
  public procurement reform initiatives, 272
audits
  anti-corruption, 355–6

banks *see* development banks
best value *see* value for money
bidding for contracts *see* tendering
Botswana
  contract award criteria, 43–4
  law and regulation

conflict with treaty obligations, 33–4
historical development of legal system, 25–6
international organisations and initiatives, 37–8
official guidance, 32, 33
oversight bodies, 31
primary sources of law, 27–8, 31–3
procurement regime overview, 31–6
procurement rules overview, 38–9
regional integration, 37
secondary sources of law, 31–2, 33
and Uganda procurement reform, 33–4
use of UNCITRAL Model Law, 33–4, 41, 265–6, 279, 280–1

procuring entities
organisation of, 30–1
rules as to, 38

public procurement
anti-corruption, 31
central bodies, 26, 28–9
committees, 29–30
final relief, 326–7
introduction to, 26
legal regime *see* law and regulation *above*
organisation of, 28–31
policy objectives, 26–8
preferential rules, 26–8, 32
procedures
contract award criteria, 43–4
introduction to, 39
methods *see* tenders *below*
planning, 40–1
suppliers *see* suppliers *below*
regulatory context, 36–8
rules, 38–9
and social policy, 27–8, 380–2, 385–6
StatExtract data (table), 256
summary of analysis, 44–5
suspension of procedures, 320–1
regulated procurement types, 38–9
single-source (direct) procurement, 284–5
suppliers
compensation to, 328
registration and listing, 40–1, 302–3
remedies, 34–6, 310–11, 314, 320–1, 326–7
tenders
consultancy services, 294
contract award criteria, 43–4
direct procurement, 42–3, 284
distinction between national/international bidding, 291
formats, 43
generally, 41
micro procurement, 42, 283
open domestic bidding, 41
open international bidding, 41–2
request for quotations, 42, 283
restricted domestic bidding, 42, 282
restricted international bidding, 42
single-source (direct) procurement, 275

bribery *see* corruption

Burkina Faso
framework agreements, 299

Cameroon
framework agreements, 299

challenge proceedings *see* supplier remedies

COMESA (Common Market for Eastern and Southern Africa)
distinction between national/international bidding, 292
public procurement reform initiatives, 2–3, 270–2
use of UNCITRAL Model Law, 265–6, 272

common use items
framework agreements, 300–2

community participation in tendering

as preferred method, 290–1
World Bank guidelines, 290–1
compensation *see* supplier remedies
competition
as procurement driver, 19
complex tendering
methods, 285–90
Comprehensive Development Framework (CDF)
use of, 239
conditionality as to aid
definition of tied aid, 241
environmental conditionality, 244–6
tied aid, 219, 241–4
consultancy services
tendering and, 292–5
UNCITRAL Model Law and, 269
World Bank selection methods, 294
contracts
bidding for *see* tendering
coordination of aid policies
Ghana as example, 240
international initiatives, 238–9
procurement reform, 251
corruption
anti-corruption measures in procurement regulation
administrative measures, 348–50
introduction to, 348
regulatory measures, 351–4
social measures, 354–5
specific countries *see* public procurement, anti corruption *under specific countries*
combating corruption
link with other objectives, 13
as policy objective, 11–13
tension with other objectives, 13–15
consequences of, 342–4
definition of, 337–8
detection of
audits, 355–6
introduction to, 355
investigations, 356–7
reporting mechanisms, 357–8
economic theories on, 339
international measures
African Union Convention on Preventing and Combating Corruption, 364–6
Economic Community of West African States (ECOWAS) Protocol on the Fight Against Corruption, 368–9
introduction to, 358–60
OECD Anti-Bribery Convention, 360–3
Organization of American States Corruption Convention, 363–4
Southern Africa Development Community Protocol Against Corruption, 367–8
United Nations Convention Against Corruption, 366–7
introduction to, 336–7
political theories on, 340–1
public procurement and
corruption incidence and types, 345–7
definition of public procurement, 344–5
introduction to, 344
social theories on, 341
theories on
economic theories, 339
introduction to, 338
political theories, 340–1
social theories, 341
country systems
declarations on use of, 237–8, 240
donors' influence on reform of
direct influence, 250–1
indirect influence, 251–8
introduction to, 246–50
OECD data on use of, 255–8
World Bank Pilot Program, 253
see also specific countries
Country Procurement Assessment Reports (CPARs)
contribution to procurement reform, 250–1

decentralisation of procurement responsibilities
trend for, 295–7
Development Assistance Committee (DAC)
donors' aid to Africa (table), 227
Methodology for Assessing Procurement Systems (MAPS), 37–8
Recommendation on untying aid to LDC and Highly Indebted Poor Countries, 242–3
survey on Paris Declaration implementation, 134, 237–8, 253–4, 315–16
development banks
influence on procurement systems, 268–9
use of country systems, 255–8
see also African Development Bank; World Bank
development goals
achievement of MDGs in Africa, 225–6
direct procurement *see* single-source (direct) procurement
dispute resolution *see* supplier remedies
donors' influence on procurement
aid to Africa generally, 225–31
donor projects in specific countries, 233–4
introduction to, 219–25
procurement practices
aid structure, 232–5
environmental conditionality, 244–6
international initiatives on aid policies, 238–40
introduction to, 225–31
procurement rules, 235–8
tied aid conditionality, 241–4
procurement reform
coordination of efforts, 251
development aid as incentive, 248, 251
direct influence, 250–1
donors' commitment to, 250
donors' influence generally, 249–50
importance of, 246
indirect influence, 251–8
international initiatives, 249, 250–1
introduction to, 246–50
survey on, 248–9
theories on, 247–8
procurement rules, 20–1
summary of analysis, 258–60
supplier remedies, 316–17

e-procurement
use of, 295–304
East African Community (EAC)
public procurement reform initiatives, 272–3
Economic Community of West African States (ECOWAS) Protocol on the Fight Against Corruption
overview, 368–9
economic theories on corruption
overview, 339
efficiency
efficient procurement and horizontal policies, 378–9
as procurement objective, 9–10, 223–4
Egypt
framework agreements, 299
environmental conditionality for aid
donors' influence, 244–6
equal treatment
as procurement objective, 10–11
Ethiopia
COMESA initiatives, 67, 270–2
contracts
award criteria, 71–2, 73–4
international contracts, 74–5
with outside funding, 66–7
signing, 74
standstill period, 74, 318
defence procurement, 65–6
law and regulation
conflict with treaty obligations, 66

Ethiopia (*cont.*)
exceptions to procurement rules, 65–6
framework agreements, 299
historical development of legal system, 46–8
international organisations and initiatives, 67
procurement regime overview, 61–4
procurement rules overview, 64–7
regional integration, 67
sources of law, 49–51
use of UNCITRAL Model Law, 67, 69, 72–3, 279–82
procuring entities, 64
public procurement
anti-corruption, 55–6
central bodies, 53–61
e-procurement, 305
exceptions to rules, 65–6
final relief, 324–6
foreign donors' use of country system, 255–8
introduction to, 49–51
legal regime *see* law and regulation *above*
organisation of, 53–61
oversight bodies, 55–7, 58–61
phases, 61–4
policy objectives, 51–3
preferential rules, 52–3
procedures *see* tenders *below*
rules, 64–7
and social policy, 380–2
StatExtract data (table), 256
summary of analysis, 75–6
regulated procurement types, 65–7
suppliers
compensation to, 328–9
qualification and participation, 70
registration and listing, 70–1, 302–3
remedies, 58–61, 316, 324–6
tenders
consultancy services, 292–3
distinction between national/ international bidding, 292
formats, 73
open proceedings, 73
open tendering, 67–8
rejection, 72–3
request for proposal (RFP), 68–9
request for quotation (RFQ), 68
restricted tendering, 68, 282
single-source (direct) procurement, 69–70, 285
'specially-permitted procurement' procedure, 70
two-stage tendering, 69, 287, 288–9
European Union (EU)
African Caribbean Pacific Partnership Agreement (2000), 88–9
aggregation rules, 299–300
anti-corruption measures, 359–60
compensation provisions, 328–9
conformity with EU procurement law, 272
European Development Fund (EDF), 156
framework agreement rules, 299–300
harmonisation of aid policies, 239
horizontal policies, 371–3
and Malawi framework agreement rules, 299–300
and Nigeria
assessment of procurement systems, 154
development projects, 146
preferential procurement law in member states, 270
Public Sector Directive, 273
regional integration as stimulus for reform, 248
Remedies Directive, 327–8
social policy and public procurement, 15–16

fairness
link with other objectives, 13

as procurement objective, 10–11
tension with other objectives, 13–15
foreign aid *see* aid, donors' influence on procurement
'foreign' procurement systems
influence on national systems, 269–73
framework agreements
aggregation rules and, 299–300
common use items, 300–2
national rules on, 273
types, 298–9
use of, 295–304
France
aid system, 233
fraud *see* corruption

Gambia
use of UNCITRAL Model Law, 265–6
GDP
aid as percentage of, 226
Ghana
aid as percentage of government expenditure, 222–3
contracts
advertising of, 94–5
award criteria, 96–8
coordination of aid policies, 240
law and regulation
common law principles of contract and commercial law, 85
conflict with treaty obligations, 88–9
constitutional provisions, 83
courts' role, 85
exceptions to procurement rules, 91–2
framework agreements, 299
historical development of legal system, 77–9
international organisations and initiatives, 88–9
official guidance, 84
primary sources of law, 79–81, 84–6
procurement regime overview, 83–6
procurement rules overview, 89–92
regulatory context, 87–9
secondary sources of law, 84
use of UNCITRAL Model Law, 88, 92, 95–6, 265–6, 279, 280–2
Multi-Donor Budgetary Support Programme (MDBS), 240
procuring entities, 89–90
public procurement
anti-corruption, 84
central bodies, 81–3, 87–8, 295–6
committees, 82–3
decentralisation, 296–7
enforcement mechanisms, 85–6
exceptions to rules, 91–2
foreign donors' use of country system, 255–8
introduction to, 79–89
legal regime *see* law and regulation *above*
organisation of, 81–3
policy objectives, 79–81
preferential rules, 84
procedures
contracts *see* contracts *above*
responsibility determinations, 95–6
suppliers *see* suppliers *below*
tenders *see* tenders *below*
regulatory context, 87–9
rules, 89–92
and social policy, 380–3
StatExtract data (table), 256
summary of analysis, 98–9
suspension of procedures, 319–20
World Bank CPAR, 250–1
regulated procurement types, 90–1
request for quotations, 283
suppliers
compensation to, 328
registration and listing, 95–6, 302–3
remedies, 85–6, 310–11, 312–13, 316–17, 319–20

Ghana (*cont.*)
tenders
advertising of, 94–5
award criteria, 96–8
community participation, 94
competitive tendering, 92
consultancy services, 94, 292–3, 294–5
distinction between national/international bidding, 291
introduction to, 92
open tendering, 276
request for quotations, 93–4
restricted tendering, 93, 282
single-source (direct) procurement, 93, 285
two-stage tendering, 287
GPA *see* WTO Agreement on Government Procurement (GPA)
gross domestic product (GDP)
aid as percentage of, 226

harmonisation of aid policies
international initiatives, 238–9
High Level Forum on Harmonisation
purposes, 238–9
horizontal policies
efficient procurement and, 378–9
need for clear procurement rules, 379–80
range of mechanisms, 374–7
social policy and public procurement, 15, 371–80
taxonomy
mechanisms, 374
table, 374–6
tensions with procurement, 377–8

integrity
link with other objectives, 13
as procurement objective, 8, 10–11
tension with other objectives, 13–15
interim relief
importance of, 323–4
provision for, 319–24
international community
anti-corruption measures *see* corruption
contracts funded by international development agencies, 134
initiatives on aid policies, 222, 237–40
initiatives on procurement reform, 249, 250–1
procurement methods, 291–2
see also aid; donors' influence on procurement
international competitive bidding (ICB)
national competitive bidding distinguished, 291–2
use of, 235–7
International Conference on Public Procurement Reform in Africa (1988), 2–3
international trade
openness to, as procurement objective, 15–16
internet *see* e-procurement
invalidation *see* supplier remedies
investigations
anti-corruption, 356–7
Italy
aid system, 232–3

Joint Venture on Procurement
procurement reform initiatives, 249

Kenya
COMESA initiatives, 110–11, 270–2
contracts
advertising of, 117
award criteria, 119–20
funded by international development agencies, 114–15
defence procurement, 112–14
law and regulation
framework agreements, 299
historical development of legal system, 100–1
international organisations and initiatives, 110

official guidance, 107
primary sources of law, 102–3, 107
procurement regime overview, 107–9
procurement rules overview, 111–15
regulatory context, 109–11
secondary sources of law, 107, 109
use of UNCITRAL Model Law, 102, 110–11, 115–17, 265–6, 279, 280–1
preferential procurement rules, 386–93
procuring entities, 104, 111–12
public procurement
anti-corruption, 103, 104–5, 110, 120–1
committees, 104
common use items, 300–1
community participation, 120
consultancy services, 292–3
direct procurement, 284
e-procurement, 120
introduction to, 102–11
legal regime, 107–9
market size, 103–4
organisation of, 103–6
oversight bodies, 104–6
policy objectives, 102–3
preferential rules, 102–3, 386–93
procedures, 115–21
regulatory context, 109–11
restricted tendering, 282
rules, 111–15
and social policy, 102–3, 380–2
StatExtract data (table), 256
summary of analysis, 121–2
suspension of procedures, 319–21
two-stage tendering, 288–9
regulated procurement types, 112–15
social policy and public procurement, 386–93
suppliers
compensation to, 328
debarment, 120–1
registration and listing, 117–19, 302–3
remedies, 107–9, 310–11, 312–13, 319–21

legal systems *see* law and regulation *under specific countries*
Lesotho
donor projects, 233–4
lists of suppliers *see* supplier registration and listing
low-value procurement
methods, 283

Madagascar
use of UNCITRAL Model Law, 265–6
Malawi
central procurement bodies, 295–6
decentralisation, 296–7
framework agreements, 299
framework agreements rules, 273
use of UNCITRAL Model Law, 265–6, 281–2
Mali
framework agreements, 299
Mauritius
use of UNCITRAL Model Law, 265–6
Millennium Development Goals (MDGs)
achievement in Africa, 225–6
Model Law on Procurement *see entries at* UNCITRAL
Multi-Donor Budgetary Support Programme (MDBS)
use of, 240

Namibia
central government procurement, 132
contracts
advertising of, 136
award criteria, 138–9
funded by international development agencies, 134
defence procurement, 134

Namibia (*cont.*)
law and regulation
constitutional provisions, 125–6, 128–9
exceptions to procurement rules, 135–6
historical development of legal system, 123–5
international organisations and initiatives, 131
primary sources of law, 126, 128
procurement regime overview, 128–9
procurement rules overview, 131–5
regulatory context, 130–1
use of UNCITRAL Model Law, 126, 135, 265–6, 279, 280–1
local authority procurement, 132
procuring entities
central government, 132
introduction to, 131
local authorities, 132
regional councils, 132
state-owned enterprises, 133
public procurement
anti-corruption, 126, 127
central bodies, 126–7
e-procurement, 136
exceptions to rules, 135
final relief, 325–7
introduction to, 125–31
legal regime, 128–9
organisation of, 126–8
oversight bodies, 127
policy objectives, 125–6
preferential rules, 125–6, 130, 133, 138–9
procedures, 135–9
regulatory context, 130–1
rules, 131–5
and social policy, 125–6, 373–4, 380–2
StatExtract data (table), 256
summary of analysis, 140
regional councils, procurement by, 132
state-owned enterprises, procurement by, 133
suppliers
compensation to, 328–9
remedies, 312, 316–17, 325–7
tenders
advertising of, 136
award criteria, 138–9
evaluation, 137
notification, 1–6
types of regulated procurement
acquisition, sale or letting of goods or services, 133–4
contracts funded by international development agencies, 134
defence procurement, 134
exceptions to rules, 135
national competitive bidding (NCB)
international competitive bidding distinguished, 291–2
use of, 237
national procurement systems *see* country systems; *specific countries*
Niger
framework agreements, 299
Nigeria
contracts
advertising of, 158–9
award criteria, 159–60
funded by international development agencies, 156
defence procurement, 155–6
law and regulation
framework agreements, 299
historical development of legal system, 141–3
international organisations and initiatives, 153–4, 156
primary sources of law, 143–4, 150–1
procurement regime overview, 150–3
procurement rules overview, 154–6
regulatory context, 153–4

use of UNCITRAL Model Law, 143–4, 157, 158, 265–6, 279, 280–2
procuring entities, 146–8, 154–5
public procurement
anti-corruption, 144–5
community participation, 144–5
e-procurement, 160, 305
enforcement mechanisms, 151–2
final relief, 326–7
international organisations use of country system, 255–8
introduction to, 143–54
legal regime *see* law and regulation *above*
organisation of, 146–50
oversight bodies, 148–50
policy objectives, 143–6
preferential rules, 145–6, 164
procedures, 157–61
regulatory context, 153–4
rules, 154–6
and social policy, 145–6, 380–2
standard bidding/contract documents, 160–1
StatExtract data (table), 256
summary of analysis, 161
suspension of procedures, 319–21
regulated procurement types, 156
suppliers
compensation to, 328–9
qualification and participation, 159
remedies, 152–3, 312–13, 319–21, 326–7
Nordic+ Group
harmonisation of aid policies, 239–40

OECD
aid studies, 237
anti-corruption measures, 359–60
creditor reporting, 251
data on use of country systems, 255–8
definition of tied aid, 241
procurement Roundtable, 249
survey on Paris Declaration implementation, 134, 237–8, 253–4, 315–16
OECD Anti-Bribery Convention
overview, 360–3
OECD Convention on Combating Bribery of Foreign Public Officials
compliance with, 351
OECD/DAC Joint Venture on Procurement
Methodology for Assessing Procurement Systems (MAPS), 37–8, 252
OECD/DAC Recommendation on untying aid to LDC and Highly Indebted Poor Countries
agreement, 242–3
environmental conditionality, 245
scope, 243–4
online procurement *see* e-procurement
open tendering
as preferred method, 276–82
and UNCITRAL Model Law, 273–4
openness to international trade
as procurement objective, 15–16, 353
Organization of American States Corruption Convention
overview, 363–4
Organization for Economic Co-operation and Development *see entries at*, *see* OECD
overseas aid *see* aid, donors' influence on procurement

Paris Declaration on aid effectiveness
as to aid harmonisation, 239
implementation survey, 134, 237–8, 253–4, 315–16
as to procurement reform, 252
as to tied aid, 243
as to use of country systems, 237–8, 240

political theories on corruption
overview, 340–1
preferential procurement rules *see* public procurement, preferential rules *under specific countries*; social policy and public procurement
procurement methods
common use items, 295–304
consultancy services, 292–5
e-procurement, 305–6
framework agreements, 295–304
influences on, 263–73
international methods, 291–2
introduction to, 261–3
national methods, 291–2
overview of, 273–91
summary of analysis, 307
supplier lists, 295–304
use of UNCITRAL Model Law, 261–3
public procurement
academic studies on, 5–6
aim of study, 6
background, 1–6
corruption *see* corruption
decentralisation, 295–7
definition of, 1, 344–5
donors' influence *see* donors' influence on procurement
methods *see* procurement methods
objectives and drivers, 7–21
see also public procurement, policy objectives *under specific countries*
reform
donors' influence *see* donors' influence on procurement
initiatives, 1–6
regulation *see* regulation
and social policy *see* social policy and public procurement
structure of study, 6–7
supplier remedies *see* supplier remedies
see also under specific countries
regulation
aims of, 7–21
clarity and simplicity, 20–1
principles of, 7–21
UNCITRAL Model Law *see entries at* UNCITRAL
see also law and regulation *under specific countries*
relief *see* supplier remedies
remedies *see* supplier remedies
reporting mechanisms
anti-corruption, 357–8
request for quotations (RFQ)
as preferred tendering method, 283
and UNCITRAL Model Law, 275
restricted tendering
as preferred method, 282
and UNCITRAL Model Law, 274–5
Rwanda
COMESA initiatives, 270–2
contract award criteria, 174–5
contracts
standstill period, 318
law and regulation
framework agreements, 299
historical development of legal system, 162–3
international organisations and initiatives, 171
procurement regime overview, 167–9
procurement rules overview, 169–72
use of UNCITRAL Model Law, 169–70, 171–2, 265–6, 279, 280–1
procedures
restricted tendering, 282
procuring entities, 166–7, 170
public procurement
anti-corruption, 167
central bodies, 165–6, 295–6
community participation, 172–3
consultancy services, 292–3
decentralisation, 296–7
enforcement mechanisms, 175–6
introduction to, 163–9
legal regime

oversight bodies, 169
primary sources of law, 167–8
secondary sources of law, 168
market size, 164–5
organisation of, 164–7
oversight bodies, 167, 169
policy objectives, 163–4
procedures
contract award criteria, 174–5
direct procurement, 284
enforcement, 175–6
introduction to, 172–3
open tendering, 276
remedies, 175–6
two-stage tendering, 287
rules, 169–72
and social policy, 164, 380–2, 385
StatExtract data (table), 256
summary of analysis, 176–7
World Bank Pilot Program, 253
regulated procurement types, 170–2
suppliers
qualification and participation, 173–4
remedies, 175–6, 311, 314

SACU *see* Southern African Customs Union (SACU)
SADC *see* Southern African Development Community (SADC)
Senegal
framework agreements, 299
World Bank Pilot Program, 253
Sierra Leone
framework agreements, 299
supplier registration and listing, 296–7, 302–3
single-source (direct) procurement
as preferred method, 284–5
and UNCITRAL Model Law, 275
social policy and public procurement
horizontal policies, 15, 371–80
implementation mechanisms, 382–6
introduction to, 370–1
policy objectives, 380–2
preferential procurement rules
comparison of mechanisms, 383–5
introduction to, 386
Kenya, 386–93
other countries *see* public procurement, preferential rules *under specific countries*
South Africa, 393–401
summary of analysis, 401–3
widespread provision for, 380
social theories on corruption
overview, 341
South Africa
contracts
advertising of, 198
with other state bodies, 192–3
with outside funding, 193–4
standstill period, 318–19
defence procurement, 192
law and regulation
common law principles of contract and commercial law, 183
constitutional provisions, 179, 183, 184, 187–8
courts' role, 183
exceptions to procurement rules, 197
historical development of legal system, 178–9
international organisations and initiatives, 180
primary sources of law, 184–6
procurement regime overview, 183–6
procurement rules overview, 186–95
use of UNCITRAL Model Law, 186, 195, 265–6, 279, 280–2
procuring entities
constitutional provisions, 187–8
statutory provisions, 188–9
public procurement
anti-corruption, 184, 351, 352
applications for exemptions from regulation, 194–5
audits, 355, 356
central bodies, 181

South Africa (*cont.*)
common use items, 300–1
community participation, 195–6
exceptions to rules, 197
final relief, 324–7
foreign donors' use of country system, 255–8
introduction to, 179–86
investigations, 357
legal regime, 183–6
local level, 182, 196–7
low-value procurement, 283
market size, 180
organisation of, 180–2
oversight bodies, 182, 355, 357–8
policy objectives, 179–80
preferential rules, 179–80, 393–401
procedures, 195–8
regional level, 181–2, 196
reporting mechanisms, 357–8
rules generally, 186
and social policy, 179–80, 373–4, 380–3, 393–401
StatExtract data (table), 256
summary of analysis, 198–9
suspension of procedures, 321, 322
regulated procurement types
acquisition, sale or letting of goods or services, 189–92
applications for exemptions from regulation, 194–5
contracts with other state bodies, 192–3
contracts with outside funding, 193–4
defence procurement, 192
suppliers
compensation to, 328–9
registration and listing, 196, 302–3
remedies, 183–4, 311–13, 316–17, 321, 322, 324–7
Southern African Customs Union (SACU)
public procurement reform initiatives, 273
Southern African Development Community (SADC)
Protocol Against Corruption, 367–8
public procurement reform initiatives, 273
standstill period
absence of, 318
provision for, 318–19
specific countries *see specific countries*
StatExtract data (OECD)
analysis of use of, 255–8
selected countries (table), 256
supplier registration and listing
specific countries *see specific countries*
use of, 295–304
WTO guidance, 303–4
supplier remedies
challenge proceedings structure, 310–15
conflict between national and donor rules, 316–17
delays in use of, 313–14
final relief
compensation, 328–30
invalidation, 324–8
interim relief, 319–24
introduction to, 308–10
judicial intervention, differing methods of, 314
single or multiple regimes, 315–17
specific countries *see specific countries*
standstill period, 318–19
summary of analysis, 330–5
suspension of procurement, 319–24
temporary relief, 319–24
WTO guidance, 315
suspension of procurement
provision for, 319–24
Swaziland
consultancy services, 292–3, 294–5
use of UNCITRAL Model Law, 265–6
Sweden
use of country systems, 258

Tanzania
common procurement listing, 296–7
common use items, 300–1
community participation, 290–1
consultancy services, 292–3, 294–5
e-procurement, 305
framework agreements, 299
single-source (direct) procurement, 285
two-stage tendering, 287
use of UNCITRAL Model Law, 265–6
Task Force on Procurement
Methodology for Assessing Procurement Systems (MAPS), 37–8, 252
procurement reform initiatives, 249
survey on procurement reform, 248–9
temporary relief
provision for, 319–24
tendering
consultancy services and, 292–5
overview of methods, 273–91
and UNCITRAL Model Law, 273–5
tied aid conditionality
definition of, 241
donors' influence, 241–4
trade agreements
conflict with national procurement laws, 33–4, 66, 88–9
influence on procurement systems, 269–73
transparency
as procurement driver, 16–19, 352–3
two-stage tendering
as preferred method, 285–90
World Bank guidelines, 288

Uganda
central procurement bodies, 295–6
common use items, 300–1
community participation, 290–1
consultancy services, 294
decentralisation, 296–7
distinction between national/international bidding, 291
donor projects, 233–4
e-procurement, 305
framework agreements, 299
micro procurement, 283
procurement reform, 33–4
request for quotations, 283
restricted tendering, 282
single-source (direct) procurement, 284–5
supplier registration and listing, 296–7
two-stage tendering, 287
use of UNCITRAL Model Law, 265–6, 267–8, 280–2
UN *see entries at*, *see* United Nations
UNCITRAL Model Law on Procurement (1994 Model Law)
application to tendering methods, 273–5
consultancy services, 269
horizontal policies, 371–3
influence on procurement systems, 263–8, 272, 307
objective, 15–16
and procurement methods generally, 261–3
and procurement reform, 250–1
revision, 1–2
specific countries' use of *see specific countries*
standardisation of trade laws as objective, 20
UNCITRAL Model Law on Procurement (2011 Model Law)
changes under, 116–17, 171–2, 267–8, 278, 280–1, 282
common use items, 301–2
compensation, 329–30
consultancy services, 293
e-procurement, 305–6
final relief, 327–8
framework agreements, 298
influence on procurement systems, 282

UNCITRAL Model Law (*cont.*)
open tendering, 273–4
public procurement provisions, 261
single-source (direct) procurement, 284–5
supplier registration and listing, 303–4
suspension of procurement, 323
two-stage tendering, 289–90
United Kingdom
audits, 355
bilateral agreement with Ghana, 88–9
EU procurement law, 270
reporting mechanisms, 358
United Nations
anti-corruption measures, 359–60
use of country systems, 255–8
United Nations Commission on International Trade Law *see entries at* UNCITRAL
United Nations Convention Against Corruption
national implementation, 55–6
overview, 366–7
United States
aid system, 233
anti-corruption measures, 351
audits, 355
horizontal policies, 371–3
investigations, 357
use of country systems, 255–8

value for money
best value as objective, 296–7, 353–4
link with other objectives, 13
as procurement objective, 8–10
tension with other objectives, 13–15
Vietnam
donor projects, 233–4

WAEMU (West African Economic and Monetary Union)
public procurement reform initiatives, 2–3, 272
web-based procurement *see* e-procurement
World Bank
community participation guidelines, 290–1
consultancy services selection methods, 294
Country Procurement Assessment Reports (CPARs), 250–1
influence on procurement systems, 268–9
international competitive bidding (ICB), 237
national competitive bidding (NCB), 237
Pilot Program for Use of Country Procurement Systems, 253
procurement guidelines, 236–7
procurement Roundtable, 249
projects in Nigeria, 146
two-stage tendering guidelines, 288
use of country systems, 255–8
WTO (World Trade Organization)
tied aid negotiations, 244
WTO Agreement on Government Procurement (GPA)
horizontal policies, 371–3
influence on procurement systems, 269
objective, 15–16
revision, 1–2
supplier registration and listing, 303–4
supplier remedies, 315

Zambia
framework agreements, 299
use of UNCITRAL Model Law, 265–6
Zimbabwe
COMESA initiatives, 270–2
competitive quotation procedure, 213
contracts
drafting, 204
with other state bodies, 209–10
with outside funding, 209–10
formal tenders, 211–12
informal tender procedure, 212–13
law and regulation

courts' role, 204–7
historical development of legal system, 200–1
procurement regime overview, 204–8
procurement rules overview, 208–10
use of UNCITRAL Model Law, 204, 212, 279–82
local authority procurement, 214–15
procuring entities, 208
public interest procedure, 213
public procurement
anti-corruption, 207–8
central bodies, 203, 204, 296
enforcement mechanisms, 207–8
final relief, 325–7
introduction to, 201–8
legal regime, 204–8
local level, 202–3
organisation of, 203
policy objectives, 201–3
preferential rules, 202
procedures
competitive quotation procedure, 213
contracts *see* contracts *above*
formal tenders, 211–12
informal tender procedure, 212–13
lists of approved tenderers, 214
local authority procurement, 214–15
overview of, 210–11
public interest procedure, 213
special-formal tender procedure, 213–14
rules, 208–10
and social policy, 202, 380–2
summary of analysis, 215–16
suspension of procedures, 320–1
special-formal tender procedure, 213–14
suppliers
compensation to, 328
registration and listing, 214, 302–3
remedies, 207, 312–13, 320–1, 325–7
tenders
competitive quotation procedure, 213
distinction between national/international bidding, 292
formal procedure, 211–12
informal procedure, 212–13
local authority procurement, 214–15
public interest procedure, 213
special-formal procedure, 213–14
supplier lists, 214
types of regulated procurement, 209